We Learn Grammar
Intermediate

초판 1쇄 발행 2017년 9월 27일
2쇄 발행 2019년 5월 15일

저자 박상호
편집총괄 오유리

출판총괄 조순정
편집디자인 김현철 강민정 차혜린 김보경 이상현
일러스트 김선희 장하은
출판마케팅 장혜원 이성원 이윤재 김영준 위가을
제작/지원 김석성 양수지
펴낸곳 (주)에스제이더블유인터내셔널

임프린트 시원스쿨
홈페이지 www.jjannae.com
주소 서울시 영등포구 국회대로74길 12 남중빌딩

도서문의 안내
대량구입문의 02)2014-8151 **팩스** 02)783-5528
기타문의 02)6409-0878

등록번호 2010년 10월 21일 제 321-2010-0000219
이 책은 저작권법에 따라 보호받는 저작물이므로 무단복제와 무단전재를 금합니다.
이 책 내용의 전부 또는 일부를 이용하려면 반드시 저작권자와 (주)에스제이더블유인터내셔널의 서면동의를 받아야 합니다.
* 잘못된 책은 바꾸어 드립니다.
* 책값은 뒤표지에 있습니다.
* LOT SW M-190507 P01

영어회화, TOEIC, 비즈니스에 유용한
초중급 실전영문법

We Learn Grammar
Intermediate

박상효 지음

WeLearn 위런영어

저자의 말

〈*We Learn Grammar 시리즈*〉는 Basic과 Intermediate, 두 권으로 구성되어 영어 문장 구조를 통해 영어적 사고와 원리를 이해하고, 실질적으로 구사할 수 있도록 돕는 것을 목표로 쓰여진 교재입니다. 단순히 문법 규칙을 익히기 보다는, 의사소통이 되기 위한 영어 문장의 원리를 이해하고, 실제 말하기, 듣기, 쓰기, 읽기에 필요한 기초를 닦는 데에 초점이 있습니다.

그 중 〈*We Learn Grammar - Intermediate*〉은 자유로운 기본 의사소통을 위한 종합 실용 영문법을 골자로 하지만, 초급을 갓 벗어난 대부분의 한국 학생들이 실질적으로 필요로 하는 여러 영어 시험이나 기본 비즈니스 상황에 필요한 세세한 문법 사항들도 포함하고 있습니다. 한국 학생들에게 있어 영어를 활용하는 '실용'적인 상황이 이와 연결되어 있기 때문입니다.

〈*We Learn Grammar - Intermediate*〉은 특히 혼자 공부하는 학생들이 스스로 이해하고 익힐 수 있도록 하는 데에 중점을 두었습니다. 유럽이나 자연스러운 영어 노출 기회가 많은 학생들을 기준으로 만들어진 외서들은 그렇지 않은 우리 학생들에게 지나치게 많은 직관을 요구하여, 독학하기 어려운 경우가 많습니다. 〈*We Learn Grammar - Intermediate*〉은 간결한 한글 문장으로 개념을 설명하여 부담은 줄이면서 언어로서의 영어를 바라볼 수 있도록 도와준 뒤, 이를 바탕으로 보다 상세한 사항들을 구체적인 사례와 설명으로 익힐 수 있도록 하였습니다.

또한 어려운 문법 용어와 규칙을 외우느라 불필요한 에너지를 소모하거나, 화려한 설명에 비해 실제 활용 문장이 턱없이 부족한 기존 한글 문법 교재들과도 차이를 두었습니다. 〈*We Learn Grammar - Intermediate*〉에서는 설명을 최소화하고, 풍부한 예문과 예문이 활용되는 문맥, 즉 구체적인 사례를 제시하여 실질적인 문법의 습득에 초점을 두었습니다.

미처 다 싣지 못한 문장들은 연습문제에서 보강할 수 있도록 하였으며, 해당 문법 사항이 반영된 TOEIC이나 비즈니스 예문들을 특별부록으로 구성하여 다양하게 응용해 볼 수 있습니다.

또한 모든 예문들은 영국, 미국 등의 다양한 언어 배경을 가진 전문가와 원어민들이 감수하고 참여하여 정확도와 활용도를 높였습니다. 북미 영어를 기준으로 하나, 영국 영어에 대한 소개나 차이 설명을 틈틈이 추가하였고, 국내 영문법 학습에서 종종 언급되는 사항들도 포함하여, 더욱 다양한 활용이 가능합니다.

Basic에 이어 Intermediate에서도 각 Unit마다 학습한 문법 사항이 활용된 100개의 대화문(Dialogue)을 실었습니다. Intermediate이란 타이틀에 맞게 대화문의 문장과 내용도 좀 더 폭 넓고 풍부해졌습니다. 영어권의 문화나 비즈니스 상황 등을 간략하게 체험할 수 있도록 꾸며 학습의 재미와 의미를 더했습니다. 또한, Basic에 등장했던 인물들도 좀 더 성숙하고 사회 경험의 폭이 깊어졌습니다. Basic에 이어 꾸준히 공부해 오신 분이라면 이들의 성장과 변화를 발견하는 소소한 재미도 느끼실 수 있을 것입니다.

〈*We Learn Grammar 시리즈*〉는 가장 단순한 문장 구조부터 시작하여 좀 더 길고 복잡한 문장으로 단계적으로 발전하는 순서로 구성되어 있습니다. 따라서 전체적인 영문법에 대한 큰 그림을 정리하고 싶다면 처음부터 차근차근 순서대로 학습해 나가시는 것을 권합니다. 하지만, 이미 기초를 갖춘 상황이라면 필요한 부분만을 찾아서 학습하는 것도 가능합니다. 특히 〈*We Learn Grammar - Intermediate*〉은 공부하다가 확인하고픈 문법 사항들을 찾아 볼 수 있는 참고 서적(reference)으로도 부족함이 없도록 구성하였습니다.

Believe in yourself.

제가 학생들을 격려하며 드리는 말입니다. 여러분 안의 가능성과 능력을 충분히 발휘할 수 있음을 믿으세요. 영어가 여러분의 발목을 잡는 방해물이 아닌, 여러분의 꿈을 날게 해 줄 날개가 될 수 있도록 끊임없이 연구하고 노력하겠습니다. 여러분의 힘찬 날갯짓을 위한 도움닫기에 〈*We Learn Grammar*〉가 좋은 발판이 될 수 있기를 희망합니다.

저자 **박상효**

추천서

This book is an excellent study tool and resource for learners! Each unit provides multiple examples, opportunities for practice, and up-to-date topics. Each unit is also built upon previously learned information, and if there is a need to review a concept, the unit number is provided. The dialogues at the end of each unit are full of useful information and vocabulary. They include travel references, jokes and sarcasm, and small talk topics. All in all, learners can use this as a stand-alone reference guide, a chance to review or brush up on skills, or with a class or tutor. Good luck with your continued English study!

이 책은 학습자에게 탁월한 학습 도구이자 교재입니다. 각각의 Unit은 다양한 예문과 연습의 기회 및 최신 주제 등을 제공합니다. 이전에 학습한 내용들을 기반으로 차곡차곡 영어 문장 능력을 기를 수 있도록 구성되었으며, 연계된 Unit들이 표시되어 있습니다. 각 Unit의 맨 마지막에 제시된 대화문은 여행 영어, 농담과 유머, 일상의 자연스러운 대화 주제 등 유익한 정보와 함께 관련 어휘들을 풍부하게 제시하고 있습니다. 이 책은 문장 능력을 복습하고 다듬을 수 있는 독립된 영문법 가이드로, 학급이나 1:1 과외의 교재로도 적합합니다. 여러분의 계속되는 영어 학습에 행운이 깃들기를 바랍니다!

감수자 Jennifer Hirashiki, MA

이 책의 특징

생생한 예문

Watch out! You're going to fall into the hole.
조심해! 너 구멍에 빠지겠어.

〈We Learn Grammar〉는 실질적인 의사소통에 기초가 되는 문법을 지향하는 만큼, 예문들도 실생활에 관련된 유용한 문장들로 구성되어 있습니다. 생활에 밀접한 예문들을 다수 삽입하여, 즉각적으로 활용할 수 있도록 하였습니다.

Dialogue

> **Dialogue**
> 3. 주어진 단어를 이용하여 문맥에 맞게 문장을 완성하세요.
>
> Suzi is asking little Eva what her dream is.
> Suzi가 꼬마 Eva에게 장래희망이 무엇인지를 묻고 있습니다.
>
> Suzi Eva, _____ (what / your dream)?
> Eva   _____ (I / want to / a nurse).
> Suzi Why?
> Eva   Because my mom is a nurse. _____ (I / want to / like my mom).
> Suzi Wonderful. I'm sure _____ (you / will / a wonderful nurse).

〈We Learn Grammar〉는 모든 Unit에 1개의 Dialogue가 수록되어 있습니다. 따라서 〈We Learn Grammar〉 한 권을 학습하면 자연스럽게 100개의 자연스러운 대화 상황을 학습한 것이 됩니다. 이는 웬만한 회화 교재에 수록된 대화문보다 많은 양입니다. 또한 별도 대화문 외에도 틈틈이 대화형 지문이 다수 수록되어, 직접 대화를 경험하지 못하는 학습자들에게 최대한 실제 의사 소통의 상황에 맞춰 문법을 바라보고 이해하도록 초점을 두었습니다.

한국 학생들에게 필요한 내용 강화

한국인의 머릿속에 자리잡은 한국어의 체계를 이해하지 못하고 일방적으로 설명하는 외국인 저자의 교재나, 옛 일본식 영문법 교육의 영향을 받아 암기와 문법 용어 중심의 학습을 벗어나지 못하는 기존 교재들과 달리, 〈We Learn Grammar〉는 한국인이 가장 언어답게 영어를 공부할 수 있도록 설계, 구성되어있습니다. 모국어인 한국어의 체계와 달라서 이해하기 힘든 영어의 문장 구조를 한국인의 관점에서 이해할 수 있도록 설명했습니다. 무조건 외우기보다는 우리말과 다른 부분을 명확하게 알려주고, 이에 맞춰 영어 문장을 구사할 수 있도록 하는데 심혈을 기울였습니다.
예를 들어, 대부분의 문법 교재들이 능동태와 수동태를 일방적으로 소개하고 이를 무조건 받아들이도록 하는데에 비해, 〈We Learn Grammar〉에서는 우리말과 달리 왜 영어에서는 능동/수동 개념이 존재하고 분명하게 구분되는지를 동사의 개념과 차이에서부터 차근차근 짚어 줍니다.

이 책의 구성

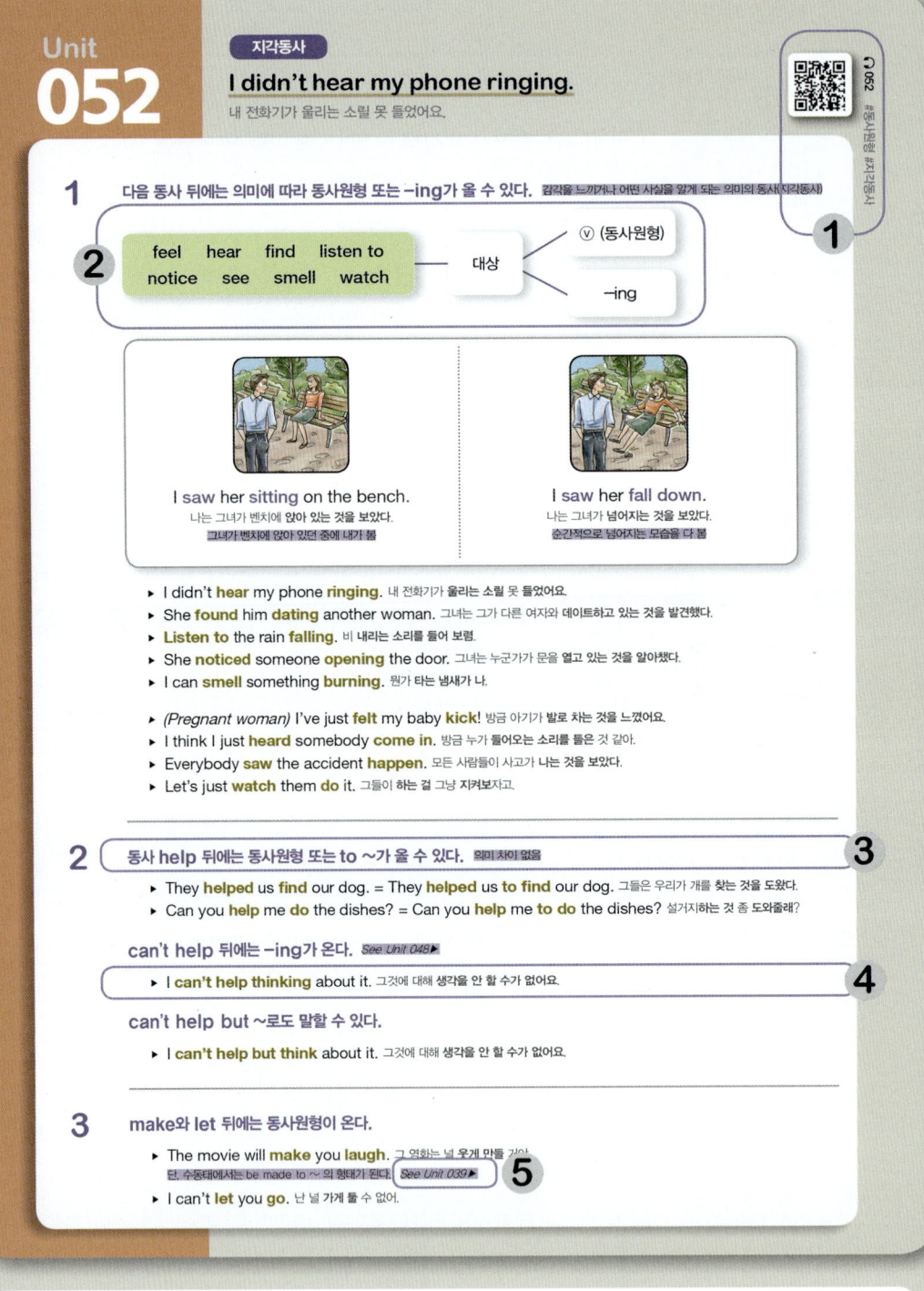

1. **#(해시태그) + MP3 QR코드**
   #(해시태그)에 해당 Unit에 관련된 문법 키워드를 실어 직관적으로 학습 목표를 알고 QR코드를 통해 MP3를 손쉽게 음원을 들을 수 있어요.
2. **다양한 삽화+표** 다양한 삽화와 표를 활용하여 쉽고 간단하게 문법 내용을 이해할 수 있어요.
3. **심플한 설명** 복잡한 설명을 최소화하여 예문과 삽화를 통해 직관적으로 문법을 이해할 수 있습니다.
4. **실용적인 예문** 당장 말하기에 사용할 수 있는 **실생활에 유용한 실용 예문**을 다양하게 공부할 수 있습니다.
5. **바로 따라가는 링크** 해당 문법 학습에 필요한 내용을 **링크로 제시**하여 그때그때 관련 내용을 확인할 수 있어요.

6 Exercises

1. 밑줄 친 부분이 틀렸다면 맞게 고치세요. 고칠 부분이 없다면 X를 쓰세요.

1. The movie's going to start soon. We'd better leave now.   X
2. I think you'd better start blogging about your business. _____
3. I can't wear shorts to a job interview. I'd better change clothes before I go. _____
4. You'd better not be late again or you'll lose your job. _____
5. It's a great sci-fi movie. You'd better see it. _____
6. I know he's been studying hard for the test. He'd better be able to pass it. _____

2. (not) supposed to와 주어진 표현을 써서 문장을 완성하세요.

1. (My wife, make dinner tonight) — My wife is supposed to make dinner tonight.
2. (You, take more than 3 books) _____
3. (Cars, be on the bike path) _____
4. (The newspaper, be delivered by now) _____

3. 문맥에 맞는 문장끼리 연결하세요.

1. My husband is getting a little overweight. •   • a. It's time he learned how to use it.
2. Mike has never used Excel at work before. •   • b. It's high time we went back home.
3. It's almost midnight. •   • c. It's time he went on a diet.
4. They've been engaged for 5 years. •   • d. It's about time I bought a new one.
5. You'll have to catch a morning train. •   • e. It's time you went to bed.
6. My laptop keeps turning off. •   • f. It's about time they got married.

🔊 Dialogue

4. 주어진 단어를 이용하여 문맥에 맞게 문장을 완성하세요.

Mike parked his car in the guest parking lot of the company.
Mike는 회사의 손님 주차 구역에 주차를 했습니다.

Trish   Mike. Is that blue car yours?
Mike   Yes, it is. Is there anything wrong with that?
Trish   Actually yes. _____ (You, not, supposed to, park your car) in the guest parking lot.
Mike   Oh, really? I'm sorry, I didn't know that. I'll move it right away.
Trish   Thank you for your understanding.

정답 p.264 ▶

이 책의 구성

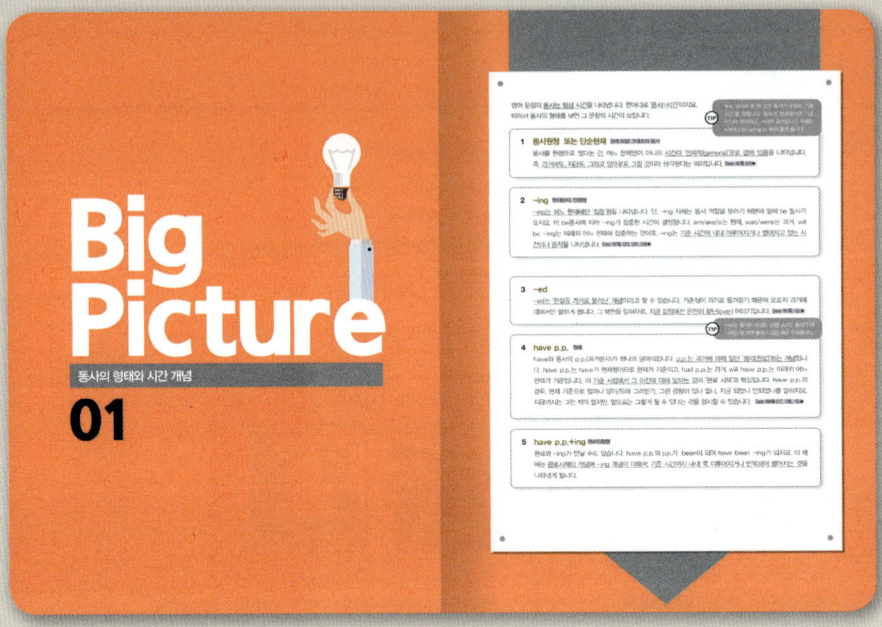

Big Picture
여러 Unit에 걸쳐 학습하게 될 문법 개념이나 사항을 먼저 큰 그림으로 아울러 살펴볼 수 있는 페이지입니다. 해당 Unit들을 학습하면서 수시로 상기하거나, 전체 학습 후 복습과 정리를 위해 간략히 훑어 볼 수도 있습니다.

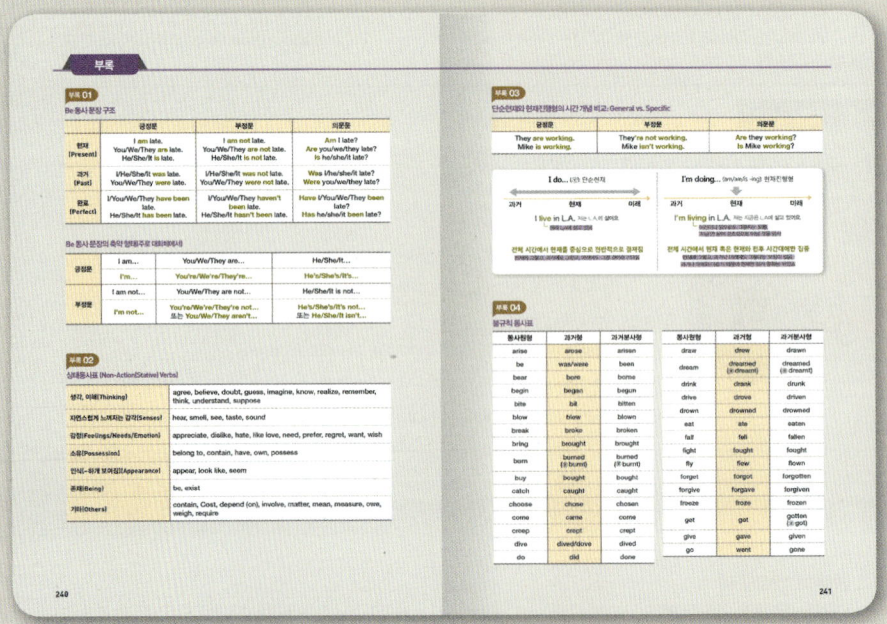

다양한 부록 + TOEIC BUSINESS SENTENCES 100
본문에 미처 수록하지 못한 다양한 문법 요소를 보강할 수 있고, 토익과 비즈니스 문장을 맛볼 수 있습니다. 부록을 활용하여 더욱 탄탄하게 영문법을 완성하세요.

Dialogue 등장인물

Naomi Yamaguchi
유학생
제시카의 집에 홈스테이 중

James Klein
Jessica의 남편,
Watson 씨와 이웃

Jessica Klein
James의 아내,
Nicole과 동료

Mr. and Mrs. Watson
Klein 부부와 이웃

Patrick Watson
Watson 씨 부부의 아들

Andy(Andrew) Watson
Watson씨 부부의 아들,
Patrick 의 남동생

Mr. Harris
James와 이웃

Erika Huang
대만계 미국인 대학생

Rachel Cruz
Mr. Cruz의 딸, Jessica의 친구

Mr. Cruz
Rachel의 아버지,
Amy, Andy 등의 학교 선생님

Amy Landers
Andy의 여자친구,
Eugene의 여동생

Eugene Landers
Amy의 오빠,
학교 밴드의 보컬

Ben
Andy의 친구,
액션 피규어 수집이 취미

Sarah
Amy의 친구

Jay Kim
한국인 유학생

Suzi Hong
한국인 유학생

Sia Turner
Mike의 누나,
John의 사촌누나

Mike Turner
Sia의 남동생,
Trish의 직장 동료

Trish Brooks
Mike의 직장동료

Julia
Nicole의 룸메이트, 승무원

Nicole
Julia의 룸메이트,
Jessica의 직장동료

목차

중급 영문법에 들어가기 전에 알아두어야 할 기초 사항 점검

Big Picture 01
동사의 형태와 시간 개념

Unit 001	Be동사	— Everything's going to be all right. **22**
Unit 002	단순현재	— My laptop works well. **24**
Unit 003	현재진행형	— The elevator isn't working. **26**
Unit 004	단순현재 vs. 현재진행형(1)	— You're always forgetting my birthday! **28**
Unit 005	단순현재 vs. 현재진행형(2)	— Let me pay this time. I insist. **30**
Unit 006	단순과거	— It rained a lot last night. **32**
Unit 007	과거진행형	— I was living abroad in 2014. **34**
Unit 008	현재완료(1)	— Have you done your homework? **36**
Unit 009	현재완료(2)	— It's the first time I've ridden a motorcycle. **38**
Unit 010	단순과거 vs. 현재완료	— You've done your hair! Awesome! **40**
Unit 011	현재완료(3)	— I've had my smartphone for two years. **42**
Unit 012	현재완료진행형	— How long have you been learning English? **44**
Unit 013	현재완료 vs. 현재완료진행형	— I've done the laundry! vs. I've been doing the laundry all day. **46**
Unit 014	과거완료	— I suddenly remembered I had left my phone in the car. **48**
Unit 015	과거완료진행형	— I'd been waiting for the bus for 20 minutes when it arrived. **50**
Unit 016	be going to ~ vs. be -ing	— When are you going on vacation? **52**
Unit 017	will	— I think I'll have an espresso. **54**
Unit 018	going to vs. will, 그 외의 미래	— I was going to call you. **56**

| Unit 019 | will be -ing vs. will have p.p. — I'll be graduating in two years. 58 |
| Unit 020 | when I do vs. when I've done — I'll ask her about it when I call her. 60 |

Big Picture 02
동사의 형태와 MODE

Unit 021	can/could(1) — I can help you with that. 64
Unit 022	can/could(2) — I'm starving. I could eat a horse. 66
Unit 023	may/might — I might be relaxing at home at this time tomorrow. 68
Unit 024	must(추측) — You must not have heard me correctly. 70
Unit 025	must vs. have to — You don't have to pay. It's free. 72
Unit 026	should — I shouldn't have said that. 74
Unit 027	기타 조동사 — You're not supposed to park here. 76
Unit 028	제안하기 — The doctor recommended that I rest for a few days. 78
Unit 029	예의 바른 요청 — Do you think you could make a little less noise? 80

Big Picture 03
현실에서 비현실로(가정법)

Unit 030	가정법 0번 vs. 1번 — Let's meet at the ticket counter if we ever get separated. 84
Unit 031	2번 가정법 — If I were you, I would accept the offer. 86
Unit 032	3번 가정법 — If he had left earlier, he would have avoided the traffic. 88
Unit 033	기타 가정법 — Unless I call you, I'll see you at 3. 90
Unit 034	wish — I wish I could, but I have other plans. 92

Big Picture 04
동사의 종류와 문장 구조

Unit 035	자동사 vs. 타동사 — I found the book quite interesting. 96
Unit 036	수동태(1) — Milk is kept in the fridge. 98
Unit 037	수동태(2) — No, thank you. I'm being helped. 100
Unit 038	수동태(3) — His company was established in 1994. 102
Unit 039	수동태(4) — The winner will be given a free trip to Norway. 104
Unit 040	사역동사 — I can't get him to understand it. 106
Unit 041	have something p.p. — Let's have a pizza delivered. 108
Unit 042	수동태(5) — It is said that life is a journey. 110

Big Picture 05
동사의 연결

Unit 043	to부정사(1) — I need to stop and think about this for a minute. 114
Unit 044	to부정사(2) — I told him to call back later. 116
Unit 045	to부정사 패턴(1) — I just called to say hello. 118
Unit 046	to부정사 패턴(2) — She is fun to be with. 120
Unit 047	-ing(1) — I miss working with you. 122
Unit 048	-ing(2) — They just went on working. 124
Unit 049	to or -ing(1) — I hate being an only child. 126
Unit 050	to or -ing(2) — I clearly remember talking about it. 128
Unit 051	to or -ing(3) — We agreed to meet again next week. 130
Unit 052	지각동사 — I didn't hear my phone ringing. 132
Unit 053	분사구문 — He took a shower, singing loudly. 134

Big Picture 06
명사의 종류와 관사

Unit 054	셀 수 있는 명사/셀 수 없는 명사(1) — I had two slices of bread and a packet of chips for lunch. **138**	
Unit 055	셀 수 있는 명사/셀 수 없는 명사(2) — The news is fake. **140**	
Unit 056	셀 수 있는 명사/셀 수 없는 명사(3) — Have a good time! **142**	
Unit 057	한정사 — Some people don't use social media at all. **144**	
Unit 058	수량형용사 — Nothing is impossible. **146**	
Unit 059	all-whole, every-each — The subway runs every five minutes. **148**	
Unit 060	both, either, neither — He is neither American nor British. **150**	
Unit 061	other, another, the other — Can I have another cup of tea? **152**	
Unit 062	The(1) — Have you seen the picture I posted? **154**	
Unit 063	The(2) — Dokdo is in the East Sea. **156**	
Unit 064	The(3) — Please go to Gate 9 for boarding. **158**	
Unit 065	The(4) — What do you usually do after school? **160**	

Big Picture 07
대명사와 반복 피하기

Unit 066	대명사(1) — If anyone calls, tell them I'm busy. **164**
Unit 067	대명사(2) — He was given one week's notice to leave the apartment. **166**
Unit 068	it — It's you that I need, not him. **168**
Unit 069	대동사, so — I might not be able to answer the phone. If so, just text me. **170**

목차

Big Picture 08
명사 꾸며 주기, 명사가 아닌 것 꾸며 주기

Unit 070   형용사 — His car looks nice.   174

Unit 071   부사 — They are all foreigners.   176

Unit 072   강조부사 — What a beautiful castle it is!   178

Unit 073   so, such — It's such a brilliant idea!   180

Unit 074   enough, too — The house isn't big enough for 4 people to live in.   182

Unit 075   비교급과 최상급(1) — I'd like to have a more powerful computer.   184

Unit 076   비교급과 최상급(2) — Busan is the second largest city in Korea.   186

Unit 077   비교급과 최상급(3) — The car is twice as expensive as this one.   188

Unit 078   관계대명사(1) — I think I deleted the email you sent me by accident.   190

Unit 079   관계대명사(2) — He has three sisters, two of whom are nurses.   192

Unit 080   관계사절(1) — Tell me how you practice English.   194

Unit 081   관계사절(2) — He works for a factory making smartphones.   196

Big Picture 09
전치사

Unit 082   시간 전치사(1) — The singer became famous in her early twenties.   200

Unit 083   시간 전치사(2) — I couldn't get up until 9:30 this morning.   202

Unit 084   장소 전치사(1) — My old car is still in good condition.   204

Unit 085   장소 전치사(2) — Does this bus go downtown?   206

Unit 086   기타 전치사(1) — You can pay by credit card or in cash.   208

Unit 087   기타 전치사(2) — Their parents don't approve of their marriage.   210

Unit 088	기타 전치사(3) — I apologized to her for what I said. **212**
Unit 089	기타 전치사(4) — Why don't we talk about it over lunch? **214**
Unit 090	구동사 — Did you look it up on the Internet? **216**
Unit 091	접속사(1) — I wear long sleeves when working in the garden. **218**
Unit 092	접속사(2) — The car was too expensive. Besides, I didn't like the color. **220**
Unit 093	접속사(3) — My brother likes dogs while I prefer cats. **222**
Unit 094	접속사(4) — I left home early so that I could catch the first bus. **224**
Unit 095	접속사(5) — Above all, I value honesty and social justice. **226**

Big Picture 10
문장의 종류와 어순

Unit 096	That S+V / It ···to/that — There is one key fact (that) you have overlooked. **230**
Unit 097	간접의문문 — How often does the app update? **232**
Unit 098	부가의문문 — You two have met before, haven't you? **234**
Unit 099	간접화법 — May both of you live a long and happy life together! **236**
Unit 100	도치법 — Little did she realize what was about to happen. **238**

- 부록 **240**
- 특별부록 **248**
- 정답 **258**
- Index **276**

중급 영문법에 들어가기 전에 알아두어야 할 기초 사항 점검

1 각 단어의 명칭

- **명사**(NOUN) — 사물, 사람 등을 가리키는 명칭. what(무엇) 또는 who(누구)에 해당하는 단어
- **대명사**(PRONOUN) — 명사를 대신 하는 단어
- **동사**(VERB) — 동작이나 상태를 서술하는 단어
- **형용사**(ADJECTIVE) — 명사나 대명사를 꾸며주는 단어
- **부사**(ADVERB) — 동사, 형용사, 부사 또는 문장 전체를 꾸며주는 표현
- **전치사**(PREPOSITION) — 문장이나 표현에 명사를 더해주는 연결어
- **접속사**(CONJUNCTION) — 문장(절)과 문장(절)을 이어주는 연결 표현

2 문장의 구성

영어 문장은 기본적으로 하나의 '주어'와 '동사'로 구성되어 있습니다. '동사'가 없으면 문장이 완성되지 않습니다. 문장의 '동사'는 단어가 아닌 '~다'를 나타내는 하나의 덩어리일 수도 있습니다.

- She **plays** the piano very well. 그녀는 피아노를 잘 쳐요.
- She **is playing** the piano now. 그녀는 지금 피아노를 치고 있어요.
- She **has been playing** the piano since she was seven.
  그녀는 7살 때부터 꾸준히 피아노를 쳐 왔습니다.

3 영어문장의 종류

주로 쓰이는 영어 문장에는 보통 일반 문장이라고 하는 긍정문과 부정문, 그리고 의문문, 이렇게 크게 세 가지가 있습니다.

이 문장들을 만드는 방법은 쓰여지는 동사의 종류에 따라 다릅니다.

동사의 종류와 각 문장 만드는 법은 다음 표를 참고하세요.

	Be type 동사	Do type 동사
일반문장(긍정문)	am, are, is, can, have (p.p.) 등 I'm an engineer. 저는 엔지니어입니다.	go, eat, like, dance, work 등 I work at a high tech company. 저는 첨단 기술 회사에서 일합니다.
부정문	I'm not hungry. 전 배고프지 않아요.	I don't have a cat. 저는 고양이가 없어요.
의문문	Are you from Canada? 당신은 캐나다에서 오셨나요?	Do you go to school by bus? 당신은 버스로 등교하나요?

Big Picture

동사의 형태와 시간 개념

01

영어 문장의 동사는 항상 시간을 나타냅니다. 한마디로 '동사=시간'이지요.
따라서 동사의 형태를 보면 그 문장의 시간이 보입니다.

 동사 덩어리 중 맨 앞의 동사가 문장의 '기준 시간'을 말합니다. 동사가 현재형이면 기준 시간이 현재이고, -ed면 과거입니다. 미래는 will이나 be going to 등이 함께 옵니다.

1 동사원형 또는 단순현재 원래 모양 그대로의 동사
동사를 원형으로 썼다는 건, 어느 한때만이 아니라 시간이 '전체적(general)'으로 걸쳐 있음을 나타냅니다. 즉, 과거에도, 지금도, 그리고 앞으로도 그럴 것이라 생각된다는 의미입니다. *See 부록03▶*

2 -ing 현재분사, 진행형
-ing는 어느 한때에만 '집중'됨을 나타냅니다. 단, -ing 자체는 동사 역할을 못하기 때문에 앞에 Be동사가 오지요. 이 Be동사에 따라 -ing가 집중한 시간이 결정됩니다. am/are/is는 현재, was/were는 과거, will be -ing는 미래의 어느 한때에 집중하는 것이죠. -ing는 기준 시간에 내내 이루어지거나 벌어지고 있는 사건이나 동작을 나타냅니다. *See 부록03, 06, 09▶*

3 -ed
-ed는 '한걸음 과거로 물러난' 개념이라고 할 수 있습니다. 기준점이 과거로 옮겨졌기 때문에 오로지 과거에 대해서만 말하게 됩니다. 그 때만을 말하므로, 지금 입장에선 완전히 끝난(over) 이야기입니다. *See 부록 05▶*

 -ed는 동사로 쓰이는 반면, p.p.는 동사가 아니라는 점 외에 둘의 느낌은 매우 유사합니다.

4 have p.p. 완료
have와 동사의 p.p.(과거분사)가 하나의 덩어리입니다. p.p.는 과거에 대해 일단 '정리(완료)'하는 개념입니다. have p.p.는 have가 현재형이므로 현재가 기준이고, had p.p.는 과거, will have p.p.는 미래의 어느 한때가 기준입니다. 이 기준 시점에서 그 이전에 대해 말하는 것이 '완료 시제'의 핵심입니다. have p.p.의 경우, 현재 기준으로 얼마나 많이/오래 그러한가, 그런 경험이 있나 없나, 지금 되었나 안되었나를 말하지요. 지금까지는 그런 적이 없지만, 앞으로는 그렇게 될 수 있다는 것을 암시할 수 있습니다. *See 부록 07, 08, 10▶*

5 have p.p.+ing 완료진행형
완료와 -ing가 만날 수도 있습니다. have p.p.의 p.p.가 been이 되어 have been -ing가 되지요. 이때에는 완료시제의 개념에 -ing 개념이 더해져, 기준 시간까지 내내 쭉 이루어지거나 반복되어 벌어지는 것을 나타내게 됩니다.

Unit 001

Be동사

Everything's going to be all right.
모든 일이 잘 될 거야.

1 대화체에서 Be동사 문장은 주어가 대명사일 때 축약된 형태로 많이 쓰인다. *See 부록 01▶*

- A: **You're** late again. 너 또 늦었어.
  B: Sorry. The bus was late. 미안. 버스가 늦게 왔어.
- A: Is he your boyfriend? 그 남자 네 남자친구니?
  B: No. **He's not** my boyfriend. **He's** my elder brother. 아냐. 그는 내 남자친구가 **아니야**. 우리 오빠야.

2 Be동사 뒤에는 보통 명사, 형용사, 전치사가 온다.

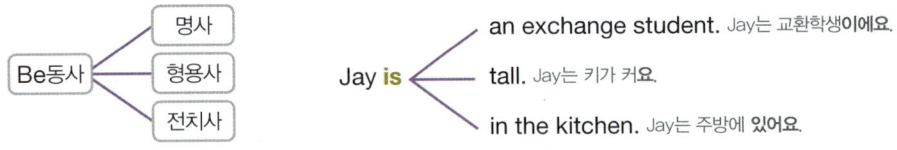

3 Be동사는 문장에서 동사 자리에 동사가 없을 때 쓸 수 있다.

- 문장을 완성하기 위해 명사, 형용사, 전치사, -ing, p.p. 앞

- His office **is** on the fifth floor. 그의 사무실은 5층에 있습니다.
- They**'re** playing basketball now. 그들은 지금 농구를 하고 있어요.
- This skirt **is** made of silk. 이 치마는 실크로 만들었어요.

- to (부정사) 뒤 전치사 to와 헷갈리지 말 것! *See Unit 085, 088▶*

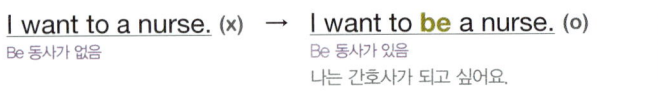

- Everything's going **to be** all right. 모든 일이 잘 될 거야.
- You don't have **to be** afraid. 두려워할 필요 없어요.
- **To be** honest, it's not quite my style. 솔직하게 말하면 그건 내 스타일은 아니야.

- will이나 조동사 뒤

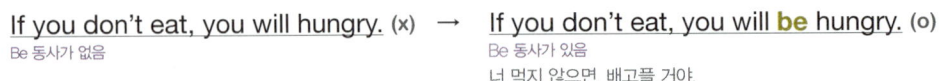

- It **can't be** true. 그건 사실일 리가 없어.
- It's 9 p.m. He **must be** at home now. 저녁 9시야. 지금쯤이면 그는 집에 있을 **거야**.
- It **might be** a good idea to cancel it. 그것을 취소하는 것이 좋은 생각일**지도 모르겠어요**.

Exercises

1. 문장의 빈칸에 들어갈 Be동사의 정확한 형태를 넣으세요.

1. The restroom _is_ is on the third floor.
2. Andy and Patrick _____ brothers.
3. _____ James still here?
4. _____ I late?
5. A: Have you swum in the ocean?
   B: No, this _____ the first time.
6. You need to _____ careful when you cross the street.
7. A: I'm looking for Amy. Have you seen her?
   B: Yes, she _____ here a minute ago.
8. What _____ you going wear to the party?
9. We _____ so tired after driving all night.
10. A: Is 11 o'clock OK for you?
    B: Yes. I'll _____ there at 11 o'clock.
11. Have you ever _____ to Venice?

2. 문장의 틀린 부분이 있다면 고쳐서 다시 쓰세요. 틀린 부분이 없다면 X를 쓰세요.

1. You don't have to afraid. — *You don't have to be afraid.*
2. Jessica and Nicole are nurses. — X
3. The children doing their homework now. — _____
4. Our headquarters in Seoul. — _____
5. The office is going to cleaned tomorrow. — _____
6. Where she from? — _____
7. The final exam wasn't difficult. — _____
8. Don't worry. Happy. — _____
9. He's been teaching English for many years. — _____
10. I'll back in an hour. — _____
11. My house used to here. — _____

🔊 Dialogue

3. 주어진 단어를 이용하여 문맥에 맞게 문장을 완성하세요.

Suzi is asking little Eva what her dream is.
Suzi가 꼬마 Eva에게 장래희망이 무엇인지를 묻고 있습니다.

Suzi Eva, _____ (what / your dream)?
Eva   _____ (I / want to / a nurse).
Suzi Why?
Eva   Because my mom is a nurse. _____ (I / want to / like my mom).
Suzi Wonderful. I'm sure _____ (you / will / a wonderful nurse).

Unit 002

단순현재

My laptop works well.
내 노트북 컴퓨터는 잘 작동합니다.

1 **Do type** 동사 문장은 다음과 같이 만든다. 부정문과 의문문에서 do를 사용한다.

	긍정문	부정문	의문문
현재 (Present)	I/You/We/They **work**. He/She/It **works**.	I/You/We/They **don't**(=**do not**) work. He/She/It **doesn't**(=**does not**) work.	**Do** I/you/we/they work? **Does** he/she/it work?

2 단순현재 시제는 -ing나 -ed 형태가 아닌 그대로의 동사 형태(현재형)는 현재를 기준으로 한 전반적인 시간대를 말한다. 특별히 어느 한때만을 이야기하지 않음

▶ A: Where **do you come** from? 어디 출신이세요?
  B: I **come** from Australia originally. 저는 원래 호주에서 **왔어요**.
  A: What **do you do**? 무슨 **일**을 하시나요?
  B: I'm a flight attendant. I **work** for World Airways. 승무원이에요. 저는 월드항공사에서 **일해요**.
  A: And so where **do you live**? 아, 그럼 어디 **사시나요**?
  B: I **live** in L.A. World Airways is an American company. L.A에 **살아요**. 월드항공사가 미국 회사거든요.

3 반복적으로 일어나는 일이나 사실, 일반적인 사항을 말할 때 동사의 현재형을 쓴다.

▶ I **get** to work at 9:00. 저는 회사에 9시에 **도착합니다**.
▶ What **do** you **do** in your spare time? 여가 시간엔 뭘 하세요?
▶ My laptop **works** well. 내 노트북 컴퓨터는 잘 **작동된다**.

● timetable(시간표)나 프로그램, 일정 등에 대해서도 동사의 현재형으로 표현할 수 있다. *See Unit 016 ▶*

▶ The train to L.A. **leaves** at 8:45 and **gets** in Union Station at 9:20.
  L.A행 기차는 8시 45분에 **출발해서** 9시 20분에 Union Station에 **도착합니다**.

4 단순현재 시제에는 다음과 같은 시간표현이 자주 함께 쓰인다.

● always, usually와 같은 빈도부사는 Be type 동사 뒤, Do type 동사 앞에 올 수 있다.

100%			50%		0%
always	usually	often	sometimes	hardly ever/seldom/rarely	never

▶ You **can always trust** him. 그 사람은 항상 믿을 수 있어.
▶ She **never forgets** a face. 그녀는 **절대 (한 번 본)** 얼굴을 잊어버리지 않아요.
▶ We **don't often drink** wine. 우리는 자주 와인을 마시진 않아요.
▶ **Sometimes** I **take** the bus to work. 저는 **가끔** 버스를 타고 회사에 갑니다. sometimes는 문장의 맨 앞에 오는 경우가 많다

● every day/week/month, daily/weekly/monthly, once a year, from time to time, most of the time 등의 표현은 보통 문장의 앞이나 뒤에 온다. *See Unit 071 ▶*

▶ **Every winter** they go to Colorado. 매해 겨울 그들은 콜로라도에 간다.
▶ We prepare a sales report **four times a year**. 우리는 **1년에 4번** 판매 보고서를 준비합니다.

Exercises

1. 주어진 동사를 적절한 형태로 바꾸어 문장을 완성하세요.

1. Americans _speak_ (speak) English.
2. I hardly ever _____ (take) the train to work.
3. I _____ (not smoke).
4. Every time prices _____ (go up), wages should increase, too.
5. My company _____ (design) and _____ (manufacture) educational toys.
6. The café _____ (open) at 8:00 a.m. and _____ (not close) until midnight.
7. The Han River _____ (flow) into the West Sea.

2. 주어진 단어를 써서 대화에 들어갈 질문을 완성하세요.

1. A: How would you like to pay?
   B: _Do you take Visa_ (you / take Visa)?
2. A: Some people can go to sleep right after closing their eyes.
   B: _____ (How / they / do that)?
3. A: _____ (Where / he / live)?
   B: In Glendale.
4. A: _____ (she / drive an SUV)?
   B: Yes. A big black one.
5. A: _____ (How often / you / call your parents)?
   B: Every weekend.

3. 주어진 빈도 부사를 문장의 맨 앞과 맨 뒤가 아닌 중간에 넣어 문장을 다시 쓰세요.

1. I get to work at 8:30 a.m. (usually) — _I usually get to work at 8:30 a.m._
2. She doesn't wear jeans. (often)
3. My dog is happy. (always)
4. He shouts at others. (never)
5. What do you do in your spare time? (usually)
6. I've wanted to be an accountant. (always)

🔊 Dialogue

4. 주어진 단어를 이용하여 문맥에 맞게 문장을 완성하세요.

Noah is on a quiz show on TV. Noah는 TV 퀴즈 프로그램에 출연하고 있습니다.

Show Host Welcome to Speed Quiz! Today's contestant is Noah Stuart. Noah. Are you ready?

Noah Yes, I'm ready.

Show host OK. Here comes the first question. _____ (Koreans / speak Korean). _____ (Italians / speak Italian). Then _____ (what language / Canadians, speak)?

Noah Uh... Canadian?

Show Host Oh no! They Speak English! _____ (Canadians / speak English)!

Unit 003

현재진행형

The elevator isn't working.
엘리베이터가 작동하지 않아요.

1 -ing 형태는 어느 한때에 '집중'하는 시간 개념을 나타낸다. am/are/is -ing는 '지금'에 초점을 두고 있다.
See 부록 03▶

▶ A: **Is** Mike **working** now? Mike 지금 근무 중인가요?
　B: No, he isn't. He's out for lunch. 아뇨, 지금은 일하고 있지 않아요. 점심 먹으러 나갔어요.

2 꼭 지금 말하고 있는 순간만이 아닌 지금 전후의 일시적인 한때를 말할 수도 있다.

These days I**'m reading** a book about the life story of Steve Jobs.
요즘 난 스티브 잡스의 생애에 대한 책을 **읽고 있어**.

▶ He**'s doing** a TESOL course at UCLA. 그는 UCLA에서 TESOL 과정을 **밟고 있다**.

3 am/are/is -ing는 다음과 같은 시간 표현과 함께 자주 쓰인다.

```
now    at the moment   currently   nowadays
right now    these days    this week/month/year…
```

▶ **This week** I'm taking the bus to work – my car is at the garage.
저 **이번 주**는 회사에 버스 타고 가요. 차가 카센터에 있거든요.

4 -ing가 집중한 시간은 그 이전이나 이후와는 '다름'이 암시된다. 따라서 am/are/is -ing는 과거나 미래에는 그렇지 않고 지금만 그렇다는 뉘앙스이다.

▶ The elevator **isn't working**. We'll have to take the stairs. 엘리베이터가 **작동하지 않아요**. 계단으로 가야겠네요.
　이전에는 작동했었고, 앞으로도 (고쳐서) 작동될 것으로 기대됨. 그러나 '지금'은 작동하지 않음

따라서 시간에 따라 달라지고 있는 변화를 말할 때에도 am/are/is -ing가 쓰인다.
▶ Prices **are going up**. 물가가 오르고 있어요.
▶ The problem of global warming **is getting** worse. 지구 온난화 문제가 더 심각해지고 있어요.

일반적으로 그런 것과 어느 한때만 그러함의 구분이 선명하지 않은 동사(상태동사)는 보통 -ing로 쓰지 않는다.
-ing 형태가 가능한 동사는 보통 "구체적"이고 "시각적"인 action을 의미 See 부록 02▶
▶ Now I **remember** her name! It's Amber. 이제 그녀의 이름이 **기억나**! Amber야.
　Now I'**m remembering** her name! It's Amber. (X)

같은 동사라도 의미에 따라 -ing를 쓸 수 있을 수도 없을 수도 있다. See Unit 005 ▶
▶ I **have** a question for you now. 지금 당신에게 질문이 하나 있는데요. 소유 의미의 상태동사
　I'**m having** a question for you now. (X)
▶ We'**re having** a wonderful time here. 우린 지금 여기서 멋진 시간을 보내고 있어. '(경험)겪다'라는 의미의 action

Exercises

1. 주어진 동사를 적절한 형태로 바꾸어 문장을 완성하세요. 주어가 대명사라면 축약형을 쓰세요.
   1. Sarah _is doing_ (do) a computer course this month.
   2. I _____ (use) a company car this week. My car is at the garage.
   3. Sea levels _____ (rise) because of global warming.
   4. Sorry, I _____ (drive) now. Can I call you back later?
   5. Look! They _____ (sell) perfume at a 30% discount!
   6. They _____ (develop) a new drug for diabetes.

2. 주어진 단어를 사용하여 문장을 완성하세요. 가능하면 축약형을 쓰세요.
   1. _The air conditioner isn't working_ (The air conditioner / not / work). Please, call the maintenance team.
   2. A: Are you OK? You look a bit tired.
      B: Well, _____ (I / not / sleep very well) these days.
   3. This is a bad line. _____ (you / call from your cell phone)?
   4. A: _____ (How / it / go)?
      B: Very well, thank you.
   5. _____ (They / not / reply to my emails). Should I call them?
   6. A: _____ (Mr. Harris / expect me)?
      B: Yes. He's waiting in the meeting room now.

3. 밑줄 친 부분이 틀렸다면 맞게 고치세요. 밑줄 친 부분이 맞다면 X를 쓰세요.
   1. Now I'm remembering his name! It's Noah.   _I remember_
   2. A: Can I help you, sir?
      B: No, thanks. I'm just looking.   _X_
   3. A: Are you enjoying this course?
      B: Yes. I'm liking it very much.   _____
   4. A: Are you enjoying your vacation?
      B: Yes! We're having a wonderful time here in Rome.   _____
   5. Sir, I'm having a question.   _____

🔊 Dialogue

4. 주어진 단어를 이용하여 문맥에 맞게 문장을 완성하세요.

Suzi is making a phone call to a company. Suzi가 어느 회사에 전화를 걸고 있습니다.

Suzi: Hello, this is Suzi Kim. May I speak to Mr. Elliot, please?
Staff member: I'm sorry, but he's not in at the moment.
Suzi: When will he be back?
Staff member: Well, he's on vacation. _____ (He / not / work) this week.
Suzi: Oh, I see. Then may I speak to someone in charge of shipping?
Staff member: Sure... Please hold.

Unit 004

단순현재 vs. 현재진행형(1)

You're always forgetting my birthday!
넌 맨날 내 생일 까먹어!

1. 시간 개념의 비교: 일반적인(general) vs. 구체적인(specific) See 부록 03 ▶

I do... (V) : 단순현재 일반적인 사실, 습관, 반복적인 것, 변치 않는 것	I'm doing... (am/are/is -ing) : 현재진행형 일시적, 현재 진행 중인 사건, 변화, 변동 상황
▶ I **work** for an American company. 저는 미국 회사에서 **일합니다**. 변동 없는 일반적 사실	▶ I**'m working** from home today. 전 오늘 재택근무해요. 오늘만 일시적으로 재택근무
▶ They **have** a meeting every Monday. 그들은 매주 월요일에 회의를 **합니다**. 반복	▶ Mike is busy right now. He**'s having** a meeting. Mike는 지금 바쁩니다. 회의 중입니다. 현재 진행 중
▶ We all **get old** one day. 우리는 모두 언젠가는 **늙는다**. 변치 않음	▶ The population of Korea **is getting older**. 한국의 인구의 연령이 높아지고 있다. 변화, 변동 중

2. 반복이 암시되는 빈도 표현(How often, 얼마나 자주)은 일반적으로 현재진행형 시제에는 쓰지 않는다.

▶ I **usually check** my email from my smartphone. 저는 보통 스마트폰으로 이메일을 확인해요.
   I**'m usually checking** my email from my smartphone. (X)

단, am/are/is always -ing는 '과도하게' 반복이 심하다는 의미로 쓸 수 있다. 종종 비난의 뉘앙스

> What's that noise? Are they having a party again?
> 저 시끄러운 소린 뭐지? 그들이 또 파티를 하고 있나?

> I think so. **They're always having a party!**
> 그런 것 같아. 그 사람들 맨날 파티야.

▶ She**'s always getting** phone calls or text messages. 걔는 허구한 날 전화 아니면 문자 **와요**.
▶ You**'re always forgetting** my birthday! 넌 맨날 내 생일 까먹어!

3. 일시적으로 그렇게 '군다'라고 말할 때 '(be)+being+형용사'로 말할 수 있다.
'~게 군다'라고 말할 수 있는 행동과 연관된 형용사에 대해서만 쓸 수 있다. 예) He is being tall. (X)

He is mean. (general)	vs.	He is being mean. (now)
그는 못됐다. (일반적)		그는 못되게 굴고 있다. (일시적 모습)

▶ My boss **is being** so **nice** to me today. He isn't usually like that.
   사장님이 오늘 나한테 너무 **잘해 주시네**. 보통 그렇지 않은데 말이야.
▶ The buyers **are being** very **difficult** at the moment. 바이어들이 지금 매우 **까다롭게 굴고 있어요**.

Exercises

1. 주어진 동사를 적절한 형태로 바꾸어 문장을 완성하세요. 주어가 대명사라면 축약형을 쓰세요.
   1. I usually ___have___ (have) dinner after 8:00 p.m.
   2. I'm afraid Ms. Turner isn't in now. She _____ (have) lunch with a client.
   3. It _____ (get) dark. Let's go back home now.
   4. It _____ (get) very cold in January in the North Sea.
   5. James _____ (work) very hard and always does his best.
   6. Steve _____ (work) very hard today. He's not usually like that.
   7. I _____ (visit) my grandmother in Vancouver every summer.
   8. A: Are you here on business?
      B: No, I _____ just _____ (visit) a friend.

2. 주어진 동사의 -ing 형태와 always를 사용하여 문장을 완성하세요.
   1. This car ___is always breaking down___ (break down)! I should trade it in for a new one.
   2. You're so forgetful. You _____ (forget) things.
   3. Everybody loves little Eva because she _____ (smile and laugh).
   4. He _____ (play) games on his phone.
   5. He isn't so popular because he _____ (tell) the same stories.
   6. I don't like Jack and Sam very much. They _____ (argue).

3. 주어진 표현 중 문장의 문맥에 가장 적합한 표현을 고르세요.
   1. I wonder why my boss (is so nice / **is being so nice**) to me today. He isn't usually like that.
   2. A: What is your new English teacher like?
      B: She (is very nice / is being very nice).
   3. I can't understand why you (are so mean / are being so mean) to me these days.
      You didn't used to be like this.
   4. They've rejected the deal. I think they (are unreasonable / are being unreasonable) in their demands now.
   5. Mike isn't at work today. He (is sick / is being sick).
   6. Look. I (am very patient / am being very patient), so please don't keep me waiting so long.

🔊 Dialogue

4. 주어진 단어를 이용하여 문맥에 맞게 문장을 완성하세요.

   Andy is shopping for a gift for his girlfriend Amy. Andy는 여자친구 Amy에게 줄 선물 쇼핑을 하고 있습니다.

   Andy I'm looking for some phone accessories for my girlfriend's new phone.
   Clerk How about this mirror screen protector?
   Andy What's good about it?
   Clerk This offers superior protection from scratches. Plus its shiny finish acts like a mirror when your phone is in sleep mode.
   Andy That's great. _____ (My girlfriend / always / fix her makeup).
   Clerk Then it's a perfect fit.

Unit 005

단순현재 vs. 현재진행형(2)

Let me pay this time. I insist.
이번엔 제가 내겠다니까요.

#ⓥ vs. be –ing #Present Simple vs. Present continuous #단순현재(제일) 진행형 비교

1 똑같이 '지금'에 초점을 둔 문장이라도 동사에 따라 형태(시제)가 달라질 수 있다.

상태동사(Non-Action Verbs) ⓥ (단순현재) general, not graphic/visual, 일반적 개념, 추상적		동작동사(Action Verbs) am/are/is –ing (현재진행형) specific, graphic/visual, 구체적 이미지	
인식, 인지	▶ Now I **know**. 이제 알겠어요.	동작	▶ I'm **learning** now. 지금 익히고 있어요.
감정 느낌	▶ I **like** this cake! Scrumptious! 이 케이크 맘에 들어! 완전 맛있어!	활동	▶ Are you **enjoying** your cake? 케이크는 맛있게 들고 계신가요?
현재 상태	▶ I'm **hungry** now. 나 지금 배고파.	변화, 변동	▶ I'm **getting** hungry. 점점 배고파지고 있어요
자연스러운 감각	▶ Do you **hear** me? 제 말 들리세요? ▶ What do you **see**? 뭐가 보이니?	의도적 행동	▶ I'm **listening** to a podcast. 저는 지금 팟캐스트를 듣고 있어요. ▶ What are you **looking** at? 뭘 보고 있니?

2 같은 단어라도 의미에 따라 달리 쓰일 수 있다.

▶ I **have** a question for you now.
  지금 당신에게 질문이 하나 **있는**데요.
▶ We're **having** a wonderful time here.
  우리는 지금 여기서 멋진 시간을 보내고 있어.

▶ I **think** that social media is a good thing for many reasons.
  저는 소셜 미디어가 여러 가지 이유로 좋은 것이라고 **생각해요**.
▶ I'm **thinking** about my next vacation.
  다음 휴가에 대해서 **생각 중이야**.

▶ A: Do you understand? 이해되나요?
  B: I **see**. 네, 이해해요.
▶ I **see** a light over there.
  저기 불빛이 **보여요**.
▶ I'm not **seeing** anyone at the moment.
  저는 지금 누구도 **사귀고 있지 않아요**.
▶ James is **seeing** the doctor now.
  그는 지금 의사를 **만나고 있어요**. (진료 중임)

▶ It **smells** terrible here. 여기 냄새가 **지독하네요**.
▶ Look! Your dog is **smelling** the ground.
  보렴. 네 개가 바닥 **냄새를 맡고 있어**.

▶ This soup **tastes** good. 이 수프 **맛이 좋네요**.
▶ The chef is **tasting** the soup.
  셰프가 수프의 **맛을 보고 있어요**.

see, hear, smell, taste 등 자연스럽게 느껴지는 감각에 대해 말하는 동사는 종종 can과 함께 쓰이기도 한다. **See Unit 021 ▶**

3 look과 feel은 ⓥ와 am/are/is –ing에 모두 쓸 수 있다.

▶ You **look** stunning today. = You're **looking** stunning today. 너 오늘 정말 멋져 **보여**.
▶ I don't **feel** well today. = I'm not **feeling** very well today. 저 오늘은 몸이 별로 안 좋아요.

4 다음 동사들은 '내가 지금 ~하는 바이다'라는 의미로 말할 때 단순현재 시제 형태로 쓰인다.

> promise apologize insist advise refuse suggest suppose swear

▶ Believe me. I **promise** I won't let you down. 믿어 줘. 널 실망시키지 않겠다고 **약속해**.
▶ Let me pay this time. I **insist**. 이번엔 제가 내겠**다니까요**. 고집, 주장하는 뉘앙스

Exercises

1. 다음 보기에서 동사를 골라 적절한 형태로 바꾸어 문장을 완성하세요. 주어가 대명사라면 축약형을 쓰세요.

> be   get   hear   learn   listen to   look   ~~understand~~

1. Now I _understand_ what you're talking about.
2. I _____ how to read Japanese now.
3. It _____ very cold now.
4. It _____ cold now.
5. Why _____ you _____ at me like that?
6. I _____ a noise now.
7. A: What are you doing?
   B: I _____ music.

2. 주어진 동사를 적절한 형태로 바꾸어 문장을 완성하세요. 주어가 대명사라면 축약형을 쓰세요.

1. I _have_ (have) a question for you now.
2. I _____ (have) dinner now. Can I call you back later?
3. We _____ (think) about moving back to Vancouver.
4. What _____ you _____ (think) about studying abroad?
5. _____ you _____ (see) anyone?
6. I _____ (see) what you mean.
7. Mmm. These cookies _____ (smell) good.
8. In the picture, she _____ (smell) the flowers.

3. 아래 보기에 주어진 동사 중 적절한 것을 골라 넣어 문장을 완성하세요.

> apologize   ~~insist~~   promise   recommend   suppose

1. Let me pay this time. I _insist_.
2. I won't make the same mistakes again. I _____.
3. I highly _____ her class.
4. I _____ prices will go up.
5. I _____ for the delays.

🔊 Dialogue

4. 주어진 단어를 이용하여 문맥에 맞게 문장을 완성하세요.

Patrick wants his brother Andy to help him with cleaning his car.
Patrick은 세차하는데 동생 Andy가 도와주길 바라고 있습니다.

Patrick Andy, how about helping me clean my car?
Andy Nah. I'm tired.
Patrick I'll buy you lunch if you help me.
Andy Really? _____ (you / promise)?
Patrick I do. Let's go to Holley's after we finish the cleaning, OK?

Unit 006

단순과거

It rained a lot last night.
어젯밤에 비가 많이 왔다.

1 과거에 이미 끝난 행동이나 사건은 동사의 -ed 형태를 써서 말한다.
동사가 -ed 형태가 되면 기준 시간이 과거로 한 걸음 물러난다고 할 수 있다.

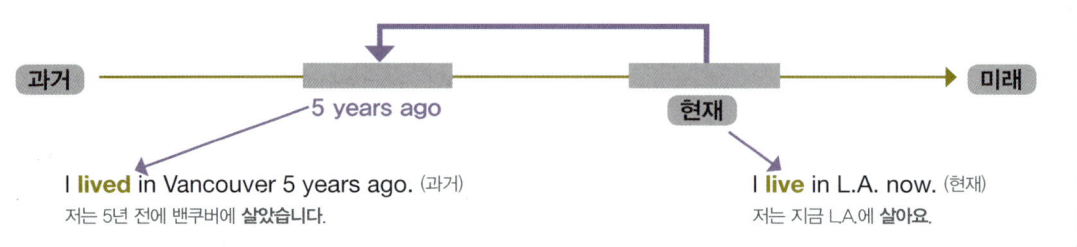

I **lived** in Vancouver 5 years ago. (과거)
저는 5년 전에 밴쿠버에 **살았습니다**.

I **live** in L.A. now. (현재)
저는 지금 L.A.에 **살아요**.

단, 불규칙 동사는 -ed가 아닌 다른 형태를 취한다. See 부록 04▶

	긍정문	부정문	의문문
Do type 동사	I worked…	I didn't work…	Did you work…?
Be type 동사	I was…	I wasn't…	Were you…?

- A: **Did** you **visit** the British Museum when you **were** in London? 런던 갔을 때 대영박물관 **방문했었니**?
  B: Yes, I **did**. On the second day of my trip. 응, 갔었어. 여행 둘째 날에.
  A: **Did** you **like** it? What **was** it like? 좋았어? 어땠니?
  B: I **loved** it! It **was** magnificent! 너무 좋았어! 정말 감명 깊었어!
- It **rained** a lot last night. 어젯밤에 비가 많이 **왔다**.
- I **didn't take** the job because the salary **was** too low. 월급이 너무 낮아서 나는 그 일자리를 **받아들이지 않았다**.
- What **did** you **study** in college? I mean, you major? 대학에서 뭘 **공부하셨죠**? 제 말은 그러니까, 전공이?

2 동사의 -ed가 쓰인 문장에서는 다음의 시간 표현들이 자주 쓰인다.

> **In** January/2016, **yesterday**, **last** week/month/year, a few days **ago**, **when** I was a child…

- Sia worked hard **last year** and she got a good bonus **in December**.
  Sia는 **작년에** 열심히 일해서 **12월에** 보너스를 두둑이 받았다.
- **When I was a child**, I wanted to be an astronaut. 나는 어릴 때 우주인이 되고 싶어했다.

3 **used to ~**는 '과거 한때 그러곤 했으나 지금은 그렇지 않다'라는 의미로 쓸 수 있다.

- Mike **used to work** in sales. (He doesn't work in sales anymore.)
  Mike는 판매 분야에서 **일했었다**. (지금은 더 이상 판매 분야에서 일하지 않는다.)

● 비슷한 의미로 would가 쓰일 수도 있으나, would는 구체적인 과거의 때와 함께 반복되던 동작 또는 행동에 대해 말할 때에만 쓸 수 있다.

- On Sundays, we **would go** out for dinner. 일요일이면 우리는 저녁을 먹으러 밖으로 나가곤 했었다.
- The building **used to be** a library. 그 건물은 한때 도서관이었다.
  *The building **would be** a library.* (X)
  구체적인 때가 드러나지 않았고, 동작이나 행동에 대해 말하는 문장이 아님

● 'be/get used to+명사/-ing'는 '~에 익숙하다'라는 의미로, used to ~와는 다른 표현이다.

- **I'm used to living** in a dorm now. 이제 기숙사에 **사는 것에 익숙해요**.

Exercises

1. 주어진 동사를 적절한 형태로 바꿔 넣어 문장을 완성하세요.
    1. The project ___finished___ (finish) two weeks ago.
    2. My sister is a designer. She _____ (go) to Milan Fashion Show last month.
    3. What _____ you _____ (do) last weekend?
    4. I _____ (graduate) from high school in 2015.
    5. I'm sorry to disturb you. I _____ (not realize) you had a visitor.
    6. _____ you _____ (study) management when you _____ (be) in college?
    7. I'm sorry I _____ (not answer) your call this morning. I _____ (be) too busy.
    8. In the Middle Ages, people _____ (eat) with their hands.

2. 주어진 표현으로 질문을 완성하세요.
    1. (When / Michael Jackson / die)   _When did Michael Jackson die_ ?
    2. (Where / the Vikings / live)   _____ ?
    3. (What / James Watt / invent)   _____ ?
    4. (How many books / Roald Dahl / write) _____ ?

    ▶ 위 질문에 대한 답을 주어진 표현을 이용하여 완성하세요.
    1. in 2009   _He died in 2009._ .
    2. in Scandinavia   _____ .
    3. the steam engine   _____ .
    4. 49 books   _____ .

3. 문장의 문맥에 가장 적합한 표현을 골라 문장을 완성하세요.
    1. When I was a child, I (**used to** / am used to) be very shy.
    2. I (used to / am used to) working alone now.
    3. There (used to / would) be a lot of frogs in this pond.
    4. We (used to / are getting used to) the new office.
    5. He (was used to / would) kick the door when he was angry.

🔊 Dialogue

4. 주어진 단어를 이용하여 문맥에 맞게 문장을 완성하세요.

Sia is visiting her aunt. Sia는 고모를 방문하고 있습니다.
Sia   Wow, the town has changed a lot!
Aunt Ann It has. It is much different than before.
Sia   _____ (What, happen to my favorite bakery)?
          It used to be over there.
Aunt Ann It moved to Main Street.
Sia   Really?
Aunt Ann Yes. Their business was so successful that they built a new store and added a cafeteria section.

Unit 007

과거진행형

I was living abroad in 2014.
나는 2014년에는 해외에서 살고 있었다.

1 was/were –ing는 과거의 어느 한때에 벌어지고 있던 사건이나 상황을 말할 때 쓸 수 있다. See 부록 06▶

I **was living** abroad in 2014. 2014년 이전이나 이후에는
나는 2014년에는 해외에서 살고 있었다. 해외에서 살지 않았다는 뉘앙스,
2014년에 대해서만 초점

과거 ——✗————✗————✗————✗————✗——→ 현재
　　　2011　　2013　　2014　　2015　　2016

2 was/were –ing는 어떤 사건이나 이야기의 배경이나 상황을 설명할 때에 자주 쓰인다.

▸ Sam and his wife had an accident in his car yesterday. Luckily, **they were wearing seatbelts** and **he wasn't driving very fast**. 사건 Sam과 그의 아내는 어제 차 사고가 났다. 상황 다행히 (사고가 났을 때) 그들은 안전벨트를 하고 있었고, 그는 과속하고 있지도 않았다.(= 안전벨트를 매고 과속하지 않고 달리던 와중에 사고가 났다)

▸ **I was talking to a client** when you called. 전화 주셨을 때 저는 고객과 상담 중이었습니다. when S+V으로 때를 나타냄

3 was/were –ing는 종종 while과 함께 사용된다. 보통 '~하다가/하는 동안에'의 의미로 이해할 수 있다.

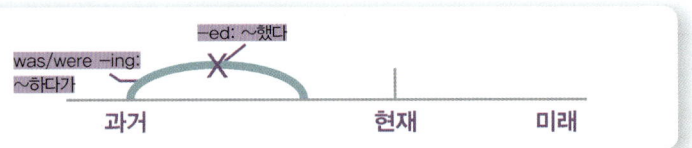

While S was/were -ing, S -ed. (=S -ed while S was/were -ing) S가 ~하다가(was/were -ing) ~했다(-ed) 간혹 when을 쓰기도 함	While A was/were -ing, B was/were -ing (=B was/were -ing while A was/were -ing) A가 ~하는 동안에 B는 ~하고 있었다 동시에 두 가지 일이 벌어지고 있었음
▸ I first **met** Ms. Kim while I **was visiting** London on a marketing trip. 나는 마케팅 출장 차 런던에 **방문했다가** Ms. Kim을 처음 **만났다**.	▸ While I **was cooking**, he **was setting** the table. 내가 요리하는 동안 그는 식탁을 차리고 있었다.

4 –ed vs. was/were –ing : 과거 기준 시간 또는 그 이후에 벌어지는 것은 –ed, 그 전에 이미 시작되어 벌어지고 있던 것은 was/were –ing로 말한다.

When the phone rang, ┌ I **was talking** to a client. 전화벨이 울렸을 때, 나는 고객과 상담 중이었다.
기준시간　　　　　　　└ I **answered** it. 전화벨이 울리자 나는 전화를 받았다.

▸ When they decided to close down the factory, they **were losing** $200,000 a week.
공장을 닫기로 결정했을 때 그들은 (이미) 주당 20만불의 **손실을** 입고 있던 와중이었다.

▸ When they decided to close down the factory, they **fired** everyone.
공장을 닫기로 결정하자, 그들은 모든 사람들을 **해고했다**.

Exercises

1. 다음 보기에서 동사를 골라 적절한 형태로 바꾸어 문장을 완성하세요.

> pay   shine   sing   ~~take~~   wear

1. A: Why didn't you answer my phone?
   B: I _was taking_ a shower.
2. A: My math teacher got angry with me during the class.
   B: Why?
   A: I _____ attention.
3. The missing boy _____ a red T-shirt when he was last seen.
4. It was a beautiful morning. The sun _____ and the birds _____.

2. 주어진 동사를 적절한 형태로 바꾸어 문장을 완성하세요.

1. I _found_ (find) the missing file while I _was looking_ (look) for something else.
2. It _____ (start) raining while I _____ (drive) home.
3. While I _____ (chat) with him, my computer _____ (crash).
4. The security guard _____ (notice) the broken lock while he _____ (walk) around the warehouse.
5. Tim Berners-Lee _____ (invent) the World Wide Web in 1989, while he _____ (work) at CERN in Geneva.
6. While you _____ (wait), I _____ (negotiate) with a client.

3. 문장의 문맥에 가장 적합한 표현을 골라 문장을 완성하세요.

1. When the fire alarm went off, everybody (**left** / was leaving) the building quickly.
2. When the fire alarm went off, everybody (danced / was dancing).
3. When he opened the door, the children (played / were playing) hide and seek.
4. When he opened the door, the children (shouted, "Yay!" / were shouting, "Yay!")
5. When he took over the business, it (lost / was losing) a lot of money.
6. When he took over the business, he (hired / was hiring) more staff.

🔊 Dialogue

4. 주어진 단어를 이용하여 문맥에 맞게 문장을 완성하세요.

Andy is asking Amy to help him.
Andy가 Amy에게 도와달라고 부탁하고 있습니다.

Andy Amy, can you help me with this bag?
Amy   That's no problem, but it doesn't look so heavy.
Andy It's not heavy, but I cannot carry anything now.
Amy   What's wrong?
Andy _____
      (I, hurt my back, while, I, move furniture yesterday).
Amy   Oh, dear. I'm sorry to hear that. Give me the bag. I'll carry it for you.

Unit 008

현재완료(1)

Have you done your homework?
너 숙제 했니?

1. **have p.p.**는 보통 '~했다'로 해석되지만, 구체적인 과거 시간이 드러나지 않거나 애매한 경우, 혹은 '지금'과도 연관이 있는 시간 개념을 나타낸다. *See 부록 07*▶

   - **I've spoken** to the manager. 저는 매니저에게 이야기를 했습니다. 언제 했는지는 밝히지 않음
   - I **spoke** to the manager **yesterday**. 저는 어제 매니저에게 이야기를 했습니다. '어제' 했음

   • have p.p.의 기준 시간은 '현재'이다. 현재를 기준으로 과거를 말한다(현재완료). 현재 기준으로 몇 번을 했는지, 또는 했는지 안 했는지를 말하고, 이 사실은 현재 이후에 바뀔 수 있다. 반면, -ed(단순과거)는 바뀌지 않는, 이미 돌이킬 수 없는 과거를 암시한다.

   - **I've been** so busy. 지금까지 정말 바빴어. 앞으로는 덜 바쁠 가능성 암시
   - I **was** so busy last week. 지난 주는 정말 바빴어. 지난 주에 바빴다는 사실은 바뀔 수 없음

2. **have p.p.**의 초점은 과거 언제 그랬는지의 시점이 아니라 그랬는지 안 그랬는지 사실 여부에 있다. O? X?

   - **Have** you **done** your homework? 숙제 했니? 숙제를 했는지 안 했는지에 초점
   - Listen! **I've passed** my driver's test! 있잖아! 나 면허 시험 합격했어! 합격했다는 그 자체에 초점
   - **I've visited** Paris twice. 전 파리를 두 번 방문해 봤어요. 두 번 방문했다는 것만 알 수 있고, 각각 언제인지는 아직 밝혀지지 않음

3. **have p.p.**는 -ed와 비슷하게 과거처럼 해석되지만, 오로지 과거에 대해서만 말하는 -ed와 달리 **have p.p.**는 현재에도 걸쳐져 있거나 현재와 연관이 있다.

   - **I've lived** in L.A. for 10 years. 저는 L.A.에서 10년째 살고 있어요. '지금'까지 10년
   - **I've lost** my car key. 차 열쇠 잃어버렸어. 그래서 '지금 운전할 수 없다'는 말의 우회적인 표현

4. **have p.p.**는 구체적인 과거의 때를 나타내지는 못하나, (지금까지의) '기간'은 말할 수 있다. 이를 통해 과거의 시간을 우회적으로 추측할 수 있음

   - **I've been** married **for 5 years**. 저는 결혼한 지 5년 되었어요. 5년 전에 결혼했음
   - **I've lived** here **since 2016**. 저는 2016년부터 여기 살았어요. 2016년에 이사 왔고 그때부터 여기 살기 시작했음

5. **have p.p.**는 구체적인 과거의 때를 나타내지는 못하나, 대략의 범위를 암시할 수는 있다.

   - The train **has just arrived**. 기차가 방금 도착했다. 오래 전은 아니고 몇 분 전 정도일 것으로 추측할 수 있음
   - **I've already had** lunch. 전 벌써 점심 먹었어요. 상대가 예상한 식사 시간보다는 이른 시간에 먹었음
   - I **haven't seen** him **recently**. 최근에 그를 못 봤다. 정확하게 언제인지는 몰라도 가까운 시일 내임을 추측 가능

6. 과거에 아예 안 한 것, 일어나지 않은 것은 **haven't p.p.**로 말한다. 과거에 구체적으로 '집을' 시간 자체가 없음

   - I **haven't finished** the report yet. 아직 보고서를 못 마쳤습니다.
   - **I've never seen** a whale. 나는 고래를 본 적이 없다.

   • 어느 한때에만 그러지 않은 것은 -ed로 말한다.

   - I **didn't sleep** well last night. 나는 어젯밤 잘 자지 못했다. 어젯밤만 해당함. 다른 때에도 모두 잘 자지 못한 것은 아님

Exercises

1. 주어진 동사를 적절한 형태로 바꾸어 문장을 완성하세요. 주어가 대명사라면 축약형을 쓰세요.

    1. I _haven't spoken_ (not speak) to the boss about your proposal, but I will soon.
    2. I _____ (visit) the headquarters several times so far.
    3. We _____ (live) in L.A. for 10 years.
    4. He still _____ (not pay) the rent.
    5. Morning _____ (break). Wake up.
    6. I _____ (see) that man before, but I don't remember when.
    7. Oh no. My car _____ (break down) again.
    8. A: Is David here? David
       B: No. He _____ (not arrive) yet.
    9. _____ you _____ (find) your cell phone?
    10. I _____ (not do) my homework yet.
    11. Look. You _____ (make) the same mistake again.

2. 문장의 문맥에 가장 적합한 표현을 골라 문장을 완성하세요.

    1. I ((didn't sleep) / haven't slept) well last night.
    2. Rachel is a travel writer. She (visited / has visited) Europe many times.
    3. Jessica (moved / has moved) to L.A. after she got married.
    4. A: Do you know anything about deep learning?
       B: Well, I (never heard / have never heard) of it.
    5. I (lost / have lost) my cell phone again.
    6. When I was a child, I (liked / have liked) climbing trees.
    7. My parents (never traveled / have never traveled) abroad.
    8. Where (did you live / have you lived) before you came here?
    9. Long time no see. How (were you / have you been)?
    10. They (arrived / have arrived) fifteen minutes ago.

◆ Dialogue

3. 주어진 단어를 이용하여 문맥에 맞게 문장을 완성하세요.

Sia is introducing her brother Mike to Rachel at a party.
Sia가 파티에서 남동생 Mike를 Rachel에게 소개하고 있습니다.

Sia   Rachel, _____ (you, not meet) my brother Mike, have you?
Rachel No. Hi, I'm Rachel. Nice to meet you.
Mike   Hi, Rachel. Nice to meet you, too. _____ (I, hear) a lot about you from Sia.
Rachel You have? Hope that it's all positive.
Mike   She said that you're a wonderful travel writer.
Rachel Did she say that? Oh, I think I'm flattered.

Unit 009

현재완료(2)

It's the first time I've ridden a motorcycle.
오토바이는 처음 타 봐요.

1. have p.p.를 써서 과거에 그랬던 경험을 말할 수 있다. 상대방은 이 문장만으로 언제인지 모름

긍정문	부정문	의문문
I/You/We/They **have worked**... He/She/It **has worked**...	I/You/We/They **haven't worked**.... He/She/It **hasn't worked**...	**Have** I/you/we/they **worked**...? **Has** he/she/it **worked**...?

- Rachel **has visited** the British Museum twice. Rachel은 대영박물관을 두 번 **방문한 적이 있다**.
- I **haven't tried** horse meat. 저는 말고기는 먹어 본 적 없어요.

전혀 해 보지 않았다는 의미를 강조하기 위해 never가 자주 쓰인다.

- Humans **have never traveled** to Mars or Venus. 인류는 화성이나 금성으로 가 본 적이 없다.

ever는 have p.p. 질문에서 '(그럴 것 같지는 않지만) 혹시나 (한 번이라도)'의 뉘앙스를 준다. See Unit 072▶

- **Have** you **ever seen** a U.F.O.? 혹시 U.F.O.를 본 적이 있니?

경험에 대해 다음과 같이 말할 수도 있다.

> It's the first/second/... time 주어 have p.p. ~를 해 본 것이 처음/두 번째/... 이다.

- **It's the first time I've ridden** a motorcycle. (= I've never ridden a motorcycle.) 오토바이는 **처음 타 봐요**.
- **Is it the first time you've seen** this error? 이런 에러를 본 것이 **처음인가요**?

> It's the best/most .../... 주어 have ever p.p. ~해 본 것 중에 가장 ...하다.

- It's **the best** smartphone **I've ever used**. 내가 써 본 것 중 최고의 스마트폰이에요. See Unit 076▶
- *Old Boy* is **the most shocking** movie **I've ever seen**. 올드보이는 내가 본 것 중에서 가장 충격적인 영화예요.

2. just를 써서 '방금', already를 써서 '벌써' 또는 '이미 끝난(완료) 것'을 말할 수 있다. 보통 have와 p.p. 사이에 온다.

- **I've just seen** Suzi. (= I just saw Suzi.) 나 방금 Suzi 봤어. 미국 영어에서는 이런 경우 -ed를 쓰기도 함
- Little Eva **has already learned** how to read. 꼬마 Eva는 벌써 읽는 법을 익혔답니다.
- **Have** you **finished** the game **already**? 벌써 게임을 마친 거야? 대화체에서는 already가 질문 맨 뒤에 오기도 함

3. yet을 써서 '아직 아닌' 또는 '끝나지 않은 것'에 대해 말하거나 물을 수 있다. 보통 문장의 맨 끝에 온다.

- The rain **hasn't stopped yet**. 비가 아직 안 그쳤어요.
- **Have** you **fixed** your phone **yet**? 전화기 아직 안 고쳤니?

4. 과거의 행동이나 사건을 통해 현재의 상황을 말할 때 have p.p.를 쓸 수 있다.
과거에 언제 그랬느냐가 중요하지 않고, 지금 어떠한 상황이라는 데에 초점이 있음

- **I've given** the report to the director. (= He has it now.) 보고서 부장님께 **드렸어요**. (보고서가 부장님께 있음)
- **We've run** out of coffee. (= We need to buy some.) 커피가 다 **떨어졌어요**. (커피를 사야 함)
- A: Is Mr. Harris in? Harris 씨 계신가요?
  B: Sorry. He's **just stepped** out. (= He's not in.) 죄송합니다만, 방금 **나가셨어요**. (지금 안 계심)

Exercises

1. 주어진 표현을 이용하여 경험에 대한 질문을 완성하세요.

1. (you, ever, study abroad) — *Have you ever studied abroad?*
2. (you, ever, see, a celebrity, in person) — _____
3. (you, ever, swim, in the ocean) — _____
4. (you, ever, stay up, all night) — _____

▶ 완성된 질문에 대해 본인의 답을 문장으로 말해 보세요.

1. *Yes, I have. I studied in Australia in 2016.* or *No, I haven't. I've never studied abroad.*
2. _____
3. _____
4. _____

2. 다음 보기처럼 주어진 표현을 사용하여 질문에 대한 응답 문장을 만드세요.

1. A: Have you seen a whale before?
   B: No. *It's the first time I've seen a whale*. (the first time)
2. A: Have you ever stayed in the Blueridge Hotel?
   B: No. _____. (the first time)
3. A: You haven't eaten sashimi before, have you?
   B: Yes, I have once. _____. (the second time)
4. A: What is your favorite movie?
   B: *Interstellar is the best movie I've ever seen*. (Interstellar, the best movie, see)
5. A: So… do you like the steak?
   B: Wow! _____. (This, the best steak, eat)
6. A: Jay is so kind.
   B: Yes. _____. (He, the kindest person, meet)

3. 주어진 표현을 넣어 문장을 다시 말해 보세요.

1. The manager has spoken to me. (already) — *The manager has already spoken to me.*
2. He hasn't finished the November sales report. (yet) — _____
3. I've sent him an email. (already) — _____
4. The company has announced it is going to close the Beijing factory next year. (just) — _____

◆ Dialogue

4. 주어진 단어를 이용하여 문맥에 맞게 문장을 완성하세요.

Suzi is taking a ballet lesson. Suzi는 발레 수업을 받고 있습니다.

A woman   I think you're a wonderful dancer!
Suzi   Oh, thanks.
A woman   _____ (you, learn) ballet before?
Suzi   No, _____ (I, just, start).
A woman   Really? You don't look like a beginner at all!
Suzi   Thank you. I'm flattered.

Unit 010

단순과거 vs. 현재완료

You've done your hair! Awesome!
너 머리(손질)했구나! 멋진데!

1 -ed와 have p.p.의 기준 시간, 초점

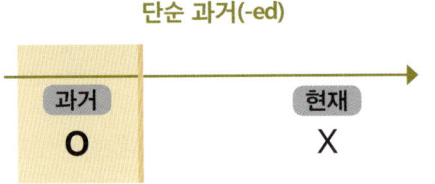

단순 과거(-ed)	현재완료(have p.p.)
기준이 현재에서 과거로 이동	현재를 기준으로 과거를 말함
현재와는 더 이상 직접적인 연관 없음. 과거로 끝난(over) 사항. 과거에서 그랬다고 지금도 그러한지는 알 수 없음.	과거 사실이 현재와도 연관 있음. 현재를 기준으로 그러하며, 기준이 바뀌면 내용이 달라질 수 있음.

끝남(OVER)	아직 안 끝남(NOT OVER)
▶ I **was** busy yesterday. 나는 어제 바빴다. 오늘도 바쁜지 안 바쁜지는 이 문장만으로는 확실히 알 수 없음. 어제 바빴다는 사실만 전달	▶ I**'ve been** busy recently. 나는 최근에 바빴다. 과거부터 지금까지 바쁨. (지금 이후에도 바쁠지 안 바쁠지는 모름)
명확한 과거의 때가 있음	**언제인지 모호함**
▶ I **visited** New York last month. 나는 지난 달에 뉴욕을 방문했다. 방문한 때가 '지난 달'임을 명확히 밝힘	▶ I**'ve visited** New York several times. 나는 뉴욕을 여러 번 방문했다. 방문을 했다는 것만 알 수 있고 정확하게 언제였는지는 알 수 없음
과거를 나타내는 시간 표현: in 2015, last night/Monday/week/month/year/…	**지금이 포함된 시간 표현:** today, this week/month/semester/year/…
▶ She **interviewed** 10 people last week. 그녀는 지난 주에 10명을 면접 보았다.	▶ She **has interviewed** 10 people this week. 그녀는 이번 주에 10명을 면접 보았다.
과거 이야기에 초점	**그로 인한 현재의 상황(결과)에 초점**
▶ I **did** my hair last week. 나 지난 주에 머리(손질)했어. 과거(지난 주)에 있었던 일을 말함	▶ You**'ve done** your hair! Awesome! 너 머리(손질) 했구나! 멋진데! 머리를 손질해서 지금 멋져 보인다는 것에 초점

2 -ed 와 have p.p.의 기간

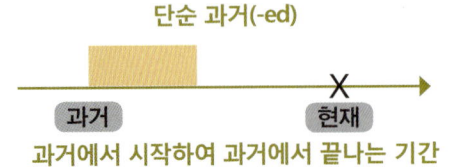
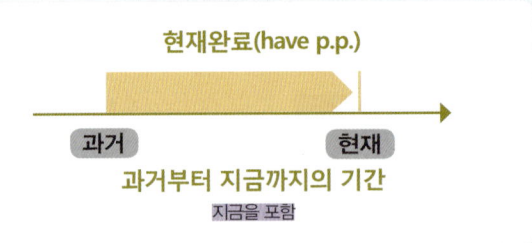

단순 과거(-ed)	현재완료(have p.p.)
과거에서 시작하여 과거에서 끝나는 기간 현재와는 더 이상 직접적인 연관 없음	과거부터 지금까지의 기간 지금을 포함

from… to ~	since…
▶ I **lived** in Seattle from 2014 to 2015. 나는 2014년부터 2015년까지 시애틀에서 **살았다**. 현재는 다른 곳에 살고 있음 암시	▶ I**'ve lived** in Denver since 2015. 나는 2015년부터 덴버에서 살고 있다. 지금까지 덴버에 살고 있음 (단, 지금 이후에도 덴버에 살지 안 살지는 알 수 없음)
for …	**for …**
▶ I **lived** in Seattle for two years. 나는 시애틀에서 2년간 **살았다**. 현재가 포함되지 않은 과거의 2년간	▶ I**'ve lived** in Denver for a few years. 나는 몇 년째 덴버에서 살고 있다. 지금을 포함한 몇 년간임

Exercises

1. 문장의 문맥에 가장 적합한 표현을 골라 문장을 완성하세요.
   1. (Did you see / Have you seen) Erika yesterday?
   2. I'm looking for Erika. (Did you see / Have you seen) her today?
   3. Claire is a New Yorker. She (lived / has lived) in New York all her life.
   4. Dinosaurs (lived / have lived) all over the Earth.
   5. I (stayed / have stayed) in the Blueridge hotel last year.
   6. I (stayed / have stayed) in the Blueridge hotel a couple of times.

2. 주어진 표현을 사용하여 have p.p. 문장을 만들어 현재 상황을 다시 말해 보세요.

   1. Patrick isn't at home now.   _He's gone out._   (He, go out)
   2. There are no cookies in the jar.   _____   (Someone, eat, all the cookies)
   3. Now Alice has a new car.   _____   (She, buy, a new car)
   4. The window is broken.   _____   (Someone, break, the window)
   5. Your shoes are missing.   _____   (Someone, take, my shoes)
   6. I'm full.   _____   (I, eat, a lot)

3. 주어진 표현들을 문맥에 맞게 연결하여 문장을 완성하세요.
   1. Mike worked as programmer   •   • a. since 1992.
   2. Andy has been in the hospital   •   • b. from 2010 to 2012.
   3. James has worked for JJ International •   • c. for only two hours.
   4. Last night I slept   •   • d. for three days.

🔊 Dialogue

4. 주어진 단어를 이용하여 문맥에 맞게 문장을 완성하세요.

   Julia is offering coffee to Nicole. Julia가 Nicole에게 커피를 권하고 있습니다.

   Julia   Would you like some coffee? I've got some fresh beans.
   Nicole No, thanks.
   Julia   Are you sure? It's your favorite – Hawaiian Kona.
   Nicole Sounds tempting, but _____ (I, already, drink) 5 cups of coffee today.
   Julia   Five cups? That's too much!
   Nicole Yes. I'm already over the limit for the day, so no thanks, Julia.

Unit 011

현재완료(3)

I've had my smartphone for two years.
내 스마트폰은 산 지 2년 되었다.

1
과거에서 시작되어 지금까지 계속 이어져 온 상태에 대해서 **have p.p.**로 표현할 수 있다.
주로 상태동사 *See 부록02*▶

- **I've known** her since we were in college together. 저는 함께 대학 다닐 때부터 그녀를 **알고 지냈습니다**.
- **We've loved** each other for a long time. 우리는 오랫동안 서로 **사랑해 왔습니다**.

구체적인 행동이 지속되거나, 꾸준히 반복되어 온 경우에는 보통 **have been –ing**로 말한다. *See Unit 012*▶

- He**'s been using** this app for a month. 그는 이 앱을 한 달간 **사용해 왔습니다**.

지속되거나 꾸준히 반복된 상태나 동작의 '기간'에 보다 초점을 두어 다음과 같이 말할 수 있다.

- **It's been a long time since** I **met** her. 그녀를 만난 지 오랜 시간이 흘렀다.
- **It's been 5 years since** I last **saw** him. 그를 마지막으로 본 지 5년이나 되었다.
- **How long has it been since** Marilyn Monroe **died**? 마릴린 먼로가 **사망한 지 얼마나 되었죠**?

2
우리말 해석과 상관없이 시간 개념에 따라 동사가 달리 쓰일 수 있다.

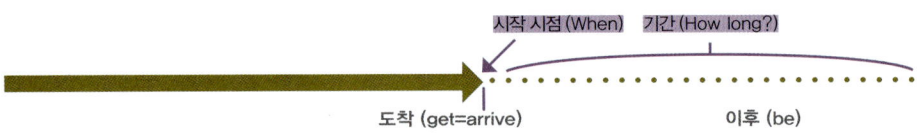

- We **got** to the airport at noon. 우리는 정오에 공항에 **도착했다**.
- **Have** you ever **been** to Russia? 혹시 러시아에 **가 본 적 있어요**?

- My brother **got married** last month. 우리 오빠는 지난 주에 **결혼했다**.
- We**'ve been married** for 7 years. 우리는 **결혼한 지 7년 되었어요**. (7년째 결혼한 상태)

- When **did** you first **meet** your wife? 아내 분은 언제 처음 **만났나요**?
- How long **have** you **known** each other? 너희 둘은 서로 **알고 지낸** 지 얼마나 오래 되었니?

- I **bought** my smartphone two years ago. 나는 내 스마트폰을 2년 전에 **샀다**.
- I**'ve had** my smartphone for two years. 내 스마트폰은 **산 지 2년 되었다**. (2년째 소유 중)

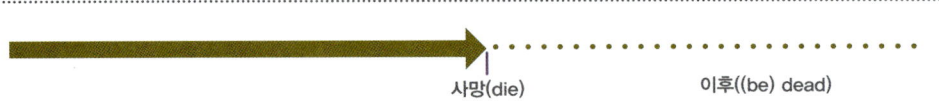

- His grandfather **died** 8 years ago. 그의 할아버지는 8년 전에 **돌아가셨다**.
- Michael Jackson **has been dead** for many years. 마이클 잭슨이 **사망한 지 여러 해가 되었다**.

Exercises

1. 주어진 단어를 사용하여 문장을 완성하세요. 가능하면 축약형을 쓰세요.

1. (We, love each other, for a long time) — *We've loved each other for a long time.*
2. (Andy, know Amy, since third grade) — _____
3. (Mr. Cruz, be, a teacher, for thirty years) — _____
4. (There, be, a strong wind, all day) — _____
5. (There, be, a high-tech revolution, in China, since 1997) — _____

2. 주어진 문장을 It's been ~ since…를 사용하여 다시 써 보세요.

1. I haven't seen him for 5 years. → *It's been 5 years since I last saw him.*
2. I haven't gone to the movies for a year. → _____
3. We haven't visited him for a long time. → _____
4. Sia hasn't eaten meat for over 10 years. → _____
5. I haven't gone shopping for ages. → _____
6. He hasn't called her for two weeks. → _____

3. 다음 문장을 for나 since를 사용한 have p.p. 문장으로 바꾸세요.

1. She moved to L.A. 4 years ago. — *She has lived in L.A. for 4 years.*
2. They got married 7 years ago. — _____
3. Steve Jobs died in 2011. — _____
4. I first met him when I was in elementary school. — _____

▶ 다음 의문을 How long…?으로 시작하는 have p.p. 의문문으로 바꾸세요.

5. When did you buy your cell phone? — *How long have you had your cell phone?*
6. When did they get married? — _____
7. When did you arrive here? — _____

◆ Dialogue

4. 주어진 단어를 이용하여 문맥에 맞게 문장을 완성하세요.

Rachel is in Hawaii on vacation now. She is talking on the phone with Jessica.
Rachel은 하와이에서 휴가 중입니다. 그녀는 지금 Jessica와 통화하고 있습니다.

Jessica What's the weather like there?
Rachel Great! I think I'm lucky. I heard it rained a lot last week, but _____ (it, not, rain) so far this week.
Jessica Good for you.
Rachel Yeah. _____ (It, be, sunny and warm, since, the moment I arrived at the airport).
Jessica I hope you enjoy the sunshine and have a relaxing holiday.

Unit 012

현재완료진행형

How long have you been learning English?
영어는 얼마나 오랫동안 공부해 오셨나요?

1 지금까지 구체적인 행동이 지속되거나, 꾸준히 반복되어 온 경우에는 보통 have been –ing로 말한다.

과거 ─────── 현재 ─────── 미래

- I**'ve been waiting** for him for 20 minutes. 저는 그를 20분째 기다리고 있어요. 지속
- He**'s been using** this app since January. 그는 1월부터 이 앱을 사용해 왔습니다. 반복

긍정문	부정문	의문문
I have been working…	I haven't been working… I haven't worked.	Have you been working?

- I**'ve been thinking** about your offer all week. 당신의 제안을 일주일 내내 생각해봤습니다.
- The price of oil **has been going up** steadily since last year. 유가가 작년부터 꾸준히 오르고 있어요.
- **Have** you **been waiting** long? 오래 기다렸니?
- How long **have** you **been learning** English? 영어는 얼마나 오랫동안 공부해 오셨나요?

2 have been –ing는 얼마나 오랫동안 그래 왔는지를 말하는 기간 표현과 함께 자주 쓰인다. have p.p.와도 쓰임

> over the last few days/weeks/years/…, all day/week/my life/…,
> for ten years, for ages, since 9 o'clock

- We**'ve been working** on the project **over the last few weeks**. 우리는 최근 몇 주간 그 프로젝트 작업을 해 왔다.
- She**'s been looking for** a nice gift for her nephew **all day**.
  그녀는 하루 종일 남자 조카를 위한 멋진 선물을 찾고 있다.

3 have been –ing는 지금까지 그래 왔다는 것만을 말할 뿐, 앞으로도 계속 그럴지 안 그럴지는 문맥으로 판단한다.

- Where have you been? I**'ve been waiting** for ages!
  지금껏 어디 있었니? 나 엄청 오래 기다렸거든. 더 이상 기다리지 않음
- I**'ve been waiting** for ages! I'll stay just another five minutes.
  나 엄청 오래 기다렸거든! 앞으로 딱 5분만 더 있을 거야. 5분 더 기다릴 것임

4 know, like, seem, want와 같은 상태동사는 have p.p. 형태로 말한다. See Unit 011▶

- I**'ve** always **wanted** to be a dancer. 전 항상 무용수가 되고 싶었어요.
  I've always wanting to be a dancer. (X)

live나 work의 경우 have p.p.와 have been –ing 모두에 쓰일 수 있다.

- The Watsons **have lived** in L.A. for 5 years. Watson 씨네 가족은 L.A.에 산 지 5년 되었다.
  = The Watsons **have been living** in L.A. for 5 years.
- I**'ve worked** in marketing all my life. 저는 평생을 마케팅 분야에서 일해 왔습니다.
  = I**'ve been working** in marketing all my life.

Exercises

1. 문맥에 맞는 문장끼리 연결하세요.

1. He's out of breath.
2. The ground is wet.
3. He's so tired.
4. The world is all white.
5. His clothes are covered with paint.
6. He's overweight.
7. His hands are dirty.

a. It's been snowing.
b. He's been painting the kitchen.
c. He's been running.
d. It's been raining.
e. He's been working hard all day.
f. He's been fixing his bicycle.
g. He's been eating too much recently.

2. 주어진 단어를 사용하여 문맥에 맞게 문장을 완성하세요. 주어가 대명사라면 축약형을 쓰세요.

1. They're still dancing. _They've been dancing all night_ (They, dance, all night).
2. We're still working on the project. _____ (We, work on it, for months).
3. Is he still waiting? _____ (How long, he, wait)?
4. They're still negotiating. _____ (They, negotiate, since early this year).
5. Are you still looking for it? _____ (How long, you, look for it)?
6. Andy is still watching YouTube videos. _____ (He, watch them, for hours).

✨ Dialogue

3. 주어진 단어를 이용하여 문맥에 맞게 문장을 완성하세요.

Sarah is asking Andy why Amy is so upset today.
Sarah는 Andy에게 왜 Amy가 오늘 속상해하는지를 묻고 있습니다.

Sarah Amy is so upset today. Do you know why?
Andy Well, she's angry with me because I forgot our date yesterday.
Sarah Uh-oh. Did you apologize to her for that?
Andy Not yet, but I'm going to.
Sarah You should do that right now. _____ (She, be, so upset) all day today. Don't let it last long.

Unit 013

현재완료 vs. 현재완료진행형

I've done the laundry! vs. I've been doing the laundry all day.
빨래 했다! vs. 나는 하루 종일 빨래를 했다.

1. have p.p.와 have been –ing의 비교

have p.p.	have been -ing
계속된 상태 (be, want, know, have…) 상태동사	**계속/반복된 행동/사건** (do, go, work, wait…) 동작(action) 동사
▶ She's **been** an English teacher for 10 years. 그녀는 10년간 영어 선생님으로 일해 왔다.	▶ She's **been teaching** English for 10 years. 그녀는 10년간 영어를 가르쳐 왔다.
▶ Ben **has had** his action figures since second grade. Ben은 2학년 때부터 액션 피규어를 소장해 왔다.	▶ Ben **has been collecting** action figures since second grade. Ben은 2학년 때부터 액션 피규어를 수집해 왔다.
▶ We've **known** each other for several years. 우리는 서로 알고 지낸 지 여러 해 되었어요.	▶ We've **been dating** for several years. 우리는 수 년째 데이트 해 오고 있어요.
완료	**완료 또는 계속**
▶ I've **done** the laundry! 빨래 했다! 빨래를 마쳤음	▶ I've **been doing** the laundry all day. 나는 하루 종일 빨래를 했다. 빨래를 다 했을 수도 있고, 아직도 안 끝났을 수도 있음
▶ I've **written** a report for the director. 부장님께 드릴 보고서를 썼다. 보고서 작성을 마쳤음	▶ I've **been writing** a report for the director. 부장님께 드릴 보고서를 내내 쓰고 있다. 아직 작성 중
현재의 결과에 초점	**쭉 해온 행동/사건 자체에 초점**
▶ I've already **had** lunch. I'm full. 이미 점심 먹었어요. 배불러요. 점심을 먹어서 배가 부르다는 것에 초점	▶ I've **been having** lunch with Mr. Gatsby. 지금껏 Gatsby 씨와 점심을 먹었어요. Gatsby 씨와 점심을 먹었다는 자체에 초점
▶ I've **done** my homework. 전 숙제 했어요. 숙제를 다 했음. 다른 것을 해도 됨	▶ I've **been doing** my homework. 내내 숙제 했어요. 숙제를 마쳤을 수도 마치지 않았을 수도 있음. 계속 숙제하고 있었다는 데에 초점
How many? / How much?에 초점	**How long?에 초점**
▶ Rachel **has written** 2 books. Rachel은 2권의 책을 썼다.	▶ Rachel **has been writing** books since 2012. Rachel은 2012년부터 책을 써 왔다.
▶ Jay **has run** 10 kilometers. Jay는 10킬로미터를 뛰었다.	▶ Jay **has been running** for two hours. Jay는 2시간째 뛰고 있다.
부정문: 얼마나 오래 그러지 않았나에 초점 for나 since와 함께 쓰임	**부정문: 내내 그러지 못한 행동/사건 자체에 초점**
▶ We **haven't had** a vacation for two years. 우리는 휴가를 안 간 지 2년이나 되었다.	▶ Amy **hasn't been feeling** very well recently. Amy는 최근에 내내 컨디션이 썩 좋지 못하다.
▶ They **haven't talked** to each other since Wednesday. 그들은 수요일부터 서로 말을 안 하고 있다.	▶ She **hasn't been sleeping** well these day. 그녀는 요즘 내내 잠을 잘 자지 못했다.

2. have p.p.의 부정문에서는 for 대신 in이 쓰일 수 있다.

▶ We haven't had a vacation **in** two years. 우리는 휴가 안 간 지 2년이나 되었다.
▶ I haven't heard from them **in** decades. 나는 그들로부터 소식을 못 들은 지 수십 년이 되었다.

● all day, all my life와 같이 all로 시작하는 표현 앞에서는 for를 쓰지 않는다.

▶ I've been waiting for his phone call **all day**. 나는 하루 종일 그의 전화를 기다렸다.
I've been waiting for his phone call **for all day**. (X)

Exercises

1. 주어진 동사를 have p.p. 또는 have been –ing 형태로 바꾸어 문장을 완성하세요. 두 가지 형태가 모두 가능한 경우 have been –ing를 쓰세요. 주어가 대명사라면 축약형을 쓰세요.

1. Alice __*has been*__ (be) a wonderful secretary for six years.
2. Alice _____ (work) as a secretary for six years.
3. I _____ (have) lunch at the canteen so far.
4. A: Are they enjoying themselves?
   B: Yes! The children _____ (have) a great time in the swimming pool.
5. I _____ (have) the miniature cars for a long time.
6. I _____ (collect) the miniature cars for a long time.
7. He _____ (wait) here for thirty minutes.
8. He _____ (be) here for thirty minutes.

2. 주어진 동사를 적절한 형태로 바꾸어 문장을 완성하세요.

1. A: So, which car are you going to buy?
   B: Well, My husband and I __*have been talking*__ (talk) about it over the weekend, but we __*haven't decided*__ (not decide) yet.
2. I _____ (not feel) very well these days.
3. A: _____ you _____ (finish) your meal?
   B: Yes. Let's leave now.
4. I _____ (look) around the museum for two hours, but there are still more to see.
5. A: Why are you sweating?
   B: I _____ (exercise).
6. I know I need to start exercising because I _____ (not do) it lately.
7. How many books _____ you _____ (read) this year?
8. How long _____ you _____ (read) that book?
9. A: Your eyes are red. _____ you _____ (cry) or something?
   B: Nah. I _____ (peel) onions.
10. We _____ (not hear) from her in years.

🔊 Dialogue

3. 주어진 단어를 이용하여 문맥에 맞게 문장을 완성하세요.

Mike is talking with his boss in the office. Mike는 사무실에서 상사와 이야기 중입니다.

Boss   Mike, have you finished the report?
Mike   Um… Sir, _____ (I, work on it) for the past week, day and night, but it's not ready yet.
Boss   Hmm. When can it be done?
Mike   I think I need a few more days.
Boss   I need that report by this Thursday morning. Can you do that by then?
Mike   Yes. It will be ready on your desk on Thursday morning.

Unit 014

과거완료

I suddenly remembered I had left my phone in the car.
차에 전화기를 두고 내렸다는 것이 갑자기 기억났다.

1 had p.p.는 과거의 어느 기준 시간 이전의 과거에 대해 말할 때 쓸 수 있다(과거완료, Past Perfect). *See* 부록 08 ▶

- 과거 어느 기준 시간 이전에 있었던 사건이나 행동

The meeting **had already started** by the time I **arrived**.
내가 도착했을 쯤에는 회의가 이미 시작되었다.

▶ I suddenly **remembered** I **had left** my phone in the car.
  차에 전화기를 두고 내렸다는 것이 갑자기 기억났다. 기억났던 순간(과거) 이전의 행동

▶ I **thought** I'**d seen** her somewhere before, but I was wrong.
  나는 내가 그녀를 전에 어딘가에서 봤다고 생각했으나 아니었다. 생각했던 때(과거) 이전의 사건

- 과거 어느 기준 시간 이전까지의 지속되었던 상태

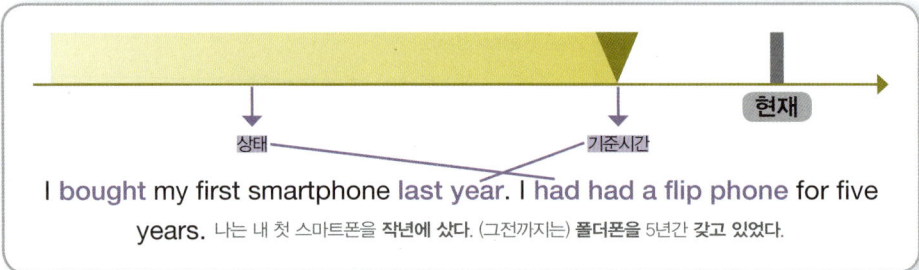

I **bought** my first smartphone last year. I **had had** a flip phone for five years. 나는 내 첫 스마트폰을 작년에 샀다. (그전까지는) 폴더폰을 5년간 갖고 있었다.

▶ Jessica and James **had known** each other for years **when they got married**.
  Jessica와 James는 **결혼했을 때**, 수년간 서로 알고 지낸 사이였다. 결혼하기 이전의 상태

2 과거의 사건이나 상태 등을 일어나는 순서대로 말하는 경우에는 had p.p.를 쓰지 않는다.

▶ I **left** my phone in the car. Luckily, the driver **found** it and **called** me at work.
  나는 차에 전화기를 두고 내렸다. 다행히 기사가 발견하여 사무실로 전화를 주었다.

before나 after 등의 시간 표현으로 인해 시간 순서가 분명히 드러나는 경우에도 굳이 had p.p.를 쓰지 않아도 된다.

▶ The meeting **(had) started before I arrived**. 회의는 내가 도착하기 전에 시작되었다.
▶ I **arrived after** the meeting **(had) started**. 나는 회의가 시작한 뒤에 도착했다.

3 have p.p.와 had p.p.는 기준 시간에 차이가 있다.

⎡ You're late, Mike. The meeting **has** already **started**. Mike, 늦었군요. 회의가 이미 **시작되었어요**. 지금 상황
⎣ The meeting **had** already **started** by the time I arrived.
   내가 도착했을 쯤에는 회의가 이미 **시작되었다**. 지나간 이야기

⎡ I'**ve had** my smartphone for a half year. It's quite new.
  전 스마트폰을 **산 지** 반 년 되었어요. 꽤 새 거죠. 지금 기준으로 반 년째 소유
⎣ I bought my first smartphone last year. I **had had** a flip phone for five years.
  나는 내 첫 스마트폰을 작년에 샀다. 그전까지는 5년 동안 폴더폰을 갖고 있었다. 작년까지의 이야기

Exercises

1. 보기와 같이 주어진 내용과 had p.p.를 써서 문장을 완성하세요.

1. I've seen him before. → I thought ___I had seen him before___ .
2. I didn't send them an email. → I realized that _____.
3. There was traffic jam. → He arrived late because _____.
4. His late grandfather left him a fortune. → Did he know that _____?
5. I already had dinner. → I didn't want to eat because _____.
6. I've had my first cell phone for years. → _____ until I bought a new smartphone.
7. She locked the door. → She wasn't sure if _____ before she left.
8. The children have never been to the amusement park. → The children were excited because _____.

2. 문장의 문맥에 가장 적합한 표현을 골라 문장을 완성하세요.

1. When Jessica got home from work, James (already prepared the dinner / (had already prepared the dinner)).
2. When he asked her to marry him, she (said yes / had said yes).
3. When I arrived at the office this morning, the door (was smashed / had been smashed), so I (called the police / had called the police).
4. When the police arrived, the thieves (already left the house / had already left the house).
5. When it started raining, everybody (opened their umbrella / had opened their umbrella).

🔊 Dialogue

3. 주어진 단어를 이용하여 문맥에 맞게 문장을 완성하세요.

Jessica and James are waiting for a guest.
Jessica와 James는 손님을 기다리고 있습니다.

Jessica Hasn't he arrived yet?
James No. I've just gotten a call from him. He's stuck in traffic on 74.
Jessica Oh no. 74? 74 is always jammed at this time.
James I know. I wanted to tell him not to take 74, but it was too late.
_____ (He, already, turn into the road).

Unit 015

과거완료진행형

I'd been waiting for the bus for 20 minutes when it arrived.
저는 버스가 도착할 때까지 20분째 기다리고 있었습니다.

1
과거의 어느 기준 시간까지 구체적인 행동이나 사건이 지속되거나, 꾸준히 반복되어 온 경우에 **had been -ing**로 말한다.

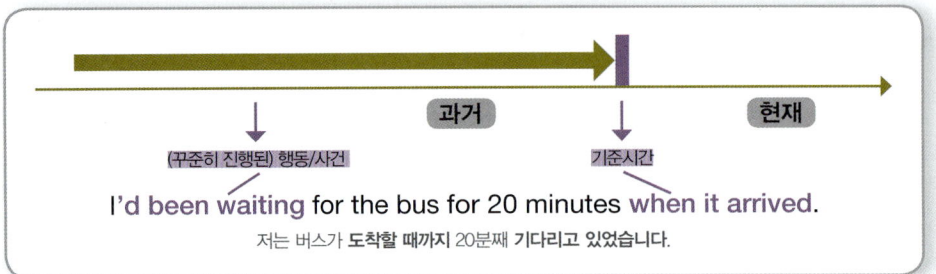

I'd been waiting for the bus for 20 minutes when it arrived.
저는 버스가 **도착할 때까지** 20분째 **기다리고** 있었습니다.

- He**'d been using** a flip phone by the time he bought a new smartphone.
  그는 새 스마트폰을 살 때까지 폴더폰을 **사용해 왔습니다**. 스마트폰을 산 시점(과거) 이전까지 내내 폴더폰을 사용했음
- She**'d been cooking** for an hour when we arrived.
  우리가 도착했을 때 그녀는 한 시간째 **요리 중이었다**. 우리가 도착한 때(과거) 이전에 내내 요리 중이었음
- I could tell it **had been raining**. 나는 내내 비가 왔었음을 알 수 있었다. 내가 알 수 있던 시점(과거) 이전에 비가 내내 왔음
- Mr. Cruz reported that Ben **had been preparing** very well for the final exam.
  Cruz 씨는 Ben이 기말고사를 아주 잘 **준비해 왔다고** 보고했다(성적표에 적었다). 성적표가 나오기 이전에(과거) Ben이 시험공부를 꾸준히 했음

2
have been -ing는 현재, **had been -ing**는 과거의 기준 시간까지 꾸준히 또는 얼마나 오래 행동이나 사건이 지속, 반복되었는가를 말한다.

- I **have been working** here for two years. 저는 여기서 2년째 일하고 있어요. 지금까지 2년간 근무해 옴
- When I left my last job, I **had been working** there for two years.
  제가 마지막 직장을 관둘 때 거길 2년째 **다니고 있었습니다**. 그만 둔 시점까지 2년간 근무했음

3
know, like, seem, want와 같은 상태동사는 **had p.p.**로 말한다. *See Unit 014▶*

- Jessica and James said they **had known** each other for nine years.
  Jessica and James said they they **had been knowing** each other for nine years. (X)
  Jessica와 James는 그들이 9년째 **알고 지냈던** 사이라고 말했다.

live나 work의 경우 **had p.p.**와 **had been -ing** 모두에 쓰일 수 있다.

- The Watsons moved to L.A. 3 years ago. They **had lived** in Vancouver before.
  = The Watsons **had been living** in Vancouver before.
  Watson 씨네 가족은 3년 전에 L.A로 이사 왔다. 그들은 그 전에는 밴쿠버에서 **살았었다**.

4
기준 시간 전까지 행동이나 사건 자체가 내내 일어나지 않았다고 말할 때 **hadn't been -ing**를 쓴다.

- I went to the doctor this morning. I **hadn't been feeling** very well for some time.
  나는 오늘 아침에 병원에 갔다. 한동안 몸이 내내 안 좋았기 때문이다. 내내 컨디션을 좋게 느낀 적이 없었다는 것에 초점

그러나 얼마나 오래 그러지 않았는지에 대한 '기간'에 초점을 둔 경우, **hadn't been -ing**가 아닌 **hadn't p.p.**로 말한다. *for a long time과 같은 기간을 나타내는 시간 표현과 함께 쓰이는 경우*

- He recognized his high school sweetheart at once even though he **hadn't seen** her for over 10 years. 그는 10년이 넘도록 **못 봤는데도** 불구하고 고등학교 때 여자친구를 한 번에 알아 보았다. 10년이 넘는 기간에 초점
  He recognized his high school sweetheart at once even though he **had been seeing** her for over 10 years. (X)

Exercises

1. 문맥에 맞는 문장끼리 연결하세요.

   1. She was out of breath.
   2. The ground was wet.
   3. The report was finally done.
   4. The world was all white.
   5. Her clothes were covered with paint.
   6. Her eyes were red.
   7. Her hands were dirty.

   a. It had been snowing all night.
   b. She had been crying.
   c. She had been painting the kitchen since early morning.
   d. She had been fixing her car.
   e. She had been exercising for hours.
   f. It had been raining all day.
   g. She had been working on it day and night.

2. 주어진 동사를 had p.p. 형태로 바꾸어 문장을 완성하세요.

   1. When the bus finally arrived, I _had been waiting_ (wait) for almost an hour.
   2. Patrick _____ (try) to open the door for an hour when his brother Andy found his key.
   3. By the time his mom told him to stop, he _____ (play) video games for four hours.
   4. I _____ (work) for almost 10 hours when my boss told me to go home.
   5. When the company went public, they _____ (develop) education software for 10 years.

3. 문장의 문맥에 가장 적합한 형태를 골라 문장을 완성하세요.

   1. I (have been using / (had been using)) my old flip phone for five years by the time I bought a new smartphone.
   2. Amy said that she (had known / had been knowing) him since high school.
   3. When I left my last job, I (was working / had been working) there for nine years.
   4. Recently my company (has been using / had been using) the program a lot.
   5. Police (has been looking / had been looking) for the missing boy for hours until they found him safe near his home.
   6. When I arrived at the station, the train (had already left / had already been leaving).

✦ Dialogue

4. 주어진 단어를 이용하여 문맥에 맞게 문장을 완성하세요.

Trish has just come back from a meeting, and Mike is asking about it.
Trish는 방금 회의에서 돌아왔고, Mike가 이에 대해 물어 보고 있습니다.

Mike Trish, how did the meeting with ABS go?
Trish It went quite well.
Mike Then, why was the boss so upset when he was back in the office?
Trish _____ (He, sit in traffic, for three hours).
Mike Oh, I see.

Unit 016

be going to ~ vs. be -ing

When are you going on vacation?
휴가는 언제 갈 거예요?

1 이미 결심했거나 계획한 미래에 대해 **am/are/is going to ~**로 말할 수 있다.
- ▶ I**'m going to study** business in college. 저는 대학에서 비즈니스를 공부할 계획이에요.
- ▶ I**'m not going to accept** the job offer. 저는 그 일자리 제안은 받아들이지 않을 생각이에요.
- ▶ **Are** you **going to take** the exam? 너 그 시험 볼 거니?
- ▶ When **are** they **going to move out**? 그들은 언제 이사 나갈 거예요?

• am/are/is going to go는 am/are/is going으로 말할 수 있다.
- ▶ When **are** you **going** on vacation? (=When **are** you **going to go** on vacation?) 휴가는 언제 갈 거예요?

2 지금 어떤 일이 벌어질 징조가 보이는 경우에도 **am/are/is going to ~**로 말할 수 있다.

Watch out! You**'re going to** fall into the hole.
조심해! 너 구멍에 빠지겠어.

- ▶ I'm not feeling very well. I**'m going to be** sick. 몸이 안 좋아요. 병 날 것 같아요.
- ▶ The traffic is heavy. We**'re going to be** late. 교통 체증이 심하네요. 우리 늦겠어요.

3 이미 그렇게 하기로 정해진(arranged) 미래에 대해서는 **am/are/is -ing**로 말할 수 있다. 보통 언제(때), 어디서(장소) 그렇게 하기로 약속한 경우이다. 아주 가까운 미래로 거의 변동될 여지가 없는 미래에 대해서도 **am/are/is -ing**로 말할 수 있다.
- ▶ I**'m** not **working** tomorrow. 저는 내일 근무하지 않습니다.
- ▶ **Are** you **doing** anything tonight? 오늘 밤 뭐 할 거니?
- ▶ We**'re having** a meeting this afternoon. 우리는 오늘 오후에 회의를 할 것입니다.

am/are/is -ing는 종종 am/are/is going to ~로 말하기도 한다.
- ▶ What **are** you **going to do** this weekend? 이번 주말에 뭐 할 거니?

4 개인이 아닌 대중에게 적용되는 일정, 프로그램, 시간표 등에 대해 말할 때 단순현재 시제를 쓸 수 있다.
- ▶ The plane **arrives** at 5. 그 비행기는 5시에 도착합니다. 모두에게 적용되는 비행 일정
- ▶ What time **does** the game **begin**? 경기는 몇 시에 시작하나요? 모든 이들에게 적용되는 경기 일정

그러나 개인적인 일정은 am/are/is -ing로 말한다.
- ▶ I**'m leaving** tomorrow. 전 내일 떠나요. 나만의 일정
- ▶ We**'re going** skiing this weekend. 우린 주말에 스키 타러 가요. 우리들만의 일정

5 when, as soon as, until 등의 시간표현 뒤에 오는 미래도 단순현재 시제로 말한다. *See Unit 091* ▶
- ▶ Please wait here **until the manager returns**. 매니저가 돌아올 때까지 여기서 기다려 주세요.
   *Please wait here **until the manager will return**.* (X)

Exercises

1. 보기와 같이 문장을 다시 쓰세요. 주어가 대명사라면 축약형을 쓰세요.

1. I've decided not to accept the job offer. → *I'm not going to accept the job offer.*
2. I've decided to buy a smartphone. → _____
3. They've decided to spend the weekend in San Diego. → _____
4. We're planning to redesign our website. → _____
5. The company is planning to hire 100 people. → _____

2. 주어진 단어를 사용하여 문맥에 맞는 문장을 완성하세요. 가능하면 축약형을 쓰세요.

1. The traffic is really bad today. → *We're going to be late.* (We / be late)
2. There are dark clouds in the sky. → _____ (It / rain)
3. We're running out of gas. There's no gas station around here. → _____ (The car / stop soon)
4. The company is in serious financial trouble. → _____ (It / go bankrupt)

3. 밑줄 친 부분이 틀렸다면 맞게 고치세요. 틀린 부분이 없다면 X를 쓰세요.

1. When you're going to see him, please tell him I called.   *you see*
2. What time does the plane arrive?   _____
3. I leave tomorrow.   _____
4. We'll discuss it again after the boss will return.   _____
5. Mr. Cruz is retiring next year.   _____
6. The concert begins at 7:40.   _____
7. I will contact you as soon as I am getting the information, OK?   _____

✦ Dialogue

4. 주어진 단어를 이용하여 문맥에 맞게 문장을 완성하세요.

A secretary is telling her boss about his schedule.
비서가 사장님에게 그의 스케줄을 얘기하고 있습니다.

Boss Have you arranged everything?
Secretary Yes. In 10 minutes, _____ (you / interview) three applicants for the manager's position.
Boss _____ (What / I / do) after that?
Secretary After the interview, Mr. Smith from AUX _____ (be / come) to the office at 12.
Boss _____ (we / have) lunch together?
Secretary Yes. It's going to be a power lunch*.

* power lunch 회사 중역들이 중요한 계획, 아이디어, 결정 등을 논의하며 하는 점심식사

Unit 017

will

I think I'll have an espresso.
에스프레소로 한 잔 할까 해요.

1 will은 미리 계획한 것이 아닌 즉석에서 미래에 그러겠다고 하는 결심이나 제안에 대해 쓴다.

긍정문	부정문	의문문
I **will** work…	I **won't** work…	**Will** I work…?

- **I'll wait** for you outside. 밖에서 기다릴게요.
- **I'll email** you the information. 정보를 이메일로 보내 줄게요.

Will you ~?는 요청의 의미로 쓰일 수 있다. 즉석에서 그래 줄 것이냐고 묻는 것이므로
- **Will you get** me an espresso, please? 에스프레소 한 잔 갖다 주시겠어요?

Shall I ~?와 **Shall we ~?**를 써서 즉석에서 제안을 할 수도 있다.
- **Shall I get** you something to drink? 뭐 마실 것 좀 갖다 드릴까요? 뭔가를 해 주겠다는 제안
- **Shall we have** a beer? 맥주나 한 잔 할까? 함께 뭔가를 하자는 제안

2 미래에 그럴 것이라고 예상할 때에도 will을 쓸 수 있다. 현재 어떤 징조가 있다면 am/are/is going to로 말한다
- The store **will be closed** on Sunday. 그 가게는 일요일에는 문을 닫을걸.
- I **won't stay** long. I've got a meeting at 2:30. 전 오래 있지는 않을 거예요. 2시 30분에 회의가 있거든요.

3 will 앞에 종종 believe, be sure, expect, know, suppose, think 등의 표현이 올 수 있다.
- I **think I'll have** an espresso. 에스프레소 한 잔 할까 해요.
- I **think** it **will** be quite cold tomorrow. 내 생각엔 내일 날씨가 좀 추울 것 같다.
- I **guess** he **won't be** home until late. 그가 늦게까지 집에 안 올 것 같다.
- Do you **suppose** she **will marry** him? 그녀가 그와 결혼할 것 같나요?
- Everybody**'s sure** that she **will pass** the exam. 모두가 그녀가 시험에 붙을 거라 확신한다.
- I **doubt** they **will accept** your offer. 그들이 당신의 제안을 받아들일지 의심스럽네요. (받아들일 것 같지 않다)
- I **wonder** what she **will say**. 그녀가 뭐라 할지 궁금합니다.
- He **expects** the economy **will improve**. 그는 경제가 발전할 것이라고 예상한다.
- We **hope** they**'ll agree** to the deal. 우리는 그들이 거래에 동의하기를 바란다.

단, think 뒤에는 부정문을 쓰지 않고 don't/doesn't think ~로 말한다.
- I **don't think I'll call** him now. 지금 그에게 전화하진 않을래요.
- I **don't think** it **will take** long to finish the job. 그 일을 마치는 데에 오래 걸릴 것 같지 않아요.

hope 뒤에는 will을 안 쓰는 경우가 많다.
- Here's little something for you. I **hope** you **like** it. 이거 작은 선물인데, 네 맘에 들길 바라.
- I **hope** you **don't mind** me asking, but how old are you? 질문이 불쾌하지 않으시다면 나이가 어떻게 되시나요?

maybe나 probably 등의 부사가 함께 쓰이기도 한다. probably의 위치에 주의하자. See Unit 071▶
- She**'ll probably say** yes. 그녀는 아마도 Yes라고 말할 거예요. will 뒤에 위치
- She **probably won't say** no. 그녀는 아마도 No라고 말하진 않을 거예요. 부정문의 경우 won't 앞에 위치

4 won't ~는 좀처럼 의지나 바람대로 되지 않는 것을 말할 때 쓸 수 있다.
- Help! My car **won't start**. 도와줘! 내 차 시동이 안 걸려.
- Eva **won't stop** crying. I've tried everything and I'm really exhausted.
Eva가 도통 울음을 그치려 하질 않아요. 모든 시도를 다 했는데, 정말 지치네요.

Exercises

1. 문맥에 맞게 대화를 연결하세요.

1. A: Would you like a glass of wine?
2. A: It's getting dark.
3. A: I'm afraid he's on another line.
4. A: Don't worry about the meeting.
5. A: Here's my proposal.
6. A: Do you need any help?

a. B: OK, no problem. I'll call back later.
b. B: I'll support you.
c. B: Thanks. I'll have a look at it later.
d. B: I'll turn on the light.
e. B: No, thanks. I'm driving. I'll just have a coffee.
f. B: Yes please. Will you carry that chair for me?

2. 문장의 문맥에 가장 적합한 표현을 골라 문장을 완성하세요.

1. (Shall /(Will)) you give me a hand with these boxes?
2. (Shall / Will) I get you some tea?
3. (Shall / Will) you please move your car?
4. What time (shall / will) we meet?
5. When (shall / will) I see you again?

3. 주어진 표현을 써서 문장을 다시 써 보세요.

1. I'll have an espresso. (think) → *I think I'll have an espresso.*
2. She will accept the proposal. (doubt) → _____
3. My boss won't be happy about it. (guess) → _____
4. What happened to him? (wonder) → _____
5. She doesn't mind waiting in the car. (hope) → _____
6. I won't stay here tonight. (think) → _____

4. 문맥에 맞는 문장끼리 연결하세요.

1. Can you help me with my car?
2. Ben is angry with me.
3. It's almost 9 o'clock.
4. My son is picky.
5. I've been working all day.

a. It won't start.
b. I think I'll stop now.
c. He won't eat vegetables.
d. He won't talk to me.
e. Shall we leave now?

🔊 Dialogue

5. 주어진 단어를 이용하여 문맥에 맞게 문장을 완성하세요.

Naomi and Erika are grocery shopping for a barbecue party.
Naomi와 Erika는 바비큐 파티를 위해 장을 보고 있습니다.

Naomi I hope it doesn't rain for our barbecue tomorrow.
Erika Don't worry. I'm sure _____ (it, not). The forecast says _____ (it, be dry).
Naomi Great. By the way, _____ (one chicken, be enough)?
Erika Well, I think _____ (we, need) two.
There _____ (be) at least 6.
Naomi OK. I'll buy two then.

Unit 018

going to vs. will, 그 외의 미래

I was going to call you.
너한테 전화하려고 했었는데.

1 will ~ vs. am/are/is going to ~

will ~	am/are/is going to ~
즉석에서 결심, 약속, 제안	이전에 해 놓은 계획, 결심
▶ A: How about this. It's only $12. 이건 어떤가요? 단돈 12달러입니다. B: It looks nice. OK, **I'll take** it. 괜찮아 보이네요. 좋아요, 그걸로 할게요. ▶ **I'll do** it now. 지금 바로 하겠습니다.	▶ I've made up my mind. **I'm going to buy** a Volkswagen. 전 결정했어요. 폭스바겐을 살 거예요. ▶ **I'm going to study** marketing in college. 저는 대학에서 마케팅을 공부할 계획입니다.
생각이나 믿음에 근거한 예상, 예측	현재의 징조에 따른 예상, 예측
▶ Do you think it**'ll be hot** tomorrow? 내일 더울 것 같니?	▶ It's already 28 degrees Celsius. It**'s going to be** very **hot** today. 벌써 28도네. 오늘 엄청 덥겠어.

미래에 대한 예상이나 추측에 대해 종종 will ~과 am/are/is going to ~가 모두 쓰일 수 있다.
▶ Everything **will be** all right. = Everything**'s gonna be** all right. 모든 일이 잘 될 거예요.
└ 대화체에서 going to는 종종 gonna로 발음한다.

2 과거 시간을 기준으로 그 뒤에 올 미래에 대해 말할 때 다음과 같이 말할 수 있다.

● will → would 과거에 그럴 것이라 예상 또는 결심. 이후의 상황은 문맥을 통해 파악해야 함
  - I know you **will make** it. 난 네가 해낼 것임을 알아.
  - I knew you **would make** it. 난 네가 해낼 줄 알았어. 실제로 해 냈음

▶ He promised that he **would come** to the party. 그는 파티에 올 거라고 약속했다. 파티에 왔을 수도 안 왔을 수도 있음. 실제로 파티에 왔는지는 이 문장만으로는 알 수 없음

● am/are/is going to ~ → was/were going to ~
과거에 그러려고 했거나 그런 일이 벌어질 것이라 예상했는데 실제로는 그렇게 되지 않음을 암시
  - You don't have to email her. **I'm going to call** her tomorrow. 그녀에게 이메일 보내지 않아도 돼요. 제가 내일 전화할 거예요.
  - A: Hello, Jay. It's me, Naomi. 여보세요, Jay. 나야, Naomi.
    B: Hi, Naomi. **I was going to call** you. 안녕, Naomi. 너한테 전화하려고 했었는데.

▶ I thought it **was going to snow** on Christmas, but it didn't. 난 성탄절에 눈이 올 줄 알았는데 안 왔어.

3 be about to ~ 는 '막 ~하려던 참', 즉 ~이 아주 임박했을 때 쓸 수 있다.

▶ Hurry up! The game **is about to begin**. 서둘러! 경기가 막 시작하려고 해.
▶ A: Were you doing something? I don't want to bother you. 뭐 하고 있었니? 방해하고 싶진 않은데.
B: I **was about to watch** a movie, but that can wait. 영화를 하나 막 보려던 참이지만 뭐 이따 해도 돼.

4 be to ~는 공식적인 일정이나 반드시 그렇게 되어야(or 되지 말아야) 한다는 뉘앙스의 미래로 쓰일 수 있다.
주로 신문이나 기타 미디어의 미래 사건에 대한 보도에서 많이 볼 수 있다. 미래 외의 다른 의미로도 쓰임 See Unit 045▶

▶ President Moon **is to meet** Pope Francis next week. 문 대통령은 다음 주에 프란시스코 교황을 만날 것입니다.
▶ You **are not to do** that again. 너 다시는 그래선 안 돼.
▶ If you **are to catch** the train, you must leave now. 그 기차를 타야겠다면, 지금 떠나야 한다. See Unit 031▶

Exercises

1. 보기에서 동사를 골라 적절한 형태로 바꾸어 문장을 완성하세요. 주어가 대명사라면 축약형을 쓰세요.

1. A: _Are_ you _doing_ (do) anything tonight?
   B: Not really. I'm free.
2. A: Have a wonderful trip!
   B: Thanks. I _____ (send) you a postcard!
3. A: I'm out of the office this afternoon.
   B: _____ you _____ (visit) a customer?
4. A: Could you make sure that Ms. Turner gets my message?
   B: Sure. I _____ (tell) her myself when she gets in.
5. A: We've chosen a name for our dog!
   B: Really? What _____ you _____ (call) him?

2. 문맥에 맞게 대화를 연결하세요.

1. A: Are you free tonight? — a. B: Sorry. I am visiting my sister's.
2. A: How about tomorrow at 3:30? — b. B: Sure. I'll do it now.
3. A: What are you plans for the summer? — c. B: I'm going to a summer camp.
4. A: Can you type these documents? — d. B: OK. I'll see you then.

3. 문장의 문맥에 가장 적합한 표현을 골라 문장을 완성하세요.

1. I knew you (will / **would**) make it.
2. Hurry up! The game (will / is about to) begin.
3. I (would / was going to) write an email to them, but I forgot.
4. I'm waiting for her call because she said she (would / was going to) contact me this afternoon.
5. The Irish president (is about to / is to) visit the Scottish Parliament on Wednesday.
6. He (would / was going to) leave on Monday, but he couldn't get a flight until Thursday.
7. You promised that you (wouldn't / weren't to) be late.
8. You (are about to / are not to) start the test until the teacher tells you to.

🔊 Dialogue

4. 문장의 문맥에 가장 적합한 표현을 보기에서 골라 문장을 완성하세요.

It's sunny today. Amy is wondering why Sarah is wearing rain boots.
오늘은 날씨가 화창합니다. Amy는 왜 Sarah가 장화를 신고 있는지 궁금해하고 있습니다.

❶ is going to   ❷ was going to   ❸ was about to   ❹ was to

Amy   Why are you wearing those rain boots? It's not rainy today.
Sarah Well, I thought it _____ rain when I left home.
Amy   I see. It's true that it was quite cloudy early this morning.
Sarah It was. But it just got sunny and dry.
Amy   It's not easy to predict the weather these days.

Unit 019

will be -ing vs. will have p.p.

I'll be graduating in two years.
전 2년 뒤면 졸업할 거예요.

1 will be -ing는 미래의 어느 한때에 벌어지고 있을 거라 예상되는 사건이나 상황을 말할 때 쓸 수 있다.

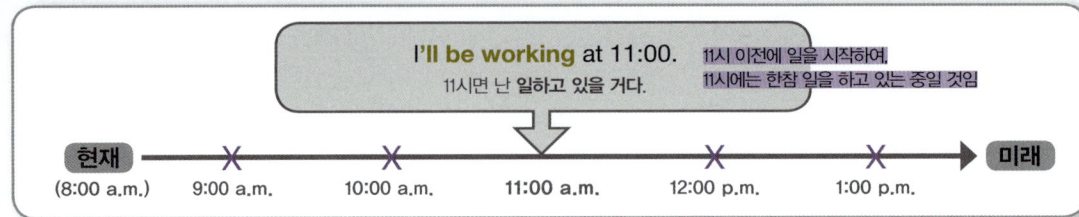

- I'm going to Hawaii tomorrow. This time next week, I'll be sunbathing on the beach.
  난 내일 하와이에 가. 다음 주 이 시간이면 난 해변에서 **일광욕 중일 거야**.

2 미래에 벌어질 거라 예상되는 사건에 대해서도 will be -ing를 쓸 수 있다. 진행 중이 아님. be going to와 비슷

- I'll be graduating in two years. 전 2년 뒤면 졸업할 거예요.
- President Moon will be making a statement in the press room at 11:00 a.m.
  문 대통령이 11시에 기자회견실에서 성명을 **발표할 것입니다**.

3 will you be -ing는 다소 조심스럽게 상대방의 미래 행동에 대해 묻는 뉘앙스이다.
질문에 묻는 이의 바람이 깔려 있는 뉘앙스일 수 있다

- A: **Will you be using** your bicycle tomorrow? 내일 자전거 쓸 거니?
  B: No. Do you want to borrow it? 아니. 빌리고 싶니?

4 will have p.p.는 미래의 어느 기준 시간 이전에 벌어질 일에 대해 쓸 수 있다.

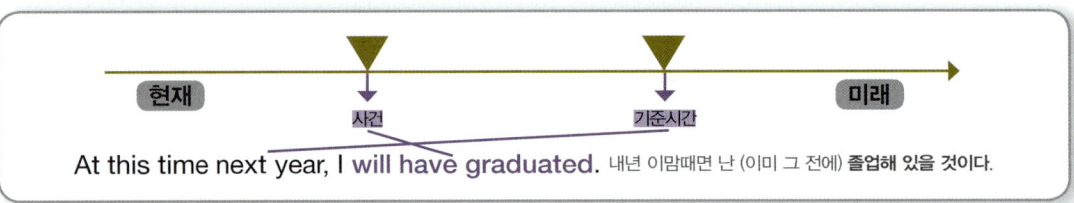

At this time next year, I will have graduated. 내년 이맘때면 난 (이미 그 전에) 졸업해 있을 것이다.

- Oh, dear. I'm late. The meeting will already have started by the time I arrive.
  이런, 늦었어. 내가 도착할 즈음이면 이미 **시작했겠어**. 내가 도착하기 전에 회의가 시작
- Mr. Cruz will have retired by 2030. 2030년이면 Cruz 씨는 이미 **은퇴했을 것이다**. 은퇴 시점이 2030년 전

will have p.p.는 미래의 어느 기준 시간까지 지속되고 있을 상태에 대해서도 쓸 수 있다.

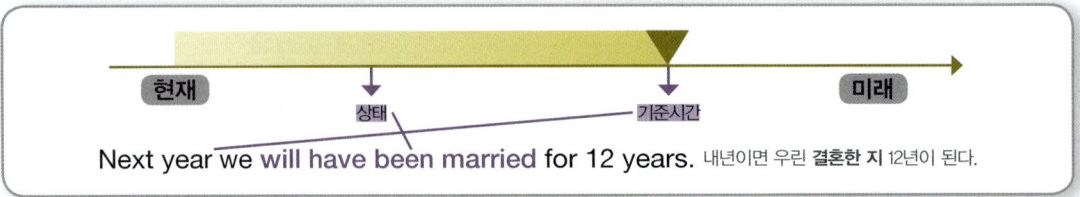

Next year we will have been married for 12 years. 내년이면 우리 **결혼한 지** 12년이 된다.

- I probably won't have had much experience by then. 그 때까지는 제가 경력이 많이 **쌓여 있을 것 같지 않아요**.
- He will have been playing the game for 5 hours by midnight. 자정이면 걔는 그 게임을 5시간째 **하고 있을 거야**.
  미래의 어느 기준 시간까지 지속 또는 반복될 행동이나 사건에는 will have been -ing를 쓸 수 있다.

Exercises

1. 다음 Mr. Harris의 일정표를 보고, 주어진 표현을 사용하여 그의 하루에 대해 예상하는 문장을 완성해 보세요.

	May 27th (Tuesday)
10:00 ~ 12:00	Business Seminar: How to be successful
12:00 ~ 12:50	Lunch
1:00 ~ 2:40	Meeting with Mr. Branson
3:00	Leave for the airport
4:50 ~ 7:45	Flight to Seattle
7:45	Arrive in Seattle

1. The seminar _will begin_ (begin) at 10:00.
2. The seminar _____ (finish) by 12:00.
3. At 12:30, Mr. Harris _____ (have) lunch.
4. At 2:00, he _____ (meet) with Mr. Branson.
5. At 3:00, he _____ (leave) for the airport.
6. At 6:00, he _____ (fly) to Seattle.
7. He _____ (arrive) in Seattle by 8:00.

2. 문장의 문맥에 가장 적합한 표현을 골라 문장을 완성하세요.

1. They (will be married / will have been married) for 10 years by 2022.
2. By the time I get to the station, the train (will be leaving / will have left).
3. A: (Will you pass / Will you be passing) the stationery shop when you're out?
   B: Probably. Why?
   A: I need some staples. Can you get me some?
4. Tomorrow at this time, I (will be taking / will have taken) my final exam.
5. I (will be waiting / will have been waiting) here for an hour by 5:30.
6. (Will they be attending / Will they have attended) the training next Thursday?
7. Do you think you (will be doing / will have done) the same job in ten years' time?
8. James, how long (will you be working / will you have been working) for JJ International by the time you retire?

🔊 Dialogue

3. 주어진 단어를 이용하여 문맥에 맞게 문장을 완성하세요.

Jay wants to talk to Erika, but she's busy now.
Jay는 Erika와 이야기를 하고 싶어하는데, Erika가 지금은 바쁩니다.

Jay   Erika, do you have time to talk?
Erika Sorry. I'm going to a class now. Actually I'm late. Can we do it later?
Jay   All right. Will you be free at lunchtime?
Erika Sure. The class _____ (end) by then.
Jay   OK, then I'll see you at lunchtime. Shall we talk over lunch?
Erika Sounds good. I'll see you then.

Unit 020

when I do vs. when I've done

I'll ask her about it when I call her.
그녀에게 전화하면 그것에 대해 물어볼게요.

1 동사원형은 현재(기준시간)부터 그 이후의 시간 흐름을 의미하는 반면, have p.p.는 현재(기준시간)부터 그 이전의 시간 흐름을 의미한다.

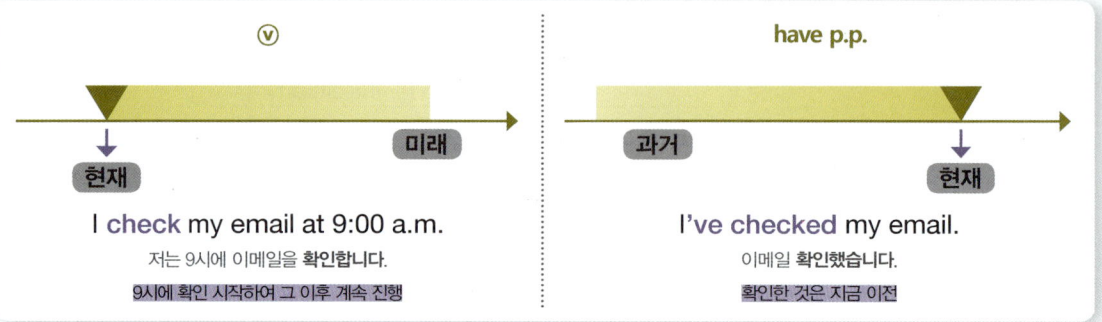

I **check** my email at 9:00 a.m.
저는 9시에 이메일을 확인합니다.
9시에 확인 시작하여 그 이후 계속 진행

I**'ve checked** my email.
이메일 확인했습니다.
확인한 것은 지금 이전

when I ~는 ~가 시작되는 시점이 기준이지만, when I've p.p.는 해당 동작, 사건이 끝나는(완료, p.p.) 되는 시점이 기준이다.

▶ I'll ask her about it **when I call** her.
그녀에게 전화하면 그것에 대해 물어볼게요.
전화를 걸어서 통화가 연결된 후

▶ I'll have dinner **when I've called** her.
그녀와 전화 끝나면 저녁 먹을게요.
그녀와의 통화가 다 끝난 시점

▶ (in a class) When you**'ve read** the story, tell your partner about it.
이야기를 읽고 나면 짝꿍에게 그에 대해 이야기해 주세요.

▶ Don't say anything until he**'s left** the room. 그가 방을 (완전히) 나설 때까지 아무 말도 하지 말아라.

after나 as soon as, finish 등 '이후'를 암시하는 표현이 쓰이는 경우, have p.p.를 쓰지 않아도 된다.

▶ You can turn off the light **after she leaves**. or You can turn off the light **after she has left**.
그녀가 떠난 뒤에 불을 꺼도 됩니다.

▶ I'll send you the report **as soon as I finish it**. or I'll send you the report **as soon as I've finished it**. 마치는 대로 보고서를 보내드리겠습니다.

2 have p.p.는 동사의 과거형(-ed)을 쓸 수 없는 자리에서 과거를 표현해야 할 때 쓸 수 있다.

● **to have p.p** See Unit 043▶
  ▶ She seems **to have lost weight**. 그는 살이 빠진 것 같다. 지금 그렇게 보인다고 말하기 이전에 살이 빠졌음
  ▶ I would like **to have seen** it. 그걸 봤었더라면 좋을 텐데. 과거에 그랬으면 지금 좋겠다는 의미

● **조동사+have p.p.** 조동사의 -ed 형태가 과거 아닌 다른 의미로 쓰인 상황에서 뒤에 올 동사의 have p.p.로 과거 의미 표현
  ▶ I **could have taken** the earlier train. 나는 그 이전 기차를 탈 수도 있었다. could take은 현재의 의미를 나타낸다.
  See Unit 022▶
  ▶ He **might have been busy**. 그는 바빴었을지도 몰라. might는 과거의 의미로 쓰이지 않는다. See Unit 023▶

● **having p.p.** -ing 자리에서 과거 의미를 나타냄
  ▶ **Having washed** the car, I noticed a small scratch on the door.
  차를 세차하고 나니, 문짝에 작은 스크래치가 난 것을 발견했다. See Unit 053▶
  ▶ **Without having done** your homework, you can't go out. 숙제를 다 마치지 않았으면, 넌 나갈 수 없단다.

Exercises

1. 문맥에 맞게 연결하여 문장을 완성하세요.

1. We need to get to the hotel • • a. when you've called him.
2. The door will open • • b. after the bus stops.
3. Please, don't leave your seat • • c. until the bus has stopped.
4. Don't say anything • • d. until he's left the room.
5. Let's have dinner • • e. before it gets dark.

2. 문장의 문맥에 가장 적합한 표현을 골라 문장을 완성하세요.

1. He is poor now, but he seems to (be / (have been)) rich.
2. He seems to (be / have been) rich. I saw him in a Ferrari last Sunday.
3. My grandfather could (speak / have spoken) 3 languages.
4. Don't you think he looks slimmer than before? He seems to (lose weight / have lost weight).
5. (Seeing / Having seen) the film before, I know the ending.
6. It seems to (rain / have rained). The ground is wet.

3. 다음 보기처럼 두 문장을 한 문장으로 만드세요. 주어가 대명사라면 축약형을 쓰세요.

1. I'll finish the report. I'll send you the report right away.
   → __I'll send you the report__ as soon as __I finish it__ .
2. You're going on vacation. What are you going to do?
   → _____ when _____ ?
3. He'll recover. Then he'll get back to work.
   → _____ when _____ .
4. I'll learn everything. I will keep trying.
   → _____ until _____ .
5. I'll see it. I won't believe it until then.
   → _____ until _____ .

🔊 Dialogue

4. 주어진 단어를 이용하여 문맥에 맞게 문장을 완성하세요.

Andy is sick in bed. Amy has come to see him.
Andy는 아파서 자리에 누워 있습니다. Amy가 그를 보러 왔습니다.

Amy	How are you feeling, Andy?
Andy	Terrible.
Amy	Did you have breakfast?
Andy	No. I didn't want to eat.
Amy	Oh dear. Get up. Let's eat something.
Andy	No, Amy. I've lost my appetite.
Amy	Come on. You'll feel better when _____ (you, have) something to eat.

Big Picture

동사의 형태와 MODE

02

동사의 형태는 시간뿐 아니라 말의 태도나 현실성도 나타냅니다. 더 많은, 다양한 문장을 다루고 소화하는 중급 단계에서는 이를 잘 구분하는 것이 중요합니다. -ed(때로는 p.p.)는 다음과 같은 태도와 현실성을 표현합니다.

1 태도

동사가 -ed 형태로 변하면 말하는 사람의 태도가 한걸음 물러납니다. 공손하고 조심스럽거나 양보하는 느낌을 나타낼 수 있습니다. 특히 분위기와 느낌을 나타내는 '조동사'들이 한걸음 물러나는 경우가 그렇지요. can보다 could가 더 예의 바르게 들리는 이유입니다.

- **Could** you do me a favor? 제 부탁 좀 들어 주시겠어요? '과거' 문장이 아님에 주의
- I **would like** to talk to Mr. Harris. Harris 씨와 이야기하고 싶습니다. want보다 예의바른 느낌
- We **could** go out to eat tonight. 오늘 밤 나가서 외식할 수도 있을 것 같은데요. 다소 조심스럽게 제안

2 현실 → 비현실

동사의 -ed 형태는 현실에서 한걸음 떨어져 비현실로 물러나는 것을 의미할 수도 있습니다. 영어는 우리말과 달리 현실과 다르거나 비현실적인 상상을 동사의 형태로 나타냅니다.

- If I **were** a millionaire, I **would buy** a private jet.
  내가 백만장자라면 개인 비행기를 살 거야. 비현실적인 상상
- It's time we **went** home. 우리 이제 집에 가야 할 시간이거든. 현실은 집에 가지 않고 있음

3 조동사

동사 중에는 홀로 동사 역할을 하지 못하고, 다른 동사를 돕는 역할을 하는 것들도 있습니다. 이런 동사들을 '조동사'라고 합니다. 조동사에는 의문문의 Do처럼 기능적인 역할만 하고 따로 의미를 갖지 못하는 조동사(Auxiliary verbs)와 본동사에 보조적인 분위기를 더해주는 조동사(Modal verbs)가 있습니다. 분위기(Mode)를 나타내는 주요 동사 표현은 부록 11을 참고하세요.

기본적으로 조동사는 동사를 '돕는' 동사입니다. 동사 앞에서 '추측, 가능성, 허락, 의무, 필요' 등의 의미를 더해 주지요. 또한, 맨 앞에 오기 때문에 문장의 시간도 표현하죠. 덕분에 본동사는 조동사 뒤에서 항상 원형으로 오게 됩니다.

Unit 021

can/could(1)

I can help you with that.
그거 제가 도와드릴 수 있어요.

1 can은 '~할 수 있다' 또는 '~할 줄 안다'라는 능력을 표현할 때 쓸 수 있다.
- I **can play** the drums. 나는 드럼 칠 줄 알아.
- He **can't speak** Spanish. 그는 스페인어는 할 줄 모릅니다.
- **Can you stand** on your head? 물구나무 설 수 있니?

can은 또한 '~이 가능하다' 또는 '그럴 수 있다'라는 가능성을 표현할 때에도 쓸 수 있다.
- I **can help** you with that. 그거 제가 도와드릴 수 있어요.
- A: How about going to the movies tonight? 오늘 밤에 영화 보러 가는 거 어때?
  B: I'm sorry I **can't**. I'm having dinner with my parents. 미안하지만 안 되겠어. 부모님과 식사 약속이 있어.
- I don't believe it. It **can't be** true. 믿을 수 없어요. 그건 사실일 리가 없어요. `가능성의 강한 부정`
- **Can you give** me a hand? 나 좀 도와줄 수 있어? `가능하다면 해 달라는 요청의 의미`

2 am/are/is able to ~는 다음과 같을 때 can 대신 쓸 수 있다.
- ● 문장 구조상 can을 쓸 수 없을 때
  - I'**ll be able to see** you this weekend. 이번 주말에 널 볼 수 있을 것 같아.
  - She **hasn't been able to sleep** well recently. 그녀는 최근에 계속 잠을 잘 자지 못했어요.
  - To **be able to speak** fluent English, you must practice a lot.
    영어를 유창하게 말할 수 있기 위해서는 연습을 많이 해야만 합니다.

- ● 현재 할 수 있거나 그럴 수 있음을 강조할 때 `일반적인 능력이나 가능성에 대해서는 쓰지 않음`
  - We'**re** finally **able to buy** our own home! 마침내 우리만의 집을 살 수 있게 되었어요!
    이전에는 집을 살 수 없었으나 이제는 살 수 있음을 암시

3 could는 과거의 일반적으로 할 수 있었던 것에 말할 때 쓴다.
- I **could play** the piano quite well when I was a child. 어릴 땐 내가 피아노를 꽤 잘 쳤었는데 말이지.
- Erika **couldn't speak** English when she lived in Taiwan. 대만에 살았을 때 Erika는 영어를 할 줄 몰랐다.

4 과거 특정한 상황에서 그럴 수 있었던 것에 대해서는 was/were able to ~를 쓴다.
그때에만 가능했고, 다른 때에도 늘 그럴 수 있다고 보장할 수 없음. managed to나 succeed (in ~ing)를 대신 쓸 수도 있다.
- The traffic was bad, but I **was able to get** to the airport in time.
  교통이 안 좋았지만, 나는 제시간에 공항에 도착할 수 있었다.
- We **were** finally **able to persuade** our client. 우리는 마침내 고객을 설득할 수 있었다.

단, 부정문의 경우에는 couldn't와 wasn't/weren't able to를 모두 쓸 수 있다.
- I **wasn't able to finish** the report by the deadline. = I **couldn't finish** the report by the dead line.
  나는 마감 시한까지 보고서를 마칠 수가 없었다.

5 see, hear, understand 등 일반적인 신체 또는 지각 기능에 대해 말할 때에는 can이나 could가 쓰인다.
be able to를 쓰지 않음
- You **can see** the ocean from the window. 창문을 통해 바다를 볼 수 있어요.
  You **are able to see** the ocean from the window. (X)
- When he came close to me, I **could smell** the garlic on his breath.
  When he came close to me, I **was able to smell** the garlic on his breath. (X)
  그가 내게 가까이오자 숨에서 마늘 냄새가 났다.

Exercises

1. 문맥에 맞게 can이나 be able to를 넣어 문장을 완성하세요. 문맥에 따라 부정 형태로 쓰일 수 있습니다.

1. Erika __can__ speak three languages.
2. I'm afraid that I won't _____ make it to the seminar tomorrow.
3. She _____ see anything without her glasses.
4. Dr. Singh might _____ see you this afternoon.
5. I'd like to _____ speak better English.
6. Our products _____ be customized according to your needs.
7. I'm quite good at reading English, but I _____ understand when people speak too fast.

2. 문장의 문맥에 가장 적합한 표현을 골라 문장을 완성하세요.

1. Michael Jackson was a singer who ((could) / was able to) dance.
2. After climbing for several hours, I (could / was able to) get to the top of the mountain.
3. We (could / were able to) cover the main points at the meeting although we didn't have much time.
4. Most hotels were fully booked, but we (could / were able to) find one to stay.
5. He spoke out loud so that everyone (could / was able to) hear him well.
6. The negotiation broke down because we (couldn't / weren't able to) agree on the price.

3. 밑줄 친 부분이 틀렸다면 맞게 고치세요. 고칠 게 없다면 X를 쓰세요.

1. After trying several times, I was finally able to open the door.   __X__
2. Can you hear the sound of rain?   _____
3. When I'm in Hawaii, I enjoy can swim every morning.   _____
4. You aren't able to smoke here, but you're able to smoke in the garden.   _____
5. A: Did you get your cast removed?
   B: Yes. Now I'm finally able to walk!   _____

🔊 Dialogue

4. 문장의 문맥에 가장 적합한 표현을 골라 문장을 완성하세요.

Julia is a flight attendant. She's just come back from her flight.
Julia는 승무원입니다. 그녀는 방금 비행을 마치고 돌아왔습니다.

Nicole How was the flight?

Julia It wasn't good this time. It took much longer because of the delay.

Nicole What was the reason for the delay?

Julia The fog. Everybody had to sit on the airplane waiting for it to clear up for hours.

Nicole Oh dear.

Julia The boarding finished at 6, but the plane (could / was able to) take off at 9.

Nicole That must have been awful.

Unit 022

can/could(2)

I'm starving. I could eat a horse.
배고파 죽겠다. 말 한 마리라도 먹을 수 있겠어.

1 **could는 '과거'가 아닌 현재나 미래에 대해서도 쓸 수 있다.** 태도나 현실적임에서 한걸음 물러섬

- **could는 좀 더 예의 바른 요청이나 제안에도 쓰일 수 있다.** 과거의 의미가 아님. can을 쓸 수도 있음
  - **Could you give** me a hand? 저 좀 도와주시겠어요? Can you give me a hand?보다 예의 바름
  - A: I haven't heard from her for days. 그녀에게 며칠 동안 연락을 못 받았어요.
    B: You **could call** her. 전화를 해 보세요. You can call her보다는 다소 조심스러운 느낌 See Unit 029▶

- **could는 지금 또는 미래에 '그럴 수 있는' 가능성에 대해 말할 때에도 쓰인다.** can보다 덜 확신하는 느낌
  - It **could be** true, but I'm not sure. 그게 사실일 수도 있겠지만, 전 확신할 수 없네요.

- **상상 속 또는 비현실적인 것에 대해 말할 때에도 쓰인다.** can을 쓰지 않음
  - I'm starving. I **could eat** a horse. 배고파 죽겠다. 말 한 마리라도 먹을 수 있겠어.
  - I love this place. I **could stay** here forever. 여기 너무 좋다. 영원히 있을 수도 있겠어.
  - If I were a millionaire, I **could buy** whatever I want. 내가 백만장자라면 원하는 건 뭐든지 살 수 있을 텐데. See Unit 031▶

2 **과거에 그럴 수 있었던 가능성에 대해서는 could have p.p.로 말한다.** 현실로 이루어지지는 않았음

- I was starving. I **could have eaten** a horse.
  나는 배고파 죽을 지경이었다. 말 한 마리라도 먹을 수 있었을 거다. 실제로 말을 먹지는 않았음
- If I had had enough money, I **could have bought** it.
  내가 그 때 돈이 있었더라면, 그걸 살 수 있었을 텐데. See Unit 032▶
- You **could have tried** harder. 너는 더 열심히 노력했을 수도 있었어. 실제로는 그러지 않았음

couldn't have p.p.는 과거에 그럴 수 없었을 것이라는 의미이다.
실제로 그랬거나, 때로는 '~라 해도 그럴 수 없었을 것'이란 의미로도 쓰임

- We **couldn't have done** it without you. 너 없이는 우리가 그걸 할 수 없었을 거야. 네가 있어서 우리가 해냈음
- Things **couldn't have been** better.
  상황이 (그보다) 더 좋아질 수는 없었을 겁니다(최고였습니다). 가장 좋은 상태였음 See Unit 076▶
- I didn't know about the party, but I **couldn't have gone** anyway. I was busy.
  파티에 대해서는 몰랐지만 어쨌거나 못 갔을 거야. 바빴거든. 알았다 해도 안 갔음

	능력(ability)	가능성(possibility)
현재/미래 (Present/Future)	**can** 일반적 ▶ She **can speak** 3 languages. 그녀는 3개국어를 할 수 있다.	**can** 현실적 ▶ You **can have** it if you want. 원하면 그거 가져가 돼.
	am/are/is able to 강조, can을 못 쓸 때 ▶ Now I'**m able to walk**. 이제는 걸을 수 있어. 이전에 어떤 이유로 걷지 못하다가 지금은 걸을 수 있음을 암시	**could** 예의, 조심스러움, 덜 확신, 비현실적 ▶ I'm so mad I **could scream**. 너무 화나서 소리라도 지를 수 있을 것 같아. 실제로 소리를 지를 것은 아니고 그 정도로 화났다는 의미
과거(Past)	**could** 일반적, 전반적 ▶ My late grandmother **could speak** 3 languages. 돌아가신 우리 할머니는 3개국어를 하실 수 있었다.	**could have p.p.** 비현실, 가정, 상상, 실제와 다름 ▶ I loved the place. I **could have stayed** there forever. 거기 너무 좋았다. 영원히 있을 수도 있었겠다.
	was/were able to 특정한 상황에서만 ▶ Luckily, I **was able to catch** the sunrise yesterday! 운 좋게도 어제 일출을 볼 수 있었어.	

Exercises

1. 문맥에 맞는 문장끼리 연결하세요.

1. He could have gotten a job in Australia.
2. He was wearing a seatbelt.
3. He was an excellent salesperson.
4. He could have killed the dog.
5. He was driving too fast.
6. He couldn't have gone to Australia anyway.
7. Last year was very successful.

a. He could sell anything to anybody.
b. Otherwise, he could have been killed.
c. However, he decided not to take it.
d. Things couldn't have been better.
e. He couldn't have avoided the accident.
f. Luckily, he was able to stop the car in time.
g. He was in the hospital.

2. 밑줄 친 부분이 틀렸다면 맞게 고치세요. 고칠 것이 없다면 X를 쓰세요.

1. I love seafood. I can eat it every day.   *could eat*
2. I couldn't have done it without you.   _____
3. A: What shall we do on the weekend?
   B: We could have visited my mother.   _____
4. Could you give me a hand?   _____
5. If I were a millionaire, I can buy a private jet. _____

3. 문장의 문맥에 가장 적합한 표현을 골라 문장을 완성하세요.

1. It (was able to be / (could be) / could have been) true, but I'm not sure.
2. I was starving. I (was able to eat / could eat / could have eaten) a horse.
3. Luckily, I (was able to arrive / could arrive / could have arrived) at the station in time.
4. I (was able to swim / could swim / could have swum) about 70 meters in my teens.
5. I (was able to call / could call / could have called) him, but I decided to text him.

✦ Dialogue

4. 주어진 단어를 이용하여 문맥에 맞게 문장을 완성하세요.

Suzi recently took her driver's test. Patrick is asking about it.
Suzi는 최근에 운전면허시험을 보았습니다. Patrick이 이에 대해 묻고 있습니다.

Patrick Suzi, how did your driver's test go?
Suzi   I passed!
Patrick Congratulations! I knew you could do it.
Suzi   Thanks, Patrick. I _____ (not, do) it without your help.
Patrick You're welcome, Suzi. We should buy some champagne to celebrate.
Suzi   Yay! Can I drive you to the liquor store?

Unit 023

may/might

I might be relaxing at home at this time tomorrow.
내일 이 시간에는 나 집에서 쉬고 있을지도 몰라.

1 may나 might는 둘 다 '~일지도 모른다' 또는 '~할지도 모른다'라는 현재와 미래에 대한 추측에 쓰인다.
- He **might be** at home now. = He **may be** at home now. 그는 지금 집에 있을지도 몰라요.
- I **might not be** here tomorrow. = I **may not be** here tomorrow. 저는 내일 여기 오지 않을지도 몰라요.

May I ~?는 정중하게 '~해도 되겠냐'고 물을 때 쓸 수 있다.
- **May I come** in? 들어가도 되겠습니까?

2 현재 또는 미래에 '~하고 있을지도 모른다'라는 의미로 **may/might be -ing**를 쓸 수 있다.
- Don't call him now. He **may/might be having** dinner. 그에게 지금은 전화하지 마. 저녁식사 중일지도 몰라.
- I **may/might be relaxing** at home at this time tomorrow. 내일 이 시간에는 나 집에서 쉬고 있을지도 몰라.

3 과거에 '~했었을지도 모른다'는 추측은 **may/might have p.p.**를 써서 표현할 수 있다.
- A: I can't find my phone. Have you seen it? 전화기를 못 찾겠어. 내 전화기 본 적 있어?
  B: No. You **may/might have forgotten** it at school. 아니. 네가 학교에서 잊어버리고 왔는지도 모르지.
- A: Why is Sarah eating so little for lunch today? 오늘 Sarah가 왜 이리 점심을 적게 먹는 거지?
  B: She **may/might have eaten** a lot for breakfast. 아침에 많이 먹었는지도 몰라.
- Alice didn't come to the party. She **may/might not have known** about it.
  Alice는 파티에 오지 않았어요. 파티에 대해 알지 못했을지도 몰라요.

4 **might**는 비현실적인 상황에서 쓰인다. `may는 쓰지 않음. could와 비슷`
- If I were a millionaire, I **might buy** him a yacht. 내가 백만장자라면 그에게 요트를 사 줄지도 모르지.
- If I had had enough money, I **might have bought** it. 내가 돈이 충분히 있었더라면 그걸 샀을지도 몰라.

5 **maybe, perhaps, possibly, probably**를 써서 추측의 의미를 나타낼 수도 있다.
`may나 could 등과 함께 쓰이기도 함`

- **maybe**와 **perhaps**는 확실치 않다는 뉘앙스를 띈다. (50% 또는 그 이하)
  `perhaps보다는 maybe가 일상적인 대화에서 더 많이 쓰임`
  - **Maybe/Perhaps** I'll see him at the party. 아마 파티에서 그를 보게 되지 않을까.
  - A: Are you going to the concert? 그 콘서트 갈 거니?
    B: **Maybe or Maybe not**. 갈지도 모르고, 안 갈지도 몰라.

- **possibly**는 다소 딱딱하고 격식 있는 뉘앙스로, 확률이 아주 높지는 않지만 그럴 수 있다는 의미이다. (50% 이하)
  - This could **possibly** be the last time we ever see each other.
    이번이 아마도 우리가 서로를 보는 마지막일지도 모르겠습니다.

- **probably**는 Be type 동사 뒤, Do type 동사 앞에 오며, 꽤 그럴 가능성이 있다는 뉘앙스가 있다. (50% 이상)
  `부정문에서는 not 앞에 옴`
  - The plane will **probably** arrive late. 그 비행기는 아마도 늦게 도착할 것이다.
  - He **probably won't** answer this question. 그는 아마도 이 질문에 답하지 않을 거야.

6 **may/might as well**은 '(그 외에 달리 더 나은 게 없으니) 그렇게 해야겠다'라는 의미로 쓰인다.
- The TV is broken. We **may/might as well listen to** the radio. TV가 고장 났어. 라디오나 들어야겠어.

Exercises

1. 같거나 비슷한 의미의 문장끼리 연결하세요.

1. Our local nursery school may close.   •   • a. He may know about it.
2. Maybe he is busy.   •   • b. Our local nursery school might close.
3. Perhaps he was busy.   •   • c. He might be busy.
4. Perhaps he knows about it.   •   • d. He might have been busy.
5. Perhaps I'll join a football team.   •   • e. I might join a football team.
6. Maybe I won't join a football team.   •   • f. I may not join a football team.
7. It is possible he didn't know about it.   •   • g. He might not have known about it.

2. might와 주어진 동사를 써서 문맥에 맞게 문장을 완성하세요. 문맥에 따라 not을 쓸 수 있습니다.

1. Naomi said that she ___might go___ (go) back to Japan in November or December.
2. A: Ben walked past me without saying hello.
   B: Well, he _____ (see) you.
3. A: Where's Sarah?
   B: I don't know. She _____ (be) in the library.
4. A: Can I try that puzzle? It seems quite simple.
   B: It _____ (be) as easy as you think.
5. It's almost midnight. They _____ (go) to bed already.

3. 밑줄 친 부분이 틀렸다면 맞게 고치세요. 고칠 것이 없다면 X를 쓰세요.

1. She <u>might be</u> in the garden now.   ___X___
2. I <u>might go</u> to Spain next year.   _____
3. He <u>might be</u> late yesterday because of the traffic.   _____
4. Don't call me at 8:00. I <u>might have been taking a bath</u>.   _____
5. Take an umbrella with you. It <u>may rain</u> today.   _____

🔊 Dialogue

4. 주어진 단어를 이용하여 문맥에 맞게 문장을 완성하세요.

Andy is looking for his phone.
Andy는 전화기를 찾고 있습니다.

Andy   I can't find my phone. Have you seen it?

Patrick   No. Isn't it on your bed? You usually leave it there.

Andy   No. Not this time.

Patrick   You _____ (might, forget) it at school, then. When was the last time you saw it?

Andy   I don't remember.

Patrick   Try calling it with my phone.

Unit 024

must(추측)

You must not have heard me correctly.
네가 분명 잘못 들었던 게야.

1 must는 '(분명) 그럴 것'이라고 확신하는 추측에 쓰인다. [must는 의문문으로 쓰이지 않음]

- He never goes out on weekday evenings, so he **must be** at home now.
  그는 평일 저녁엔 절대 안 나가요. 그러니 지금 **틀림없이** 집에 **있을** 거예요.
- No one's answering the doorbell. They **must not be** at home.
  벨을 눌렀는데 아무도 답을 안 하네요. 사람들이 집에 **없나 봐요**.

2 must be –ing는 '(분명) 지금 ~하고 있을 것이다'라는 의미이다.

- The traffic is heavy today. They **must be repairing** the road again.
  오늘 차가 막히네. 분명 또 도로를 보수 중인 게야.
- She doesn't look so happy. Something **must be bothering** her.
  그녀는 기분이 좋아 보이지 않는다. 뭔가가 그녀의 **신경을 거스르고 있나** 보다.

3 과거에 '(분명) ~했을 것이다'는 추측은 must have p.p.를 써서 표현할 수 있다.

- No one's answering the doorbell. They **must have gone out**.
  벨을 눌렀는데 아무도 답을 안 하네요. 사람들이 **외출했나 봐요**.
- My phone is missing. I **must have dropped** it somewhere. 전화기가 없어졌어. 내가 어딘가에 **떨어뜨렸나 봐**.
- I said "ship," not "sheep." You **must not have heard** me correctly.
  난 'sheep'이 아니라 'ship'이라고 했어. 네가 분명 **잘못** 들었던 게야.

4 그럴 것이라는 추측이나 가능성의 may, might, must, could는 종종 유사하게 쓰이기도 하고, 차이가 나기도 한다.

현재 (Present)	**may, might, could** 확실치는 않음(not sure)	▶ Ask Patrick. He **may/might/could know** the answer. Patrick에게 물어 봐. 그가 답을 **알지도 몰라/알 수도 있어**.
	must 분명 그럴 것 **must not** 분명 아닐 것 **can't** 그럴 리가 없음	▶ Mike isn't at work today. He **must be** sick. Mike는 오늘 회사에 오지 않았어요. 분명 아픈 **거예요**. ▶ Mike isn't at work today? He **must not be feeling** well today. Mike가 오늘 회사에 오지 않았다고요? 그는 분명 오늘 컨디션이 안 좋은가 봐요. ▶ $1000 for a secondhand phone? It **can't be** right. 중고폰이 1000달러라고? 그 가격이 맞을 리가 없어.
미래 (Future)	**may, might, could** 미래에 대해 장담하지는 않음	▶ The new vaccine **may/might/could save** thousands of lives. 새 백신이 수 천명의 목숨을 **살릴 지도 모릅니다/살릴 수도 있습니다**.
과거 (Past)	**may/might have p.p.** 확신할 수 없음	▶ Well, he **may/might not have seen** it. 글쎄, 그는 그걸 **못 봤을지도 몰라**.
	must have p.p. 그랬을 거라 확신 **must not have p.p.** 안 그랬을 거라 확신 **couldn't have p.p.** 과거에 그랬을 가능성이 없거나 그랬을 리 없음. (가정, 상상)	▶ She sold her stock at its peak. She **must have made** a lot of money. 그녀는 최고가에 주식을 팔았다. 분명 많은 돈을 **벌었을 것이다**. ▶ He **must not have gone** to the party. 그는 분명 파티에 **가지 않았던 게야**. ▶ I wasn't invited, but even if I had been invited, I **couldn't have gone** anyway. 초대를 받진 못했지만, 초대를 받았다 해도 나는 어쨌거나 **안 갔을 것이다**.

Exercises

1. 주어진 단어를 사용해서 적절하게 변형하여 문장을 완성하세요.

   1. She never stops talking about her new boyfriend.
      → _She must be in love with him._ (She, must, be in love, with him)
   2. The music next door is so loud.
      → _____ (They, must, have a party)
   3. When I called her, a stranger answered.
      → _____ (She, must, change her phone number)
   4. Nobody's answered the doorbell.
      → _____ (They, must, not, be, at home)
   5. Naomi's bedroom light it still on.
      → _____ (She, must, read a book or study)
   6. They say they definitely sent my order, but I never received it.
      → _____ (It, must, lose, on the way)
   7. Mike has come for a 2 o'clock meeting. It's now 2:20 and nobody else is there.
      → _____ (The meeting, must, be canceled)

2. 문장의 문맥에 가장 적합한 표현을 골라 문장을 완성하세요.

   1. She sold her stock at its peak. She (could / (must)) have made a lot of money.
   2. Alice isn't coming tonight. She (may / must) come tomorrow, I hope.
   3. I can hear some voices. Someone (might / must) be in the house.
   4. You (could have been / must have been) a beautiful baby.
   5. You (might / must) be right, but I'm going to check anyway.
   6. The café is always empty. It (might not / must not) be very good.
   7. It (can't / may not) be true. I don't believe it.
   8. She's just started learning English. She (might not / must not) be very fluent yet.
   9. He's been working over 10 hours a day for weeks. He (can / must) be exhausted.

🔊 Dialogue

3. 주어진 단어를 이용하여 문맥에 맞게 문장을 완성하세요.

   Jay is at a store. He's just realized that his umbrella's gone.
   Jay는 가게에 있습니다. 그는 막 그의 우산이 사라졌음을 알았습니다.

   Server Can I help you, sir?
   Jay Yes. Someone _____ (must, pick up) my umbrella.
   Server Is it a black, foldable, automatic umbrella?
   Jay Yes. It was here five minutes ago.
   Server It's kept in the umbrella stand over there. I put it there because someone might trip over it.
   Jay Oh, I see. Thank you.

Unit 025

must vs. have to

You don't have to pay. It's free.
돈 안 내셔도 돼요. 무료입니다.

1 **must와 have to**는 '반드시 그래야 한다'는 의미를 나타내는 데에 쓰인다. _{하지 않을 경우 문제가 생길 수 있음을 암시}

- must는 보통 규칙이나 지시 사항 등에 쓰이며, 대화보다는 글에서 더 자주 쓰인다(문어체).
  - ▶ Drivers **must drive** carefully. 운전자들은 조심히 운전해야 합니다.
  - ▶ You **must login** first to access this page. 이 페이지에 접속하려면 먼저 로그인하셔야 합니다.

- must는 '강력히 추천' 할 때에도 쓰인다.
  - ▶ You **must watch** this video. It's fun. 이 비디오 보는 거 강추해. 재미있어.

- have to는 일반적인 대화에서 많이 쓰인다. 대화체에서는 have to 대신 have got to도 종종 쓰인다.
  - ▶ Sorry. I **have to go** now. = Sorry. I**'ve got to go** now. 미안해요. 저 이제 가야만 해요.
  - ▶ He **has to finish** the report by Monday. = He**'s gotta finish** the report by Monday.
    그는 월요일까지 보고서를 마쳐야 합니다. _{have/has got to는 발음 그대로 have/has gotta로 표기하기도 한다.}

- have to는 외부적인 요인으로 인해 그럴 수밖에 없다는 뉘앙스를 줄 수 있고, must는 말하는 사람이 그럴 수밖에 없다고 생각한다는 뉘앙스를 줄 수 있다. _{단, 이 차이가 언제나 분명한 것은 아니다.}
  - ▶ I **have to** stop smoking. It's my doctor's order. 저는 담배를 끊어야 합니다. 의사 선생님의 지시예요.
  - ▶ I **must** stop smoking. I think it's bad for me. 전 담배를 끊어야 해요. 몸에 안 좋은 것 같아서요.

2 부정문의 **mustn't**와 **don't/doesn't have to**는 의미가 다르다.

- mustn't는 '그래서는 안 된다'라는 의미이다.
  _{보통 추측의 must not은 줄여서(축약) 말하지 않고, 의무감의 must not은 mustn't로 줄여 말한다.}
  - ▶ You **mustn't be** late for class. 수업에 늦어서는 안 됩니다.

- don't/doesn't have to는 '그러지 않아도 된다'라는 의미이다.
  - ▶ You **don't have to pay**. It's free. 돈 안 내셔도 돼요. 무료입니다.
  - ▶ She **doesn't have to wear** a suit every day. The dress code at her work is casual.
    그녀는 매일 정장을 입지 않아도 됩니다. 회사의 드레스코드는 캐주얼입니다.

3 '~해야만 하는지'를 묻는 의문문은 **have to**를 사용한다. _{must는 의문문에 쓰이지 않음}

- ▶ **Do we have to pay** for that? 그거 돈 내야 하나요?
- ▶ **Does everyone have to do** military service in your country? 당신의 나라에선 모두가 군대에 가야 하나요?

4 **have to**는 과거나 미래 시제, 조동사 등과 함께 쓰일 수 있다. _{must는 쓸 수 없음}

- ▶ I **had to take** a taxi last night. The bus never came. 나는 어젯밤에 택시를 타야 했어. 버스가 오질 않더라고.
- ▶ We**'ll have to wait** and see what happens next. 다음에 무슨 일이 일어날지는 우리가 두고 봐야 할 겁니다.
- ▶ He **might have to leave** work early. 그는 일찍 회사를 나서야만 할지도 모릅니다.

5 **have to**와 비슷한 의미로 **need to**가 쓰이기도 한다.

- ▶ He **needs to do** more exercise. 그는 운동을 더 할 필요가 있다.
- ▶ You **don't need to hurry**. 서두를 필요 없어요.

6 '~해선 안 된다'라는 금지의 의미로 **can't** ~나 **be not allowed to** ~를 쓸 수도 있다.

- ▶ I'm sorry, but you **can't smoke** in here. = I'm sorry, but you**'re not allowed to smoke** in here.
  죄송합니다만, 여기 안에서는 흡연을 하실 수 없습니다.

Exercises

1. 주어진 단어와 have to를 사용하여 문장을 완성하세요. 필요한 경우 have to의 형태를 바꾸세요.

   1. _I have to take_ (I, take) this medicine every morning. The doctor told me so.
   2. _____ (We, go) now. Otherwise we'll miss the last bus.
   3. What time _____ (I, arrive) at the airport if I've already checked in online?
   4. _____ (Jessica and Naomi, go) to the supermarket because they didn't have enough food for dinner.
   5. _____ (she, work) nights?
   6. _____ (They, get) an interpreter in Japan because none of them could speak Japanese.
   7. _____ (Mike, finish) his report quickly because the deadline is today at 5:00 p.m.
   8. _____ (I, finish) this essay today. _____ (It, be) handed in by tomorrow.

2. mustn't나 don't have to를 넣어 문장을 완성하세요. 필요한 경우 동사의 형태를 바꾸세요.

   1. I _don't have to_ go to work tomorrow. It's Sunday.
   2. Children _____ play in this dangerous place.
   3. You _____ come if you don't want to.
   4. We _____ wait outside because the gate was open.
   5. Shhh! Everyone's sleeping. We _____ wake them up.
   6. People _____ stand on this bus.

3. 밑줄 친 부분이 틀렸다면 맞게 고치세요. 틀린 부분이 없다면 X를 쓰세요.

   1. Drivers must stop at stop signs. — X
   2. You must get a visa if you want to visit China. — _____
   3. I can't set my alarm tonight. I don't want to oversleep tomorrow morning. — _____
   4. In order to log on to the Internet, you must enter your user I.D. — _____
   5. Sorry. I don't need to call you back later. My cell phone battery is dying. — _____
   6. You can't smoke here. It's a school. — _____
   7. This bus is free. You're not allowed buy a ticket. — _____
   8. You've got to smoke in a gas station. — _____

✦ Dialogue

4. 문장의 문맥에 가장 적합한 표현을 골라 문장을 완성하세요.

Andy is going to a rock festival tomorrow. Andy는 내일 록 페스티벌에 갈 예정입니다.

Andy I (don't have to / mustn't) forget to set my alarm for 5.

Patrick Why do you have to get up that early?

Andy Eugene and I are going to a rock festival in San Diego. To get the best seats we decided to leave early.

Patrick Shall I give you a ride to the station?

Andy Thank you, but you (don't have to / mustn't). We're going by car. Eugene is driving.

Unit 026

should

I shouldn't have said that.
난 그 말 하지 말아야 했어.

1 should는 '~하는 것이 낫다' 또는 '~하는 것이 옳다'라는 의미를 나타낸다.
보통 권유나 조언 등 의견을 표현할 때에 많이 쓰임

- When you're in London, you **should** definitely **check out** Camden. 런던에 가면 캠든은 꼭 **가는 게 좋아**.
- My hair is too long. I **should get** a haircut. 머리가 너무 길어. **잘라야겠어**.
- You **shouldn't be** here. 여기 계시면 안 **되거든요**.
- He **shouldn't watch** too much TV. 걔는 TV를 너무 많이 보지 않는 게 좋겠더라.
- **Should I buy** a S phone or K phone? S phone을 **사는 게 나을까**, 아니면 K phone을 **사는 게 나을까**?
- What **should I do**? 제가 어떻게 **하는 게 좋을까요**?

should는 I think와 자주 쓰인다.
- **I think** I **should** eat more vegetables. 저는 채소를 더 많이 먹어야 할 것 같아요.
- **I don't think** you **should** tell him about it. 그에게 그것에 대해 말하지 않는 게 나을 것 같아.
  think 뒤에는 부정문이 오지 못하므로 I don't think S+ should ~ 로 말한다.
- **Do you think** I **should** wear a suit? 정장을 입는 것이 **나을까**?

should는 must나 have to처럼 '반드시' 해야만 한다는 뉘앙스는 아니다.
- I **must get** back to work now. The deadline is tomorrow. 이제 다시 일로 돌아**가야겠어**. 마감이 내일이야.
  일로 돌아가지 않으면 마감 안에 일을 못 마쳐서 문제가 생길 수 있음 암시
- I **should get** back to work now. Talk to you later. 이제 다시 일로 돌아**가야겠어**. 다음에 얘기하자.
  지금 일로 돌아가지 않는다고 문제가 생긴다기 보다는 대충 대화를 끝낼 때가 되었다 싶을 때 쓰는 표현

2 should have p.p.는 과거에 그랬어야 했다는 아쉬움이나 후회의 의미로 쓰인다.
- I missed the train. I **should have left** home earlier. 기차를 놓쳤어. 좀 더 일찍 집을 나서야 **했는데**.
- This book is overdue. You **should have returned** it to the library yesterday.
  이 책 기한이 지났어. 어제 도서관에 **반납했었어야 했어**.
- I **shouldn't have said** that. I regret it now. 난 그 말 하지 말아야 했어. 지금 후회돼.
- You **shouldn't have sold** your car. I really liked it. 넌 차를 팔지 말아야 했어. 정말 맘에 들었었는데.

3 should는 논리나 근거에 의해 그것이 사실이거나 그렇게 될 것이란 의미로도 쓰인다.
보통 문맥이나 대화에서 그럴 만한 이유가 제시되거나, 상식적으로 그럴 만한 것임

- Ask Erika. She **should know**.
  Erika에게 물어보렴. 걔는 **알 거야**. Erika가 충분히 알 만한 사항이거나, 아주 똑똑해서 알 것이라 기대함
- Patrick's on his way. He **should be** here soon. Patrick은 오는 길이에요. (그러니) 곧 여기 **도착할 거예요**.

과거에 그랬을 거라 기대했으나 그렇게 되지 않은 것에 대해서는 should have p.p.로 말한다.
- Where's Trish? She **should have arrived** by now.
  Trish는 어디 있죠? 지금쯤이면 도착했어야 하는데요. 올 것이라고 예상한 시간에 오지 않았음

4 should 대신 ought to가 쓰이기도 한다.
- I **ought to eat** more vegetables. 저는 채소를 더 많이 **먹어야 할 것 같아요**.
- Patrick's on his way. He **ought to be** here soon. Patrick은 오는 길이에요. (그러니) 곧 여기 **도착할 거예요**.

Exercises

1. 아래의 보기에 주어진 동사와 should나 shouldn't를 써서 문장을 완성하세요.

> cross   eat   email   knock   put   ~~visit~~

1. If you have time, you ___should visit___ the British Museum.
2. Kids _____ the street alone until they're 14.
3. Late-comers _____ on the door before entering the classroom.
4. That model is too skinny. I think she _____ more.
5. You _____ him about the changes. Otherwise he won't know what's happening.
6. In the U.K. you _____ your elbows on the table while you're eating.

2. 문맥에 맞는 문장끼리 연결하세요.

1. Haven't they given you the money back yet?
2. The movie left the theater.
3. The government lost the election.
4. I'm in a difficult position.
5. It's a pity he sold the stock.
6. She often has trouble getting up.

a. They shouldn't have raised taxes.
b. They should have done it last week.
c. He should have kept it for another month.
d. It should be available online soon.
e. She shouldn't stay up late at night.
f. What do you think I should do?

3. 문장의 문맥에 가장 적합한 표현을 골라 문장을 완성하세요.

1. I (**must** / should) get back to work now. The deadline is tomorrow.
2. You (must / should) clean your room more often.
3. I think you (must / should) think carefully before you sell the stock.
4. Late-comers are NOT allowed to take the exam. So you (mustn't / shouldn't) be late.
5. Ask Erika. She (has to / should) know.
6. My flight to Moscow leaves at 7:40, so I (have to / should) be at the airport by 6:00 at the latest.
7. The plane (must / should) have arrived at 9:00, but it was almost an hour late.

🔊 Dialogue

4. 주어진 단어를 이용하여 문맥에 맞게 문장을 완성하세요.

Mr. Watson is cooking dinner. Mr. Watson이 저녁을 요리하고 있습니다.

Mrs. Watson   Is dinner ready?

Mr. Watson   Um… Honey, _____
(I, tonight, we, eat out, should, think).

Mrs. Watson   What do you mean? I thought you were cooking.

Mr. Watson   I did, but the steak burned to a crisp.

Mrs. Watson   Can I have a look? Oh, it's…black.

Mr. Watson   _____
(I should, earlier, from the grill, have removed the steak).

Unit 027

기타 조동사

You're not supposed to park here.
여기 주차하시면 안 되는 거라서요.

1
had better는 특정한 상황에서 '그렇게 하지 않을 경우 문제가 생길 수 있으므로 해야 한다'라는 의미를 나타낸다.
should보다는 강하고, must나 have to보다는 다소 약한 의무감

You**'d better take** an umbrella with you today. The forecast says it's going to rain this afternoon.
오늘 우산 **가져가는 게 좋을걸**. 예보에서 오후에 비 올 거래. 우산을 안 가져가면 곤란할 수 있음

We**'d better leave** now or we'll miss the train.
지금 **떠나지 않으면** 기차를 놓칠 거야.

had better의 부정문은 **had better not ~**이다.

▶ He**'d better not forget** his wife's birthday this year.
그가 올해는 아내의 생일을 잊지 않아야 할 텐데. 잊어버리면 올해는 문제가 생길 수 있음 암시

특정 상황에만 걸쳐진 것이 아닌 일반적인 조언이나 의견에는 **should**를 쓴다. had better를 쓰지 않음

▶ All passengers **should wear** seatbelts. 모든 승객들은 안전벨트를 **착용해야 한다**.
All passengers **had better wear** seatbelts. (X)

2
(be) supposed to ~는 '그렇게 하기로 예정, 허락, 의도된 것'에 대해서 말할 때 쓸 수 있다. 주로 대화체에서 쓰임

▶ All members **are supposed to attend** today's meeting. 모든 회원들은 오늘 회의에 **참석하기로 되어 있습니다**.
▶ Children **are not supposed to earn**, but to learn. 어린이들은 **돈을 버는 게 아니라** 배워야 하는 것이죠.
▶ **Are you supposed to meet** him today? 오늘 그를 만나기로 되어 있나요?

종종 '그렇게 되어야 하지만 되지 않은 것'에 대해 말한다.

▶ He **was supposed to be** here half an hour ago. 그 분은 30분 전에 여기 **와 있어야 했는데요**. 30분 전에 오지 않았음
▶ Could you please move your car? You**'re not supposed to park** here.
차 좀 이동시켜 주시겠습니까? 여기 **주차하시면 안 되는 거라서요**. 주차하면 안 되는 곳에 주차해 놓은 상황
▶ **Was** that **supposed to be** funny? I felt it was quite rude.
그거 재미**있었어야 했나**? 난 좀 무례하다고 느꼈는데. 재미있지 않았음

(be) supposed to는 이외에도 '~라고 (사람들이) 말한다'라는 의미로도 쓰인다.

▶ The new Bong Joon-Ho movie **is supposed to be** good. 봉준호 감독 새 영화 **좋다던데**.

3
It's time 뒤에 '주어+-ed'가 오는 경우, '~해야 한다'라는 재촉의 의미를 갖는다.
이때 동사의 -ed는 과거와는 상관없고, 실제로 벌어져야 할 일이 벌어지지 않고 있음을 암시

▶ **It's time** we **started** packing. We have to leave in an hour. 짐 싸기 **시작해야 해**. 한 시간 뒤면 떠나야 해.

about이나 **high**가 더해지면 빨리 해야 한다는 재촉의 의미가 좀 더 강해진다.

▶ It's **about** time you got a haircut. It's too long. 넌 머리 좀 **빨리** 잘라야겠다. 너무 길어.
▶ It's **high** time he started working. 그는 **어서** 일을 시작해야 해.

Exercises

1. 밑줄 친 부분이 틀렸다면 맞게 고치세요. 고칠 부분이 없다면 X를 쓰세요.

1. The movie's going to start soon. We'd better leave now.   X
2. I think you'd better start blogging about your business.   _____
3. I can't wear shorts to a job interview. I'd better change clothes before I go.   _____
4. You'd better not be late again or you'll lose your job.   _____
5. It's a great sci-fi movie. You'd better see it.   _____
6. I know he's been studying hard for the test. He'd better be able to pass it.   _____

2. (not) supposed to와 주어진 표현을 써서 문장을 완성하세요.

1. (My wife, make dinner tonight)   *My wife is supposed to make dinner tonight.*
2. (You, take more than 3 books)   _____
3. (Cars, be on the bike path)   _____
4. (The newspaper, be delivered by now)   _____

3. 문맥에 맞는 문장끼리 연결하세요.

1. My husband is getting a little overweight.   •   • a. It's time he learned how to use it.
2. Mike has never used Excel at work before.   •   • b. It's high time we went back home.
3. It's almost midnight.   •   • c. It's time he went on a diet.
4. They've been engaged for 5 years.   •   • d. It's about time I bought a new one.
5. You'll have to catch a morning train.   •   • e. It's time you went to bed.
6. My laptop keeps turning off.   •   • f. It's about time they got married.

🔊 Dialogue

4. 주어진 단어를 이용하여 문맥에 맞게 문장을 완성하세요.

Mike parked his car in the guest parking lot of the company.
Mike는 회사의 손님 주차 구역에 주차를 했습니다.

Trish   Mike. Is that blue car yours?

Mike   Yes, it is. Is there anything wrong with that?

Trish   Actually yes. _____ (You, not, supposed to, park your car) in the guest parking lot.

Mike   Oh, really? I'm sorry, I didn't know that. I'll move it right away.

Trish   Thank you for your understanding.

Unit 028

제안하기

The doctor recommended that I rest for a few days.
그 의사는 내가 며칠 간 쉴 것을 권했다.

1
제안이나 요구, 주장 등의 의미를 가진 동사 뒤에 오는 S+V(절)의 동사는 원형이다. ~하는 것이 좋다/옳다라는 의미 암시

ask demand insist propose recommend suggest → (that) S + 동사원형

he, she, it 등의 주어가 와도 동사원형을 쓴다. 동사 뒤에 s/es를 더하지 않음

- I **insist she come** with us. 나는 그녀가 우리와 함께 가야 한다고 주장하는 바야.
  I **insist she comes** with us. (X)

문장 전체의 시제와 상관없이 동사원형을 쓴다.

- The mayor **asked** that **all residents continue** to look for the lost cat.
  The mayor **asked** that **all residents continued** to look for the lost cat. (X)
  시장님은 모든 주민들이 계속해서 잃어버린 고양이를 찾을 것을 요청했다.
- The old man **demanded** that **the manager apologize** to him.
  The old man **demanded** that **the manager apologizes** to him. (X)
  그 노인은 매니저가 자신에게 사과할 것을 요구했다.
- The doctor **recommended** that **I rest** for a few days.
  The doctor **recommended** that **I rested** for a few days. (X)
  그 의사는 내가 며칠 간 쉴 것을 권했다.

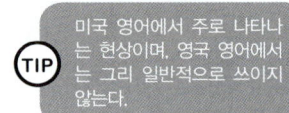

TIP: 미국 영어에서 주로 나타나는 현상이며, 영국 영어에서는 그리 일반적으로 쓰이지 않는다.

Be동사의 경우 am/are/is 또는 was/were가 아닌 be를 쓴다.

- He **proposed** that **the event be** held again in 2020. 그는 2020년에 그 행사를 다시 개최할 것을 제안했다.
  He **proposed** that **the event is** held again in 2020. (X)

부정문의 경우에 'not+동사원형'이 온다.

- She **suggested** that **they not argue** anymore. 그녀는 그들이 더 이상 언쟁하지 않을 것을 제안했다.
  She **suggested** that **they don't argue** anymore. (X)

suggest, propose, insist 등은 뒤에 다른 구조가 올 수도 있다. See Unit 047, 051 ▶

- I **suggested having** another meeting. 나는 회의를 한 번 더 하자고 제안했다.

2
'~해야 한다'라는 의미가 암시되는 형용사 뒤의 'S+V(절)'도 동사원형을 쓴다.

It's essential/imperative/important/necessary/vital/... → (that) S + 동사원형

- It's **essential** that **everyone be** here on time. 모든 사람이 제시간에 이곳으로 오는 것이 아주 중요합니다.
- It's **imperative** that **the government do** something about health care.
  정부는 보건의료에 관련하여 뭔가 조치를 취해야만 한다.
- It's **important** that **you not miss** class. 여러분이 수업을 빼먹지 않는 것이 중요합니다.
- It was **necessary** that **I take care** of the garden. 내가 정원을 돌봐야 할 필요가 있었다.

It's essential/important… for … to ~ 형태로도 말할 수 있다. See Unit 046 ▶

- It's **essential for everyone to be** here on time. 모든 사람이 제시간에 이곳으로 오는 것이 아주 중요합니다.

3
간혹 '~해야 한다'라는 의미가 암시되는 명사 뒤에 'S+V(절)'이 오는 경우에도 동사원형을 쓴다.

- There was a **request** that **all phones be** turned off during class.
  수업 중에 모든 전화기가 꺼져 있어야 한다는 요청이 있었습니다.

Exercises

1. 보기와 같이 문장을 다시 쓰세요.

1. "How about eating out at Paula's Kitchen?"
   → He proposed that we _eat out at Paula's Kitchen._
2. "I think it would be a good idea for Mike to learn how to use Excel."
   → He recommended that Mike _____.
3. "Apologize to me!"
   → She demanded that he _____.
4. "Don't make personal calls during business hours."
   → The company asked that all employees _____.
5. "We must invite him to the wedding."
   → She insisted that _____.
6. "Why don't we have a word with the boss?"
   → He suggested that _____.

2. 주어진 동사를 적절한 형태로 바꾸어 문장을 완성하세요.

1. It is necessary that a life guard ___keep___ (keep) watching the toddler pool.
2. The protesters insisted that more money _____ (be) invested in education.
3. It's vital that you _____ (neglect, not) your own health.
4. The customer was upset. He demanded that we _____ (refund) his money.
5. Please be on time. It's important you _____ (make) a good impression.
6. There was a request that we _____ (provide) more information.

3. 주어진 표현을 문맥과 문장 구조에 맞게 연결하여 문장을 완성하세요.

1. It's essential for everyone • • a. for kids to eat healthy.
2. It's essential • • b. that everyone be here on time.
3. He suggested • • c. to be here on time.
4. He asked • • d. her to marry him.
5. It's important • • e. having a party.

🔊 Dialogue

4. 주어진 단어를 이용하여 문맥에 맞게 문장을 완성하세요.

Ben and Sarah are talking about a movie. Ben과 Sarah는 영화에 대해 이야기하고 있습니다.

Ben　Have you seen the new Marvel movie?
Sarah　No, not yet. Have you?
Ben　I saw it last Sunday. I highly _____
　　　(recommend, that, you, see it too).
Sarah　But I'm not a big fan of superhero movies.
Ben　It's not just a superhero movie. It's really deep and profound.
Sarah　Is that so? Then, I'll give it a try this weekend.

Unit 029

예의 바른 요청

Do you think you could make a little less noise?
소리를 조금만 작게 해 내 주실 수 있을까요?

1. 조동사의 -ed(과거) 형태는 좀 더 예의 바르거나 정중한 느낌을 나타낼 수 있다.

❶ 조심스러운 가능성이나 제안, 바람 See Unit 022 ▶

- We **could** have dinner at The Plaza tonight.
  우리 오늘 저녁에 The Plaza에서 저녁을 먹어요. `We can ~보다 예의 바르고 조심스러운 느낌`
- I **would like to** get some fresh air. 바람 좀 쐬고 싶네요. `I want ~보다 예의 바른 느낌`

❷ 요청 `please가 함께 쓰임`

- **Could** you close the door, please? 문 좀 닫아 주시겠습니까? `Can you ~?보다 예의 바름`
- **Could** you **possibly** close the door, please? 문 좀 닫아 주실 수 있을까요? `possibly가 더해지면 더욱 예의 바른 요청이 됨`
- **Would** you do me a favor, please? 부탁 하나 들어 주시겠어요? `Will you ~?보다 예의 바름`

Do you think you could ~? `Do you think you can ~?은 부정확한 표현`

- **Do you think you could** make a little less noise? 소리를 조금만 작게 해 내 **주실 수 있을까요?**

mind -ing를 써서 말할 수도 있다.

- A: **Would you mind** repeat**ing** that? 그거 다시 한 번 말씀해 주시겠어요?
  B: No, of course not. 물론이죠.
  `mind의 의미가 '꺼리다', '신경 쓰이다' 등의 부정적인 의미이기 때문에 mind가 들어간 질문에 대한 긍정적인 대답에는 No 또는 Not을 사용`

❸ 허락

- A: **Could I** have a word with you? 이야기 좀 나눌 수 있을까요? `Can I ~?보다 예의 바름`
  B: Yes, of course **you can**. `Could I ~?로 물어도 대답은 you can으로 답한다.`

May I ~?는 허락을 얻는 격식 있는 표현이다.

- How **may I** help you, ma'am? 도와드릴**까요**, 여사님?
- **May I** have a word with you? 이야기 좀 나눌 수 있겠습니까?

mind를 써서 말할 수도 있다.

- A: **Would you mind if** I **asked** you something? 뭐 좀 여쭤봐도 실례가 안될까요?
  `Do you mind if I ask you something?으로 말할 수도 있다.`
  B: Of course not. Please, go ahead. 물론 (실례가) 안 되죠. 말씀하세요.

Would it be all right/OK/possible if ~? 또는 I wonder if I could ~의 형태로도 말할 수 있다.

- **Would it be all right if** I **moved** the table? 제가 탁자를 치워도 괜찮을까요?
  `Is it all right if I move this table, please?로 물을 수도 있다.`
- **I wonder if I could** change my ticket. 제 표를 바꿀 수 있는지 궁금합니다.

I would like (to) ~를 써서 표현할 수도 있다.

- **I would like to** have a word with you. 이야기 좀 나누고 싶습니다.

❹ 초대, 초청

- **Would you like to** have dinner with us tomorrow? 내일 저희와 저녁 식사**하실래요**?

Exercises

1. 문장의 문맥에 가장 적합한 표현을 골라 문장을 완성하세요.
   1. (Do you like / **Would you like**) some coffee?
   2. I'm very busy. Would you mind (to give / giving) me a hand?
   3. (May I / Would I) ask you a personal question?
   4. Would it be all right if I (leave / left) class a little early today?
   5. Do you think you (can / could) wait a few more minutes?

2. 보다 예의 바르거나 정중한 문장에 V 표시를 하세요.
   1. ⓐ Let's have dinner at The Plaza tonight.
      ⓑ We could have dinner at The Plaza tonight.   V
   2. ⓐ Could you please turn down the TV?
      ⓑ Can you turn down the TV?
   3. ⓐ What's your name?
      ⓑ May I ask who's calling?
   4. ⓐ Would you mind waiting a few minutes?
      ⓑ You can wait a few minutes, can't you?

3. 문맥과 문장 구조에 맞게 각각의 표현을 연결하여 문장을 완성하세요.
   1. Would you mind if   a. waiting outside?
   2. May I   b. you could help me with that?
   3. Would you   c. I turned on this light?
   4. Would you mind   d. have a word with you?
   5. Do you think   e. do me a favor?

4. 문맥에 맞는 문장끼리 연결하세요.
   1. Could I have a seat here?   a. Sure. Thanks.
   2. Would you mind if I sat here?   b. Yes, of course you can.
   3. Would you like to sit here?   c. No, not at all.
   4. May I have your name?   d. Certainly. I'll do it right away.
   5. Could you possibly move your car?   e. Yes. It's Dion Park.

🔊 Dialogue

5. 주어진 단어를 이용하여 문맥에 맞게 문장을 완성하세요.

Eugene is applying to a college. He's asking Mr. Cruz to be his reference.
Eugene은 대학에 지원했습니다. 그는 Mr. Cruz에게 추천인이 되어주기를 부탁하고 있습니다.

Eugene Mr. Cruz. _____ (I, Could, use your name) as a reference on my college application?

Mr. Cruz Sure. Please go ahead.

Eugene Thank you very much.

Big Picture

현실에서 비현실로(가정법)

03

[Big Picture 2]에서 이야기했듯이, 우리말과 달리 영어는 문장이 직접 현실과 비현실을 나타냅니다. 동사가 -ed인데 시간이 '과거'가 아니라면, 이것은 현실과 거리가 먼(한걸음 물러난) 비현실, 가상의 이야기일 수 있지요.

그래서 우리말로 '만약에 ~하면 …한다'라는 말도 영어로는 현실성이 있는가의 여부와 시간 배경에 따라 여러 가지 문장 형태로 표현하게 됩니다. 다음은 소위 '가정법'이라고 하는 '만약에~'를 말하는 문장 형태를 정리한 표입니다.
일단 먼저 모양을 익혀 두면, 본 unit에서 하나 하나 자세하게 살펴보고 문장을 접하면서 감각을 확인하는 데에 도움이 될 수 있답니다.

0번 가정법	If/When S ~, S ~. 100% 확률. 반드시 일어나는 일	**When** you heat ice, it melts. 얼음을 가열<u>하면</u> 녹는다.
1번 가정법	If S ~, S will ~ 50% 확률. 두고 봐야 알 수 있음.	**If** it rains tomorrow, I'**ll** just stay home. 내일 비가 오<u>면</u> 그냥 집에 있<u>을 거야</u>.
2번 가정법	If S -ed, S would ~ 0%에 가까움. 현재/현실과 다른 상상	**If** I **had** a lot of money, I **would** travel around the world. 내가 돈이 많<u>다면</u> 세계 여행을 <u>할 거야</u>.
3번 가정법	❶ If S had p.p., S would have p.p. 과거에 그랬더라면 그때 그랬을 것이라는 실제와는 다른 상상	**If** I **had gone** to the party last night, I **would have seen** him. 어젯밤 그 파티에 <u>갔었더라면</u> 그를 <u>만났었을 텐데</u>.
	❷ If S had p.p., S would ~ 과거에 그랬더라면 지금 이럴 것이라는 실제와 다른 상상	**If** I **had gone** to the party last night, I **would** be tired now. 어젯밤 그 파티에 <u>갔었더라면</u> 난 지금 피곤했<u>을 거야</u>.

Unit 030

가정법 0번 vs. 1번

Let's meet at the ticket counter if we ever get separated.
혹시라도 우리가 떨어지게 되면 티켓 카운터에서 만나자.

1. '일반적인 사실'이나 '항상 그렇게 되는 것'에 대해서는 다음과 같이 말한다.

0번 가정법	If S + ⓥ (단순현재),	S + ⓥ (단순현재).
	If it **rains**, 비가 오면	the ground **gets** wet. 땅이 젖는다.

▶ Ice **melts** if you **heat** it. 얼음은 가열하면 녹는다. `If S+V 부분이 뒤로 갈 수도 있음`

2. '그렇게 될지 안 될지 두고 봐야 하는 것'에 대해서는 다음과 같이 말한다.

`실제로 가능한 상황`

1번 가정법	If S + ⓥ (현재시제),	S+will ~
	If it's sunny tomorrow, 내일 날씨가 화창하면,	we'**ll go** to the beach. 우리는 해변에 갈 거야.

└ 내일 날씨가 화창할지 아닐지는 내일이 돼 봐야 함. 반반의 확률

▶ If you**'re** thirsty, I**'ll get** you something to drink. 목이 마르면 마실 것을 갖다 **드릴게요**.
▶ **Will** you **help** me if I **have** a problem downloading it? 그거 다운받는 거에 문제 **생기면 도와 줄 거니?**

will 대신 조동사가 올 수도 있다.
▶ If you want, I **can** help you. 네가 원하면 내가 도와줄 **수도 있어**.
▶ I **may** arrive home late if the traffic is bad. 교통이 안 좋으면 나 집에 늦게 도착할지도 몰라.

S+will ~ 대신에 명령문이 올 수도 있다.
▶ If you see Mike, **tell** him that I'm looking for him. Mike를 보면 내가 찾는다고 **말해 주세요**.
▶ **Ask** Trish if you're not sure what to do. 무엇을 해야 할지 잘 모르겠으면 Trish에게 **물어보세요**.

If S+ⓥ의 내용이 미래라도 will을 쓰지 않는다. `See unit 091▶`
▶ **If** it's sunny tomorrow, we'll go to the beach. 내일 날씨가 화창하면, 우리는 해변에 갈 거야.
If it **will be** sunny tomorrow, we'll go to the beach. (X)

If S+ⓥ의 시제는 단순현재 외에 현재진행형도 올 수 있다.
▶ If you**'re not feeling** very well, call your doctor. 몸이 안 좋으면 담당 의사에게 전화하세요.

If … be to ~는 '굳이 그래야겠다면, 반드시 그래야겠다면'의 뉘앙스로 쓰일 수 있다.
▶ If you **are to catch** the train, you must leave now. 그 기차를 **타야겠다면**, 지금 떠나야 한다.

3. 실제로 반드시 또는 그렇게 될 것에 대해서는 if 대신 when을 쓴다.

┌ I'll cook dinner **when** I get home. 집에 도착하면 내가 저녁 요리할게. `집에 반드시 도착함`
└ I'll cook dinner **if** I get home earlier. 집에 일찍 도착하게 되면 내가 저녁 요리할게. `일찍 도착할지는 두고 봐야 함`

때로는 말하는 사람의 믿음에 따라 when과 if의 선택이 달라진다.
┌ **When** he calls, tell him to meet me at the station.
│ 그가 전화**하면** 역에서 나랑 만나자고 말해 주세요. `그가 전화할 것이라고 확신함`
└ **If** he calls, tell him to meet me at the station.
   그가 전화**하면** 역에서 나랑 만나자고 말해 주세요. `그가 전화할지 안 할지 확신하지는 않음`

4. ever를 써서 If S+ⓥ에 '혹시' 또는 '행여나'의 의미를 강조할 수 있다. `See unit 072▶`

▶ Let's meet at the ticket counter if we **ever** get separated. 혹시라도 우리가 떨어지게 되면 티켓 카운터에서 만나자.

Exercises

1. 문맥에 맞게 각각의 표현을 연결하여 문장을 완성하세요.

1. He always flies business class
2. I'll pay the bill
3. If you're still considering Korea for your honeymoon,
4. When you get to the airport,
5. If you send somebody an email,
6. Don't drink too much alcohol
7. I'll be disappointed

a. it usually arrives in seconds.
b. please go to the check-in counter.
c. when he goes on a long flight.
d. if I'm not promoted this year.
e. when I get paid.
f. when you fly business class.
g. I'll suggest Jeju.

2. 주어진 상황과 표현을 사용하여 보기처럼 문장을 쓰세요. 가능하면 축약형을 쓰세요.

1. The traffic may be OK. – we / get to the station in time.
   → _If the traffic is OK, we'll get to the station in time._

2. He may be late again. – I / be angry.
   → _____

3. It may stop raining. – we / go out for a walk.
   → _____

4. I may see Jay today. – I / give him your message.
   → _____

5. The government may raise taxes. – people / consume less
   → _____

3. if 또는 when을 넣어 문장을 완성하세요.

1. ___If___ you ever arrive early, please wait in the lounge.
2. Sales will improve _____ summer begins.
3. Mike says he's on the way. Could you please send him up _____ he arrives?
4. What can I do _____ I forget my password?
5. We won't be able to see the comet tonight _____ it rains.

🔊 Dialogue

4. 주어진 단어를 이용하여 문맥에 맞게 문장을 완성하세요.

Amy is excited to meet Sarah's cat. Amy는 Sarah의 고양이를 보고 신났습니다.

Amy Your cat is lovely! Can I pet her? I've never petted a cat before.
Sarah Sure. I think she likes you.
Amy Oh! She's making some sound.
Sarah She's purring.
Amy Purring?
Sarah Yes. _____ (Cats, purr, when, they, be, happy).

Unit 031

2번 가정법

If I were you, I would accept the offer.
내가 너라면 그 제안 받아들일 거야.

1. 현재 현실적으로 이루어질 수 없거나 힘든 것에 대해서는 다음과 같이 말한다.

2번 가정법	If S+-ed,	S+would ~
	If I **had** a spaceship, 만일 내게 우주선이 있다면,	I **would fly** to Venus. 나는 금성으로 날아갈 거예요.

▶ If I **knew** the answer, **I'd tell** you. 답을 알면 너에게 말해 줬을 거야. `지금 답을 모름`
▶ If Patrick **was** here, **he'd know** what to do.
　Patrick이 지금 여기 있었더라면 어떻게 해야 할지 알 텐데. `Patrick은 지금 여기에 없음`

would 대신에 might이나 could가 쓰일 수도 있다.

▶ I **could** buy a house if I **had** enough money. 돈만 충분히 있었어도 집을 살 수 있을 텐데.
▶ If you **went** to bed a little earlier, you **might** not be so tired.
　네가 조금만 더 일찍 잠자리에 들어도 그렇게 피곤하지 않을지도 몰라.

If S+Ⓥ의 동사가 Be동사인 경우 were가 종종 쓰인다. `요즘에는 대화체에서 If S was…로도 많이 씀`

▶ If I **were** you, I would accept the offer. 내가 너라면 그 제안 받아들일 거야.
▶ If James **were** here, he would help us. James가 지금 여기 있다면 우리를 도와줄 텐데.

If S+Ⓥ에는 일반적으로 would를 쓰지 않는다.

▶ If the shoes **were** cheaper, I would definitely buy them. 그 구두가 좀 더 저렴하다면 난 분명 그걸 살 거야.
　If the shoes **would be** cheaper, I would definitely buy them. (X)

2. 말하는 사람의 믿음에 따라 가정법 문장 구조가 달라질 수 있다.

1번 가정법	2번 가정법
충분히 가능하다고 믿음	당장에 일어날 수 없는 비현실적인 것이라 믿음
▶ If you **ask** her nicely, she **will** say yes. 네가 정중하게만 부탁하면 그녀는 좋다고 할 거야. `상대방이 충분히 정중하게 부탁할 수 있을 거라 믿음`	▶ If you **asked** her nicely, she **might** say yes. 네가 정중하게만 부탁해도 그녀가 좋다고 할지도 모를 텐데. `상대방이 정중하게 부탁할 것이라고 생각하지 않음`

3. 2번 가정법은 예의 바르거나 격식 있는 표현에서도 종종 사용된다.

❶ 예의 바른 요청이나 허락을 구하는 표현 `See Unit 029▶`

▶ **Would** it **be** all right **if** I **took** the day off tomorrow? 제가 내일 하루 쉬어도 괜찮겠습니까?
▶ **Would** you **mind if** I **used** your phone charger? 휴대폰 충전기 좀 사용해도 괜찮을까요?
▶ I **would appreciate** it **if** you **could** help me with this matter.
　이 건에 대해 저를 도와주실 수 있다면 대단히 감사하겠습니다.

❷ If S were to ~는 매우 일어나기 힘든 일을 강조할 때 쓰는 격식 있는 표현이다.

▶ If the president **were to** resign, things would be more difficult.
　대통령이 만에 하나 하야**한다면**, 상황은 더욱 나빠질 것이다. `대통령이 하야하기는 매우 가능성이 적음을 강조`

❸ 비즈니스 등에서 Should you ~가 자주 쓰인다.
`If S should ~의 도치. 가정법 If S+Ⓥ에 쓰인 should는 '행여라도 우연히 그렇게 된다면'의 뉘앙스를 준다.` `See Unit 100▶`

▶ **Should you have** any questions, please feel free to contact me.
　혹시 질문이 있으시면 편하게 제게 연락 주십시오.

Exercises

1. 주어진 상황에 대해 읽고 적절한 문장을 만들어 보세요.

1. I can't buy the new S-phone. It's so expensive.
   → *If the new S-phone wasn't/weren't so expensive, I could buy it.*

2. She doesn't enjoy her job. That's why she doesn't work hard.
   → _____

3. I can't open the door because I don't have the key.
   → _____

4. The reason you're tired in the morning is that you never go to bed early.
   → _____

5. I don't speak perfect French, so I can't work in France.
   → _____

2. 문맥에 맞게 각 표현을 연결하여 문장을 완성하세요.

1. Should you have any questions, •   • a. it would be a disaster to the city.
2. If Congress were to pass the bill •   • b. if you could take a few minutes to fill out this form.
3. We would appreciate it •   • c. if the terms of the contract were different.
4. Would it be all right •   • d. I'll buy the apartment.
5. They might accept it •   • e. if I came at 10:00 a.m.?
6. If the bank lends me the money •   • f. I'd buy the apartment.
7. If the bank lent me the money •   • g. please contact us.

🔊 Dialogue

3. 주어진 단어를 이용하여 문맥에 맞게 문장을 완성하세요.

Andy and Patrick are in Colorado on vacation. Unfortunately they both have the flu now.
Andy와 Patrick은 콜로라도에 휴가를 왔습니다. 불행하게도 둘 다 독감에 걸려 있습니다.

Andy   I'm so bored and miserable.

Patrick   Me, too.

Andy   _____ (If, we, not, have this terrible flu, we, go out skiing).

Patrick   I can't believe we both have the flu on our first day in Colorado.

Andy   Just our luck.

Unit 032

3번 가정법

If he had left earlier, he would have avoided the traffic.
그가 좀 더 일찍 떠났더라면, 교통체증을 피했을 것이다.

1 과거에 실제로 이루어지지 않았던 것에 대해 다음과 같이 말한다.

3번 가정법 (1)	If S+had p.p.,	S+would have p.p. 과거의 상황
	If he **had left** earlier, 그가 좀 더 일찍 떠났더라면,	he **would have avoided** the traffic. 교통체증을 피했을 것이다.

▶ If I **had known** you were in the hospital, I **would have gone** to see you.
  네가 입원한 것 **알았더라면**, 문병 **갔을 거야**.

▶ If he **hadn't gone** to the casino, he **wouldn't have lost** the money.
  카지노에 안 **갔었더라면**, 그는 그 돈을 잃지 않았을 거예요.

▶ If I **had taken** an umbrella with me, I **wouldn't have been** wet in the rain.
  우산만 **가져갔었어도** 빗속에 젖지 **않았었을** 텐데.

S+would 또는 S+would have p.p.의 would 대신에 might나 could가 쓰일 수도 있다.

▶ If they had left earlier, they **might** have avoided the traffic.
  그들이 좀 더 일찍 떠났더라면, 교통체증을 피했었을지도 모른다.

▶ If the weather had been good, we **could** have gone out. 날씨가 좋았더라면, 우린 외출할 수 있었을 것이다.

▶ I **might** have stayed there longer if it hadn't been so cold.
  그렇게 춥지만 않았었어도 나는 거기에 좀 더 오래 머물렀을 것이다.

2 과거에 그랬었다면, 현재 이러했을 것이라는 상상은 다음과 같이 말한다.

3번 가정법 (2)	If S+had p.p.,	S+would ~ 지금의 상황
	If he **had left** earlier, 그가 좀 더 일찍 떠났더라면,	he **would be** here by now. 지금쯤이면 여기 와 있었겠죠.

▶ If he **had followed** your advice, he **would be** much healthier.
  그가 네 조언을 들었더라면, 지금 훨씬 더 건강했을 텐데.

▶ If they **had warned** him, he **wouldn't be** in prison now.
  그들이 그에게 경고했었더라면, 그는 지금 감옥에 있지 않을 것이다.

▶ If I **had gone** to drama school, I **might be** an actor now.
  연기 학교를 갔었더라면, 지금 나는 배우를 하고 있었을지도 모른다.

3 과거에 실제로 그랬는지 안 그랬는지 모르거나 그랬을 가능성이 있다고 생각될 때에는 If S -ed를 쓸 수 있다.

▶ I'm sorry **if** I **was** rude. 제가 무례했다면 죄송합니다. 자신이 무례했을 수도 있다고 생각함. 확신하지 못함

▶ Mom would have made me apologize **if** I **had been** rude.
  내가 만일 무례했었다면 엄마가 사과하게 만들었을 것이다. 무례하지 않았음

Exercises

1. 주어진 상황에 대해 읽고 적절한 문장을 만들어 보세요.

1. I lost my passport. I'm not in Norway now.
   → _If I had not lost my passport, I would be in Norway now._

2. My brother didn't study law. He's not a lawyer now.
   → _____

3. She arrived late. Her boss was angry.
   → _____

4. He sold his car. Now he has to take the bus every day.
   → _____

2. 문장의 문맥에 가장 적합한 표현을 골라 문장을 완성하세요.

1. If he (leaves / left /(had left)) earlier, he would be here by now.
2. I'm expecting a call from Ms. Turner. If she (calls / called / had called) today, please let me know immediately.
3. I would apply for the internship if I (have / had / had had) an MBA, but unfortunately I don't.
4. If I started this project again, I think I (will do / would do / would have done) it differently.
5. If I (was / were / had been) there, I would have seen everything.
6. I'm not sure if I interrupted you. I'm sorry if I (do / did / had done).
7. We bought a small house, but we (would buy / would have bought) a bigger one if we had had more money.

3. 주어진 표현을 문맥에 맞게 연결하여 문장을 완성하세요.

1. If she had had the correct information,   •   • a. if she had been more prepared.
2. I would have accepted the job   •   • b. she probably wouldn't have made the error.
3. Her presentation could have been better   •   • c. she might have studied law.
4. If the company had offered a 10% pay raise, •   • d. if they offered a better salary.
5. If she hadn't studied management,   •   • e. they could have avoided the strike.

🔊 Dialogue

3. 주어진 단어를 이용하여 문맥에 맞게 문장을 완성하세요.

Amy is asking Andy about his holiday in Colorado. Amy가 Andy의 콜로라도 휴가에 대해 묻고 있습니다.

Amy   Andy, did you have a lot of fun in Colorado?
Andy   No. Patrick and I were sick all holiday long.
Amy   I'm sorry to hear that.
Andy   We just had to stay in the cabin and watched TV. _____ (If, we, not, have the flu, it, be, a wonderful vacation). There were a lot of things to do, but we just couldn't do any.
Amy   What a shame.

Unit 033

기타 가정법

Unless I call you, I'll see you at 3.
내가 전화하지 않는다면, 3시에 보자.

1. '아니라면'이라는 의미로 or나 otherwise가 쓰일 수 있다.
- We've got to leave now, **or** we'll be late. 우린 지금 떠나야 해요. **아니면** 늦을 거예요.
- Luckily I caught the train. **Otherwise**, I would have been late. 다행히 기차를 탔다. **안 그랬으면**, 난 늦었을 것이다.

2. unless는 '만일 그렇지 않다면'의 의미로 If … not과 유사하다.
- **Unless** it rains tomorrow, we'll go to the beach. 내일 비가 오지 **않는다면**, 우리는 해변에 갈 것이다.
  (= **If** it **doesn't** rain tomorrow, we'll go to the beach.)
- I'll cook dinner tonight **unless** someone wants to. 누가 원하**지만 않는다면**, 오늘 저녁은 내가 요리할게.

unless는 불가능한 상황에서는 쓰지 않는다. `2번과 3번 가정법에 쓰이지 않음`
- **Unless I call you**, I'll see you at 3. 내가 전화하지 않는다면, 3시에 보자.
  Unless I called you, I'll see you at 3. (X)

3. in case는 '만약에 ~할 것에 대비하여'라는 의미로 쓰인다.
- Take an umbrella with you **in case** it rains. 비가 올 것에 대비해서 우산 가져가렴.
- Let me say thank you ahead of time for helping me out **in case** I forget later.
  나중에 까먹을 것에 대비해서 미리 도와줘서 고맙다고 말할게.

'in case of+명사'는 '~의 경우에는'의 의미로 in case와 구별된다.
- **In case of emergency**, don't panic. Call 911. 응급상황에서는 당황하지 마세요. 911로 전화하세요.

4. as if 또는 as though는 '마치 ~인 것처럼'의 의미로 쓸 수 있다. `as if가 더 일반적임`
- She acted **as if** she didn't hear me. 그녀는 마치 내 목소리를 못 들은 것처럼 행동했다.
- It looks **as if** it's going to rain. 비가 올 것처럼 보이네.
- I felt **as though** I had been born again. 나는 마치 다시 태어난 것처럼 느껴졌다. `as if는 look과 feel 뒤에 자주 옴`

5. '~하는 조건하에' 또는 '~하는 한'의 의미로 다음의 표현들을 쓸 수 있다.

❶ as long as `so long as로 쓰기도 함`
- We'll be safe **as long as** we all stay together. 우리 모두가 함께 하는 한, 우린 안전할 겁니다.

❷ providing (that) 또는 provided (that) `대화에선 providing (that)이 더 많이 쓰임`
- **Providing that** the weather is fine, we'll go hiking to Runyon Canyon.
  (= **Provided that** the weather is fine …) 날씨가 좋다면 우리는 러니언 캐년으로 하이킹 갈 거야.

6. supposing은 '만약 ~라고 상상해보라'라는 의미로 쓸 수 있다. `현실성의 판단에 따라 시제가 달라질 수 있음`
- **Supposing** you didn't have a phone, it'd be so inconvenient, eh?
  네게 전화기가 없다고 **상상하면** 무척 불편할 거야, 그치?
- **Supposing** he hadn't come to help us, we'd have been in trouble.
  그가 우릴 도와주러 오지 않았다고 **상상하면** 우린 곤란했을 거야.

Exercises

1. 주어진 표현을 사용하여 같은 의미의 문장으로 다시 쓰세요.

    1. The machine will start working if you press that button. (unless)
       → _The machine won't start working unless you press that button._
    2. I'll call you if I have a problem. (unless)
       → _____
    3. The hotels may be fully booked. Book a room in advance. (in case)
       → _____
    4. I might get hungry later, so I'll keep some salad. (in case)
       → _____

2. 빈칸에 들어갈 가장 적절한 표현을 보기에서 골라 넣어 문장을 완성하세요.

    > ~~just in case~~   otherwise   unless   as if   as long as   supposing

    1. Here's my number _just in case_ you need to contact me.
    2. You will not be able to pass the exam _____ you study.
    3. He got a pay raise. _____ he couldn't have afforded the rent.
    4. Live _____ you were to die tomorrow.
    5. _____ you were a millionaire, what would you do?
    6. I'll support you _____ you're honest with me.

3. 문맥에 맞게 각 표현을 연결하여 문장을 완성하세요.

    1. In case of fire,   • • a. as though I hadn't slept for days.
    2. My eyes felt heavy   • • b. follow this procedure.
    3. You may go to the party   • • c. provided that you're home by midnight.
    4. The soldiers will stay   • • d. or you'll regret it.
    5. Don't go to that hairdresser,   • • e. as long as it's necessary.
    6. Unless you have a valid license,   • • f. you cannot drive a car.

🔊 Dialogue

4. 보기 중 빈칸에 들어갈 가장 적합한 표현을 골라 넣어 문장을 완성하세요.

    Andy is always dropping things. He's just dropped his new phone.
    Andy는 항상 뭔가를 떨어뜨립니다. 방금 새 휴대폰을 떨어뜨렸습니다.

    > ❶ if   ❷ unless   ❸ in case   ❹ supposing

    Patrick It's the second time you've dropped your phone, Andy.
    Andy I know, but I just can't help it. I'm such a klutz.
    Patrick Get a phone case _____ you drop it again.
    Andy I don't want to waste my money on buying an ugly case.
    Patrick Well, it would be much better than a cracked smartphone.

Unit 034

wish

I wish I could, but I have other plans.
그럴 수 있으면 좋겠는데 다른 선약이 있어요.

1 wish는 바람을 나타내며 다음과 같이 쓸 수 있다.

❶ wish to ~ `want to보다 격식 있음`

- I **wish to** speak to Mr. Harris, please. Harris 씨와 이야기하고 싶습니다.
- Who do you **wish to** talk to? 어느 분과 말씀하시길 원하시는지요?

❷ wish+someone+명사 `주로 축복의 의미의 표현에서 쓰임`

- I **wish you a merry Christmas**. 즐거운 크리스마스가 되기 바라요.
- A: Are you going to the interview? 면접 가는 거니?
  B: Yes. **Wish me luck**! 응. 내게 행운을 빌어 줘!

❸ wish S −ed : 현재 이루어질 수 없는 것에 대한 바람 `현실적이지 않으므로 뒤의 동사가 −ed임`

- I **wish** I **had** a Ferrari. 페라리 자동차가 있다면 좋겠다. `현실은 페라리가 없음`
  I **wish** I **have** a Ferrari. (X)
- A: How about having dinner with us tonight? 오늘 밤 우리랑 저녁 먹는 거 어때요?
  B: I **wish** I **could**, but I have other plans.
  그럴 수 있으면 좋겠는데, 다른 선약이 있어요. `그럴 수 있었으면 하는 아쉬움의 의미로 I wish 뒤에 could가 자주 옴`
- Do you ever **wish** you **were** someone else? 다른 누군가가 되었으면 하고 바라는 때가 있나요?

가능한 것을 바랄 때에는 hope를 쓴다. `현실적이므로 뒤에 현재시제 또는 will이 옴`

- I **hope** the weather is fine tomorrow. 내일 날씨가 좋았으면 좋겠어.
  I **wish** the weather is fine tomorrow. (X)
- I **hope** you get better soon. 네가 곧 낫기를 바라.
- I **hope** she didn't miss her flight. 그녀가 비행기를 놓치지 않았기를 바란다.

❹ wish S had p.p. `과거에 이루어졌었더라면 좋았을 거라는 바람`

- I **wish** I **had bought** the phone. 그 전화기를 샀더라면 좋았을 텐데.
- I **wish** he **hadn't left**. 그가 떠나지 않았었더라면 좋았을 것을.

과거에 그렇게 할 수 없어서 아쉬웠던 것에 대해 I wish I could have p.p.로 말할 수 있다.

- I **wish** I **could have gone** to the party. 내가 그 파티에 갈 수만 있었어도…

---

2 wish 뒤에 would가 오는 경우, 어떤 상황에 대한 강한 아쉬움을 나타낼 수 있다.
`어떤 동작이나 변화에 대한 강한 바람. 상태에 대해서는 쓸 수 없음`

- I **wish** the Watson brothers **would come**. Watson 네 형제가 왔으면 좋겠는데.
  I **wish** the Watson brothers **would be here**. (X)
- I **wish** you'd stop interrupting me. 너 그만 좀 끼어들었으면 좋겠어.

---

3 if only는 wish보다 강한 아쉬움과 바람을 나타낸다.

- **If only** I could turn back time. 시간을 뒤로 돌릴 수만 있다면.
- **If only** I hadn't said that. 내가 그 말만 안 했었어도.

if only 뒤에 wish처럼 would가 쓰일 수 있다.

- **If only** you **would** listen to me. 네가 내 말 좀 제발 들어 줬으면.

Exercises

1. hope 또는 wish를 넣어 문장을 완성하세요.

1. Who do you ___wish___ to talk to?
2. I _____ you a happy New Year.
3. I _____ you like the flowers I sent you.
4. We _____ you arrived back in London safely.
5. Do you ever _____ you had a time machine?
6. I _____ I could stay longer.

2. 문장의 문맥에 가장 적합한 표현을 골라 문장을 완성하세요.

1. I wish I (didn't drink / **hadn't drunk**) so much last night.
2. He drinks like a fish. I wish he (doesn't drink / didn't drink / hadn't drunk) so much.
3. I hate sharing a room with my brother. I wish I (would have / had / had had) my own room.
4. I hope you (enjoy / would enjoy / enjoyed) the rest of your stay.
5. I've been waiting for the bus for over an hour. I wish I (would take / took / had taken) a taxi.
6. I'm not a good dancer. I wish I (could / would / might) dance better.
7. My neighbors have been arguing since morning.
   I wish they (would stop / stop / had stopped) shouting at each other.
8. I bought a second-hand phone and it keeps freezing and restarting.
   I wish I (didn't buy / hadn't bought / wouldn't have bought) it.
9. He received a ticket for reckless driving yesterday.
   If only he (would be / was / had been) more careful.

3. 문맥에 맞게 각 표현을 연결하여 문장을 완성하세요.

1. If only   •   • a. good luck and success in everything.
2. I don't wish to be rude,   •   • b. I had listened to my parents.
3. I hope   •   • c. everything is going well with you.
4. We wish you   •   • d. but I need to go back to my work now.

🔊 Dialogue

4. 주어진 단어를 이용하여 문맥에 맞게 문장을 완성하세요.

Mrs. Watson is making dinner. Andy has just come into the kitchen.
Mrs. Watson이 저녁을 만들고 있습니다. Andy가 막 부엌에 들어왔습니다.

Andy Macaroni and cheese again?

Mrs. Watson Don't you like macaroni and cheese?

Andy Well, you know I do. But sometimes _____
_____ (I, wish, you, would, cook something else).

Mrs. Watson Like what?

Andy Steak! I'd like some steak!

Mrs. Watson OK. I'll cook some steak tomorrow.

Big Picture

동사의 종류와 문장 구조

04

영어 문장에서 동사는 시간을 나타내고, 예의와 같은 태도를 나타내기도 하고, 현실적인지 비현실적인지를 알려 주기도 합니다. 뿐만 아니라 동사는 문장 구조를 결정하기도 합니다.

1 자동사

- **Birds fly.** 새는 납니다.

자동사(Intransitive)는 위 문장처럼 주어와 동사만으로도 완전한 문장이 되게 하는 동사입니다. '높이(high)'라든가 '하늘에서(in the sky)'와 같이 꾸며주는 말들을 더할 수는 있지만 필수는 아닙니다.

2 타동사

동사 뒤에 무엇인가가 뒤따라야 문장이 완전해지는 동사에는 크게 두 가지가 있습니다. Be동사, become, seem과 같은 '연결동사(linking verbs)'와 타동사(transitive)입니다.

타동사는 동사 뒤에 어떤 '대상(목적어)'이 와야 하는 동사입니다. 즉, 주어(주체)와 대상 간의 '상호 작용'을 암시하는 동사라고 할 수 있지요. 우리말에서는 주체와 대상 사이의 상호작용을 크게 의식하지 않다 보니 타동사에 익숙하지 않을 수 있습니다. 그러므로 가능한 계속 머리 속에 상호작용인지 아닌지를 떠올리는 연습을 하는 것이 좋습니다. 타동사에도 종류가 여럿이 있습니다.

- **I like apples.** 나는 사과를 좋아해요.

위 문장은 '사과'라는 대상이 와서 문장이 완성되었습니다. 어떤 경우에는 give처럼 '~를'뿐만 아니라 '~에게'에 해당하는 대상이 추가로 필요할 수도 있어요.

- **I gave him a book.** 나는 그에게 책을 줬어요.

대상만으로 문장이 여전히 불완전한 경우도 있습니다. I made him.(나는 그를 만들었다.)은 문법적으로는 문제가 없지만 의미상으로 납득이 되지 않습니다. 다음처럼 동사 뒤에 대상뿐 아니라 의미를 보완해 주는 다른 표현(보어)도 함께 와 줘야 하죠.

- **I made him laugh.** 나는 그를 웃게 만들었다.

3 동사의 p.p.

동사의 p.p.는 직접 하는 것이 아니라 '당하거나 받는' 수동적인 의미를 나타냅니다. -ing와 마찬가지로 Be동사가 함께 해야 합니다.

Unit 035

자동사 vs. 타동사

I found the book quite interesting.
저는 그 책이 꽤 흥미롭다고 생각했어요.

1 문장에서는 동사가 그 뒤에 오는 구조를 결정한다.

동사	+ 구조	
① fly, sleep,… 자동사(Intransitive)	X 주어와 동사만으로 문장이 완전함	▸ Birds **fly**. 새는 난다. ▸ The baby is **sleeping**. 아기는 자고 있다.
② be, become, seem, sound, feel, remain… 연결동사(Linking Verb)	명사 (Noun) 형용사 (Adjective) 전치사구 (Preposition+N) -ing p.p. 보어 *더 이상 동사가 아님. 명사나 형용사*	▸ She **became** a travel writer. 그녀는 여행작가가 되었다. ▸ He **seems** afraid. 그는 두려워하는 것 같다. ▸ The milk **is** in the fridge. 우유는 냉장고에 있어요. ▸ They**'re** dancing. 그들은 춤추고 있어요. ▸ I**'m** interested in music. 전 음악에 관심이 있어요.
③ like, kick, watch… 타동사(Transitive)	명사 (Noun) -ing 동명사	▸ I **like** cheese. 저는 치즈를 좋아합니다. ▸ Do you **watch** TV every evening? 매일 저녁마다 TV 보세요?
④ get, tell, send… 타동사(Transitive)	명사 (Noun) + 명사 (Noun) ⇨ 간접목적어+직접목적어	▸ I'll **get** you some coffee. 커피 좀 가져다 드릴게요.
⑤ find, make, keep… 타동사(Transitive)	명사 (Noun) + 형용사 (Adjective) 명사 (Noun) + 동사(Verb) 명사 (Noun) + 명사 (Noun) 목적어+목적보어	▸ She **makes** me happy. 그녀는 나를 행복하게 해요. ▸ Mom **made** me clean the room. 엄마는 내가 방을 치우게 했다. ▸ They **made** their daughter an actor. 그들은 딸을 배우로 만들었다.

2 같은 동사라도 의미와 기능에 따라 문장 구조가 달라질 수 있다.

- I usually **read** in my spare time. 저는 여가 시간에 보통 독서합니다. ①
- I'm **reading a magazine**. 잡지 읽고 있어요. ③

- I **bought a pair of shoes**. 전 신발 한 켤레를 샀어요. ③
- I **bought him a pair of shoes**. 저는 그에게 신발 한 켤레를 사 줬어요. ④

- I've **found the book**! It's here. 그 책 찾았어요! 여기 있네요. ③
- I **found the book quite interesting**. 저는 그 책이 꽤 흥미롭다고 생각했어요. ⑤

> **TIP** describe, explain, introduce, propose, say, suggest 등은 ③으로만 쓰이고, '~에게'는 to ~로 나타낸다.
> 예) She explained the situation to me. (She explained me the situation.) 그녀가 제게 상황을 설명해 주었습니다.

3 대상이 둘인 문장(④)은 두 가지 형태가 가능하다.

> **bring, give, lend, pass, sell, send …**

▸ He gave **me a book**. 그는 내게 책을 한 권 주었다.
   = He gave **a book** (**to me**).

> **buy, cook, get, make …**

▸ Can you get **me some water**? 물 좀 갖다 줄래?
   = Can you get **some water** (**for me**)?
▸ I bought **him a pair of shoes**. 저는 그에게 신발 한 켤레를 사 줬어요.
   = I bought **a pair of shoes for him**. for him을 생략하면 의미가 달라질 수 있음

'~에게'에 해당하는 전치사+대상'은 생략 가능. ③ 형태

Exercises

1. 문장의 문맥에 가장 적합한 표현을 골라 문장을 완성하세요.
   1. Can I get (you some tea / some tea you)?
   2. I showed (him my vacation photos / my vacation photos him).
   3. I described (them the whole situation / the whole situation to them).
   4. He sold (his old car his neighbor / his old car to his neighbor).
   5. Did she tell (you the truth / the truth you)?
   6. She bought (for him a book / a book for him).
   7. I've recovered (the file from the hard disk / from the hard disk the file).
   8. I'll make (you coffee / you for coffee).
   9. Kate, can I introduce (you Mike Turner / you to Mike Turner)?

2. 주어진 단어를 맞는 순서대로 배열하여 문장을 완성하세요.
   1. (clean / the room / me / made) Mom _made me clean the room_.
   2. (yesterday / an email / sent / her) I _____.
   3. (his report / gave / the managing director / this morning / to) Mike _____.
   4. (it / you / explain / to / Can / me?) _____?
   5. (promised to / a full refund / me) They _____.

3. 문맥에 맞게 각 표현을 연결하여 문장을 완성하세요.
   1. What are you reading   a. interesting?
   2. Mom made me   b. magazines.
   3. I'll cook dinner   c. now?
   4. I don't read   d. the salt?
   5. Will you pass me   e. a cake.
   6. Can you bring it back   f. tired?
   7. Are you feeling   g. to me?
   8. Did you find the book   h. for you.

🔊 Dialogue

4. 주어진 단어를 이용하여 문맥에 맞게 문장을 완성하세요.

Naomi is about to go to a supermarket. Naomi는 지금 슈퍼마켓에 가려는 참입니다.

Naomi   Ms. Klein. I'm going to the supermarket now.
        Is there anything you want from there?

Jessica _____ (you, Can, get, some, mayonnaise, me)?

Naomi   No problem. Anything else?

Jessica Don't we need margarine?

Naomi   Yeah, that's what I'm going to buy.

Unit 036

수동태(1)

Milk is kept in the fridge.
우유는 냉장고에 보관된다.

1 수동의 의미를 나타내는 동사의 p.p.(과거분사)를 써서 수동태 문장을 만들 수 있다.

| We | keep milk in the fridge. → 능동(active) 동사 keep의 주체 가 중심(주어)
우리는 우유를 냉장고에 **보관한다**.

| Milk | is kept in the fridge. → 수동(passive) 동사 keep의 대상 이 중심(주어)
우유는 냉장고에 **보관된다**.

수동태 문장에서는 Be동사가 문장의 동사 역할을 한다. `p.p.는 더 이상 동사가 아님`

▶ The FIFA World Cup **is held** every 4 years. 피파 월드컵은 4년마다 **개최된다**.
   The FIFA World Cup **held** every 4 years. (X)   `Be동사가 빠지면 held나 built가`
▶ The church **was built** 300 years ago. 그 교회는 300년 전에 **지어졌다**.   `p.p.가 아닌 동사로 보여`
   The church **built** 300 years ago. (X)   `어색하게 해석될 수 있음`

주로 대화체에서 Be동사 대신 get이 쓰이기도 한다. `'되었다'는 변화 의미 강조`

▶ Trish **got promoted** last month. Trish는 지난 달에 **승진되었다**.
▶ Luckily, the driver didn't **get injured** in the accident. 운 좋게도 그 운전자는 사고에서 **부상당하지 않았다**.

by를 써서 수동태 문장의 주체(누가, 무엇이)를 나타낼 수 있다.

▶ The microwave was invented **by** Percy Spencer. ← Percy Spencer invented the microwave.
  전자레인지는 Percy Spencer**에 의해 발명되었다**. ← Percy Spencer는 전자레인지를 발명했다.
▶ Honey is made **by** bees. ← Bees make honey.
  꿀은 벌**에 의해 만들어진다**. ← 벌은 꿀을 만든다.

---

2 다음은 보통 거의 수동태 형태로 쓰이는 표현들이다.

❶ **be born** : 태어나다

▶ A: Where were you born? 어디서 태어나셨어요?
  B: I **was born** in Gwangju. 저는 광주에서 **태어났습니다**.
▶ Their first son, Neil, **was born** in 2011. 그들의 장남 Neil은 2011년에 **태어났습니다**.

❷ **get + p.p.**

▶ Now, let's **get started**. 이제 **시작합시다**.
▶ Wait, I'm **getting dressed**. 기다려. 나 **옷 입고 있어**.
▶ We're **getting married**. 우리 **결혼합니다**!
▶ They **got divorced** last year. 그들은 작년에 **이혼했다**.

❸ p.p.가 형용사로 쓰이는 경우에도 문장 형태가 수동태처럼 보인다. `See Unit 041▶`

▶ I **was** very **tired** yesterday. 나는 어제 무척 **피곤했다**.
▶ I'm not **finished** yet. 저 아직 안 **끝났어요**.
▶ I'm **interested** in world history. 저는 세계사에 **관심이 있습니다**.
▶ My phone **is gone**! 내 전화기가 **사라졌어**!
▶ Nobody **was hurt**. 아무도 **다치지 않았어요**.

Exercises

1. 보기와 같이 문장을 수동태로 다시 쓰세요.

1. People speak English in New Zealand.
   → English ___is spoken___ in New Zealand.
2. People grow corn a lot in my hometown.
   → Corn _____ a lot in my hometown.
3. Somebody often steals cars in this neighborhood.
   → Cars _____ in this neighborhood.
4. Percy Spencer invented the microwave.
   → The microwave _____ by Percy Spencer.
5. J. R. R. Tolkien wrote *The Lord of the Rings*.
   → *The Lord of The Rings* _____ by J. R. R. Tolkien.

2. 밑줄 친 부분이 틀렸다면 맞게 고치세요. 고칠 부분이 없다면 X를 쓰세요.

1. The Channel Tunnel built in the late 1980s.   ___was built___
2. Cheese is made of milk.   _____
3. Frederic Auguste Bartholdi was designed the Statue of Liberty.   _____
4. My package was damaged in transit.   _____
5. Garbage collects every other week.   _____

3. 빈칸에 들어갈 가장 적절한 표현을 보기에서 골라 넣어 문장을 완성하세요.

| born | ~~gone~~ | interested | married | tired |

1. Just spray apple cider vinegar around. The smell will be ___gone___ soon.
2. Anna and her fiancé got _____ last month.
3. The U.S. Census Bureau reports that about 360,000 babies are _____ each day around the world.
4. Most young people are _____ in politics but are alienated by politicians.
5. If you're overweight, you'll get _____ when you climb a flight of stairs.

◆ Dialogue

4. 주어진 단어를 이용하여 문맥에 맞게 문장을 완성하세요.

Julia is asking Nicole about her hometown. Julia는 Nicole에게 고향에 대해 묻고 있습니다.

Julia   _____ (Where, you, bear), Nicole?
Nicole   _____ (I, bear, in Lyon).
Julia   _____ (Where, it, locate)?
Nicole   Lyon is in the southeast of France. It's the third largest city in France.
Julia   Did you grow up there, too?
Nicole   Just until I was four.

Unit 037

수동태(2)

No, thank you. I'm being helped.
고맙지만 괜찮습니다. 저는 다른 직원의 도움을 받고 있습니다.

1 수동태 문장에서는 Be동사가 시제를 나타낸다.

① 단순 현재: am/are/is p.p.
- I'm paid weekly. 저는 주급을 받습니다.

② 단순 과거: was/were p.p.
- The microwave was invented in 1946. 전자레인지는 1946년에 발명되었다.

③ 현재 진행: am/are/is being p.p.
- A: May I help you, sir? 선생님, 도와드릴까요?
  B: No, thank you. I'm being helped. 고맙지만 괜찮습니다. 저는 다른 직원의 도움을 받고 있습니다.
- The road is being repaired. 도로가 지금 보수되는 중이다.

④ 과거 진행: was/were being p.p.
- All the computers in the library were being used. 도서관의 모든 컴퓨터들이 사용 중이었다.
- Princess Diana was being followed by paparazzi when she was killed in a car accident.
  다이애나비는 파파라치에게 쫓기다가 차 사고로 숨졌다.

⑤ 현재 완료: have/has been p.p.
- Many shops have been closed over the last year. 지난 1년간 많은 가게들이 문을 닫았다.
- Listen, everyone. James has been promoted to Sales Director! 여러분, James가 판매부장으로 승진했어요!

⑥ 과거 완료: had been p.p.
- When I got to the theater, I found out that the concert had been canceled.
  극장에 도착하자 나는 콘서트가 취소되었다는 것을 알았다.
- I emailed them that the shipment had been delayed. 제가 그들에게 출하가 연기되었다고 이메일을 보냈어요.

⑦ 미래: will be p.p.
- The project will be finished next month. 프로젝트가 다음 달에 끝날 것입니다.
- Your order will be delivered soon. 귀하의 주문상품은 곧 배송될 것입니다.

2 조동사+수동태

① 조동사+be p.p.: 현재 or 미래
- Something must be done right now. 뭔가 조치가 당장 취해져야만 해요.
- Your goods can be damaged in transit. 귀하의 상품은 수송 중에 파손될 수 있습니다.

② 조동사+have p.p.: 과거
- Your email might have been lost. 당신의 이메일은 분실되었을지도 모릅니다.
- My computer must have been hacked. 내 컴퓨터는 분명 해킹 당했던 게야.
- If I hadn't locked the door, my car would have been stolen.
  내가 문을 잠그지 않았었더라면 내 차는 도난 당했을 것이다.

3 수동태의 -ing 형태는 being+p.p.이고, to부정사의 수동태 형태는 to be p.p.이다.
- I'm afraid of being left alone. 저는 홀로 남겨지는 것이 두려워요.
- I don't want to be fired. 저는 해고되길 원치 않아요.

Exercises

1. 보기와 같이 밑줄 친 동사 부분을 수동태로 다시 쓰세요.

1. They pay me weekly. → I _'m paid_ weekly.
2. His boss has fired him. → He _____.
3. They invited Julia and Nicole to the party. → Julia and Nicole _____ to the party.
4. We must do something immediately. → Something _____ immediately.
5. The kitchen smelled nice while she was baking cookies.
   → The kitchen smelled nice while cookies _____.
6. He realized that someone had stolen his camera.
   → He realized that his camera _____.
7. When will you deliver my package?
   → When _____ my package _____?
8. We can give you a loaner phone while we are repairing your phone.
   → We can give you a loaner phone while your phone _____.
9. She wants her boss to promote her. → She wants to _____.
10. You should have saved the file. → The file _____.

2. 주어진 단어를 사용하여 문장을 완성하세요. 가능하면 축약형을 쓰세요.

1. (are / All our pies / made with / fresh ingredients)
   → _All our pies are made with fresh ingredients_.
2. (Has / to the hospital / he / taken / been)
   → _____?
3. (The Mona Lisa / by / painted / Leonardo Da Vinci / was)
   → _____.
4. (When / tea / served / be / will)
   → _____?
5. (not / His cancer / have / discovered / might / been)
   → _____.

🔊 Dialogue

3. 주어진 단어를 배열하여 문맥에 맞게 문장을 완성하세요.

Sia is shopping at a clothes shop.
Sia는 옷 가게에서 쇼핑 중입니다.

Sia _____ (What, this jacket, made of, is)?

Clerk _____ (It, made of, is, top-grade leather).

Sia How much is it?

Clerk $500.

Sia That's too expensive. Do you have a cheaper one of similar style?

Clerk We have one with the same design, made of faux-leather. It's $125.

Unit 038

수동태(3)

His company was established in 1994.
그의 회사는 1994년에 설립되었다.

1 다음과 같은 경우에 수동태로 말할 수 있다.

❶ 주어가 명확하지 않거나, 일반적이거나, 너무 뻔한 경우

▸ The office **is cleaned** every day. 사무실은 매일 **청소됩니다**.
  ← Somebody cleans the office every day. 누군가 사무실을 매일 청소합니다. 막연

▸ English is **spoken** all over the world. 영어는 전 세계에서 **쓰인다**.
  ← People speak English all over the world. 사람들은 전 세계에서 영어를 쓴다. 너무 뻔함

❷ 타동사의 대상에 초점을 두고 말할 때

▸ Honey **is made** by bees. 꿀은 벌에 의해 **만들어진다**. '꿀'에 초점
  ← Bees make honey. 능동태 벌이 꿀을 만든다. '벌'에 초점

▸ His company **was established** in 1994. 그의 회사는 1994년에 **설립되었다**.
  회사에 초점. 설립자가 누구인지는 이 문장에서 중요하지 않음

❸ 수동태는 일상 대화보다는 주로 시스템이나 과정 등을 설명할 때 쓰인다.

▸ White sand, soda and lime **are mixed** together and heated into thick syrup. As the syrup **is cooled**, it becomes glass. While the glass is not hard, it **is rolled** into flat sheets or **molded** into different shapes by machines. 흰 모래, 소다, 석회가 **섞이고** 가열되어 진한 시럽이 됩니다. 시럽이 **식으면서** 유리가 됩니다. 유리가 아직 굳지 않았을 때 롤러로 **밀어** 납작한 판이 **되거나** 기계에 의해 다른 모양으로 **주조됩니다**.

❹ 수동태는 개인적인 느낌이 적고, 보고서나 계약서 등 격식 있는 문어체에서 많이 볼 수 있다.

▸ After the contract **is made**, every employee will **be given** a written statement of terms and conditions of employment. 계약이 **체결되면**, 모든 직원들에게 고용 조건이 적힌 서류가 **주어질 것입니다**.

2 일상 대화나 '상호작용'에 초점이 없다면 능동태로 말하는 것이 보다 일반적이다.

⎡ He **received** the notice yesterday. 그는 어제 그 통지서를 받았습니다. 보다 자연스러움
⎣ He **was given** the notice yesterday. 그는 어제 그 통지서를 받았습니다. 딱딱하고, 격식 있는(Formal) 느낌

⎡ She **learned** to read when she was 5. 그녀는 다섯 살 때 읽는 법을 배웠다. 익혔다는 사실에 초점
⎣ She **was taught** to read when she was 5. 그녀는 다섯 살 때 읽는 법을 배웠다. 누군가에게 배웠다는 암시(상호작용)

⎡ I **heard** that he would be here tomorrow. 그가 내일 여기 올 거라고 들었어요. 내가 어떤 소식이나 내용을 접함
⎣ I **was told** that he would be here tomorrow. 그가 내일 여기 올 거라고 들었습니다.
  누군가가 나에게 소식이나 내용을 전달, 통보했음 암시(상호작용)

3 의미가 비슷해 보이는 동사라도 구체적 의미나 기능에 따라 쓰임이 다를 수 있다.

⎡ The ticket price **was raised** to $50 last month.
⎣ The ticket price **raised** to $50 last month. (X) ─ 티켓 가격이 지난 달에 50달러로 **올랐다**.

⎡ The ticket price **went up** to $50 last month.
⎣ The ticket price **was gone up** to $50 last month. (X)

Exercises

1. 주어진 문장 뒤에 이어지기 가장 자연스러운 문장에 V 표시를 하세요.

1. **Last year I visited the Houses of Parliament's clock tower in London.**
   _____ People commonly call it Big Ben.
   ___V_____ It is commonly called Big Ben.

2. **Wilson and Clark is a training and education company.**
   _____ It employs more than 50 employees.
   _____ More than 50 employees are employed.

3. ***The Starry Night* is one of the world's most well-known works of art.**
   _____ Vincent Van Gogh painted it.
   _____ It was painted by Vincent Van Gogh.

2. 주어진 동사를 적절한 형태로 바꾸어 문장을 완성하세요.

1. The first papermaking machine _____ (develop) in France around 1798. Since then papermaking machines _____ (be) greatly _____ (improve) and _____ (enlarge). However, the basic processes remain the same.

2. Chocolate begins with the seeds of the cacao tree. When the seeds _____ (collect), they _____ (dry) in the sun. The dry seeds _____ (call) cocoa beans. The cocoa beans _____ then _____ (ship) to processing plants or chocolate factories.

3. 주어진 동사를 적절한 형태로 바꾸어 문장을 완성하세요.

1. I ___*heard*___ (hear) that you're from Australia.
2. He _____ (give) a pay raise last month.
3. We've _____ (lose) the game.
4. They _____ (defeat) in the final last year.
5. He _____ (receive) a ticket for speeding yesterday.
6. I _____ (tell) that the manager was busy.

🔊 Dialogue

4. 동사 pay의 적절한 형태를 넣어 문장을 완성하세요.

James and Jessica are talking about the bills to pay.
James와 Jessica는 지불해야 할 고지서들에 대해 얘기하고 있습니다.

James	Honey, these bills aren't due until next week, right?
Jessica	No. They should _____ immediately.
James	Alright. Can we pay the bills online, or should I go to the bank?
Jessica	You can _____ the bills online using a credit card.
James	How about the credit card bill?
Jessica	Oh, that should _____ from our bank account.

Unit 039

수동태(4)

The winner will be given a free trip to Norway.
우승자에게는 노르웨이 무료 여행이 주어질 것입니다.

1 타동사는 능동태와 수동태, 두 가지 문장으로 쓰일 수 있다. *See Unit 035 ▶*

- 능동태 : Everybody **likes** <u>her</u>. 모든 사람들이 **그녀를** 좋아합니다.
- 수동태 : <u>She</u> **is liked** by everybody. 그녀는 모든 사람들에게 **사랑 받습니다**.

2 대상이 둘인 경우 각각의 대상을 주어로 두 가지 수동태 문장이 가능하다. *See Unit 035 ▶*

We'll pay <u>you</u> <u>$120</u> for your old phone. 당신의 오래된 전화기에 120달러를 지불하겠습니다.

- <u>You</u> **will be paid** $120 for your old phone.
  당신에게 오래된 전화기에 $120이 **지불될 것입니다**.
- <u>$120</u> **will be paid** for your old phone.
  $120이 오래된 전화기에 **지불될 것입니다**.

대상(직접목적어)이 주어가 되는 수동태에서 '~에게'에 해당하는 대상(간접목적어) 앞에 전치사가 온다.

- We'**ll give** <u>you</u> two hours to think about it. 그것에 대해 생각할 시간으로 당신에게 두 시간을 **드리겠습니다**.
  → <u>You</u> **will be given** two hours to think about it. 당신에게 두 시간이 **주어질 것입니다**.
- We'**ll give** <u>two hours</u> **to** you to think about it. 그것에 대해 생각할 시간으로 당신에게 두 시간을 **드리겠습니다**.
  → <u>Two hours</u> **will be given to** you. 두 시간이 당신에게 **주어질 것입니다**.

사람을 주어로 한 수동태가 사물을 주어로 한 수동태보다 더 자주 쓰인다.

- ▶ **The winner will be given** a free trip to Norway. 우승자에게는 노르웨이 무료 여행이 **주어질 것입니다**.
- ▶ **He was offered** a position at Google, but he decided not to take it.
  그에게 Google 사에서의 일자리가 **제안되었으나**, 그는 받아들이지 않기로 결심했다.

3 'make+대상+동사'의 수동태는 **be made to ~**이다. ⑤ 유형의 문장은 수동태로 잘 쓰이지 않는다. *See Unit 035 ▶*

- ▶ I **was made to** clean the room. 나는 (엄마가 시켜서) 방을 치워**야 했다**.
  ← 능동태 : Mom made me clean the room. 엄마는 내가 방을 치우게 했다.

동사 **elect**는 다음과 같은 수동태 형태로 종종 쓰인다.

- ▶ He **was elected** president in 2017. 그는 2017년에 대통령으로 **선출되었다**.

Exercises

1. 주어진 문장을 밑줄 친 부분을 주로 한 문장으로 다시 쓰세요.

1. We'll pay you $120 for your old phone.
   → You _____will be paid $120 for your old phone_____.

2. Eugene lent me this book.
   → I _____.

3. A friend told me about the party.
   → I _____.

4. They haven't paid me for the work yet.
   → I _____.

5. They took the injured driver to the hospital immediately.
   → The injured driver _____.

6. They promised us delivery within 5 days of our order.
   → We _____.

7. They made me wait in the lobby for an hour.
   → I _____.

2. 문장의 틀린 부분이 있다면 고쳐서 다시 쓰세요. 고칠 부분이 없다면 X를 쓰세요.

1. A free trip to Norway will be given the winner. ... will be given to the winner
2. He was offered a position at Google, but he decided not to take it. _____
3. The order was sent to us through our website. _____
4. I was given to this sample at the trade fair in Austria. _____
5. She was asked very difficult questions at the interview. _____
6. Nothing can make me to feel better now. _____
7. They were told to leave immediately. _____
8. Angela Merkel was elected to chancellor twice. _____

🔊 Dialogue

3. 주어진 단어를 이용하여 문맥에 맞게 문장을 완성하세요.

Julia and Nicole are talking about their friend Alice.
Julia와 Nicole은 친구 Alice에 대해 이야기하고 있습니다.

Julia Have you heard?

Nicole What?

Julia Alice may leave the company.

Nicole Why?

Julia She _____ (offer, a position at Henson's) with better pay, and she'll probably accept it.

Nicole Good for her. She deserves to _____ (give, a good chance).

Unit 040

사역동사

I can't get him to understand it.
난 그에게 그것을 이해시키지 못하겠어요.

1 주어가 대상에게 '~하라고 시키거나 하도록 만드는' 경우에 다음의 동사들을 쓸 수 있다. **사역동사**

❶ make somebody ~ : 누군가가 ~하도록 만들다 대상의 의지와 관계없음. 때로는 다소 강제적인 뉘앙스

make ─ **somebody/something** ─ **ⓥ(동사원형)**

- He **makes me laugh** a lot. 그는 나를 많이 웃게 만들어요.
- What **makes you think** so? 왜 그렇게 생각해?(무엇이 너를 그렇게 생각하게 했지?)
- You can't **make me do** it. 넌 내가 그걸 하게 만들 수 없어.

● 비슷한 의미로 force를 쓸 수도 있다. 물리적 힘이나 강제적인 뉘앙스가 좀 더 강함

force ─ **somebody/something** ─ **to ~**

- You can't **force me to make** a decision. 당신은 내게 결정하라고 강요할 수 없어요.

❷ have somebody ~ : 누구에게 ~하라고 시키다/설득하다

have ─ **somebody/something** ─ **ⓥ(동사원형)**

- My English teacher **has her students speak** to each other every day.
  우리 영어 선생님은 매일 학생들이 서로 말을 하도록 시킨다.
- I'll **have Alice book** a meeting room. Alice에게 회의실을 예약하라고 하겠습니다.

❸ get somebody to ~ have와 비슷하나, 대화체에서 더 흔하게 쓰임

get ─ **somebody/something** ─ **to ~**

- A: My laptop keeps turning off. 내 노트북이 계속 꺼져.
  B: I'll **get Patrick to come** and **have** a look. Patrick이 와서 좀 보도록 할게.
- I can't **get him to understand** it. 난 그에게 그것을 이해시키지 못하겠어요.

❹ let somebody ~ : 누가 ~하도록 허락하다

let ─ **somebody/something** ─ **ⓥ(동사원형)**

- **Let me introduce** myself. 제 소개를 하겠습니다.
- Don't **let him go**. 그가 가게 하지 마세요.

● 비슷한 의미로 allow를 쓸 수도 있다. 격식 있는 표현이나 문어체에서 많이 쓰임

allow ─ **somebody/something** ─ **to ~**

- Please **allow** me **to introduce** myself. 제 소개를 하겠습니다.

Exercises

1. 문장의 문맥에 가장 적합한 표현을 골라 문장을 완성하세요.

   1. A: I'm too busy to clean my house.
      B: Why don't you (have / (get)) someone to do it for you?
   2. I (had / got) the shop deliver the food.
   3. Mr. Harris often (has / gets) Alice type letters.
   4. He didn't (make / force) me to do it. It was my decision.
   5. Mom always (makes / forces) us do our homework before we have dinner.
   6. Yoga (allows / lets) your body relax.
   7. My parents won't (allow / let) me to stay out late.
   8. Exercise makes you (learn / to learn) better.
   9. Little Eva got everyone she knows (sign / to sign) her mom's birthday card.
   10. Please allow me (express / to express) my sincere apology.
   11. We need to have a plumber (repair / to repair) the leak in the sink as soon as possible.
   12. Police forced the man (leave / to leave) the bar.

2. 주어진 단어를 맞는 순서대로 배열하여 문장을 완성하세요.

   1. (What / you / so / think / makes)
      → _What makes you think so?_ ?
   2. (I'll / a mechanic / have / my car / look at)
      → _____.
   3. (made / His ex-boss / overtime every day / work / him)
      → _____.
   4. (my cousin / got / my dog / I / to / look after / while I was away)
      → _____.
   5. (I / allow / only family members / see me / want to / to / on Facebook)
      → _____.
   6. (have / I'll / up to your room / your suitcases / someone / bring)
      → _____.
   7. (me / you / around our new house / Let / show)
      → _____.

🔊 Dialogue

3. 주어진 표현 중 가장 적합한 표현을 골라 문장을 완성하세요.

Mike is out at the moment, and Trish is answering his phone.
Mike는 지금 자리에 없습니다. Trish가 그의 전화를 받고 있습니다.

Kate   Hello, this is Kate Morgan in Accounting. Could I speak to Mike?

Trish Hello, Kate. Well, he's not in at the moment, I'm afraid.
       Can I ask what this call is about?

Kate   There's something I need to check with him. It is quite urgent.

Trish OK, I'll have him (call / to call / called) you when he gets back.

Unit 041

have something p.p.

Let's have a pizza delivered.
피자 시켜 먹자.

1 본인이 직접 하지 않고 누군가의 손을 빌려 무엇을 할 때 have/get something p.p.의 형태로 말할 수 있다. 주로 금액을 지불하고 받는 서비스들에 해당. something이 수동의 입장이므로 p.p.를 씀

have/get ── somebody/something ── p.p.

I usually **have my hair cut** at a hairdresser nearby.
나는 보통 근처 미용실에서 **머리를** 자른다.

I **cut** my hair myself.
나는 **스스로** 머리를 **자릅니다**.

- We **have our office cleaned** every day. 우리는 **사무실을** 매일 **청소합니다**.
- He **had his car repaired** yesterday. 그는 어제 **차를 수리했다**.
- She's **having the kitchen painted**. 그녀는 지금 **부엌을 칠하고** 있다.
- Let's **have a pizza delivered**. 피자 시켜 먹자.
- I'll **have the Internet installed** as soon as possible. 나는 가능한 빨리 **인터넷을 설치할** 거야.
- I like taking pictures and I like **having my pictures taken**, too. 나는 사진 찍는 것도 **찍히는 것도** 좋아해요.

누군가에게 하라고 시키는 경우에는 have somebody ~의 형태로 말한다. *See unit 040▶*

- We **have them clean** the office every day. 우리는 매일 그들에게 청소를 시킨다.

get은 대화체에서 자주 볼 수 있다.

- A: When will the report be ready? 보고서는 언제쯤 준비될 것 같나?
  B: I'll **get it done** by tomorrow. 내일까지 **끝내 놓겠습니다**.
- Don't **get your hair cut** at the hairdresser. 그 미용실에선 **머리 자르지** 마.
- When are you going to **get your car repaired**? 차는 언제 수리시킬 거예요?
- I need to **get the jacket dry-cleaned**. 재킷을 드라이클리닝 해야겠어.
- He **got his car washed** at a car wash near the station. 그는 역 근처 세차장에서 **차를 세차했다**.

누군가를 시킨다고 할 때에는 get somebody to ~의 형태임에 유의한다. *See unit 040▶*

- I'll **get them to repair** my car. 그들한테 차를 고치도록 시킬 거야.

2 have/get something p.p.는 우발적인 사고를 당하거나, 어쩔 수 없이 겪은 것에 대해서도 쓸 수 있다.

- He **had his ankle twisted** in Colorado. 그는 콜로라도에서 **발목을 접질렀다**.
- Don't drink and drive. You'll **get your driver's license taken away**.
  술 마시고 운전하지 마세요. **면허증을 압수당할** 거예요.
- They **got their car stolen** while camping. 그들은 캠핑 중에 **차를 도난당했다**.

Exercises

1. 그림에 맞게 주어진 단어를 이용하여 문장을 완성하세요. 필요한 경우 have 또는 get을 쓰세요.

   1. Let's ___have a pizza delivered___ (deliver, a pizza)!
   2. She's ___painting the kitchen___ (paint, the kitchen).
   3. I have to _____ (fix, my camera) because I dropped it in the water.
   4. I can _____ (repair, my car) myself. I'm a mechanic.
   5. I _____ (change, my phone number) because I had kept receiving spam calls.
   6. I need to _____ (shorten, these pants). They're too long.
   7. I _____ (check, my teeth) regularly.
   8. He's _____ (cut, the grass) now.

2. 문장의 문맥에 가장 적합한 표현을 골라 문장을 완성하세요.

   1. When are you going to have the pool (cleaning /(cleaned))? Summer's coming.
   2. You can get your mail (forward / forwarded) to your new address.
   3. I (let / had / made) my apartment broken into last night.
   4. If you use your cell phone in class, you will have it (take / taken) away.
   5. I'm afraid to get my ears (piercing / pierced).

◀ Dialogue

3. 주어진 단어를 이용하여 문장을 완성하세요.

   Trish is asking Mike a favor. Trish는 Mike에게 부탁을 하고 있습니다.

   Trish Mike, could you do me a favor?
   Mike   Sure. What is it?
   Trish Could you please take this document to the copy store and have _____ (make, 10 copies)?
   Mike   OK. No problem. 10 copies, right?
   Trish Thank you. Please get _____ (spiral-bind, them).

Unit 042

수동태(5)

It is said that life is a journey.
인생은 여정이라고들 한다.

---

1 다음 상호작용이 암시된 동사들은 수동태로 자주 쓰인다. 보통 주체보다는 대상을 중심(주어)으로 말함. p.p.가 아예 보편적인 형용사가 되기도 함 See Unit 036 ▶ 상호작용이 드러나지 않는 동사가 상호작용이 있을 때는 사역동사를 쓴다. See Unit 040 ▶

When **were** you **born**?
당신은 언제 **태어났나요**?

원인(주체)없이 저절로 일어날 수 없음
- He **was injured** in the car accident. 그는 차 사고에서 **부상당했다**.
- I **was** so **scared**. 나는 너무 **무서웠다**.
- You will **be surprised** to know who she is.
  그녀가 누군지 알게 되면 너 **놀랄** 거야.
- I don't **get frightened** easily. 나는 쉽게 **겁먹지** 않는다.
- We **were shocked** when they lost the game.
  그들이 경기에 지자 우리는 **충격을 받았다**.

---

2 주체나 대상이 불분명한 경우 수동태로 쓰지 않는다. 상호작용이 모호, 우리말 해석이 수동태가 되는 경우에 주의

The door **opened**.
문이 **열렸다**.
저절로(원인 불명) 열림

The door **was opened** by the guard.
그 문은 경비에 의해 **열렸다**.
경비가 주체, 문이 대상

- This pen **writes** well. 이 펜은 잘 **써진다**.
- My computer **works** fine. 내 컴퓨터는 잘 **작동된다**.

---

3 다음 동사들은 주어가 일반적인 사람일 경우 수동태 문장으로 자주 쓰인다. 동사의 주체가 너무 뻔함

> believe, claim, consider, expect, know, report, say, think...

- **It is said that** life is a journey. (← People say that life is a journey.) 인생은 여정이라고들 **한다**.
- **It is believed that** the fire started in the kitchen. 화재가 주방에서 시작되었다고 **믿어진다**.
- **It is considered that** love is the main theme in his poetry. 그의 시에서는 사랑이 주요 테마라고 **간주된다**.
- **It is expected that** the storm will pass through Cuba. 폭풍이 쿠바를 통과할 **것으로 예상됩니다**.
- **It is reported that** 12 people were missing. 12명이 실종되었다고 **보도되었다**.
- **It is thought that** Ronaldo is one of the best soccer players in the world.
  호나우두가 세계에서 가장 훌륭한 축구선수 중의 하나라고 **생각된다**.

동일한 문장을 다음과 같은 형태로도 말할 수 있다.

- Life **is said to be** a journey. be said to ~는 be supposed to ~로도 말할 수 있다. See Unit 027 ▶
- The fire **is believed to have started** in the kitchen.
- Love **is considered to be** the main theme in his poetry.
- The storm **is expected to pass through** Cuba.
- 12 people **are reported to be** missing.
- Ronaldo **is thought be** one of the best soccer player in the world.

Exercises

1. 주어진 동사를 적절한 형태로 바꾸어 문장을 완성하세요.

1. Fortunately nobody __was injured__ (injure) in the accident.
2. I _____ (not, scare) of dogs. They're just adorable.
3. This pen won't _____ (write) well.
4. The news of Princess Diana's death _____ (shock) the world.
5. I _____ (surprise) that the game is still popular.
6. A: Boo! / B: Hey, you _____ (frighten) me!
7. She walked to the elevator and waited for the door to _____ (open).
8. Andy and Patrick _____ (bear) in Canada.
9. This machine _____ (work) by electricity.

2. 문장의 문맥에 가장 적합한 표현을 골라 문장을 완성하세요.

1. People say that there is a ghost in the theater.
   → __It is said that there is a ghost in the theater.__
2. The media reported that crime had increased over the past five years.
   → _____
3. Many people think that empathy is a special emotion that only humans show.
   → _____
4. It is expected that the storm will pass through Cuba.
   → __The storm is expected to pass through Cuba.__
5. It is thought that chocolate contains a lot of fat.
   → _____
6. It is alleged that he robbed the bank.
   → _____
7. It is considered that knowledge is power.
   → _____

🔊 Dialogue

3. 주어진 동사를 적절한 형태로 바꿔 넣어 문장을 완성하세요.

Rachel is upset. Rachel은 화가 났습니다.

Jessica Why are you upset?

Rachel I think my package is missing. The tracking says that it's been delivered but I don't have my package.

Jessica How can that be possible?

Rachel I don't know. I _____ (not, sign) for the package.

Jessica That's strange.

Rachel I suspect it _____ (sign) by someone else.

Jessica Who was that?

Rachel I don't know.

Big Picture

동사의 연결

05

기본 문장 구조에 추가로 명사나 동사, 또는 다른 절(S+V, 문장)을 더해서 보다 풍부하고 구체적인 의미를 나타낼 수 있습니다. 이 때 더해지는 표현의 종류에 따라 각각 다른 연결 장치가 쓰입니다. *See 부록 12▶*

이 중 동사가 추가로 이어지는 형태는 크게 세 가지로 나눌 수 있습니다. Big Picture 04에서 동사가 그 뒤에 올 구조를 결정한다고 했듯, 마찬가지로 뒤에 이어지는 추가 동사의 형태도 첫 동사가 결정합니다.

1 to로 연결하기

동사가 등장하는 순서대로 사건이 벌어지는 개념, 즉, 본동사가 먼저 일어나고 다음 동사가 일어나는 시간 순이라면, 다음 동사를 앞으로의 목적지나 미래를 암시하는 to로 이어줄 수 있습니다.

> I've <u>decided</u> <u>to get</u> a job.   나는 <u>취업하기로</u> <u>결심했어요</u>.
> ❶ → ❷   결심 후 취업

반대로 위치는 동사 뒤에 오지만 실제로는 그 전에 있었던 사건이나 행동에 대한 동사는 –ing를 취합니다.

> I've just <u>finished</u> <u>cleaning</u> the room.   방금 방 <u>치우는 것을</u> <u>마쳤다</u>.
> 방을 치운 것이 먼저, 그 다음에 마침

2 동사를 –ing 형태로 만들어 연결하기

–ing는 어느 하나에 '집중'하기 때문에, 보다 생생한 시각적인 느낌을 줍니다. '형용사'의 역할을 하기도 하고, '명사'로 쓰이기도 합니다. 명사 자리에 –ing가 오면 보통 '~하는 것'으로 해석되는 경우가 많습니다.

> We're interested in <u>working</u> with you.   저희는 귀하와 함께 <u>일하는 것</u>에 관심이 있습니다.

3 동사원형으로 연결하기

끝으로 영어에는 예외적인 것들이 있습니다. 본동사 뒤에 오는 두 번째 동사가 to도 –ing도 아닌 원형이 오는 경우도 있습니다.

> Don't make me cry.   날 울리지 말아요.

to ~와 –ing가 모두 가능한 경우도 있고요.

> I'll help you to do it. = I'll help you do it.   네가 그것 <u>하는 거</u> 도와줄게.

각각의 동사를 큰 틀에서 기억하고 구사하되, 예외적이거나 사용이 낯선 것들은 자주 쓰는 것들부터 일단 많이 접하고 연습하여 습관적으로 쓸 수 있게 익히는 것을 권합니다.

Unit 043

to부정사(1)

I need to stop and think about this for a minute.
난 이 문제에 대해서 잠시 멈추고 생각할 필요가 있어.

1 다음 동사들 뒤에는 to ~가 온다.

> afford agree* appear arrange attempt claim
> decide* demand deserve expect* fail forget*
> guarantee hesitate hope* learn* manage
> mean* need* neglect offer* plan* prepare
> pretend promise* refuse* seem tend threaten
> train try* want* would like*

+ to ~

* 표시 단어들은 이미 Basic에서 소개되었습니다. 이 단어들이 익숙하지 않다면 먼저 익힌 뒤에 나머지 단어들을 학습하는 것을 권합니다.

보통 동사 → to ~ 로의 시간적 순서를 따른다.

> We agreed to be just friends.
>   ①   ②
> to ~는 앞으로 있을 미래를 암시
> 사건의 시간적 순서가 ① → ②
> 우리는 그냥 친구가 되기로(지내기로) 했다.

▶ He can't **afford to buy** a car. 그는 차를 살 형편이 못 된다.
▶ Don't **attempt to change** everything at once. 모든 것을 한 번에 **바꾸려고 시도하지** 마라.
▶ Have you **arranged to meet** him this Friday? 이번 주 금요일에 그를 **만나기로 하셨나요**?
▶ You **deserve to win**. 넌 이길 자격이 돼.
▶ We **expected to finish** by 4:00p.m. 우리는 오후 4시까지는 **끝낼 것으로 예상했습니다**.
▶ We **guarantee to deliver** your order within five days. 우리는 주문하신 것을 5일 안에 **배송할 것을 보장합니다**.
▶ Don't **hesitate to ask** me for help. 제게 **주저 말고** 도움을 **청하세요**.
▶ We're **hoping to find** a cheaper option. 우리는 보다 싼 선택을 **찾기를 희망하고** 있습니다.
▶ I **managed to get** to the station in time. 나는 겨우 제시간에 역에 **도착했다**.
▶ I **need to stop and think** about this for a minute. 난 이 문제에 대해서 잠시 **멈추고 생각할 필요가 있어**.
▶ He **neglected to pay** the rent last month. 그는 지난 달 집세를 **내는 것을 깜박했다**.
▶ We're **preparing to move** our office. 우리는 사무실을 옮길 준비 중이다.
▶ They **refused to help** me. 그들은 나를 **돕는 것을 거절했다**.
▶ My uncle **tends to repeat** the same stories when he is drunk.
  우리 삼촌은 술에 취하면 같은 얘기를 **반복하는 경향이 있다**.
▶ My landlord is **threatening to take** legal action if I don't pay her this week.
  집주인이 이번 주에 내가 돈을 내지 않으면 법적인 조치를 **취하겠다고 위협하고 있다**.
▶ She's **training to be** a pilot now. 그녀는 지금 비행사가 **되는 훈련 중이다**.

to ~ 앞에 not을 더해 부정의 의미를 나타낼 수 있다.

▶ They **agreed not to work** after 6:00 p.m. 그들은 오후 6시 이후에 **일하지 않기로 합의했다**.
▶ He **promised not to waste** money. 그는 돈을 **낭비하지 않겠다고 약속했다**.

2 to be -ing와 to have p.p.로 진행 중이거나 이전에 있었던 사건임을 나타낼 수 있다.
주로 seem, pretend 등의 동사 뒤에서 쓰임

▶ The wifi seems **to be working** now. 와이파이가 이제 **작동하고 있는 것 같다**.
▶ The farmer claimed **to have seen** a U.F.O. 그 농부는 U.F.O.를 **보았다고 주장했다**.

114

Exercises

1. 보기에서 동사를 골라 적절한 형태로 바꾸어 문장을 완성하세요.

   | afford guarantee claim threaten neglect seem wait |

   1. We __guarantee__ to refund your money if you're not satisfied with your purchase.
   2. Don't _____ to vote in any elections.
   3. There _____ to be an error here.
   4. Are you _____ to use the bathroom?
   5. We can't _____ to miss this opportunity.
   6. The hackers are _____ to erase all the data on the hard disk.
   7. North Korea _____ to have succeeded in nuclear fusion.

2. 주어진 표현들에서 적절한 표현을 골라 to로 연결하여 문장을 완성하세요.

1. ~~What time have you arranged~~	a. be in his early thirties.
2. He offered	b. fix the TV but failed.
3. I believe I deserve	c. be happy.
4. They agreed **to**	d. ~~meet her?~~
5. He attempted	e. buy me a drink, but I refused.
6. Sorry. I didn't mean	f. give us more time.
7. The man appeared	g. hurt your feelings.

   1. _What time have you arranged to meet her?_
   2. _____
   3. _____
   4. _____
   5. _____
   6. _____
   7. _____

✦ Dialogue

3. 주어진 단어를 이용하여 문맥에 맞게 문장을 완성하세요. 필요하면 동사 형태를 바꾸세요.

   Sarah is talking about her boyfriend. Sarah가 자신의 남자친구에 대해 이야기하고 있습니다.

   Sarah _____ (My boyfriend, forget, tend, to, dates).

   Amy Forget dates?

   Sarah Yes. He forgot our 50th day anniversary last time.

   Amy Uh-huh.

   Sarah I was so disappointed. Then _____
   (he, to, not, promise, forget, our 100th day anniversary), but he did.

   Amy Maybe he's just too busy?

   Sarah I guess so. I just hope he won't forget our 111th day anniversary.

Unit 044

to부정사(2)

I told him to call back later.
나는 그에게 나중에 전화해 달라고 말했다.

1 동사 뒤에 대상이 오는 경우 동사 + 대상 + to~ 의 순서로 말한다. `대상이 to ~ 하기를 ~하다`

> ask* advise* allow* enable encourage force get
> invite need* order* persuade* remind tell* warn

* 표시 단어들은 이미 Basic에서 소개되었습니다. 이 단어들이 익숙하지 않다면 먼저 익힌 뒤에 나머지 단어들을 학습하는 것을 권합니다.

주어	동사	대상(목적어)	to~
I	told	him	to call back later

나는 그에게 나중에 전화해 달라고 말했다.

- She **advised me to contact** you. 그녀가 당신한테 **연락하라고** 제게 조언했습니다.
- My parents never **allow me to stay** out late. 우리 부모님은 내가 늦게까지 밖에 **있는 것을** 절대 허락하지 않으신다.
- This app **enables you to watch** live TV. 이 앱은 라이브 TV를 볼 수 있게 해 줍니다.
- He **encouraged me to apply** to the company. 그는 내가 그 회사에 **지원하도록** 격려했다.
- Don't **force me to eat** this and that. 나한테 이거 저거 먹으라고 강요하지 마.
- Dad always **gets me to try** something new. 아빠는 내가 항상 뭔가 새로운 것을 **시도하게 한다**. *See Unit 040▶*
- They **invited me to go** to Vancouver with them. 그들은 내게 그들과 함께 밴쿠버에 가자고 초대했다.
- I **asked her to call** on Monday. 저는 그녀에게 월요일에 전화해 달라고 요청했습니다.
- He **warned me to stop**. 그는 내게 멈추라고 경고했다.

---

2 동사에 따라 뒤에 대상 없이 쓰일 수도 있고 대상이 올 수도 있다. `자동사도 되고 타동사도 되는 동사`

> ask* beg choose expect mean want would like

- He **expects to leave** Manchester United soon. 그는 맨체스터 유나이티드를 곧 떠날 거라고 예상된다.
- Many people **expect him to leave** Manchester United soon.
  많은 사람들이 그가 곧 맨체스터 유나이티드를 떠날 것으로 예상한다.

- I **chose to do** it. 나는 그것을 하기로 선택했다.
- They **chose her to do** it. 그들은 그녀가 그 일을 하도록 선택했다.

---

3 to ~ 앞에 not을 넣어 부정의 의미를 나타낸다. `대상이 to ~ 하지 않기를 ~하다`

주어	동사	대상(목적어)	not	to~
I	told	him	not	to call back later

나는 그에게 나중에 전화하지 말라고 말했다.

- He **advised me not to buy** the car. 그는 내게 그 차를 사지 말라고 조언했다.
- The judge **ordered him not to drive**. 판사는 그에게 운전하지 말라고 명령했다.

단, want나 need 같이 to ~ 앞에 not을 쓰지 않는 경우도 있다.
- I **don't want you to leave**. 나는 네가 떠나는 것을 원치 않는다.
  I want you not to leave. (X)
- I **didn't need you to tell** me what to do. 나는 네가 내게 뭘 할지 말해 줄 필요가 없었다.

Exercises

1. 주어진 단어를 맞는 순서대로 배열하여 문장을 완성하세요.
   1. (I / do that / ask / you / to / didn't)   *I didn't ask you to do that.*
   2. (wear jeans / at work / to / doesn't / Our boss / allow / us)   _____
   3. (What / expecting / you / are / them / to / do / ?)   _____
   4. (Mr. Cruz / his students / to / gets / think critically)   _____
   5. (you / remind / Can / at the supermarket / me / to / buy toilet paper)   _____
   6. (use a smartphone / persuade / I'm / my grandmother / to / trying / to)   _____
   7. (take a few days off / The doctor / to / me / advised)   _____
   8. (to / call back later / me / He / told)   _____

2. 문장의 틀린 부분이 있다면 고쳐서 다시 쓰세요. 고칠 부분이 없다면 X를 쓰세요.
   1. He advised me to not buy the car.   *He advised me not to buy the car.*
   2. My parents chose him be my godfather.   _____
   3. I warned her not to trust him.   _____
   4. I wanted him not to know about it.   _____
   5. The police officer ordered me not leave my house.   _____
   6. Don't expect to learn a language overnight.   _____

Dialogue

3. 주어진 단어를 맞는 순서대로 배열하여 문장을 완성하세요.

   Eugene is talking to one of his apartment mates, Nate.
   Eugene은 아파트 메이트 중 하나인 Nate와 이야기하고 있습니다.

   Nate _____ (to, seem, have something, You) on your mind.

   Eugene Yes, Nate, I do.

   Nate What is it?

   Eugene _____ (I, you, need, be, more considerate, to) about the amount of time you spend in the shower.

   Nate Uh...

   Eugene I don't know what you're doing in the shower for fifty minutes every morning, but there are five of us sharing this apartment, and we've got only two bathrooms.

   Nate Sorry. I never realized that I was spending that much time in the shower.

Unit 045

to부정사 패턴(1)

I just called to say hello.
그냥 안부 인사하려고 전화했어.

---

1 to ~는 '목적이나 이유'를 나타낼 수 있다: V to V (동사 to 동사) See Unit 094 ▶

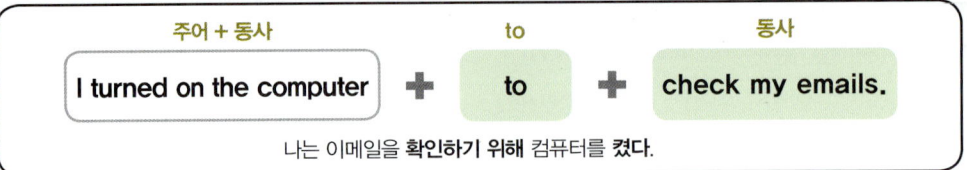

나는 이메일을 확인하기 위해 컴퓨터를 켰다.

- I just **called to say** hello. 그냥 안부 **인사하려고** 전화했어.
- He **got up** early **to catch** the morning train. 그는 아침 기차를 타기 위해 일찍 **일어났다**.

in order to를 쓰기도 한다. See unit 094 ▶

- He retired **in order to spend** more time with his children. 그는 자녀들과 좀 더 시간을 **보내기 위해** 은퇴했다.

'~하지 않기 위해서'의 의미로 to 앞에 not을 쓸 수 있다.

- We talked quietly **not to** wake the baby. 우리는 아기를 깨우지 **않기 위해** 조용히 얘기했다.

Be동사 뒤에 to ~가 오는 경우, '~하는 것'으로 이해할 수 있다. 명사적 용법

- Her job **is to help** other people. 그녀의 일은 다른 사람들을 **돕는 것이다**.
- The purpose of life **is to live** it. 삶의 목적은 그것을 **살아내는 것이다**.

---

2 to ~는 앞의 명사를 꾸며줄 수 있다: N to V (명사 to 동사) 보통 '동사'할 '명사'로 해석

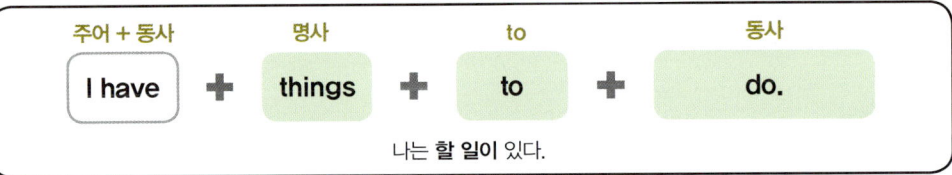

나는 할 일이 있다.

- I couldn't find **time to call** you. 너한테 **전화할 시간**이 나질 않았어.
- It was a great **chance to learn** English. 그것은 영어를 **배우기에** 훌륭한 **기회**였다.

It이나 There 등이 주어일 때 'for+사람'이 to ~ 앞에 쓰일 수 있다.

- It was a great chance **for me to learn** English. 그것은 내가 영어를 **배우기에** 훌륭한 기회였다.
- There were many places **for us to go**. 우리가 갈 곳은 많았다.

what, when, how 등 의문사 뒤에 to ~를 써서 다음과 같이 말할 수도 있다.
주로 ask, advice, decide, show, tell, learn, think 등의 동사 뒤에 쓰임

- I don't know **what to do**. 나는 무엇을 해야 할지 모르겠다.
- Can you tell me **how to delete** this app? 이 앱을 어떻게 지워야 하는지 알려 줄 수 있니?
- I'm thinking **whether to take** a taxi. 나는 택시를 탈지 말지 고민 중이다.

다음 표현들 뒤에 to ~가 자주 쓰인다. 이때 명사가 종종 생략될 수 있다.

> the first/second/last/...   the only   a lot/much/little + to ~

- I promise if anything happens, you'll be **the first** (person) **to know**. 무슨 일이 생기면 너에게 **제일 먼저 알려줄** 거라고 약속할게.
- **The only** thing to fear is yourself. 두려워할 **유일한** 것은 당신 자신이다.
- I have **a lot** (of things) **to say**. 난 할 말이 많다.

Exercises

1. 주어진 표현에서 적절한 표현을 골라 to 또는 not to로 이어 문장을 완성하세요.

	to or not to	
1. He's studying hard		a. pass his exam.
2. She works out at a gym every day		b. demand a pay raise.
3. I need a day off next week		c. miss the train.
4. I left early		d. have the annual check-up.
5. The union went on a strike		e. keep fit.
6. Use a map		f. get lost.

1. _He's studying hard to pass his exam._
2. _____
3. _____
4. _____
5. _____
6. _____

2. 빈칸에 들어갈 가장 적절한 표현을 보기에서 골라 넣어 문장을 완성하세요.

> who   what   when   where   ~~how~~   whether

1. He's learning ___how___ to play the guitar.
2. It's always hard for me to decide _____ to make for dinner.
3. She didn't know _____ to laugh or cry.
4. I set my cellphone timer to know _____ to stop.
5. Have you decided _____ to vote for?
6. Have you decided _____ to go?

3. 문장의 틀린 부분이 있다면 고쳐서 다시 쓰세요. 고칠 부분이 없다면 X를 쓰세요.

1. I don't have time for argue with you.   _I don't have time to argue with you._
2. He asked someone to bring a chair to sit on for me.   _____
3. Mr. Branson is always the last person to leave the office.   _____
4. My dream is to become a successful YouTuber.   _____
5. I don't have much say, but thank you very much.   _____

✦ Dialogue

4. 주어진 단어를 맞는 순서대로 배열하여 문장을 완성하세요.

Sia has been invited to go bowling, but she's going to class.
Sia는 볼링 치러 가자고 초대받았지만 그녀는 수업을 가기로 되어 있습니다.

Colleague   We're going bowling after work. Do you want to join us?

Sia   Sounds good but not today. I'm going to class.

Colleague   What class?

Sia   _____ (I, learn, how, to, perform CPR).

Colleague   CPR? Sounds interesting, but … why?

Sia   Well, I just wanted to learn. You know, someday it may be one of my family members that need help.

* CPR(Cardiopulmonary Resuscitation) 심폐소생술

Unit 046

to부정사 패턴(2)

She is fun to be with.
그녀는 함께 어울리기에 재미있는 사람이야.

---

1 to ~는 형용사를 꾸며줄 수 있다. : to ~하기에 형용사하다. *to ~가 형용사를 꾸며주는 부사적 용법*

주어 + 동사 / 형용사 / to / 동사
The problem was + easy + to + solve.
그 문제는 풀기 쉬웠어요.

▶ The town is **dangerous to go** out at night. 그 동네는 밤에 나가기엔 위험하다.
▶ She is **fun to be** with. 그녀는 함께 어울리기에 재미있는 사람이야.

---

2 'It's+형용사+to ~'로도 말할 수 있다. : to ~하는 것은 형용사하다.

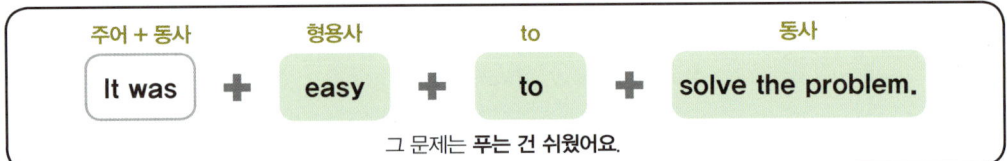

주어 + 동사 / 형용사 / to / 동사
It was + easy + to + solve the problem.
그 문제는 푸는 건 쉬웠어요.

▶ **It is dangerous to go** out at night in this town. 이 동네에서 밤에 나가는 것은 위험하다.
▶ **Is it impossible to** live forever? 영원히 사는 것은 불가능한가요?

'for+사람'이 to ~ 앞에 올 수 있다.
▶ It was easy **for me to solve** the problem. (=The problem was easy **for me to solve**.)
그 문제를 푸는 건 내게 쉬웠다.

---

3 'It's+형용사+of+사람+to ~'는 형용사를 강조한다.

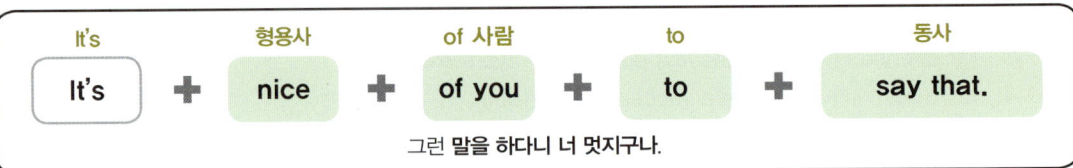

It's / 형용사 / of 사람 / to / 동사
It's + nice + of you + to + say that.
그런 말을 하다니 너 멋지구나.

▶ It was really **generous of them to forgive** the thief. 그 도둑을 용서하다니 그들은 정말 너그러웠어.
▶ It's **unfair of him to blame** her. 그가 그녀를 원망하다니 불공평해.

---

4 to ~는 감정을 나타내는 형용사의 이유나 원인 등을 나타낼 수 있다. : to ~하여 형용사하다.

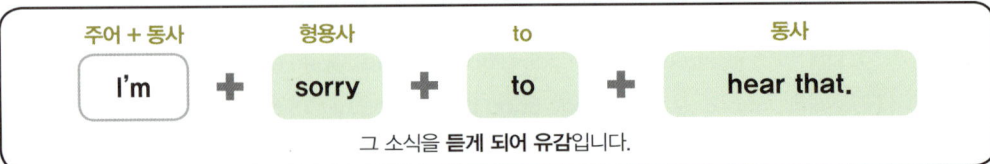

주어 + 동사 / 형용사 / to / 동사
I'm + sorry + to + hear that.
그 소식을 듣게 되어 유감입니다.

▶ I was **surprised to know** that. 나는 그 사실에 대해 알게 되어 놀랐다.
▶ We're **happy to be** back. 우리는 돌아와서 기뻐요.

---

5 Be sure/likely/certain/bound to ~는 미래에 그럴 확률이 높다는 의미로 쓰이는 표현이다.

▶ His new business **is sure to** be successful. 그의 새 사업은 확실히 성공할 것이다.
▶ Who **is most likely to** win the Oscar this year? 올해 오스카상을 탈 확률이 가장 높은 사람은 누구일까?

Exercises

1. 주어진 표현들을 문맥에 맞게 연결하여 문장을 완성하세요.

   1. Suzi is fun — a. to be with.
   2. It's impossible — b. of you to invite us.
   3. We're delighted — c. to be late for an interview.
   4. The video was not appropriate — d. for me to leave now.
   5. It's very kind — e. to break out this year.
   6. Trade war is very likely — f. to launch our new website.
   7. It would be terrible — g. for children to watch.
   8. Pleased — h. to meet you.

2. 주어진 단어를 맞는 순서대로 배열하여 문장을 완성하세요.

   1. (difficult / drive / on a rainy day / to / It / is)   *It's difficult to drive on a rainy day.*
   2. (eat / are / to / Some wild berries / dangerous)
   3. (of / It / the whole cake / eat / was / you / selfish / to)
   4. (me / It / read / is / hard / for / to / your handwriting)
   5. (I / was / the dentist / to / go / to / scared)
   6. (is / everyone / The news / make / sure / happy / to)

🔊 Dialogue

3. 주어진 단어를 맞는 순서대로 배열하여 문장을 완성하세요.

Sarah went on a blind date yesterday. Amy wants to know about it.
Sarah는 어제 소개팅을 했습니다. Amy는 소개팅에 대해 알고 싶어 합니다.

Amy How was your blind date?

Sarah The guy was a terrible complainer.

Amy Why? Tell me.

Sarah We met at Golden Grill, my favorite restaurant, and he complained about everything. First, he complained that the air conditioning in the restaurant wasn't cool enough.

Amy Well, it's kind of true that Golden Grill's air conditioning system is quite old. I think it's quite understandable.

Sarah That's not all. He kept finding fault with everything I wanted to order. He said meat dishes isn't healthy, _____ (is, eat, seafood, unsafe, to, in the summer), and fried chicken is fattening… I ended up just having salad.

Amy Oh, dear…

Unit 047

-ing(1)
I miss working with you.
여러분하고 일했던 것이 그리워요.

1 다음 동사들 뒤에는 -ing가 온다.

> avoid   can't help   can't stand   carry on
> consider   delay   deny   dislike   enjoy*   finish*
> involve   justify   keep   like   mind*
> miss   postpone   practice   put off
> regret   risk   suggest*

+ **-ing**

* 표시 단어들은 이미 Basic에서 소개되었습니다. 이 단어들이 익숙하지 않다면 먼저 익힌 뒤에 나머지 단어들을 학습하는 것을 권합니다.

▸ Don't **avoid making** mistakes. 실수하는 것을 피하지 마세요.
▸ I **can't help falling** in love with you. 그대와 사랑에 안 빠질래야 안 빠질 수가 없어요.
▸ I **can't stand waiting** for people. 나는 사람 기다리는 거 못 견디겠어요.
▸ You can **carry on working** without me. 저 없이 계속해서 작업하셔도 돼요.
▸ She **considered transferring** to another school. 그녀는 다른 학교로 옮기는 것을 고려했다.
▸ He often **delays making** decisions. 그는 자주 결정하는 것을 미룬다.
▸ He **denied lying**. 그는 거짓말했다는 것을 부정했다.
▸ I've just **finished doing** the laundry. 난 방금 빨래를 끝냈다.
▸ Her job **involves filing** and **organizing** meetings. 그녀의 일은 파일 정리와 회의를 준비하는 것을 포함한다.
▸ You can't **justify cheating**. 부정행위를 정당화할 순 없어.
▸ I don't **mind eating** alone. 전 혼자 식사하는 거 괜찮아요.
▸ I **miss working** with you. 여러분하고 일했던 것이 그리워요.
▸ **Practice interviewing** with a friend. 친구와 인터뷰하는 것을 연습하세요.
▸ Do you **regret coming** with me? 나랑 온 것 후회하니?
▸ He doesn't want to **risk losing** money. 그는 돈을 잃는 위험을 감수하길 원하지 않는다.
▸ I **suggested waiting** and **going** another day. 나는 기다렸다가 다른 날에 가자고 제안했다.

2 -ing는 명사처럼 쓰일 수 있다. 문장에서 명사 자리에 쓰임

- I like sports. 나는 스포츠를 좋아한다.
- I **like swimming**. 나는 수영을 좋아한다.

-ing는 문장의 주어로도 쓰일 수 있다.

▸ **Studying** in the morning is difficult for me. 아침에 공부하는 것은 제게 어려워요. ─ing가 주어일 때 동사는 단수를 쓴다.

전치사 뒤에도 -ing 형태를 쓴다.

▸ We're interested **in working** with you. 저희는 귀하와 일하는 것에 관심이 있습니다.
▸ I'll look forward **to seeing** you next week. 다음 주에 뵙기를 기대하겠습니다.

by -ing는 '~함으로써'라는 의미이다.

▸ You can change laws **by voting**. 투표를 함으로써 법을 바꿀 수 있다.
▸ **By using** this app, I edited a lot of photos. 이 앱을 써서 저는 많은 사진을 편집했습니다.

Exercises

1. 주어진 표현 중 맞는 표현을 골라 문장을 완성하세요.

1. I considered (to call / **calling**) him, but I decided it was better to write.
2. You deserve to (be paid / being paid) more.
3. You can't justify (to cheat / cheating).
4. Her job involves (to make / making) contact with the media.
5. Is Mr. Branson busy? OK, I don't mind (to wait / waiting) for a few minutes.
6. Will they agree (to give / giving) us discount?
7. May I suggest (to postpone / postponing) the meeting until Friday?
8. When mom opened the door, I pretended (to be / being) asleep.
9. Can I join you later? I need to finish (to write / writing) this report.
10. If you don't decide soon, you risk (to lose / losing) the opportunity.

2. 빈칸에 들어갈 가장 적절한 동사를 보기에서 골라 –ing 형태로 넣어 문장을 완성하세요.

> buy   crash   do   ~~draw~~   leave   make   sleep   work

1. Children usually enjoy _drawing_ .
2. I'm interested in _____ stock.
3. My computer keeps _____ .
4. Don't be afraid of _____ mistakes when you speak English.
5. _____ too much makes you tired.
6. I'm fed up with _____ the same thing every day.
7. He still regrets _____ her.
8. By _____ together, we can and will make the world a better place.

◆ Dialogue

3. 주어진 동사를 적절한 형태로 바꿔 넣어 문장을 완성하세요.

Andy has just got his exam grade and he's not happy about it.
Andy는 시험 점수를 막 받았는데, 즐겁지가 않습니다.

Jay   Andy, why are you sighing?

Andy   It's because of my calculus class.

Jay   What's wrong with it?

Andy   I just got my midterm exam grade and it wasn't great. It was a C.

Jay   If you're worried about _____ (fail) the class, why don't you get a tutor?

Andy   How can I get a tutor?

Jay   Well… You know what? I'm pretty good at math. I think I can help you.

Unit 048

-ing(2)

They just went on working.
그들은 그저 계속해서 일만 했다.

1 다음 표현들 뒤에도 –ing가 온다.

> give up   go on   keep (on)   put off
> look forward to   can't help
> **+** –ing

- They just **went on working**. 그들은 그저 계속해서 일만 했다.
- He **kept (on) looking** at the clock during the meeting. 그는 회의 중에 계속 시계를 보았다.
- She **put off calling** the plumber until the leak got really bad.
  그녀는 물이 새는 것이 정말 심해질 때까지 배관공을 부르는 것을 미루었다.
- She **couldn't help crying**. 그녀는 안 울래야 안 울 수가 없었다.

> spend time/money (on)   have a good/hard time   waste time
> It's no use   have trouble/difficulty   It's (not) worth
> There's no point (in) (It's) a waste of time/money
> **+** –ing

- We **had a good time talking** with her. 우리는 그녀와 이야기를 나누며 즐거운 시간을 보냈다.
- It's **no use complaining**. 불평하는 건 소용이 없다.
- **There's no point arguing** with him. 그 사람이랑 언쟁하는 것은 아무 의미가 없다.
- The movie **was not worth paying** for. 그 영화는 돈을 낼 가치가 없었다.

(be) busy 뒤에도 –ing가 올 수 있다.
- I'm sorry I didn't answer your call. I was **busy driving**. 전화 못 받아서 미안해. 운전하느라 바빴어.

2 –ing 앞에 **not**을 더해 부정의 의미를 나타낼 수 있다.
- She suggested **not leaving** early today. 그녀는 오늘 일찍 떠나지 말자고 제안했다.

3 동사와 –ing 사이에 대상이 올 수도 있다: 대상이 to ~ 하기를 ~하다 `타동사`
- I can't **imagine him dancing**. 그가 춤추는 건 상상할 수가 없어.
- Sorry to **keep you waiting**. 계속 기다리게 해서 미안해요.
- I **don't mind them staying** here. 저는 그들이 여기 머무는 것 괜찮아요.

4 여러 가지 다양한 활동에 대해 **go –ing**로 말할 수 있다.
- They **go skiing** in Colorado every winter. 그들은 겨울마다 콜로라도로 스키를 타러 간다.

5 **having p.p.**를 써서 이미 끝난 사건이나 활동임을 강조할 수 있다. `-ing로 써도 됨`
- I **regret having said** no to them. (= I **regret saying** no to them.) 그들에게 아니라고 말한 것을 후회해.
- He **admitted having cheated** on the test. (= He **admitted cheating** on the test.)
  그는 시험에서 부정행위를 한 것을 인정했다.

6 'It's 형용사+–ing'는 주로 격식 없는 대화체에서 경험이나 상황에 대해 말할 때 종종 쓰일 수 있다.
- **It was nice meeting** you again. 다시 만나게 되어 반가웠습니다.

Exercises

1. 빈 칸에 들어갈 가장 적절한 동사를 보기에서 골라 –ing 형태로 넣어 문장을 완성하세요.

   cry   develop   replace   shout   ~~sing~~   wait   yawn

   1. Everybody had a good time ___singing___ Christmas carols.
   2. Don't put off _____ your tires.
   3. I don't want to waste my time _____ for their reply.
   4. She's always calm and composed. I can't imagine her _____ at others.
   5. I was so sleepy. I just couldn't help _____.
   6. They spent a lot of money _____ a new website.
   7. It's no use _____ over spilt milk.

2. 주어진 표현을 문맥에 맞게 연결하여 문장을 완성하세요.

   1. Do you regret   a. me sitting here?
   2. Have you ever had trouble b. to going home?
   3. Where did you go   c. working now?
   4. Do you mind   d. not having gone to the parties?
   5. Are you looking forward   e. sleeping?
   6. Are you busy   f. skiing last winter?

3. 주어진 단어를 맞는 순서대로 배열하여 문장을 완성하세요.

   1. (worth / was / watching / The video / not)   ___The video was not worth watching.___
   2. (can't / me / You / staying / here / keep)   _____
   3. (I / it / anymore / not / suggested / about / arguing)   _____
   4. (this afternoon / I / shopping / with / went / Mom)   _____

Dialogue

4. to meet 또는 meeting을 넣어 대화문 속의 문장을 완성하세요.

Sia is at a conference reception.
Sia는 컨퍼런스 접수처에 있습니다.

Sia   Hello. My name's Sia Turner. Nice _____ you.
Steve Nice _____ you, too, Ms. Turner. I'm Steve Burns. Which branch do you come from? I'm from Toronto, Canada.
Sia   I'm from the headquarters.
Steve Oh, you work in London. Do you like working there?
Sia   Yes, I enjoy working in London. I'm sorry, but I see my boss over there and I need to speak with him. Please excuse me.
Steve It's OK. Nice _____ you, Ms. Turner.

Unit 049

to or -ing(1)

I hate being an only child.
나는 외동인 것이 정말 싫다.

1. 다음의 동사 뒤에는 to ~와 -ing가 모두 올 수 있다. 의미의 차이가 거의 없음

> **begin   start   continue   bother   intend**

- She began **to sing**. = She began **singing**. 그녀는 노래를 시작했다.
- I want to continue **to work**. = I want to continue **working**. 저는 계속해서 일하고 싶습니다.
- Don't bother **to knock**. = Don't bother **knocking**. 굳이 노크하지 마세요.

단, 다음과 같은 경우에는 to ~만 사용한다. 동일 구조 반복을 피하기 위함

- It's beginning **to rain**. 비가 오기 시작하고 있어요.

2. 다음의 동사 뒤에도 to ~와 -ing가 모두 올 수 있다.

> **like   love   hate**

- He **hates to drive**. = He **hates driving**. 그는 운전하는 것을 싫어한다.

그러나, 이미 하고 있는 것에 대해 말할 때에는 -ing만을 쓴다.

- Do you **like living** here? 여기 사는 것 좋으세요? 이미 살고 있는 사람에게 묻는 것임
- I **hate being** an only child. 나는 외동인 것이 정말 싫다.

3. and나 or 등으로 이어질 때에는 양쪽의 동사 형태를 같게 한다.

- He doesn't like **walking or riding** a bike to school. 그는 걷거나 자전거를 타고 학교 가는 것을 좋아하지 않는다.
- I like **to plan and attend** meetings. to ~의 경우 종종 생략
  = I like **planning and attending** meetings. 저는 기획하고 회의에 참석하는 것을 좋아합니다.

4. prefer는 다음과 같이 쓸 수 있다.

- prefer 명사 to 명사
  - I prefer **tea to coffee**. 저는 커피보다 차를 더 좋아합니다.

- prefer -ing to -ing
  - Do you prefer **driving to walking**? 당신은 걷는 것보다 운전하는 것을 더 선호하나요?

- prefer to ~ rather than to ~
  - She prefers **to drive rather than walk**. 그녀는 걷는 것보다는 운전을 선호한다.

단, would like/love/prefer 뒤에는 to ~만 쓸 수 있다.

- **Would** you **prefer to have** tea or coffee? 차로 드시겠어요? 아니면 커피로 드시겠어요?

5. would rather는 다음과 같이 말한다.

- **would rather ~ (than ~)**: I'd **rather walk** than run. 나는 뛰느니 차라리 걸을래요.
  I'd **rather not take** a taxi. 나는 차라리 택시를 안 타겠어요.
- **would rather S -ed**: I'd **rather you finished** it today. 오늘 그것을 끝내주셨으면 좋겠습니다.
- **would rather S didn't ~**: I'd **rather she didn't know** about it. 그녀가 차라리 그것에 대해 모르는 게 낫겠어요.

Exercises

1. 밑줄 친 부분이 틀리거나 어색하다면 맞게 또는 자연스럽게 고치세요. 고칠 부분이 없다면 X를 쓰세요.
   1. I love to watch horror movies. ___X___
   2. It's starting getting dark. _____
   3. Don't bother coming back. _____
   4. They continued to sing. _____
   5. Do you like singing and dance? _____
   6. What do you intend to do about it? _____
   7. Would you like coming to dinner tonight? _____
   8. I really like to work here. My boss is a nice person. _____

2. 아래 보기처럼 주어진 표현을 이용하여 문장을 완성하세요.
   1. (tea / coffee)　　　　　　　　　　　　 I prefer __tea to coffee__.
   2. (beer / wine)　　　　　　　　　　　　　 Does he prefer _____?
   3. (listen / speak)　　　　　　　　　　　　 I'd rather _____.
   4. (shop online / go to a store)　　　　　 Many people prefer _____.
   5. (have a private tutor / learn in a large classroom) Would you prefer _____?

3. 주어진 단어를 맞는 순서대로 배열하여 문장을 완성하세요.

   1. (than / have a cat / a dog / I'd / rather)　　__I'd rather have a cat than a dog.__
   2. (I'd / became / a scientist / she / rather)　　_____
   3. (not / say / anything / rather / I'd)　　_____
   4. (rather / you / I'd / anything / didn't / say)　　_____

🔊 Dialogue

4. 주어진 표현 중 맞는 표현을 골라 문장을 완성하세요.

It's starting to rain. Amy and Andy have decided not to go out.
비가 오기 시작합니다. Amy와 Andy는 나가지 않기로 결정했습니다.

Amy　Uh-oh. It's starting (raining / to rain).

Andy　It is? Then, why don't we just stay home?

Amy　Good idea. Let's just watch a movie online.

Andy　Alright. What kind of movie would you like, action or romance?

Amy　I'd prefer (seeing / to see) some action movie today.

Andy　How about the new Z Men movie?

Unit 050

to or -ing(2)

I clearly remember talking about it.
난 그것에 대해 얘기한 것 분명히 기억해요.

1 다음 동사들은 두 가지 형태로 쓰일 수 있다.

| advise | allow | encourage | permit | recommend | require | urge |

▶ I wouldn't **advise buying** a used car. 나는 중고차를 사라고 조언하지는 않겠어.	▶ I wouldn't **advise you to buy** a used car. 나는 네게 중고차를 사라고 조언하지는 않겠어.
(수동태: Buying a used car is not advised.)	(수동태: You're not advised to buy a used car.)
▶ They don't **allow smoking** in this building. 이 건물에서 흡연하는 것을 허락하진 않아.	▶ They don't **allow people to smoke** in this building. 이 건물에서 사람들이 흡연하는 것을 허락하진 않아.
(수동태: Smoking is not allowed in this building.)	(수동태: You're not allowed to smoke in this building.)
▶ Many experts **encourage eating** healthy food. 많은 전문가들이 건강한 음식을 먹을 것을 권장한다.	▶ Many experts **encourage people to eat** healthy food. 많은 전문가들이 사람들에게 건강한 음식을 먹으라고 권장합니다.
(수동태: Eating healthy food is encouraged.)	(수동태: You're encouraged to eat healthy food.)
▶ This position **requires working** nights. 이 일자리는 야간 근무를 요구합니다.	▶ This position **requires you to work** nights. 이 일자리는 당신이 야간 근무 하는 것을 요구합니다.
(수동태: Working nights is required.)	(수동태: You're required to work nights.)

2 다음 동사들은 의미에 따라 쓰이는 형태가 다르다.

▶ I clearly **remember talking** about it. 난 그것에 대해 **얘기한 것** 분명히 **기억해요**.	▶ **Remember to talk** about it later. 나중에 그것에 대해 **얘기하는 거 기억하세요**.
▶ I didn't get your text message because I **forgot turning off** my cell phone. 휴대폰을 꺼 놓은 걸 잊어서 네 문자 메시지를 못 받았어.	▶ I'm sorry I **forgot to turn off** my cell phone. 죄송합니다. 휴대폰 꺼 놓는 것을 잊었네요.
▶ **Stop talking**! 그만 떠들어!	▶ We **stopped to talk** for a while. 우리는 잠시 이야기하기 위해 멈추었다.
▶ Why don't you **try using** a different app? 다른 앱을 써 보지 그래?	▶ **Try to use** polite words. 예의 바른 표현을 쓰도록 노력하세요.
▶ I **regret telling** him the truth. 나는 그에게 사실을 말한 것을 후회해.	▶ We **regret to tell you** that your flight has been canceled. 귀하의 비행편이 취소되었다는 사실을 알려드리게 되어 유감입니다.
▶ He **went on explaining** the details. 그는 계속해서 세부사항을 설명했다.	▶ He introduced the topic and **went on to explain** the details. 그는 주제를 소개하고 세부사항 설명으로 넘어갔다.

3 동사 need는 다음과 같이 쓸 수 있다.

❶ **need to ~**: ~할 필요가 있다 `대체로 주어가 사람`

▶ You **need to get** some sleep. 넌 잠 좀 잘 필요가 있어.

❷ **need to be p.p. = need -ing**: …에게 ~가 필요하다 `주어가 받는(수동) 입장`

▶ My smartphone **needs to be charged** again. = My smartphone **needs charging** again.
내 스마트폰은 또 충전이 필요하다.
▶ The dog **needs to be washed**. = The dog **needs washing**. 그 개는 씻길 필요가 있다.
▶ The players **need to be trained**. = The players **need training**. 선수들은 훈련이 필요하다.

Exercises

1. 아래 보기처럼 문장을 다시 써 보세요.

1. I wouldn't advise you to buy a used car. → _I wouldn't advise buying a used car._
2. I would advise you to visit their website. → _____
3. The landlord doesn't allow you to paint the walls. → _____
4. I wouldn't advise you to buy from this seller. → _____
5. We encourage you to apply as early as possible. → _____
6. Most American colleges require you to take one of the most common tests, the SAT or the ACT. → _____

2. 문장의 문맥에 가장 적합한 표현을 골라 문장을 완성하세요.

1. Stop (to talk /(talking)).
2. I don't remember (to say / saying) anything like that.
3. We stopped in London for two days (to meet / meeting) Sia and Mike.
4. I'm sorry I forgot (to call / calling) you, but I was really busy.
5. We regret (to announce / announcing) the death of Prof. Zach Barclay.
6. Why don't you try (to talk / talking) to her? Maybe she'll change her mind.
7. Frist, I'll tell you about the history of our academy, then I'll go on (to explain / explaining) our courses.
8. I regret (to quit / quitting) my PhD.
9. The soldiers went on (to fight / fighting) even though they were wounded.
10. I've been trying (to lose / losing) weight for weeks, but nothing seems to work.

3. 주어진 동사를 적절한 형태로 바꿔 넣어 문장을 완성하세요.

1. The office needs to _be cleaned_ (clean).
2. The office needs _____ (clean).
3. You need to _____ (cut) your nails.
4. The batteries in the radio need _____ (change).
5. His car needs to _____ (repair).

🔊 Dialogue

4. 주어진 표현 중 가장 적합한 표현을 골라 문장을 완성하세요.

Naomi has just spilled some coffee on her shirt. Naomi는 방금 셔츠에 커피를 쏟았습니다.

- **Jessica** Why are you so upset?
- **Naomi** I just spilled a drop of coffee on my shirt.
- **Jessica** Oh dear. Can I have a look?
- **Naomi** Do you know how to get rid of coffee stains?
- **Jessica** Why don't you try (to use / using) some lemon juice on the stain?
- **Naomi** Lemon juice? Does it work on coffee stains?

Unit 051

to or -ing(3)

We agreed to meet again next week.
우리는 다음 주에 다시 만나는 것에 동의했다.

1 동사에 따라 뒤에 다양한 구조가 올 수 있다.

❶ agree, claim, decide 등

동사+(that) S+V	동사+to ~ *See unit 043*
▶ Everybody **agrees that** money isn't everything. 돈이 전부가 아니라는 것에 모두가 **동의한다**.	▶ We **agreed to meet** again next week. 우리는 다음 주에 다시 **만나는** 것에 동의했다.
▶ I **decided that** I want to study music. 나는 음악을 공부하고 **싶다고** 결정했다.	▶ I **decided to go** to New York. 나는 뉴욕으로 **가기로** 결정했다.

❷ tell, encourage, warn 등

동사+대상+(that) S+V	동사+대상+to ~ *See unit 044*
▶ I **told him that** I was all right. 나는 그에게 나는 **괜찮다고** 말했다.	▶ I **told you to be** here. 내가 너에게 여기 **오라고** 했잖아.
▶ She **warned me that** the oven was still hot. 그녀는 내게 오븐이 아직도 **뜨겁다고** 경고했다.	▶ She **warned me not to touch** the oven. 그녀는 내게 오븐을 **만지지 말라고** 경고했다.

❸ admit, deny, suggest 등

동사+(that) S+V	동사+-ing *See unit 047*
▶ You have to **admit that** you were wrong. 넌 네가 **틀렸다는** 것을 인정해야만 해.	▶ I **admitted making** a mistake. 나는 실수를 **했다는** 것을 인정했다.
▶ What do you **suggest** I do? 제가 뭘 해야 **한다고** 제안하시나요?	▶ We **suggest taking** some time to think about it. 우리는 그것에 대해 생각할 시간을 좀 **갖자고** 제안하는 바입니다.

2 'to부정사'와 '전치사 to'의 구분에 유의한다.

- We **used to work** as a team. 우리는 한때 한 팀으로 **일했었다**.
- We**'re used to working** as a team. 우리는 한 팀으로 **일하는** 것에 익숙하다.
- What app **was used to get** this effect? 이 효과를 내기 위해 어떤 앱이 **쓰였죠**?

▶ I **look forward to hearing** from you. 당신으로부터 소식 듣기를 기대하고 있습니다.
I look forward to hear from you. (X)
▶ I **can't afford to stay** in a five-star hotel. 나는 5성급 호텔에 **묵을** 형편이 안 된다.
I can't afford to staying in a five-star hotel. (X)

3 형용사도 뒤에 오는 구조(형태)에 따라 의미가 달라질 수 있다.

- I**'m afraid of losing** my cat. 내 고양이를 잃을까 두려워요.
- Don't be **afraid to ask** questions. 질문을 하는 것을 꺼리지 마세요.

- My brother is **interested in studying** law. 우리 오빠는 법 공부에 관심이 있다.
- I would be **interested to find** out more about it. 저는 그것에 대해 좀 더 **알게 되면** 관심이 갈 것 같아요.

4 to ~의 수동태는 to be p.p.이고, -ing의 수동태는 being p.p.이다. *See unit 037*

Exercises

1. 주어진 단어를 맞는 순서대로 배열하여 문장을 완성하세요.

1. (agrees / money / isn't / Everybody / everything / that)
   → *Everybody agrees that money isn't everything.*

2. (I / going / suggested / for a swim)
   → _____

3. (scared / He / didn't / that / he / was / admit)
   → _____

4. (His teacher / more / him / encouraged / to / read)
   → _____

5. (was / She / time / that / for a change / decided / it)
   → _____

6. (me / that / had seen / a U.F.O. / He / told / he)
   → _____

2. 주어진 동사를 적절한 형태로 바꿔 넣어 문장을 완성하세요.

1. The building used to __*be*__ (be) a church.
2. We look forward to _____ (meet) you soon.
3. Are you used to _____ (use) chopsticks?
4. The house is used to _____ (host) many events.
5. I can't afford to _____ (have) a private tutor.

3. 문장의 문맥에 가장 적합한 표현을 골라 문장을 완성하세요.

1. Are you interested (to learn / ⓘn learning) English?
2. He was afraid (to miss / of missing) the last bus.
3. Everybody was interested (to hear / in hearing) the news.
4. Are you afraid (to be forgotten / of being forgotten)?
5. She's not afraid (to say / of saying) what she thinks.

🔊 Dialogue

4. 보기 중 빈칸에 들어갈 가장 적합한 표현을 골라 문장을 완성하세요.

Andy is having a trouble with his computer.
Andy는 컴퓨터로 곤란을 겪고 있습니다.

Andy This computer doesn't seem to be working.

Ben What's wrong?

Andy It started lagging and then froze.

Ben I suggest (to restart / restarting) the computer. I think that's the only way.

Andy Darn… I regret not saving the file I was working on.

Unit 052

지각동사

I didn't hear my phone ringing.
내 전화기가 울리는 소리 못 들었어요.

1
다음 동사 뒤에는 의미에 따라 동사원형 또는 -ing가 올 수 있다. 감각을 느끼거나 어떤 사실을 알게 되는 의미의 동사(지각동사)

feel hear find listen to
notice see smell watch
— 대상 — V (동사원형) / -ing

I **saw** her **sitting** on the bench.
나는 그녀가 벤치에 앉아 있는 것을 보았다.
그녀가 벤치에 앉아 있던 중에 내가 봄

I **saw** her **fall down**.
나는 그녀가 넘어지는 것을 보았다.
순간적으로 넘어지는 모습을 다 봄

- I didn't **hear** my phone **ringing**. 내 전화기가 울리는 소리 못 들었어요.
- She **found** him **dating** another woman. 그녀는 그가 다른 여자와 데이트하고 있는 것을 발견했다.
- **Listen to** the rain **falling**. 비 내리는 소리를 들어 보렴.
- She **noticed** someone **opening** the door. 그녀는 누군가가 문을 열고 있는 것을 알아챘다.
- I can **smell** something **burning**. 뭔가 타는 냄새가 나.

- (Pregnant woman) I've just **felt** my baby **kick**! 방금 아기가 발로 차는 것을 느꼈어요.
- I think I just **heard** somebody **come in**. 방금 누가 들어오는 소리를 들은 것 같아.
- Everybody **saw** the accident **happen**. 모든 사람들이 사고가 나는 것을 보았다.
- Let's just **watch** them **do** it. 그들이 하는 걸 그냥 지켜보자고.

2
동사 help 뒤에는 동사원형 또는 to ~가 올 수 있다. 의미 차이 없음

- They **helped** us **find** our dog. = They **helped** us **to find** our dog. 그들은 우리가 개를 찾는 것을 도왔다.
- Can you **help** me **do** the dishes? = Can you **help** me **to do** the dishes? 설거지하는 것 좀 도와줄래?

can't help 뒤에는 -ing가 온다. See Unit 048▶

- I **can't help thinking** about it. 그것에 대해 생각을 안 할 수가 없어요.

can't help but ~로도 말할 수 있다.

- I **can't help but think** about it. 그것에 대해 생각을 안 할 수가 없어요.

3
make와 **let** 뒤에는 동사원형이 온다.

- The movie will **make** you **laugh**. 그 영화는 널 웃게 만들 거야.
  단, 수동태에서는 be made to ~ 의 형태가 된다. See Unit 039▶
- I can't **let** you **go**. 난 널 가게 둘 수 없어.

Exercises

1. 문맥에 맞춰 주어진 동사를 적절한 형태로 바꿔 넣어 문장을 완성하세요.
   1. Can you smell something ___burning___ (burn)?
   2. I didn't see him _____ (go) out.
   3. Dad watched me _____ (play) football last Sunday.
   4. He could sense someone _____ (follow) him.
   5. I was so scared. I could feel myself _____ (shake) with fear.
   6. Suddenly he felt something _____ (bite) his ankle.
   7. Have you lost something? I noticed you _____ (look) under the table.
   8. We all saw the sun _____ (rise) on the hill.
   9. I think I heard her _____ (snore) when I walked past her room.
   10. Have you heard the door _____ (bang)?
   11. The police found the suspects _____ (hide) in an abandoned warehouse.
   12. He laughed when he saw me _____ (slip) on the ice.

2. 문장의 틀린 부분이 있다면 고쳐서 다시 쓰세요. 고칠 부분이 없다면 X를 쓰세요.

   1. Please help us find our dog.   ___X___
   2. I couldn't help but to look at his face. _____
   3. Let me taking care of the bill.   _____
   4. I couldn't help laughing at his joke. _____
   5. I'll help you to do your homework.   _____
   6. What made you changed your mind?   _____

🔸 Dialogue

3. 보기 중 가장 적합한 표현을 골라 문장을 완성하세요.

James is asking his neighbor, Mr. Cruz, for a piece of advice.
James는 이웃 Mr. Cruz에게 약간의 조언을 묻고 있습니다.

James   My family is thinking of adopting a dog from a shelter.

Mr. Cruz   Oh. That's great.

James   Is there anything you want to tell us about keeping a dog?

Mr. Cruz   Well, don't let your dog (run / to run / running) around outside. I always take my Max for walks on a leash because he might get run over by a car.

James   That makes sense. I'll keep that in mind.

Unit 053

분사구문

He took a shower, singing loudly.
그는 큰 소리로 노래를 부르며 샤워를 했다.

1 -ing로 시작되는 표현이 문장에 종종 더해질 수 있다. `접속사 S+V로 바꿀 수 있음`

① 동시에 일어나는 동작이나 사건을 덧붙일 때
- I cut myself, **shaving**. 나는 면도를 하다가 베었다. `while -ing와 비슷`
- He took a shower, **singing** loudly. 그는 큰 소리로 노래를 부르며 샤워를 했다.
- We were just sitting there, **doing** nothing. 우리는 아무것도 안 하면서 거기에 그냥 앉아 있었다.

`보통 문장의 뒤에 위치`

② 문장 내용에 뒤따르는 결과나 효과를 덧붙일 때
- Strong acids are dangerous, **causing** severe burns. 강한 산은 위험하며, 심한 화상을 일으킨다.
- Cars are convenient, **making** travel easier. 자동차는 편리하며, 이동을 쉽게 한다.

③ 문장의 내용에 대한 이유나 원인을 덧붙일 때
- **Living** in Alaska, they're used to cold weather.
  알래스카에 살기 때문에 그들은 추운 날씨에 익숙하다.
- **Being** an only child, I felt like a foreigner. 외동이라서 전 이방인처럼 느껴졌어요.
- **Using** apps, you can push out notifications to customers.
  앱을 써서 고객에게 알림을 보낼 수 있다. `by -ing와 비슷`

`주로 문장의 앞에 위치`

④ 직전의 사건이나 행동을 덧붙일 때 `보통 두 개의 짧은 동작/사건이 바로 이어질 때에 쓰임`
- **Sitting** at her desk, she turned on the computer. 그녀는 자리에 앉자 컴퓨터를 켰다. `after -ing로 말할 수 있음`

2 having p.p.는 이전의 상황이나 사건, 행동임을 나타낼 때 쓸 수 있다.
- **Having locked** the door, I went to bed. 문을 잠그고 나서 나는 잠자리에 들었다.
  `보통 둘 사이에 시간 간격이 있음. 이전의 사건/행동 등이 완전히 끝난 뒤에 이후 사건/행동이 이어짐`
- **Having been** there before, I want to go somewhere else this time.
  거기는 전에 가 봤기 때문에 난 이번에는 다른 곳에 가고 싶다.

3 -ing 앞에 not을 더해 부정의 의미를 나타낼 수 있다.
- **Not having** enough money, he had to get a loan. 돈이 충분히 없어서 그는 대출을 받아야 했다.

4 being은 종종 생략될 수 있다.

① (being) 형용사
- **(Being) Both kind and generous**, she always thought of others before herself.
  친절하고 너그러워서 그녀는 항상 자신보다 남을 생각했다.

② (being) p.p. `수동의 의미`
- **(Being) Confused and frightened**, the little girl ran away. 혼란스럽고 겁을 먹어서 소녀는 도망쳤다.

5 -ing는 문장과 주어가 같을 때에 쓸 수 있다. `주어가 다른 경우 주어를 덧붙일 수 있지만, 대화체에서는 매우 드물게 쓰임`
- ~~Sitting at her desk~~, the light went out. → **As soon as** she sat at her desk, the light went out.
  `she가 주어임` 그녀가 자리에 앉자 불이 나갔다.

Exercises

1. 주어진 내용을 적절한 형태로 바꾸어 그림에 맞는 문장을 완성하세요.

1. James was walking around the park.
2. She opened the envelope.
3. The soup made me hungrier.
4. He is always hardworking and honest.
5. I didn't know what to say.
6. She has lived in London.
7. She was surrounded by her fans.

James lost his keys, _walking around the park_.
_____, she found a $10 bill.
The soup smelled good, _____.
_____, he is trusted by everyone.
_____, I kept silence.
_____, she speaks fluent English.
_____, she started singing.

Dialogue

2. 주어진 표현의 동사를 적절한 형태로 바꾸어 문장을 완성하세요.

Dialogue 1

Andy and Amy are talking together. Andy와 Amy가 대화를 하고 있습니다.
Andy My mom and dad asked me the silly question again.
Amy Silly question?
Andy Yes. They asked me who I love more - mom or dad.
Amy Haha. So, did you answer it?
Andy Of course not. I didn't say anything, _____ (not wish to) offend either of them.

Dialogue 2

Sia is doing stretches with her fitness instructor. Sia는 피트니스 강사와 함께 스트레칭을 하고 있습니다.
Instructor Start on all fours with your hands and feet spaced shoulder-width apart.
Sia Uh-huh…
Instructor Push your hips up toward the ceiling. Keep your head between your arms and straighten your legs as much as possible.
Sia Like this?
Instructor Yes. Now press into the floor with your hands, _____ (put pressure) on the calves and hamstrings.

135

Big Picture

명사의 종류와 관사

06

1 명사의 구분

영어 문장 하나하나가 하나의 그림이라고 생각하고 항상 그 구체적인 의미를 머리 속에 떠올리는 것이 영어적 감각을 익히는 좋은 습관이 될 수 있습니다. 명사는 그 그림에 그려 넣어지는 구체적인 대상이라고 할 수 있죠.

영어에서 명사는 다음과 같이 구분합니다.

- 구체적이고 고정적인 형태가 있는 것은 <u>셀 수 있는 명사</u>
- 구체적이고 고정적인 형태가 없어 그리기 애매하거나 추상적인 것들은 <u>셀 수 없는 명사</u>

2 a, the, –s/es

명사 앞에 붙는 a, the 같은 소위 '관사'나 some과 같은 '한정사', 꾸며주는 '형용사' 등은 모두 해당 명사를 구체적으로 그려 주는(표현) 역할을 합니다. 그 중에서도 a, the 나 some 같은 것들은 가장 기본적인 윤곽선을 잡아 준다고 할 수 있는데요. 우선 셀 수 있는 명사는 하나인 것과 여럿인 것이 시각적으로 확연히 구분되기 때문에, 말(문장)에서도 구분해서 표현합니다. <u>하나를 단수, 여럿을 복수</u>라고 합니다.

영어는 불필요한 반복이나 수고를 좋아하지 않습니다. 그래서, 듣는 사람이 그 명사가 무엇인지 이미 안다면, 앞에 the를 쓰는 것으로 반복을 대신합니다. 다만, 셀 수 있는 명사로 여럿(복수)인 경우라면 뒤에 –s/es를 더해 주세요. *See 부록 13* ▶

3 한정사

영어는 또한 모호하거나 막연한 것을 좋아하지 않습니다. 아주 명확하게 못 집어도 범위를 좁혀서라도 어느 정도 구체적으로 말하고자 합니다. 구체적으로 무엇인지 집을 수 없는 일반적인, 다소 막연하게 말하는 명사에 대해서는 다음과 같이 범위를 말해 줄 수 있습니다. *See 부록 14* ▶

- **All** lives are important. <u>모든</u> 생명이 중요합니다.
- **Most** cars have four wheels. <u>대부분의</u> 자동차는 바퀴가 네 개입니다.
- **Some** people don't eat meat. <u>어떤</u> 사람들은 고기를 먹지 않습니다.
- **No** fish have wings. <u>어떤</u> 물고기도 날개를 갖고 있지 <u>않</u>다.

물론 이 표현들은 구체적인 (명사의) 범위 내의 비중을 나타낼 때에도 쓸 수 있습니다.

- **All** my friends live in Korea. 내 <u>모든</u> 친구들은 한국에 살고 있다.
- **Most** of the information from the website is incorrect.
  그 웹사이트의 정보 <u>대부분이</u> 부정확하다.
- He sold **some** of his action figures. 그는 갖고 있는 액션 피규어의 <u>일부를</u> 팔았다.
- **None** of us got hurt. 우리 중 <u>누구도</u> 다치지 <u>않았다</u>.

Unit 054

셀 수 있는 명사/셀 수 없는 명사(1)

I had two slices of bread and a packet of chips for lunch.
나는 점심으로 식빵 두 장과 감자칩 한 봉지를 먹었다.

1 셀 수 있는 명사 = Countable Nouns, 가산명사

❶ 주로 사람, 동물, 식물, 사물을 나타낸다.

- There are **three people** at the bus stop. 버스 정류장에 **세 명의 사람**이 있다.
- She has **two rabbits** and **one cat**. 그녀는 **토끼 두 마리와 고양이 한 마리**가 있어요.
- I bought **ten stamps** at the post office. 나는 우체국에서 **우표 열 장**을 샀습니다.

❷ 명사를 세는 '단위'는 셀 수 있다.

- Can I have **a cup** of coffee? 커피 **한 잔** 주시겠어요?
- Apples are $5 **a kilo**. 사과는 **1킬로그램**에 5달러입니다.

❸ 하나(단수)라는 의미로 앞에 a나 an을 쓸 수 있다. 특정한 것을 말하는 것이 아닌 경우

- There's **a** big **tree** in the back yard. 뒷마당에 큰 나무가 **한 그루** 있다.
- I'll be back in **an hour**. 한 시간 뒤에 돌아올게요. 뒤에 모음으로 시작하는 단어가 올 경우 an을 쓴다.
- I've seen **a U.F.O**. 나는 U.F.O.를 봤어. 영어의 /j/ /ɪ/ /w/ 소리는 자음임에 유의

❹ 여럿(복수)을 의미할 때에는 단어 뒤에 -e/es를 덧붙인다.

- There are many **trees** in the park. 공원에 **나무**가 많다.
- The train will arrive in two **hours**. 기차는 2**시간** 뒤에 도착할 것입니다.
- She's a nanny for two **babies**. 그녀는 2명의 **아기**를 돌보는 보모이다. 자음+y로 끝나는 단어는 y가 ies로 바뀐다.

2 셀 수 없는 명사 = Uncountable Nouns, 불가산명사

❶ 보통 고정적인 형태가 없는 액체, 기체, 덩어리, 추상적 개념 등을 나타낸다.

- Most plants need **a lot of water**. 대부분의 식물들은 **많은 물**을 필요로 합니다.
- Where do you buy **bread**? **빵**은 어디서 사세요?
- **Love** is different from **friendship**. **사랑**은 **우정**과는 다르다.
- I'm interested in **rock music** and **football**. 저는 **록 음악**과 **축구**에 관심이 있어요.

❷ 단수형태로만 쓰이고 동사도 이에 따른다.

- **Money isn't** everything. 돈이 전부가 **아니다**.
- There **was** no **milk** in the fridge. 냉장고엔 우유가 전혀 **없었다**.

3 some과 단위표현으로 수량을 표현할 수 있다. 셀 수 있는 명사와 셀 수 없는 명사 모두에 쓰임 See Unit 057 ▶

- Would you like **some cookies** and **tea**? 쿠키랑 차 좀 드시겠어요?
- I had **two slices of bread** and **a packet of chips** for lunch. 나는 점심으로 **식빵 두 장**과 **감자칩 한 봉지**를 먹었다.

4 명사에 따라 쓸 수 있는 수량표현이 다를 수 있다.

- There were too **many people** at the party and we didn't have **much fun**.
  파티에 **사람들**이 너무 **많아서** 우리는 **많이 재미있진** 않았다.
- He has **little money** and **few friends**. 그는 돈도 친구도 거의 없다.

Exercises

1. 셀 수 있는 명사 앞에는 a 또는 an, 셀 수 없는 명사 앞에는 some을 넣어 문장을 완성하세요.

   1. She has __a__ dog and __a__ hamster.
   2. Would you like _____ tea?
   3. I'm looking for _____ good hotel in central London.
   4. He's wearing _____ uniform.
   5. I need _____ time to think about it.
   6. _____ apple a day keeps the doctor away.
   7. My father gave me _____ money to buy books.
   8. I opened the window to get _____ fresh air.

2. 빈칸에 주어진 내용을 적절한 형태로 바꾸어 넣어 문장을 완성하세요.

   1. There are ___three bottles of water___ (bottle, water).
   2. I bought _____ (kilo, apple).
   3. He had _____ (slice, bread) for breakfast.
   4. He always had _____ (bowl, rice).
   5. Add _____ (spoon, oil).
   6. How much is _____ (bunch, banana)?

◆ Dialogue

3. 아래 보기 중 빈칸에 들어갈 수 있는 단어를 넣어 문장을 완성하세요.

   | bread   cheese   honey   strawberry jam   salad |

   Rachel is at a restaurant. Rachel은 식당에 있습니다.

   Server Are you ready to order, ma'am?
   Rachel Yes. I'd like the chicken pie and a _____.
   Server Would you like anything else?
   Rachel Can I see your beverage menu? That's the main reason why I like to eat here.
   Server Sure. Here you are.

Unit 055

셀 수 있는 명사/셀 수 없는 명사(2)

The news is fake.
그 뉴스 가짜야.

1 **-s/es의 형태가 아닌 복수형을 갖는 명사도 있다.**

- -fe ➡ -ves: half, knife, life, shelf, wife, wolf 등
  ▸ Many **lives** were lost in the accident. 그 사고로 많은 **목숨**을 잃었다.

- -o ➡ -oes: potato, tomato, volcano 등
  ▸ **Potatoes** and **tomatoes** are on sale. 감자와 토마토가 세일이다.

- 불규칙 명사(Irregular Nouns): child, foot, man, mouse, person, tooth, woman 등
  ▸ Violence against **women** and **children** must stop. 여성과 어린이에 대한 폭력은 멈춰야만 합니다.
  ▸ Don't forget to brush your **teeth**. 양치질 하는 것 잊지 마.

- 복수 형태에 변화가 없음: fish, sheep 등
  ▸ I counted hundreds of **sheep** last night, but couldn't sleep. 어젯밤 양을 수백 마리나 셌지만 잘 수 없었다.

  단, fish는 일반적인 복수를 말할 때와 종류를 말할 때에 따라 형태가 다르다.
  ┌ There are many **fish** in the river. 그 강에는 **물고기**가 많이 산다.
  └ There are many **fishes** in the river. 그 강에는 많은 **종류의 물고기**가 산다.

2 **-ics로 끝나는 학문, 학과목을 나타내는 단어와 news는 복수처럼 보이지만, 셀 수 없는 명사이다.**
└ economics, mathematics, gymnastics, politics, physics, electronics 등

  ▸ **Politics** is not my thing. 정치는 내 취향이 아니야.
  ▸ The **news** is fake. 그 뉴스 가짜야.

3 **다음 -s로 끝나는 단어들은 단수와 복수형이 같다.**

- means ┌ The bicycle is **a** very convenient **means** of transportation. 자전거는 매우 편리한 교통**수단**이다.
        └ There are **many means** of transportation in L.A. L.A.에는 많은 교통**수단**이 존재한다.

- species ┌ The guppy is **a species** of fish. 구피는 물고기의 **한 종류**이다.
          └ **Many species** of fish live in this lake. 이 호수에는 많은 **종류의 물고기**가 산다.

- series ┌ I'm reading about **a** new television **series**. 새 TV **시리즈**에 대해 읽고 있어.
         └ The actor has appeared in **several** television **series**. 그 배우는 **몇 개의** TV **시리즈**에 출연했다.

4 **다음 단어들은 주로 복수로 쓰인다.**

- clothes
  ▸ I'm going to buy some new **clothes**. 새 옷을 좀 살 계획이에요.

- scissors, glasses, pants, pajamas *보통 한 쌍이 한 단어로 쓰이는 것들. pair를 단위로 셀 수 있다*
  ▸ He wears **glasses**. 그는 안경을 씁니다.
  ▸ How many pairs of **jeans** do you have? **청바지**는 몇 벌이나 갖고 있니?

5 **일정량의 시간이나 돈, 거리 등을 하나의 묶음으로 말할 때에는 단수로 취급한다.**

  ▸ **Four days is** too short. I need more time. 나흘은 너무 짧습니다. 전 시간이 더 필요해요.

Exercises

1. 주어진 단어를 복수 형태로 바꾸어 문장을 완성하세요.

1. Some __people__ (person) think that age is just a number.
2. Where did you put the _____ (knife)? I can't find them.
3. There were many _____ (sheep) on the island.
4. We saw some _____ (wolf) at the zoo.
5. How many _____ (fish) did you catch?
6. How many _____ (volcano) are there in Iceland?
7. Don't forget to get your _____ (tooth) checked by a dentist regularly.
8. My _____ (child) hate spinach.

2. 문장에 맞는 Be동사의 형태를 넣어 문장을 완성하세요.

1. The news __is__ fake.
2. _____ women more emotional than men?
3. Physics _____ my favorite subject.
4. The new television series _____ supposed to be very good.
5. Clothes _____ made of different materials.
6. What _____ your favorite means of transportation?
7. Ten million dollars _____ a lot of money.

3. 문장의 틀린 부분이 있다면 고쳐서 다시 쓰세요. 고칠 부분이 없다면 X를 쓰세요.

1. Mathematics are always difficult for me.   *Mathematics is always difficult for me.*
2. It is a rare species of penguin that can fly.   _____
3. The books are on the shelfs over there.   _____
4. Do you think 4 miles is too far to walk?   _____
5. He wants to study economic in college.   _____

🔊 Dialogue

4. 주어진 단어의 적절한 형태를 써 넣어 문장을 완성하세요.

Erika is showing a photo to Patrick.
Erika가 Patrick에게 사진을 보여 주고 있습니다.

Erika This was taken in my cousin Nathan's garden.
Patrick Wow. I like the design of the garden.
Erika Do you? It's a Chinese garden.
Patrick Great! Um… Who are these _____ (child)?
Erika They're Nathan's _____ (twin), Ming and Ling. It was their birthday party.

Unit 056

셀 수 있는 명사/셀 수 없는 명사(3)

Have a good time!
즐거운 시간 보내!

1. 같은 단어라도 의미의 명사적 특성에 따라 구분이 달라질 수 있다.

셀 수 있는 명사(Countable Nouns)	셀 수 없는 명사(Uncountable Nouns)
▶ What **papers** do I need to get a passport? 여권을 발급받으려면 무슨 **서류들**이 필요합니까?	▶ Please use recycled **paper**. 재활용지를 사용해 주세요.
▶ Can I have **a glass** of water? 물 **한 잔**만 주시겠어요?	▶ The bottle is made of **glass**. 그 병은 **유리**로 만들어졌다.
▶ Can I get you **a coffee**? 커피 **한 잔** 갖다 드릴까요?	▶ I don't drink **coffee**. 저는 **커피**를 마시지 않아요.
▶ There's **a hair** in my soup. 제 국에 **머리카락**이 있어요.	▶ She has long **hair**. 그녀는 **머리**가 길어요.
▶ He's going to start **a business**. 그는 **회사**를 차릴 것입니다.	▶ **Business** is going well at the moment. 현재는 **사업**이 잘 되고 있습니다.
▶ I got **an email** from MGM this morning. 오늘 아침에 MGM으로부터 **이메일을 하나** 받았습니다.	▶ You can contact me by **email**. 제게 **이메일**로 연락하시면 돼요.
▶ My laptop is making **a strange noise**. 내 노트북에서 이상한 **소음**이 나요.	▶ I can't stand **noise**. 난 **소음**은 질색이에요.
▶ Have **a good time**! 즐거운 시간 보내!	▶ I don't have **time**. **시간**이 없어요.
▶ It was **an interesting experience**. 그것은 흥미로운 **경험**이었다.	▶ I have over twelve years' teaching **experience**. 나는 12년이 넘는 교육 **경력**을 갖고 있습니다.
▶ Have you found **a parking space**? 주차 **자리** 찾았니?	▶ The sofa takes up too much **space** in the room. 소파가 방의 **공간**을 너무 차지한다.
▶ We used to raise **chickens** in the backyard. 우리는 예전에 뒷마당에서 **닭**을 길렀었다.	▶ I like **chicken**. 저는 **닭고기**가 좋아요.
▶ Try the new bakery. Their **cakes** are nice. 그 새 제과점을 이용해봐. 거기 **케이크** 좋아.	▶ Would you like some **cake**? 케이크 좀 먹을래? 셀 수 있는 명사의 일부를 말할 때 셀 수 없는 명사처럼 쓰일 수 있다.

2. 두 단어의 의미가 비슷해도 구분이 다를 수 있다.

셀 수 있는 명사(Countable Nouns)	셀 수 없는 명사(Uncountable Nouns)
▶ Are you looking for **a job**? 지금 **일자리**를 찾고 계신가요?	▶ Are you looking for **work**? 지금 **일**을 찾고 있나요?
▶ I had some **buns** for breakfast. 아침으로 **둥근 빵**을 좀 먹었다.	▶ I had some **bread** for breakfast. 아침으로 **빵**을 좀 먹었다.
▶ She spends a lot of money on **trips**. 그녀는 **여행**에 돈을 많이 쓴다.	▶ She spends a lot of money on **travel**. 그녀는 **여행하는** 데에 많은 돈을 쓴다.
▶ I have **a suggestion** for you. 여러분께 **제안**이 하나 있어요.	▶ I have **advice** for you. 여러분께 **조언**이 있습니다.
▶ It was **a wonderful view**. 멋진 **경관**이었어요.	▶ It was wonderful **scenery**. 멋진 **경치**였어요.
▶ You need to have three **meals** a day. 넌 하루 세 **끼**를 먹을 필요가 있어.	▶ You need to have some **food**. 넌 **음식**을 좀 먹어야 해.
▶ Once upon a time, three little **pigs** lived on a farm. 옛날에 세 마리의 아기 **돼지**가 한 농장에서 살았습니다.	▶ I'm allergic to **pork**. 저는 **돼지고기**에 알레르기가 있어요.
▶ We need four **chairs**. 의자 네 개가 필요합니다.	▶ We need some **furniture**. 가구가 좀 필요합니다.
▶ Are these your **bags**? 이것들은 당신 **가방**인가요?	▶ Is this your **luggage/baggage**? 이거 당신 **짐**인가요?

Exercises

1. 문장의 문맥에 가장 적합한 표현을 골라 문장을 완성하세요.

1. (Glass / **A glass**) of wine, please.
2. I'll send the information by (email / emails).
3. Where do you have your (hair / a hair / hairs) cut?
4. I noticed (hair / a hair) on her suit.
5. Mom is baking (cake / a cake) now.
6. (Chicken / Chickens) can be pets.
7. I need more (space / a space) on my hard disk.
8. Do you have any (experience / experiences) of working with children?
9. I heard (loud noise / a loud noise) and ran into the room.
10. We're running out of (time / times).
11. He works in the IT (business / businesses).
12. He is having (hard time / a hard time) hiring people.

2. 밑줄 친 부분이 틀렸다면 맞게 고치세요. 고칠 부분이 없다면 X를 쓰세요.

1. He's been looking for a work since April.   *a job* or *work*
2. The Chinese eat a lot of pork.   _____
3. The room was full of furnitures.   _____
4. Do you have any suggestion?   _____
5. I'd like a room with a view of the sea.   _____
6. They're going on a trip to Spain next week.   _____
7. You can leave your baggages at the hotel until it is time to leave for the airport.   _____

Dialogue

3. 문장의 문맥에 가장 적합한 표현을 골라 문장을 완성하세요.

James is at customs now. James는 지금 세관 통과소에 있습니다.

Customs officer Could you come here, sir?
James Yes, sure.
Customs officer How (many luggages / much luggage) do you have?
James Just this one bag.
Customs officer Do you have any (good / goods) to declare?
James No. I have some duty-free wine. That's all.
Customs officer How (many bottles / much bottle) do you have?
James Two.
Customs officer Thank you, sir. Please move to the line on the right.

Unit 057

한정사

Some people don't use social media at all.
어떤 사람들은 SNS를 전혀 이용하지 않아요.

1 다음은 명사 앞에서 어떤 것(명사)을 말하고자 하는 것인지를 밝혀 주는 표현들이다. `특정한 것`

- **the** (정)관사 *See Unit 062▶*
  ▶ Look at **the** phone over there. Isn't it cool? 저기 전화기 좀 봐. 멋지지 않니?

- **my/your/his/her/our/its/their** *See Unit 066▶*
  ▶ **My** phone keeps freezing. What can I do? 내 전화기가 계속 (작동을) 멈춰요. 어떻게 해야 하죠?
  ▶ Where are **their** parents? 그들의 부모님은 어디 있나요?

- **this/that/these/those** *See Unit 067▶*
  ▶ Hello, is **this** your phone? 저기요, 이거 댁 전화기인가요?
  ▶ **That** café is always full. 저 카페는 항상 사람들로 가득 차 있어.

2 구체적으로 어떤 것인지를 말하지 않을 때에는 다음의 표현을 쓸 수 있다. `특정한 것이 아님`

- **a** (부정)관사. 셀 수 있는 명사 하나인 경우 *See Unit 054▶*
  ▶ I'm thinking of buying **a** smartphone. 스마트폰을 하나 살까 생각 중이야.

- **some** 명사가 있거나 있다고 생각되거나 범위가 있는 긍정적인 경우 *See Unit 054▶*
  ▶ I need go to the bank to get **some** money. 돈을 좀 찾으러 은행에 가야해요.
  ▶ **Some** people don't use social media at all. 어떤 사람들은 SNS를 전혀 이용하지 않아요.
  ▶ Can I have **some** water? 물 좀 주시겠어요?

- **any** 명사가 없거나, 있는지 없는지 모르거나 범위가 무한대로 뻗는 불분명한 경우
  ▶ He doesn't have **any** brothers or sisters. 그는 형제자매가 없다.
  ▶ Are there **any** keys in the box? 상자 안에 열쇠가 없나요?
  ▶ You can choose **any** topic to talk about. 이야기할 어느 주제라도 고를 수 있습니다.
  ▶ There is little difference, if **any**, between these two. 이 둘 사이에는 차이가 있다 해도 거의 없습니다.

3 some/any/every + thing/one(body)/where/time

  ▶ Would you like **something** to drink? 뭐 마실 것 좀 드릴까요?
  ▶ There's **someone** at the door. 문밖에 누가 와 있어요. `somebody를 쓸 수도 있다.`
  ▶ She lives **somewhere** near Seattle. 그녀는 시애틀 부근 어딘가에 살아요.
  ▶ Let's have lunch together **sometime**. 언제 점심 같이 먹자. `과거나 미래의 어느 한 때. 언젠가`

  ▶ I can't hear **anything** from my earphones. 제 이어폰에서 아무 것도 안 들려요.
  ▶ Can **anybody** help me? 누구 나 좀 도와 줄 수 있어요?
  ▶ I'm not going **anywhere**. 저 아무데도 안 가요.
  ▶ Call me **anytime** after 7:00 p.m. 저녁 7시 이후 아무 때나 전화하세요.
  `every도 같은 방식으로 쓰일 수 있다.` *See Unit 059▶*

4 some, any, this, that, these, those는 단독으로도 쓰일 수 있다. `대명사로 쓰임`

  ▶ A: I've got some cookies. Would you like **some**? 쿠키가 좀 있거든. 좀 먹을래?
     B: No, thanks. I don't want **any** at the moment. 고맙지만 사양할게. 지금은 아무것도 원치 않아.

144

Exercises

1. 문장의 문맥에 가장 적합한 표현을 골라 문장을 완성하세요.
   1. Look at (a /(the)) moon. It's so big and round.
   2. A: What does Julia do?
      B: She is (a / the) flight attendant.
   3. A: How are (some / your) parents?
      B: They're fine, thank you.
   4. There aren't (any / the) hotels here.
   5. (A / This) book is mine.
   6. I'm going out to get (some / the) fresh air.
   7. A: Who's (a / that) man over there?
      B: He's Mr. Watson.

2. some이나 any를 넣어 문장을 완성하세요.
   1. Do you have _any_ brothers or sisters?
   2. I'm having _____ problems with this app.
   3. We don't have _____ food left.
   4. _____ fish can breathe air.
   5. Are there _____ seats available?

3. 빈칸에 들어갈 가장 적절한 표현을 보기에서 골라 넣어 문장을 완성하세요.

   | something | someone | somewhere | sometime |
   | anything | ~~anyone~~ | anywhere | anytime |

   1. Did _anyone_ call while I was out?
   2. I'm looking for _____ to stay.
   3. A politician will do _____ to keep his job.
   4. She couldn't find her cat _____.
   5. I hope to visit Egypt _____.
   6. It can be a friend or _____ in your family.
   7. People can change _____.

🔊 Dialogue

4. 빈칸에 들어갈 가장 적절한 표현을 보기에서 골라 넣어 문장을 완성하세요. 필요한 경우 여러 번 쓸 수 있습니다.

   | something | somewhere | anything | anywhere |

   Eugene is looking for his tablet computer. Eugene은 본인의 태블릿 PC를 찾고 있습니다.

   Eugene Have you seen my tablet? I can't find it _____.

   Sarah No, I haven't. Perhaps you've lent it to someone?

   Eugene I don't let others borrow my tablet computer. It must be _____ in this room.

   Sarah Things are in such a mess. It could be _____.

   Eugene I know. I can never find _____ when I want it.

   Sarah We've got to do _____ about this mess first. Let's tidy it up.

Unit 058

수량형용사

Nothing is impossible.
불가능한 것은 없다.

1 모든, 대부분, 일부 등에 대해 다음과 같이 말할 수 있다.
- I like **all** kinds of music. 저는 **모든** 종류의 음악이 좋아요.
- **Most** birds can fly. **대부분의** 새는 날 수 있습니다.
- **Some** mistakes are worth making. **어떤** 실수들은 할 만한 가치가 있다.

2 not+any ~는 no ~로 쓸 수 있다.
- He has **no** brothers or sisters. (=He **doesn't** have **any** brothers or sisters.) 그는 형제자매가 **없다**.
- I'm going **nowhere**. 저 아무데도 안 가요.

not ~ any 뒤에는 명사가 오지 않을 수 있지만, no 뒤에는 반드시 명사가 온다.
- A: Have you got any money? 돈 좀 있니?
  B: No, I don't have **any**. 아니, 전혀 없어. *No, I have no.* (X)

3 none은 0의 의미로, 'no + 명사'를 의미한다.
- A: How many brothers or sisters do you have? 형제나 자매는 얼마나 있니?
  B: Well, I have **none**. I'm an only child. (= … have **no** brothers or sisters.) 음. **없어**. 난 외동이야.

4 no ~나 none은 문장의 처음이나 짧은 답변에 자주 쓰인다. not ~ any보다 단정적인 느낌
- **No** one knew the answer. 아무도 답을 몰랐다.
- **Nothing** is impossible. 불가능한 것은 없다.
- A: How many people came? 사람들은 얼마나 많이 왔나요? / B: **None**. 아무도요.

5 많고 적음에 대해서 다음과 같이 말할 수 있다.
- We sold **a lot of** cars last year. 우리는 작년에 차를 **많이** 팔았습니다.
  셀 수 있는 명사와 셀 수 없는 명사 모두에 쓸 수 있음. lots of나 plenty of로 대체 가능
- **Many** people came to the conference. **많은** 사람들이 컨퍼런스에 왔습니다. 셀 수 있는 명사에 쓰임
- We don't have **much** time. 우린 시간이 **많지** 않아요. 셀 수 없는 명사. 보통 부정문과 의문문에 쓰임
- I'm going to stay here for **a few** days. 전 여기서 **며칠** 묵을 거에요. 셀 수 있는 명사
- There were **few** people in the park. 공원에는 사람이 **거의 없었다**. 셀 수 있는 명사가 거의 없거나 0일 때
- I just had some tea and **a little** cheese. 전 차와 치즈 **조금만** 먹었어요. 셀 수 없는 명사
- I'm not very happy about it, but I have **little** choice. 그것에 대해 썩 만족스럽지 않지만 선택의 여지가 **거의 없**네요. 셀 수 없는 명사가 거의 없거나 0일 때

6 '특정한' 묶음이나 범위 내에서의 모든, 대부분, 일부, 수량을 말할 때에는 of를 더한다.
of 뒤에는 the, my, these 등 특정 명사 묶음이나 범위임을 알려주는 표현이 오거나 대명사가 옴
- **All (of) the** children here are under 5 years old. 여기 어린이들은 **모두** 5세 이하입니다.
  'all of 명사'의 경우 of가 생략될 수 있다.
- I spend **most of my** spare time reading books. 저는 여가 시간의 **대부분**을 책을 읽으며 보냅니다.
- **Some of these** cars are not for sale. 이 차들 중 **일부**는 판매용이 아닙니다.
- I know **none of them**. 나는 **그들 중 아무도** 모른다.
- How **many of you** have been to Japan? 여러분 중에 **몇이나** 일본에 가 봤나요?
- He wasted **much of his** money on gambling. 그는 **그의 돈의 많은 부분**을 도박에 낭비했다.

Exercises

1. 보기와 같이 문장을 다시 쓰세요.

1. He doesn't have any brothers or sisters. → *He has no brothers or sisters.*
2. There isn't anybody here by that name. → _____
3. I won't tell anyone about our conversation. → _____
4. They didn't buy any vegetables. → _____
5. I don't have any ideas. → _____

2. 빈칸에 들어갈 가장 적절한 표현을 보기에서 골라 넣어 문장을 완성하세요. 단어는 여러 번 쓸 수 있습니다.

> a lot (of)   many   much   (a) few   (a) little

1. Rome is an old city. There are __a lot of__ or __many__ buildings there.
2. It's been very dry this year. We've had _____ rain.
3. I'm not very busy today. I haven't got _____ to do.
4. A: How _____ oranges do you want?
   B: Just _____, please.
5. Bill is a millionaire. He's got _____ money.

3. 문장의 틀린 부분이 있다면 고쳐서 다시 쓰세요. 고칠 부분이 없다면 X를 쓰세요.

1. How about donating some of this money?   __X__
2. Most my friends are single.   _____
3. None us told him about it.   _____
4. If you are truly determined, all your dreams will come true.   _____
5. Many the kids here are under seven.   _____
6. A: Why are you single?
   B: That's none of your business.   _____

🔊 Dialogue

4. 문장의 문맥에 가장 적합한 표현을 골라 문장을 완성하세요.

Amy is a big fan of figure skating. She'd like to go and see a competition.
Amy는 피겨스케이팅의 광팬입니다. 그녀는 대회에 가서 보고 싶어 합니다.

Amy There are (a lot of / much) great skaters taking part in the National Championship this year.

Sarah Yes. There's been (a lot of / many) coverage in the newspapers.

Amy I'd like to go and see the competition, but I haven't got (many / much) time at the moment.

Sarah No, not with exams coming up.

Amy I'm hoping to go this Friday if I can get a ticket. Apparently there aren't (many / much) seats left.

Sarah I've heard the cheapest tickets are $55. I think that's too (many / much).

Unit 059

all-whole, every-each

The subway runs every five minutes.
전철은 5분마다 운행합니다.

1 **all**은 일반적인 '모든'을 의미한다.
- I like **all** kinds of music. 저는 **모든** 종류의 음악이 좋아요.

특정 묶음이나 범위 안의 '전부'를 말할 수 있다. *See Unit 058▶*
- She saved **all (of)** the messages just in case. 그녀는 만약의 경우에 대비해서 **모든** 메시지를 저장했다.

of 뒤에 대명사가 오는 경우에는 of를 생략하지 않는다.
- I love **all of you**. 전 여러분 **모두**를 사랑합니다.

2 **whole**은 하나 또는 하나로 묶은 '전체'를 의미한다. 앞에 the나 my, your 등의 표현이 온다.
특정한 하나 또는 한 묶음을 말함
- **The whole** experience was valuable. 그 경험 **전체**가 소중했습니다.
- **My whole** family likes to sing. 제 온 가족이 노래하는 것을 좋아합니다.

3 **every**는 문장에서 단수로 취급된다. *'그 어느 하나도 빠짐없이'로 이해하면 쉽다. 범위가 넓은 경우에 쓰임*
- I believe **every word** she says. 나는 그녀가 하는 **모든 말**을 다 믿는다.
- **Every player** wants to be on a winning team. 어느 선수건 다 이기는 팀에 있고 싶어 한다.

every가 시간표현과 쓰이면 '매 ~마다'의 의미를 갖는다.
- The subway runs **every** five minutes. 전철은 매 5분마다 운행합니다.
- We have a short meeting **every** day. 우리는 매일 짧은 회의를 합니다.

every+thing/one(body)/where/time
- I've looked **everywhere**. 모든 곳을 다 찾아 봤어요.
- They're so strong. They win **every** time. 그들은 정말 강해요. 매번 이기네요.

4 **each**도 every와 비슷하게 쓰일 수 있다. *'각각 모두'의 의미로 이해할 수 있다. 범위가 적은 경우에 주로 쓰임*
- Make sure **each** folder has a label. 각 폴더가 (모두) 라벨이 있는지 확인하세요.
- The oranges are fifty cents **each**. 오렌지는 **각각**(개당) 50센트입니다. *'각각'의 의미로 명사 뒤에 위치하기도 함*

강조의 의미로 **each and every**를 쓸 수 있다.
- **Each and every** child is special. 모든 아이 하나 하나가 다 특별합니다.

5 **all, whole, every + 시간표현**

▶ Ben is on the Internet **all the time**. Ben은 항상 인터넷에 접속해 있다.	▶ Ben is on the Internet **every time** I see him. Ben은 내가 볼 **때마다** 인터넷에 접속해 있다.
▶ I stayed home **all day** yesterday. = I stayed home **the whole day** yesterday. 나는 어제 **하루 종일** 집에 있었어요.	▶ Smartphones are becoming more and more popular **every day**. = Smartphones are becoming more and more popular **each day**. 스마트폰은 **나날이** 인기가 더해지고 있다.
▶ I've lived in the same town **all (of) my** life. = I've lived in the same town **my whole life**. 저는 **평생**을 한 동네에서 살아왔습니다.	

Exercises

1. 문장의 문맥에 가장 적합한 표현을 골라 문장을 완성하세요.
   1. Four players ((each) / every) have a pack of cards.
   2. (All / Every) of the files are infected by the virus.
   3. The flight and the hotel are booked. (All / Everything) is ready.
   4. The company gave their sales reps (each a tablet / a tablet each).
   5. Every (option / options) has been considered.
   6. He called (all / every) hotel in town but couldn't get a room.
   7. He had a ball in each (hand / hands).
   8. My baby boy cries (all the time / every time) I finish reading him a story.
   9. Did you all stay home the (all / whole) day?

2. 밑줄 친 부분을 주어진 표현으로 바꾸어 문장을 다시 쓰세요.
   1. Mr. Cruz loves all the students in his class. (every)
      → Mr. Cruz loves ____every student____ in his class.
   2. Every member of the team will be awarded a college scholarship. (each)
      → _____ will be awarded a college scholarship.
   3. She emailed every one of her student. (all)
      → She emailed _____.
   4. My dad has worked so hard his whole life. (all)
      → My dad has worked so hard _____.
   5. They're so strong. They always win. (every time)
      → They're so strong. _____.
   6. We spent all summer in Vancouver. (whole)
      → We spent _____ in Vancouver.

🔊 Dialogue

3. 보기 중 빈칸에 들어갈 가장 적합한 표현을 골라 넣어 문장을 완성하세요.

             all   every   whole

   Mr. Harris has just come back from his vacation. James is asking about it.
   Mr. Harris는 휴가에서 방금 돌아왔습니다. James가 그에 대해 묻고 있습니다.

   James   How was your vacation?
   Mr. Harris It was fantastic. I enjoyed _____ minute of it.
                   The Maldives were just one step away from heaven.
                   I will never forget the beauty of the islands.
   James   How about the hotel?
   Mr. Harris Great. I stayed at the Ayada Resort during the _____
                   trip, and you know what? I had my own butler!
   James   That's amazing!

Unit 060

both, either, neither

He is neither American nor British.
그는 미국인도 영국인도 아니다.

1 두 개나 두 종류 혹은 묶음의 것에 대해 말할 때 다음과 같이 말할 수 있다.

❶ **both (A and B)**: 둘 다 그러함

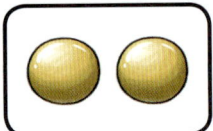

- ▶ **Both** phones look nice. 두 전화기 다 멋져 보여.
- ▶ **Both** Andy **and** Ben collect action figures. Andy와 Ben 둘 다 액션피규어를 수집한다.

❷ **either (A or B)**: 둘 중의 하나가 그러함

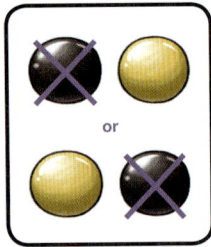

- ▶ A: Which would you like - tea or coffee? 어느 걸로 하실래요, 차 아니면 커피?
  B: **Either** is fine. 둘 중 어느 것이나 좋아요.
- ▶ You can choose **either** eggs **or** pancakes.
  달걀**이나** 팬케이크 **중 하나를** 선택하실 수 있습니다.

❸ **neither (A nor B)**: not ~ either, 둘 다 아님 `neither는 not either의 의미`

- ▶ **Neither** phone looks nice. 두 전화기 다 멋져 보이지 **않아**.
- ▶ He is **neither** American **nor** British. 그는 미국인**도** 영국인**도** 아니다.

❹ 특정한 두 개 또는 두 종류, 묶음의 것에 대해 말할 때에는 of를 쓴다.

- ▶ **Both (of) their parents** are photographers. 그들의 부모님 두 분 다 사진작가다. `both의 경우에 of가 생략될 수 있다.`
- ▶ Hey, the boss wants to talk to **both of you**. 이봐, 사장님이 너희 둘 다와 얘기하고 싶으시대.
  `뒤에 대명사가 오는 경우 of를 생략하지 않는다.`
- ▶ I'll buy **either of these phones**. 난 이 두 전화기 중의 하나를 살 거야.
- ▶ I liked **neither of the phones**. 난 두 전화기 다 맘에 들지 **않았다**.

2 셋 이상의 것들에 대해서는 다음과 같이 말한다. `See Unit 058▶`

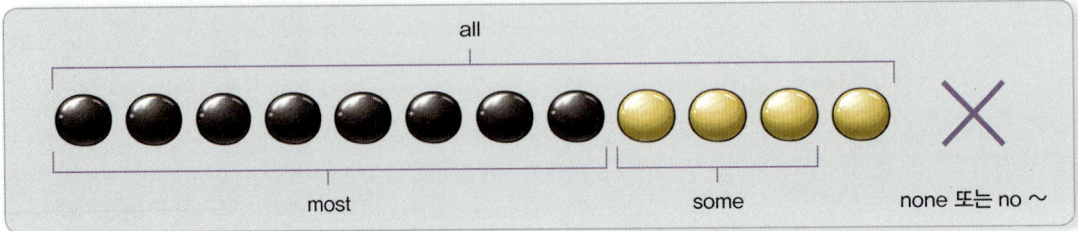

- ▶ I like **all** kinds of music. 저는 **모든** 종류의 음악이 좋아요.
- ▶ **Most** birds can fly. 대부분의 새는 날 수 있습니다.
- ▶ **Some** birds cannot fly. 어떤 새들은 날 수 없습니다.
- ▶ He solved **none** of the problems. 그는 문제 중 **아무 것도** 풀지 못했다.
- ▶ There are **no** buses today. 오늘은 (운행하는) 버스가 **없습니다**.

Exercises

1. 그림을 보고 both, either, neither를 써서 문장을 완성하세요.

1. _Both_ phones look nice.
2. _____ butter or margarine will do.
3. A: What time is it now – three or four?
   B: _____. It's five o'clock.
4. Jessica opened _____ windows.
5. I didn't see _____ movie.
6. A: Which way is it to Seoul?
   B: You can go _____ way.
7. I can't decide between these two dresses. I like them _____.

2. 밑줄 친 부분에 틀린 부분이 있다면 고쳐서 다시 쓰세요. 고칠 부분이 없다면 X를 쓰세요.

1. I speak neither Spanish nor German. I only speak English.   _X_
2. Rachel is either intelligent and beautiful.   _____
3. I invited Amy and Sarah, but both of them came.   _____
4. He didn't like both phones.   _____
5. Either buy it or lease it.   _____
6. Jay is neither Chinese or Japanese. He's Korean.   _____

✦ Dialogue

3. 보기 중 빈칸에 들어갈 가장 적합한 표현을 골라 넣어 문장을 완성하세요.

| all   most   some   any   none |

Jay and Eugene are talking together. Jay와 Eugene은 함께 얘기하고 있습니다.

Jay   What do you usually do on Sunday?

Eugene Not much. I spend _____ of the time surfing the web. How about you?

Jay   I play badminton or ping pong. Sometimes I go bowling, too. Do you play _____ of these?

Eugene No. I play _____ of them, but I play soccer and baseball online.

Jay   Online? Not in the real world?

Eugene No. I play sports only online.

Unit 061

other, another, the other

Can I have another cup of tea?
차 한 잔만 더 주시겠어요?

1 어떤 것(들)과 다른 것에 대해 다음과 같이 말할 수 있다.

❶ one – another: 어떤 것 하나와 또 다른 하나 `another는 an+other의 의미`

- Can I have **another** cup of tea? 차 한 잔만 더 주시겠어요?
- The millionaire has 10 cars. One is Ferrari. **Another** is Lamborghini. **Another** is Porche. **Another** is… 그 백만장자는 차가 10대가 있다. 하나는 페라리다. 또 하나는 람보르기니. 또 하나는 포르쉐. 또 하나는…

another 뒤에 복수표현이 올 수 있다. `기간, 거리, 개수 등이 그만큼 추가된다는 의미`

- I'll give you **another 10 minutes**. 여러분에게 10분을 더 드리겠습니다.

❷ one, some – other(s): 어떤 것 하나 또는 어떤 것들과 다른 것들

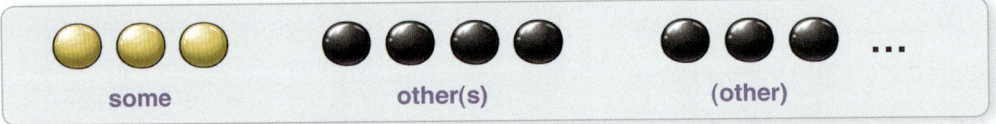

- This one is too small. Do you have it in **other sizes**? 이건 너무 작은데요. 다른 사이즈는 없나요?
- **Some** people like beef. **Others** like pork. 어떤 사람들은 쇠고기를 좋아한다. 다른 사람들은 돼지고기를 좋아한다.

❸ the other(s): 어떤 것(들)을 제외한 나머지

> **TIP** the other day는 멀지 않은 과거의 '어느 한 날'을 말한다. '일전에' 등의 의미로 해석한다.

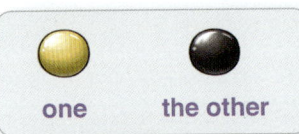

- I've talked to one of the twins, but I haven't met **the other** one. 저는 그 쌍둥이 중 한 명과는 얘기해 봤지만, 다른 한 명은 만나보지 못했어요.

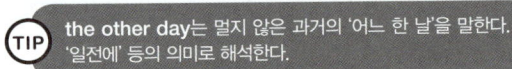

- I've just finished a report. I have to finish **the other two** by next week. 저는 방금 보고서 하나를 끝냈습니다. 다음 주까지 나머지 둘을 끝내야 합니다.
- He has five puppies. One is black, another is spotted, and **the others** are white. 그에게는 다섯 마리의 강아지가 있다. 하나는 까맣고, 다른 하나는 얼룩이고, 나머지는 하얗다.

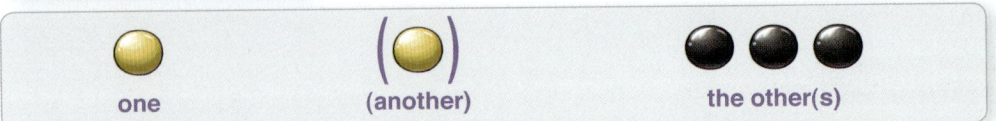

- There are five rooms in the house. Two are on the first floor. **The other three** are on the second floor. 그 집에는 방이 다섯 개가 있다. 두 방은 1층에 있다. 나머지 셋은 2층에 있다.
- Ben has many action figures. Some of them are very expensive, but **the others** are quite cheap. Ben에게는 많은 액션 피규어가 있다. 그 중 일부는 아주 비싸지만, 나머지는 꽤 싸다.

2 other 앞에 my, your 또는 no가 올 수 있다.

- They're **my other** students. 그들은 제 다른 학생들입니다.
- There is **no other** way. 다른 길(방법)은 없다.

Exercises

1. 그림을 보고 빈칸에 another, other, the other를 넣어 문장을 완성하세요.

1. They have twins. One is Anna. _The other_ is Mia.
2. She goes to school on Tuesday and Thursday. On _____ days of the week, she works in a restaurant.
3. We still have _____ 30 kilometers to go.
4. Well, we have _____ styles if you're interested.
5. He has bought _____ camera.

2. 빈칸에 들어갈 가장 적절한 표현을 보기에서 골라 넣어 문장을 완성하세요.

| another |
| other |
| others |
| the other |
| the others |

1. Would you like _another_ glass of wine?
2. She has invited some _____ people.
3. Sorry. I can't help you now because I'm busy with _____ things.
4. Why don't we meet _____ day?
5. Some people like dogs. _____ like cats.
6. He always helps _____ people.
7. I don't like this room. I'll ask for _____.
8. We had no _____ choice.
9. A: Who are those kids? / B: They're my _____ children. I have five children.
10. The bank is on _____ side of the street.

Dialogue

3. 빈칸에 공통으로 들어갈 수 있는 표현을 보기에서 골라 넣어 문장을 완성하세요.

| another   other   others   the other   the others |

Mike is calling Trish on the phone. Mike는 Trish에게 전화를 하고 있습니다.

Mike   Hello, Trish. It's Mike.
Trish   Hi, Mike. Actually, I'm on _____ line. Hang on a sec.
Mike   Sure.
Trish   Alright, Mike. I'm back. So, what's up?
Mike   Did you back up the file we were working on together _____ day? I think I just deleted it by accident.

Unit 062

The(1)

Have you seen the picture I posted?
내가 올린 사진 봤어?

1. the는 듣는 사람이 구체적으로 그 명사가 어떤 것인지 분명히 알 수 있을 때 쓸 수 있다.
셀 수 있는 명사의 단수와 복수, 셀 수 없는 명사 앞에 모두 쓰일 수 있다.

- **이미 한 번 언급되었던 명사**
  - A: We ate out at **a restaurant** on Friday. 금요일에 우리는 **식당**에서 외식했어.
    B: Was **the restaurant** nice? 그 **식당** 괜찮았어?

- **대화상의 기준 지역/장소 내의 물건, 장소나 공공 서비스 관련 시설**
  - Would you please turn down **the TV**? TV 소리 좀 줄여줄래?
  - A: Where's Dad? 아빠 어디 계시지?
    B: He is in **the kitchen**. 부엌에 계셔.
  - Does this bus go to **the airport**? 이 버스 **공항** 가나요?
  - He goes to **the movies** every weekend. 그는 주말마다 **영화** 보러 간다.

- **문장에 그 명사가 구체적으로 무엇인지를 의미하는 내용이 더해져 있을 때**
  - Have you seen **the picture I posted**? 내가 올린 사진 봤어?

- **하나뿐이거나 문맥에서 무엇을 말하는지 분명한 경우**
  - I like looking at **the sky**. 난 **하늘** 보는 것을 좋아해요.
  - I'll talk to **the boss** about it. 그것에 대해서 **사장님**과 얘기할 거야.
  - **The meeting** will begin at 9:30. 회의는 9시 30분에 시작될 거예요. 듣는 사람이 어떤 회의인지 아는 상황

- **가장 ~한 것을 나타내는 최상급 표현의 앞** See Unit 075 ▶
  - It's **the best** Korean movie I've ever seen. 그건 제가 본 한국 **영화** 중 **최고**입니다.
  - Who is **the most important** person in your life? 네 인생에서 **가장 중요한** 사람은 누구니?

- **first, second, third 등 순서를 나타내는 표현(서수) 앞** See Unit 070 ▶
  - Today is **the first day** of the rest of your life. 오늘은 당신 남은 인생의 **첫 번째** 날입니다.
  - My birthday is July **(the) 2nd**. 내 생일은 7월 2일입니다. 날짜 앞의 the는 종종 생략 가능

- **same 앞**
  - We arrived at **the same time**. 우리는 **동시에** 도착했다.

2. the는 다음과 같이 발음한다.

- **자음 소리 앞: [ðə]**
  - Please, close **the door**. 문 좀 닫아 주세요.

- **모음 소리 앞: [ði]**
  - **The oranges** are in the fridge. 오렌지는 냉장고 안에 있어요.

- **해당 명사를 강조할 때: [ðiː]** 뒤에 오는 소리와 상관없음
  - She took a picture with **THE President** of Korea. 그녀는 대한민국의 '**대통령**'과 사진을 찍었다.
    격식을 차리지 않는 대화체나 일상 문장에서는 대문자 표기로 '강조'를 나타내기도 한다.

Exercises

1. 문장의 문맥에 가장 적합한 표현을 골라 문장을 완성하세요.

1. (A /(The)) movie you recommended was great.
2. Look! (A / The) sun is rising.
3. She's been working so hard that she needs (a / the) break.
4. (A / The) presentation was wonderful. Great job, James.
5. I think you should get (a / the) new pair of jeans.
6. Ms. Watson is (a / the) photographer.
7. When is (a / the) last train to Union Station?
8. Traditionally, (a / the) mothers don't wear (a / the) same color as (a / the) bridesmaids.
9. Jupiter is (a / the) largest planet in the solar system.
10. I have (an / the) important meeting at (a / the) headquarters.
11. Excuse me, do you know where (a / the) post office is?
12. We will find (a / the) way as we always have.
13. Can I have a look at (a / the) report again?

2. 강조하는 경우를 제외하고, 밑줄 친 the의 발음에 따라 문장을 분류해서 써 보세요.

[ðə]
1

[ði]
2

1. Please, close <u>the</u> door.
2. <u>The</u> animation was made by an amateur.
3. <u>The</u> meeting will begin at 10:00 a.m.
4. I believe there is intelligent life elsewhere in <u>the</u> universe.
5. <u>The</u> umbrella is mine.
6. I really liked <u>the</u> herb tea they served.
7. Let's go back to <u>the</u> hotel. I'm getting tired.
8. A: Which shirt do you like better?
   B: I prefer <u>the</u> one with long sleeves.

Dialogue

3. 대화문에서 the가 쓰여야 하는 곳을 모두 골라 넣으세요.

Trish is asking about an order she placed on behalf of her company.
Trish는 회사를 대표하여 주문했던 건에 대해 문의하고 있습니다.

Trish	Hello. This is Trish Brooks from Wilson & Clark. I've just placed _____ order for 100 packages of copy paper. I would like to know when it will be shipped.
Representative	Can I have _____ reference number?
Trish	It was OX-970860.
Representative	Yes. _____ order is being shipped today.
Trish	How long will _____ delivery take?
Representative	We'll make sure your items arrive on _____ same day.

Unit 063

The(2)

Dokdo is in the East Sea.
독도는 동해에 있습니다.

1 **다음 명사들은 보통 the와 함께 쓰인다.**
- He's always on **the Internet**. 그는 항상 **인터넷**에 접속해 있어요.
- Are you listening to **the radio**? 지금 **라디오** 듣고 있니?

악기 앞에도 보통 the를 쓴다.
- She's been playing **the violin** since she was 6. 그녀는 여섯 살 때부터 **바이올린**을 연주해 왔다.

2 **'the+ 형용사'는 '형용사'한 사람들 전체를 의미한다.**
- The government should do more to help **the poor**. 정부는 **빈민**을 돕기 위해 좀 더 많은 일을 해야 한다.
- **The young** are the future. **젊은이들**이 미래이다.

3 **'the+ 성(last name) + s'는 '그 집안 사람들'을 의미한다.**
- **The Watsons** came from Canada. Watson 씨네 가족은 캐나다에서 왔다.

4 **지명은 보통 다음과 같이 쓸 수 있다.**
- **나라, 대륙, 도시, 동네, 도로 등 일반적인 지명 앞에는 the를 쓰지 않는다.**
  - **Seoul** is the capital of **Korea**. 서울은 한국의 수도이다.
  - **Times Square** is always busy. 타임즈 광장은 언제나 번잡하다.
- **단, 나라명에 republic이나 kingdom과 같은 국가의 유형이 포함된 경우 the를 쓴다.**
  - **The United Kingdom** is made up of England, Scotland, Wales and Northern Ireland. 영국은 잉글랜드, 스코틀랜드, 웨일즈, 북아일랜드로 구성되어 있다.
- **강이나 바다 등 물과 관련된 지명은 보통 앞에 the를 쓴다.**
  - Is **the Amazon** the longest river in the world? 아마존 강이 세계에서 가장 긴 강인가요?
  - Dokdo is in **the East Sea**. 독도는 **동해**에 있습니다.
- **사막 이름 앞에는 the를 쓰고, 호수에는 the를 쓰지 않는다.**
  - I'd love to visit **the Sahara Desert** someday. 언젠가는 **사하라 사막**을 방문해 보고 싶어요.
  - We went to **Lake Seokchon** last Sunday. 우리는 지난 주 일요일에 **석촌호수**에 갔다.
- **복수형태로 된 지명 앞에는 the를 쓴다.** 산맥, 군도 등
  - Have you been to **the Netherlands**? 네덜란드에 가 봤어요?
  - We're planning a vacation to **the Hawaiian Islands**. 우리는 하와이 제도로 휴가를 갈 계획 중이다.
- **동서남북의 방위 앞에는 보통 the를 쓰지만, 형용사형에는 쓰지 않는다.**
  - India is in **southern** Asia. Korea is in **the east**. 인도는 남부 아시아에 있다. 한국은 아시아 **동부**에 있다.
- **넓은 땅을 차지하는 공항, 대학교, 역 등의 이름 앞에는 the를 쓰지 않는다.**
  - The plane arrived at **L.A. international Airport** at 3:00 p.m. 그 비행기는 오후 3시에 L.A. **국제 공항**에 도착했다.
  - She's going to **Yale University** next year. 그녀는 내년에 **예일 대학교**로 진학한다.

Exercises

1. 문장의 문맥에 가장 적합한 표현을 골라 문장을 완성하세요.

1. He's always on (Internet / **the Internet**).
2. (The Klein / The Kleins) live in a small house.
3. She wants to go to (Stanford University / the Stanford University).
4. Why does the Sun rise in (east / the east) and set in (west / the west)?
5. The children are watching (television / the television) now.
6. I'd like to learn to play (guitar / the guitar).
7. He donated a lot of money to help (the blind / the blinds).
8. What is the largest city in (northern California / the northern California)?

2. 빈칸에 the를 넣어 문장을 완성하세요. the가 필요하지 않은 경우에는 X를 쓰세요.

1. My hometown is near ___X___ Lake Windermere.
2. Many animals live in ___the___ Gobi Desert.
3. Sia works near _____ Trafalgar Square in _____ London.
4. _____ Africa is the second largest continent in the world.
5. _____ Kingdom of Bhutan is located in _____ South Asia.
6. The climbers got lost in _____ Andes.
7. Swimming in _____ Mediterranean Sea would be wonderful.
8. Don't miss _____ Halla Mountain on _____ Jeju Island.
9. Erika is from _____ Taiwan.
10. How long does it take from London to _____ Bermuda Islands?
11. The shop is somewhere on _____ Baker Street.
12. Have you ever been to _____ Philippines?
13. _____ Dominican Republic was found in 1844.
14. Which way is it to _____ Chapel Hill?

🔊 Dialogue

3. 빈칸에 the를 넣어 문장을 완성하세요. the가 필요하지 않은 경우에는 그냥 두세요.

Nicole has just come back from her trip to New York.
Nicole은 뉴욕으로의 여행을 끝내고 막 돌아왔습니다.

Nicole I've just been to _____ New York.

Jessica Oh really? I was there at Christmas. Were you there on holiday?

Nicole Yes, and I really needed a break. It was wonderful. I walked in _____ Central Park and along _____ Broadway. I did all the sights.

Jessica What did you like most?

Nicole _____ Hudson River. I spent the whole day walking around.

Jessica Where did you stay?

Nicole I stayed at a small hotel near _____ New York University.

Unit 064

The (3)

Please go to Gate 9 for boarding.
탑승을 위해 9번 게이트로 가 주세요.

◎ 064 #without the #the 안 쓰는 경우

1
어느 특정한 것이 아닌 일반적인 것을 의미할 때에는 보통 명사 앞에 the를 쓰지 않는다.

▶ **Health** is the most important thing in **life**. 삶에 있어 건강이 가장 중요하다.

셀 수 있는 명사의 경우 보통 복수형을 쓴다.

▶ I usually reply to **emails** within 24 hours. 나는 보통 24시간 안에 이메일에 대해 답장을 보냅니다.
▶ She likes reading **books** in her spare time. 그녀는 여가 시간에 책 읽는 것을 좋아합니다.

'the+단수명사'로 말하기도 한다. 더 큰 범위 내에 속한 한 가지 전반의 개념. the 없이 복수형으로 말하는 경우가 일반적임

▶ **The telephone** was invented by Bell. (=**Telephones** were invented by Bell.)
전화기는 벨에 의해 발명되었다. 발명품 중에서 전화기
▶ **The whale** is the largest animal in the world. (=**Whales** are the largest animal in the world.)
고래는 세상에서 가장 큰 동물이다. 동물 중에서 고래

2
이름과 같은 고유명사 앞에는 일반적으로 a나 the를 쓰지 않는다.

▶ **Chris Martin** is the lead singer of **Coldplay**. 크리스 마틴은 콜드플레이의 리드 싱어이다. 사람 이름, 밴드 이름
▶ We've just finished a meeting with a buyer from **Walmart**.
우리는 방금 월마트 사에서 온 바이어와의 회의를 마쳤습니다. 회사, 기업체 명
▶ They live in an apartment on **9th Avenue**. 그들은 9번가의 아파트에 산다. 도로명, 지명 *See Unit 057▶*
▶ **Christmas** is coming! 크리스마스가 다가오고 있어요. 명절 이름
▶ They pick up garbage on **Tuesday**. 화요일에 쓰레기를 수거한다. 요일명

단, 다음과 같은 경우에는 the를 쓴다.

● **호텔이나 극장, 박물관 등의 건물명 앞**

▶ We're staying at **the Intercontinental Hotel**. 우리는 인터콘티넨탈 호텔에 묵고 있어요.

● **언론사나 단체명 앞**

▶ His father works for **the BBC**. 그의 아버지는 BBC 방송국에서 일하신다.
▶ My dream is to work at **the Red Cross**. 내 꿈은 적십자사에서 일하는 것이다.

● **The ~ of…의 패턴**

▶ **The Great Wall of China** is about 6,000 kilometers long. 중국의 만리장성은 약 6천킬로미터이다.

3
숫자가 명사 뒤에 더해진 경우에도 앞에 a나 the를 쓰지 않는다. 숫자가 이름의 역할

▶ They're in **room 503**. 그들은 503호실에 있습니다.
▶ Please go to **Gate 9** for boarding. 탑승을 위해 9번 게이트로 가 주세요.
▶ The exercise is on **page 250**. 그 연습문제는 250쪽에 있습니다.

4
breakfast, lunch, dinner 앞에는 일반적으로 a나 the를 쓰지 않는다.

▶ I usually have a bowl of cereal for **breakfast**. 나는 보통 아침으로 시리얼을 한 그릇 먹어요.

단, 앞에 형용사가 있는 경우 a를 쓴다.

▶ We had **a** wonderful **dinner** with him. 우리는 그와 멋진 저녁식사를 했어요.

Exercises

1. 보기에서 적합한 표현을 골라 넣어 문장을 완성하세요. 필요한 경우 형태를 바꾸거나 the를 추가하세요.

> Barak Obama   ~~Christmas~~   Gloria Hotel   Google
> health   Museum of Modern Art   New York Times   penguin
> television   United States of America   Wednesday

1. _Christmas_ is coming!
2. He stayed at _____.
3. Walking is good for _____.
4. Why is _____ the best place to work in America?
5. _____ is one of the largest news producers in the world.
6. _____ served as the 44th President of _____.
7. _____ is one of the greatest inventions of the 20th century.
8. Have you ever visited _____ called MOMA?
9. _____ live only in the Southern Hemisphere.
10. _____ is called 'hump day' because it is in the middle of the week.

2. 밑줄 친 부분이 틀렸다면 맞게 고치세요. 고칠 부분이 없다면 X를 쓰세요.

1. She likes reading <u>book</u> in her spare time.   _books_
2. What shall we have for <u>lunch</u>?   _____
3. Turn to <u>the page 394</u>.   _____
4. <u>The Statue of Liberty</u> is often seen in movies.   _____
5. I've just had <u>a big breakfast</u>.   _____
6. Could you tell me how to get to <u>Science Museum</u>? _____
7. <u>European Union</u> is based in Brussels, Belgium.   _____

🔊 Dialogue

3. 빈칸에 the를 넣어 문장을 완성하세요. the가 필요하지 않은 경우에는 그냥 두세요.

James is at a telecom company.
James는 전화국에 있습니다.

James Excuse me. I've got a problem with my phone bill. Can I see someone about it?

Receptionist Yes. Please go to _____ Room 3 on _____ fifth floor.

James _____ Room 3 on _____ fifth floor?

Receptionist Yes. The elevators are right next to the stairs. Take one on the left. It stops on odd numbered floors. The other is for even numbered floors only.

James Thank you.

Unit 065

The(4)
What do you usually do after school?
학교 수업 끝나고 보통 뭐 하니?

1

장소를 나타내는 셀 수 있는 명사가 그 장소의 본질적인 개념이나 추상적인 의미를 나타낼 때에는 셀 수 없는 명사처럼 쓰일 수 있다. 복수형을 쓰지 않고 앞에 a나 the를 쓰지 않음

	#with the	#without the #장소
bed	▶ There is **an** old **bed** in the room. 방에 낡은 **침대**가 하나 있다. ▶ The cat is on **the bed**. 고양이는 **침대** 위에 있다.	▶ I **go to bed** at 11:00 p.m. 저는 밤 11시에 **잠자리**에 들어요. ▶ She's sleeping **in bed**. 그녀는 **잠자리**에서 자고 있어요.
school	▶ Is there **a school** nearby? 근처에 **학교**가 있나요? ▶ **The school** I visited is an international school. 내가 방문했던 **학교**는 국제학교이다.	▶ I **go to school** by bus. 저는 버스로 **등교**합니다. ▶ What do you usually do **after school**? 학교 수업 끝나고 보통 뭐 하니? ▶ He's **at school** now. 그는 지금 **학교**에 있어요. (공부 중)
college	▶ Amherst is **a** small **college**. 암허스트는 작은 **대학교**이다.	▶ I've decided to **go to college**. 저는 **대학**에 진학하기로 결심했어요.
class	▶ We were in **the** same **class** last year. 우린 작년에 같은 **반**이었다. ▶ I have **an** English **class** in the afternoon. 나는 오후에 영어 **수업**이 있어요.	▶ He's **in class** now. 그는 지금 **수업** 중이에요.
church	▶ The town has **three churches**. 그 동네에는 **교회**가 세 개 있다. ▶ I took some pictures of **the church**. 나는 그 **교회**의 사진을 몇 장 찍었다.	▶ They **go to church** every Sunday. 그들은 일요일마다 **교회**에 갑니다. ▶ **Church** begins at 10:00 a.m. today. 예배는 오늘 10시에 시작됩니다.
prison / jail	▶ Bill went to **the prison/jail** to visit his brother. Bill은 그의 형을 면회하러 **형무소**에 갔다.	▶ His brother is **in prison/jail** for robbery. 그의 형은 강도를 저질러서 **수감** 중이다. ▶ You will **go to prison/jail** if you're convicted. 유죄판결을 받으면 너는 **감옥**에 가게 될 것이다.

2

구체적인 건물이나 장소를 나타내는 단어와 추상적인 의미를 나타내는 단어가 따로 쓰이는 경우도 있다.

- ▶ How many bedrooms are there in the **house**?
  그 **집**에 침실은 몇 개나 있나요?
- ▶ What time did you arrive at the **office**?
  사무실에 몇 시에 도착하셨나요?
- ▶ Where's your **company** located?
  당신의 **회사**는 어디에 위치해 있나요?

- ▶ They're relaxing at **home** now.
  그들은 **집**에서 쉬고 있습니다.
- ▶ He left **home** when he was seventeen.
  그는 열일곱 살 때 **집**을 나왔다.
- ▶ What time do you **get to work**?
  몇 시에 **출근**하시나요?
- ▶ Mom's at **work** now.
  엄마는 지금 **회사**에 계세요. (근무 중)

3

공공서비스와 관련된 장소들은 일반적으로 the를 쓴다.

- ▶ How often do you go to **the movies**? 영화는 얼마나 자주 보러 가세요? 문화 서비스
- ▶ A: Where are you going? 어디 가니?
  B: I'm going to **the bank**. 은행에 가요. 금융 서비스
- ▶ He's been **in the hospital** for a week.
  그는 일주일 째 **병원**에 입원해 있어요. 의료 서비스, 단, 영국 영어에서는 the를 쓰지 않음

Exercises

1. 문장의 문맥에 가장 적합한 표현을 골라 문장을 완성하세요.

   1. She goes to ((church)/ the church) every Sunday. She's a Christian.
   2. I'm taking a lot of (class / classes) this semester.
   3. I'd like a room with (single bed / a single bed).
   4. What time did you go to (bed / a bed) last night?
   5. There are more than 500 prisoners in (prison / the prison) I visited last week.
   6. A: Where's Andy?
      B: He's still in (bed / the bed).
   7. Jay used to work at a café after (school / the school).
   8. Anna and her fiancé met each other when they were in (college / the college).
   9. Columbia College is (teaching college / a teaching college).
   10. They decided to get married in (church / a church).
   11. A boy was injured in (science class / a science class).
   12. He was sent to (prison / the prison) for stealing money.
   13. Let's go to (movie / the movies) tonight.
   14. (Post office / The post office) is across from (bank / the bank).

2. 빈칸에 들어갈 가장 적절한 표현을 보기에서 골라 넣어 문장을 완성하세요.

   > company   home   ~~house~~   office   work

   1. The Watsons lived in a four-bedroom ___house___ in Vancouver.
   2. I usually go to _____ by bus.
   3. I'll call Mr. Branson when I'm back in the _____.
   4. Sit down and make yourself at _____.
   5. Her _____ was founded in 2009.

🔊 Dialogue

3. 문장의 문맥에 가장 적합한 표현을 골라 문장을 완성하세요.

   David is a pilot. He is talking with his colleague Julia.
   David은 파일럿입니다. 그는 동료인 Julia와 이야기하고 있습니다.

   Julia Have you always wanted to be a pilot?

   David Yes. I've always known what I wanted to do in life.

   Julia Since you were a little child?

   David Yes. I still remember when my dad bought me a model plane. That's when I first fell in love with airplanes.

   Julia Did you study flying in (college / the college)?

   David Yes. I took a course in aviation in (college / the college) right after leaving (high school / the high school).

Big Picture

대명사와 반복 피하기

07

1 대명사

영어는 반복을 싫어합니다. 때문에 반복을 피하는 많은 장치 또는 방법이 문법과 작문에 존재합니다.
대명사는 명사를 반복하지 않기 위한 장치입니다. 대명사는 문장에서의 자리에 따라 모양을 달리하여 혼동을 막습니다. *See* 부록 15 ▶

2 문장 반복 피하기

반복되는 내용(문장)은 문장의 가장 기본이 되는 틀인 주어와 동사 하나만을 남기는 방법으로 중복을 피할 수 있습니다. 이 때 몇 안 되는 Be type 동사는 그대로, Do type 동사는 do로 대신합니다. 부정문의 경우에는 여기에 not을 더해 줍니다.

- A: Are you interested in sports?
  스포츠에 관심이 있나요?

  B: Yes, I am. (= I am interested in sports.)
  네, 있어요. (스포츠에 관심이 있어요.)

- I asked him to turn off the TV, but he didn't (turn off the TV).
  나는 그에게 TV를 꺼 달라고 부탁했으나, 그는 그렇게 하지 않았다.

이외에도 that이나 so 같은 표현이 앞서 나온 내용을 대신하기도 합니다.

- A: Ann got married last month.
  Ann이 지난 달에 결혼했어요.

  B: Really? I didn't know that.
  (= I didn't know that she got married last month.)
  정말요? 그건 몰랐네요. (Ann이 지난 달에 결혼했다는 것은 몰랐네요.)

- A: I think she hates me.
  걔가 날 아주 싫어하는 것 같아.

  B: Why do you think so?
  왜 그렇게 생각하는데?

Unit 066

대명사(1)

If anyone calls, tell them I'm busy.
누가 전화하면 나 바쁘다고 해 줘요.

1 반복을 피하기 위해 대명사를 쓸 수 있다.

- 동일한 대상이 반복될 때에는 문장에서의 자리에 따라 대명사의 형태가 달라진다.
  - A: Have you seen **Mike** recently? I haven't seen **him** for days. 최근에 Mike 보셨어요? 며칠 째 **그를** 못 봐서요.
    B: **He**'s in L.A. on vacation now. 그는 지금 휴가 차 L.A에 가 있어요.
  - **We** are old friends. I cherish **our** friendship. 우리는 오랜 친구예요. 저는 **우리의** 우정을 소중히 여깁니다.
  - **She**'s my English teacher. Everybody likes **her** class. 그 분은 제 영어 선생님이세요. 모두가 **그녀의** 수업을 좋아해요.

- 동일한 대상은 아니나 같은 명사가 반복될 경우에 one 또는 ones를 쓸 수 있다.
  - This phone looks tacky. How about that **one**? 이 전화기는 좀 구려 보여. 저건 어때?
  - A: Which shoes are yours – these or those? 어느 게 당신 신발인가요? 이거? 저거?
    B: The red **ones** are mine. 빨간 게 제 거예요.

2 대상이 주어와 같은 경우 –self/selves 를 쓴다.

- I often talk to **myself**. 나는 종종 **혼잣말**을 해요.
- Help **yourselves**, please. 여러분 마음껏 드세요.

강조의 의미로 명사 바로 뒤에 –self/selves를 쓸 수 있다. 보통 '그 자체' 또는 '그 자신'으로 해석된다.

- I **myself** don't like hip hop music. 저 **자신**은 힙합 음악을 좋아하지 않습니다.
- The hotel **itself** was OK, but the location is terrible. 호텔 **자체**는 괜찮았는데, 위치가 나빠요.

3 일반적인 사람들(people in general)은 보통 다음과 같이 나타낼 수 있다.

- **they**
  - **They** speak Spanish in Mexico. 멕시코에서는 **사람들이** 스페인어를 씁니다.
  - That's what **they** say. 사람들이 보통 그렇게 말하지.

- **you**
  - Smoking is bad for **you**. 흡연은 몸에 안 좋아요.
  - **You** can vote in prison. 수감 중에도 투표를 할 수 있습니다.

- **one** 불특정한 한 사람을 의미, 다소 딱딱함
  - **One** should not waste **one**'s time. 사람은 자신의 시간을 낭비해선 안된다.

4 성별이 불특정한 경우 they(또는 them, their)를 쓸 수 있다.

- If **anyone** calls, tell **them** I'm busy. 누가 전화하면 나 바쁘다고 해 줘요.
- **Everybody** has **their** own opinion. 모두가 자신들만의 의견이 있다.

he or she(또는 him or her, his or her)를 쓰기도 한다.

- Each team member has to do **his or her** best. 각 팀 멤버들은 최선을 다해야 한다.

Exercises

1. one이나 ones를 넣어 문장을 완성하세요.
   1. A: Would you like an orange?
      B: Yes. I'd like __one__.
   2. This cup is dirty. Can I have another _____?
   3. These chopsticks are dirty. Can I have other _____?
   4. Liz? She is the _____ with blonde hair.
   5. The old books are in the box and the new _____ are on the shelves.

2. 적절한 대명사를 넣어 문장을 완성하세요.
   1. May I introduce __myself__?
   2. I should have been more careful. I blame _____ for what has happened.
   3. My friends say that London is an interesting city, but I _____ have never been there.
   4. Don't hurt _____ while cutting it.
   5. He couldn't believe his eyes, so he pinched _____ to make sure that he wasn't dreaming.
   6. The city _____ is very beautiful, but the people aren't very friendly.

3. 문장의 문맥에 가장 적합한 표현을 골라 문장을 완성하세요.
   1. That's what (they / one) say.
   2. (She's / Her) name is Esther.
   3. I was with a friend of (me / mine).
   4. Each student will have (one's / their) own locker.
   5. When my nephew saw my bike, he wanted one like (me / mine).
   6. Too much alcohol is bad for (you / yours).
   7. My apartment is not as modern as (you / yours).
   8. If anyone says (they / you) know what's going to happen, (they're / you're) lying.
   9. (One / They) are building a new shopping center near the community center.

✦ Dialogue

4. 빈칸에 적절한 대명사를 써 넣어 문장을 완성하세요.

Jessica and Nicole are at a party hosted by the Watsons.
Jessica와 Nicole은 Watson 부부가 주최한 파티에 있습니다.

Mr. Watson Have you two met before?

Jessica Yes, we have. Nicole and I work at the same hospital.

Mr. Watson I see. Well, I hope you enjoy _____ tonight.
Please, help _____ to a drink. Are you OK, Nicole?

Nicole Sorry. I've got this awful feeling that I've got something important to do, but I can't remember what it is.

Jessica Nicole, you worry too much. Come on. Just relax.

Unit 067

대명사(2)

He was given one week's notice to leave the apartment.
그는 일주일 내에 아파트를 비우라는 통보를 받았다.

1 this와 that은 다음과 같이 쓰이기도 한다.

this	that
처음 언급되는 것에 대해 a/an 대신	앞서 언급된 것이나 내용 전체를 대신
▶ When I was in high school, there was **this** guy who lived next door. 내가 고등학교 다닐 때, 옆 집 살던 한 남자가 있었어요.	▶ A: You're from Korea, aren't you? 한국에서 오셨죠? 그쵸? B: **That**'s right. 맞습니다.
'이 정도로' 또는 '이렇게' 부사	'그 정도로' 또는 '그렇게' 부사
▶ Things have never been **this** bad. 상황이 이 정도로 나빴던 적은 없었다.	▶ A: The new Christopher Nolan movie is a classic. 새 크리스토퍼 놀란 감독 영화는 명작이야. B: Well, I don't think it's **that** good. 글쎄, 난 그게 그렇게 훌륭하지는 않은 것 같은데.

those는 종종 관계사 who와 함께 '~한 사람들'의 의미로 쓰인다.
▶ God helps **those who** help themselves. 신은 스스로를 돕는 자를 돕는다.

2 '~의'라는 의미는 's 또는 of를 써서 나타낼 수 있다.

사람 +'s	of 사물
▶ Mike is **Sia's** younger brother. Mike는 Sia의 남동생입니다.	▶ I like the design **of your website**. 당신의 웹사이트의 디자인이 맘에 드는군요.

- 사람인 경우에도 표현이 긴 경우 's 대신 of를 쓸 수 있다.
  ▶ What was the name **of the person who called us** this morning? 오늘 아침에 우리에게 전화한 사람의 이름이 뭐였지?

- 단체나 장소에 대해서도 's를 쓸 수 있다. of를 쓰는 것도 가능
  ▶ It depends on **the government's** decision. 그것은 정부의 결정에 달려 있다.
  (= It depends on the decision **of the government**.)
  ▶ More than half of **the world's** population is bilingual. 세계 인구의 절반 이상이 2개국어를 씁니다.
  (= More than half of the population **of world** is bilingual.)

- 's는 시간표현에도 쓰일 수 있다.
  ▶ What is **today's** special? 오늘의 특별메뉴는 무엇인가요?

- 's는 누군가의 집, 가게나 사업장 등을 의미할 수 있다.
  ▶ I went to **the doctor's** yesterday. 나는 어제 병원에 갔다.

3 's를 써서 '어느 기간 동안의'의 의미를 표현할 수도 있다.
기간을 나타내는 단어가 복수를 의미하는 s로 끝난 경우에는 '(apostrophe)만 더한다.

▶ He was given **one week's** notice to leave the apartment. 그는 일주일 내에 아파트를 비우라는 통보를 받았다.
▶ It's a **ten days'** course. 그것은 10일짜리 코스입니다.

4 own은 my, your, his 등의 소유격 뒤에 쓰여서 '그 자신의'의 의미를 강조할 수 있다.

▶ I never had **my own** room until my sister moved out. 나는 언니가 이사 나갈 때까지 나만의 방을 결코 가져보지 못했다.

Exercises

1. this, that, these, those를 넣어 문장을 완성하세요.

1. A: Alice is moving to another law firm. / B: Really? I didn't know ___that___.
2. A: I hear that he has a private jet. / B: No way. He can't be _____ rich!
3. You know, I met _____ funny guy at the party last night.
4. Good things come to _____ who work hard and never give up.
5. Suddenly, there was _____ enormous crash.
6. He's never had _____ much money before.

2. 's를 써서 같은 의미의 문장으로 완성하세요.

1. It depends on the decision of the government.
   → It depends on ___the government's___ decision.
2. This camera belongs to Patrick.
   → This is _____ camera.
3. The meeting last week was successful.
   → _____ meeting was successful.
4. Who is the new president of South Korea?
   → Who is _____ new president?
5. A newborn baby needs to sleep for 16 hours a day.
   → A newborn baby needs _____ sleep a day.

3. 문장의 틀린 부분이 있다면 고쳐서 다시 쓰세요. 고칠 부분이 없다면 X를 쓰세요.

1. Please bring your own beverage.   ___X___
2. Who is this beautiful house's owner?   _____
3. They are parents of Eugene.   _____
4. I went to my sister's last Saturday.   _____
5. You will never forget the name of the teacher who touched your life. _____

🔸 Dialogue

4. 보기 중 빈칸에 들어갈 가장 적합한 표현을 골라 넣어 문장을 완성하세요.

| this   that   these   those |

Andy is so excited. Amy is asking him why. Andy는 매우 신났습니다. Amy가 이유를 묻고 있습니다.

Amy   What happened? You look excited.
Andy You won't believe _____, but I've just seen a U.F.O.
Amy   That's ridiculous.
Andy Believe me, Amy. I'm pretty sure that it was a U.F.O.
Amy   What did it look like?
Andy It looked like a star at first, but it was moving.
Amy   I think you just saw an aircraft or something.

Unit 068

it

It's you that I need, not him.
내가 필요한 건 당신이에요, 그 사람이 아니고.

---

1. it은 특별한 의미 없이 주어나 목적어(대상) 자리를 채울 때 쓸 수 있다.

- **시간, 요일, 날짜, 거리, 날씨, 사람 등**
  - ▶ **It**'s Monday morning 5:19. 지금은 월요일 아침 5시 19분입니다.
  - ▶ Is **it** far from here to the beach? 여기서 해변까지는 먼가요?
  - ▶ Look! **It**'s Mr. Cruz. 저기 봐! 크루즈 선생님이야.
  - ▶ I hate **it** when it's so cold. 나는 추운 게 너무 싫어.

- **(너무 긴) 동사표현(동사구)의 자리**

  > **It**'s terrible **to** have the flu. 독감에 걸리는 건 끔찍해요.

  - ▶ **It**'s good <u>to be home.</u> 집에 오니 좋네요.
  - ▶ **It** takes one hour <u>to get to the airport by bus.</u> 버스로 공항을 가려면 한 시간이 걸립니다.
  - ▶ **It**'s no use <u>crying.</u> 울어봐야 소용없다. See Unit 048▶

  > I find **it** interesting **to** read about historical events.
  > 저는 역사적 사건에 대해 읽는 것이 흥미로워요.

  - ▶ The Internet makes **it** possible <u>to work more effectively.</u> 인터넷은 일을 좀 더 효율적으로 하는 것을 가능하게 한다.

- **(너무 긴) S+V(절)의 자리**

  > **It**'s not true **that** cats don't like water.
  > 고양이가 물을 싫어한다는 것은 사실이 아니다.

  - ▶ **It**'s likely <u>that they will lose the game.</u> 그들이 경기에 질 가능성이 크다.
  - ▶ **It**'s good <u>that you've decided to get a job.</u> 네가 취직하기로 결심한 건 좋은 것이다.

  > I find **it** amazing **that** I can draw on my phone.
  > 전화기에서 그림을 그릴 수 있다니 신기해요.

  - ▶ He takes **it** for granted <u>that he will marry her.</u> 그는 그가 그녀와 결혼할 것이라고 당연히 믿고 있다.
  - ▶ **It** is said that he was a famous movie star.
    사람들은 그가 유명한 영화배우였다고 한다. 수동태 문장은 종종 it으로 시작된다.

---

2. '~한 사람/사물'을 강조할 때 It ~ who/that…로 말할 수 있다. See Unit 096▶

  - ▶ **It** was Andy **who** helped me move into my new apartment. 내가 새 아파트로 이사하는 것을 도운 건 Andy였어.
  - ▶ Was **it** his phone **that** kept ringing? 계속 울려댔던 게 그의 전화기였어?
  - ▶ **It**'s you **that** I need, not him. 내가 필요한 건 당신이에요, 그 사람이 아니고.

---

3. 종종 대화체에서 명사 앞에 it을 써서 매우 세련되거나 유행하는 것임을 나타낼 수 있다.

  - ▶ It's nice, but not an **It-bag**. 그거 괜찮긴 하지만, 요즘 유행하는 가방은 아냐.
  - ▶ Angelina Jolie and Brad Pitt were Hollywood's '**It**' couple.
    안젤리나 졸리와 브래드피트는 할리우드의 유명한 커플이었다.

Exercises

1. 주어진 표현을 이용하여 보기와 같이 문장을 완성하세요.

1. (good, be home) — It's _good to be home_.
2. (wear a helmet while riding on a motorcycle, essential) — It's _____.
3. (to go to the movies on Saturday night, fun) — It's _____.
4. (Erika couldn't be here tonight, a pity) — It's _____.
5. (concentrate, hard) — I found it _____.
6. (they're not coming, seem) — It _____.
7. (she is innocent, obvious to all) — It _____.
8. (be up by 7:00 a.m., a rule) — I made it _____.
9. (they'll arrive before 6:00 p.m., unlikely) — It's _____.
10. (download a video clip, about a few minutes) — It usually takes _____.

2. 보기와 같이 주어진 표현을 강조하는 문장을 완성하세요.

1. his phone — _It was his phone that_ kept ringing.
2. love — _____ brings happiness to people.
3. the boss — _____ you should talk to, not me.
4. in Hawaii — _____ I first learned to dive.
5. in 2016 — _____ you started a business?
6. Peter — _____ is always complaining.

🔊 Dialogue

3. 주어진 단어를 이용하여 문맥에 맞게 문장을 완성하세요.

Andy is talking to his school counselor Mr. Cruz.
Andy는 학교 상담사인 Mr. Cruz와 이야기를 하고 있습니다.

Andy Mr. Cruz. I need your advice.
Mr. Cruz Oh, what is it, Andy?
Andy _____ (find, to, difficult, I, it, get to class on time).
Mr. Cruz Why don't you get up a bit earlier?
Andy Well, the thing is even if I get up 15 minutes early, I still end up late to class.
Mr. Cruz Hmm, maybe you move slower because you think you have extra time?
Andy I don't know. Morning just seems rushed to me.
Mr. Cruz Well, Andy. I suggest you develop a morning routine first. Creating a consistent routine can help you stay relaxed in the mornings.

Unit 069

대동사, so

I might not be able to answer the phone. If so, just text me.
내가 전화를 못 받을지도 몰라요. 그렇게 되면 문자를 보내 주세요.

1 다음과 같이 주어와 동사만을 남기고 반복되는 내용을 생략할 수 있다. **대동사**

❶ Be type 동사: be, can, may, must, should, have (p.p.), will 등

▶ My brother isn't interested in politics, but I **am** (interested in politics).
우리 오빠는 정치에 관심이 없지만 나는 (정치에 관심이) **있다**.

▶ A: Would you like to come to my place for dinner tonight? 오늘밤에 저녁 먹으러 우리 집에 올래?
B: I wish I **could** (go to your place), but I have a test tomorrow. 그러고 싶지만 내일 시험이 있어.

▶ A: Don't tell anyone about it. 아무한테도 그것에 대해 말하지 마.
B: I **won't** (tell anyone about it). 안 할게.

▶ A: You haven't eaten horse meat, have you? 너 말고기는 안 먹어 봤지, 응?
B: I **have**. Actually, I eat it quite often. I like it. 먹어 **봤어**. 사실은 꽤 자주 먹어. 좋아하거든.

❷ Do type 동사: have, go, see, like, run, sleep, take, get 등

▶ I didn't enjoy the movie, but he **did**(=enjoyed the movie). 나는 그 영화가 재미없었지만, 그는 **재미있게 봤다**.

▶ A: I drink coffee every morning. 나는 아침마다 커피를 마셔요.
B: I **do**(=drink coffee), too. 저도요.

▶ A: Do you, Henry, take Anna to be your lawfully wedded wife?
Henry, 당신은 Anna를 당신의 합법적인 아내로 맞이합니까?
B: I **do**. 네, 맞이합니다.

▶ Amy has a cat, but I **don't** (have a cat). Amy는 고양이가 있지만 나는 **없어요**.

---

2 so는 앞서 나온 내용을 대신할 때 쓰일 수 있다.

▶ The project has been canceled because of lack of funds. Mike told me **so** yesterday.
프로젝트가 기금 부족으로 취소되었대요. Mike가 어제 제게 **그렇게** 말해 줬어요.

▶ I thought he was rude, but I didn't say **so**. 저는 그가 무례하다고 생각했지만 **그렇게** 말하진 않았어요.

▶ He wanted me to do it alone and I did **so**. 그는 제가 그것을 혼자 하길 원해서 **그렇게** 했어요.

'그렇게'의 의미로 so는 다음과 같이 쓰이기도 한다.

▶ I might not be able to answer the phone. If **so**, just text me.
내가 전화를 못 받을지도 몰라요. **그렇게** 되면 문자를 보내 주세요.

▶ A: They're going to sell their house. 그들이 집을 팔 거래요.
B: Is that **so**? 그런가요? `Is that right?으로 말하기도 함`

대화상의 짧은 대답에서 think, guess, hope 등의 동사 뒤에서도 앞서 나온 내용을 대신해 so를 쓸 수 있다.

▶ A: Does Jay come here very often? Jay가 여기 자주 오나요?
B: I think **so**. / I don't think **so**. 그런 것 같아요. / 그렇지 않은 것 같아요.

▶ A: Did she call the maintenance team? 그녀가 유지 보수팀을 불렀나요?
B: I believe **so**. / I don't believe **so**. 그런 것 같습니다. / 그렇지 않은 것 같습니다. `다소 격식 있는 느낌`

단, 다음 동사들은 부정문 형태에서는 so를 쓰지 않는다.

▶ A: Do you think it'll rain tomorrow? 내일 비가 올 것 같아요?
B: I hope **so**. / I hope **not**. 그랬으면 좋겠어요. / 안 그러길 바라요.

▶ A: Will he come? 그가 올까?
B: I'm afraid **so**. / I'm afraid **not**. 그럴 것 같아 걱정이야. / 안 그럴 것 같다고 우려되네요.

▶ A: Will you be home late tonight? 오늘 집에 늦게 올 것 같니?
B: I guess **so**. / I guess **not**. 그럴걸. / 아닐걸.

Exercises

1. 문맥에 맞는 문장끼리 연결하세요.

1. Would you like to go bowling with us tonight?
2. I passed the test!
3. Call me as soon as you arrive.
4. He is really tall.
5. We'll never make it there with all this traffic.
6. Your room is in a mess. You should tidy it up.

a. Sure we will. Rush hour is almost over.
b. I will.
c. You did? Congratulations!
d. So is his brother.
e. I can't now. Can I do it later?
f. I wish I could, but I have other plans.

2. 문장이나 대화문에 들어갈 적절한 표현을 보기에서 골라 빈칸을 채우세요.

say so
is that so
if so
~~thought so~~
think so

1. A: I thought this cold front was supposed to pass.
   B: I _thought so_, too.
2. A: I'm not sure if I should stick with my current job.
   B: I think it's time for a change, don't you?
   A: Do you really _____?
3. If you want to leave, just _____.
4. A: I've just found out that Andy's new neighbor is a former rock star.
   B: _____? Wow!
5. I might be late for the meeting. _____, please start without me.

3. 주어진 표현을 이용하여 적절하게 응답해 보세요.

1. A: Do you think it will stop raining soon?
   B: _I hope so_. (hope) I'm sick and tired of this rain.
2. A: Is Mr. Turner married?
   B: _____. (not, think) He said he's living alone.
3. A: The talent show is at 7:30, right?
   B: _____. (suppose) It has been shown at that time since the beginning.
4. A: Are there any rooms available tomorrow night?
   B: _____. (not, afraid) We're fully booked.
5. A: Will you be home early tonight?
   B: _____. (not, guess) Actually, I might work late.

🔊 Dialogue

4. 주어진 표현 중 가장 적합한 표현을 골라 문장을 완성하세요.

Suzi and Naomi are having coffee. Suzi와 Naomi는 커피를 마시고 있습니다.

Naomi   Why aren't you drinking your coffee?
Suzi   (I can't / I don't / I will). It's too hot.
Naomi   (Did it / Is it / You did)? Shall I add some cold water?
Suzi   No, thanks. I'd rather wait until it cools down a little bit. I like strong coffee.

Big Picture

명사 꾸며 주기, 명사가 아닌 것 꾸며 주기

08

1 형용사(Adjective) 명사 꾸미기

보통 명사 앞, Be동사나 seem, get 등의 동사 뒤에 종종 옵니다. -ing나 p.p.도 형용사로 쓰일 수 있습니다.

- The old man lives in a small house. 그 노인은 작은 집에 살고 있습니다.
- Rabbits are cute. 토끼는 귀여워요.
- The movie was interesting. 그 영화는 흥미로웠다.
- Suzi looks worried. Suzi는 걱정스러워 보여요.

2 명사 to 동사(Noun to Verb) 명사 꾸미기

'~할 무엇'의 의미로 명사 뒤에 'to 동사원형'을 더할 수 있습니다.

- I'm going to buy a magazine to read on the plane. 전 비행기에서 읽을 잡지를 하나 살 거예요.

3 관계사(that, which, who 등) 명사 꾸미기

명사에 대해 말하는 '문장(S+V)'을 관계사(연결 장치)를 써서 연결할 수 있습니다.

- 중심 문장 : The movie was amazing. 그 영화 끝내줬다.
- 명사에 대한 내용 : I watched the movie yesterday. 나는 어제 그 영화를 봤다.

꾸며 주고자 하는 명사 뒤에 관계사와 명사에 대한 내용을 더해 주고, 내용 속에 겹치는 명사는 생략합니다.

- The movie that I watched ~~the movie~~ yesterday was amazing.
  내가 어제 본 영화는 끝내줬다.

4 '명사+-ing' & '명사+p.p.' 명사 꾸미기

명사를 꾸며 주고자 하는 내용이 동사로 시작하는 경우(동사구) -ing나 p.p. 형태로 명사 뒤에 연결할 수 있습니다. 능동적인 경우 -ing, 수동적인 경우에는 p.p.를 씁니다.

- The woman living next door has three cats. 옆집에 사는 여자분은 고양이가 세 마리 있다.

명사를 꾸며 주는 -ing나 p.p. 부분(구)은 관계사로 시작하는 표현(절)으로 바꿀 수 있습니다.

- The woman who lives next door has three cats. 옆집에 사는 여자분은 고양이가 세 마리 있다.

5 부사 명사가 아닌 것 꾸미기

'명사'가 아닌 것을 꾸며줄 때는 '부사(adverbs)'를 씁니다. 기본적으로 위치가 자유롭습니다. 문장의 앞, 뒤 등에 모두 올 수 있습니다. 또한 일부 부사는 Be type 동사 뒤나 Do type 동사 앞에도 올 수 있습니다.

- He answered the phone quickly. 그는 재빨리 전화를 받았다.
- Unfortunately, she missed the bus. 안타깝게도 그녀는 버스를 놓쳤다.
- My mother is always kind to others. 우리 엄마는 항상 다른 사람에게 친절하시다.

Unit 070

형용사

His car looks nice.
그의 차는 멋져 보인다.

1 형용사는 명사 앞에서 명사를 꾸며 준다.
- It was a **scary** movie. 그건 무서운 영화였어.

두 개 이상의 형용사가 올 때 보통 다음의 순서대로 위치한다. 〔명사의 본질에 가까울수록 명사 가까이에 위치〕

주관적 느낌(opinion) → 크기(size) → 연령(age) → 색상(color) → 원산지(origin) → 재료(material) → 명사

- He bought a **new black German** car. 그는 새 검정색 독일차를 샀다. 〔연령-색상-원산지〕
- She was wearing a **beautiful long silk** skirt. 그녀는 아름다운 긴 실크 치마를 입고 있었다. 〔주관적 느낌-크기-재료〕

세 개 이상의 형용사를 한 번에 열거하지 않는 것이 좋다. 〔문장을 둘로 나누어 서술하는 등으로 표현〕
- She was wearing a **beautiful silk** skirt. It was **long** and **yellow**.
그녀는 아름다운 실크 치마를 입고 있었다. 길고 노란색이었다. 〔Be동사 뒤처럼 명사 없이 두 개 이상의 형용사가 쓰일 때에는 and를 쓴다.〕

some/any가 포함된 표현에는 형용사가 뒤에 더해진다.
- Let's try **somewhere new** for lunch this time. 이번엔 점심 먹을 곳으로 어딘가 새로운 곳을 시도해 보자.

2 다음 동사 뒤에는 형용사가 온다. 〔주어인 명사를 꾸며 주는 역할을 하며, '부사'가 아님에 주의〕

> appear   be   become   feel   get   look   seem   smell   taste   sound

- The movie **was scary**. 그 영화는 무서웠어.
- His car **looks nice**. 그의 차는 멋져 보인다. 〔그의 차(His car: 명사)가 멋지다는 의미〕
- It's **getting warm**. 날이 더워지고 있다. 〔날씨(the weather)가 덥다는 의미〕

3 '순서를 나타내는 표현(first, second, last 등)+수량 표현(two, three, few 등)'의 순서로 말할 수 있다.
〔앞에 보통 the가 온다. See Unit 062 ▶〕
- The **first two** days at the camp were terrible. 캠프에서의 처음 이틀은 끔찍했다.
- I haven't been feeling very well for the **past few** days. 지난 며칠간 몸이 썩 좋지 않았어요.

4 '명사+명사'의 형태로 된 하나의 명사 표현이 있다. 〔복합 명사. 앞의 명사가 뒤의 명사를 꾸며 주는 역할〕
- Sia is a **bank manager**. Sia는 은행 매니저이다.
- He wants to buy a **sports car**. 그는 스포츠카를 사고 싶어 한다.

종종 두 개의 단어가 한 단어로 합쳐지기도 한다. 〔대체로 오랫동안 사용되어 자연스럽게 한 단어처럼 인식된 것들. 별도의 뚜렷한 규칙은 없다.〕
- I've had a **headache** since the **weekend**. 주말부터 계속 두통이 있다.

5 -ing와 p.p.도 형용사로 쓰일 수 있다.

-ing (능동적 의미)	p.p. (수동적 의미)
▶ Politics is **interesting**. 정치는 흥미로워요. ▶ The news was **surprising**. 그 뉴스는 놀라웠어요. ▶ The lecture was **boring**. 그 강연은 지루했어요. ▶ The weather is **depressing**. 날씨가 침울하네요.	▶ I'm **interested** in politics. 전 정치에 관심이 있어요. ▶ We were **surprised** at the news. 우리는 그 뉴스에 놀랐어요. ▶ I was **bored** with the lecture. 난 그 강연이 지루했어요. ▶ She is feeling **depressed**. 그녀는 우울해 하고 있어요.

Exercises

1. 문장의 밑줄 친 명사에 주어진 표현을 더해 다시 써 보세요.

   1. There was a table in the middle of the room. (big, old, wooden)
      → There was _____a big old wooden table_____ in the middle of the room.
   2. Queen Elsa lives in a castle. (huge, ice)
      → Queen Elsa lived in _____.
   3. Dorothy and Toto walked along the road. (brick, yellow)
      → Dorothy and Toto walked along _____.
   4. James is a sales manager. (American, young)
      → James is _____.
   5. I'd like to meet someone. (sweet and kind)
      → I'd like to meet _____.
   6. How would you spend the days of your life? (last, ten)
      → How would you spend _____ of your life?

2. 문장의 문맥에 가장 적합한 표현을 골라 문장을 완성하세요.

   1. Your car is four years old, but still looks ((new) / newly).
   2. A: How about spending the holidays in Croatia?
      B: Croatia sounds really (exciting / excitingly).
   3. Please, look at this picture (careful / carefully).
   4. Something smells (good / well). Mom must be baking cookies or a cake.

3. 주어진 표현 중 가장 적합한 형태를 골라 문장을 완성하세요.

   1. The hotel was luxurious, but their service was quite ((disappointing) / disappointed).
   2. We were so (exhausting / exhausted) after the long journey.
   3. The poor little girl was (frightening / frightened).
   4. This math problem is really (confusing / confused). Can you help me solve this?

🔊 Dialogue

4. 보기 중 가장 적합한 표현을 골라 문장을 완성하세요.

Andy would like to help his mom cook dinner.
Andy는 엄마가 저녁을 요리하는 것을 돕고 싶어 합니다.

Andy	Can I help you with anything, Mom?
Mrs. Watson	Oh, thanks. Can you taste this soup for me?
Andy	Sure, hmm… Well, I think it's a bit bland. Let me put some salt in.
Mrs. Watson	Urgh! Andy, it tastes (strange / strangely). What did you add to the soup?
Andy	The salt on the counter.
Mrs. Watson	Oh! No, Andy. It's not salt. You put baking soda in the soup!
Andy	Did I? Oh, my… I thought it was salt. Sorry, Mom.

Unit 071

부사

They are all foreigners.
그들은 모두 외국인입니다.

1 부사는 다양한 위치에서 동사, 형용사, 부사 또는 문장 전체를 꾸며 줄 수 있다.

① 문장의 맨 앞이나 주요 문장 성분 뒤
- **Luckily**, everybody passed the exam. 운 좋게 모두가 시험에 합격했다.
- She answered the phone **quickly**. 그녀는 **재빨리** 전화를 받았다.

② 형용사나 부사 앞
- Colorado is **extremely** cold in winter. 콜로라도는 겨울에 **극도로** 추워요.
- The company is **badly** organized. 그 회사는 체계가 **허술**하다.
- You did it **very** well. 정말 잘했어.

2 빈도부사 외 일부 부사들은 Be type 동사 뒤, Do type 동사 앞에 올 수 있다. See unit 002▶

> always, usually, often, sometimes, rarely, seldom, never, ever, already, just, still, also, all, both, probably 등

- Trish **is never** late for work. Trish는 절대 회사에 지각**하지 않아요**.
- Suzi and I enjoyed the sunshine while lying on the beach. We **also swam** in the ocean.
  Suzi와 나는 해변에 누워 햇볕을 즐겼어요. 우리는 바다에서 **수영도 했습니다**.
- They **are all** foreigners. 그들은 **모두** 외국인**입니다**.

probably는 not 앞에 온다. See Unit 017▶
- The restaurant **probably** isn't the best place for a vegetarian.
  그 식당은 **아마도** 채식주의자에게 최고의 식당은 아니다.

뒤의 표현이 생략되는 경우에 어순이 달라질 수 있다.
- A: Are you up at this time? 보통 이 시간에 깨어 있어요?
  B: Yes. **I usually am**. 네. 보통 그래요. *I am usually*. (X)

> **TIP** 부정문에서의 still과 yet
> still은 not 앞에 오며, 다소 조바심이 나거나 독촉하는 뉘앙스이다.
> 반면 yet은 부정문의 맨 뒤에 오며, 아직은 아니지만 곧 그렇게 될 거라는 뉘앙스를 띤다.
> 예) He still hasn't arrived.
> 그는 아직도 도착하지 않았다.
> still … not의 어순
> He hasn't arrived yet.
> 그는 아직 도착하지 않았다.

3 다음 부사표현들은 보통 부정문이나 의문문에서 문장의 맨 뒤에 온다.

> **not** ··· yet, anymore, any longer, very often/much/well

- I haven't seen the movie **yet**. 난 아직 그 영화 **못** 봤다.
- He doesn't work here **anymore**.
  그분은 **더 이상** 여기서 근무하지 **않습니다**.

no longer는 문장 중간에 올 수 있다.
- He **no longer** works here. 그분은 더 이상 여기서 근무하지 **않습니다**.

4 부사표현이 여럿일 경우 보통 '장소+시간' 순으로 위치한다.
- We went **to Mexico last year**. 우린 작년에 멕시코에 갔다.
- They arrived **at the station at the same time**. 그들은 동시에 역에 도착했다.

시간표현은 종종 문장의 맨 앞에도 온다.
- **Last Christmas**, it snowed and the area looked very beautiful.
  작년 크리스마스에 눈이 와서 지역이 아주 아름다워 보였다.

Exercises

1. 문장의 틀린 부분이 있다면 고쳐서 다시 쓰세요. 고칠 부분이 없다면 X를 쓰세요.
   1. Colorado is cold extremely in winter.   *Colorado is extremely cold in winter.*
   2. I moved here two years, but I still don't know where everything is.
   3. Aliens probably don't exist.
   4. I trust you, and I will always.
   5. I have a bad cough and a sore throat. I have also a headache.

2. 각 박스에서 표현을 하나씩 골라 빈칸에 넣어 문장을 완성하세요.

badly	different
relatively	easy
totally	organized
~~well~~	~~paid~~
well	qualified

   1. Television writers are quite ___*well paid*___.
   2. I've decided not to take the job because the company is _____.
   3. Compared to the old one, the new system is _____ to use.
   4. James is _____ with an MBA.
   5. English is _____ from Korean.

3. 주어진 표현을 사용하여 문장을 다시 쓰세요.
   1. He shouldn't drive. (probably)   → *He probably shouldn't drive.*
   2. It's a secret. (no longer)   →
   3. I haven't received my package. (still)   →
   4. They've been waiting. (in line, for 30 minutes)   →
   5. The children had fun. (in the pool, all day)   →

✦ Dialogue

4. still 또는 yet을 넣어 문장을 완성하세요.

   Naomi is waiting for a package from Japan. Naomi는 일본에서의 소포를 기다립니다.

   Naomi   Has the mail carrier been here _____? I'm expecting a package from Japan.
   Jessica   Yes, he has, but there wasn't a package from Japan.
   Naomi   Oh, really? I thought I would get it today.
   Jessica   Perhaps it _____ hasn't arrived at the local post office.
   Naomi   Maybe you're right. I'll try tracking it online.

Unit 072

강조부사

What a beautiful castle it is!
정말 아름다운 성이야!

1 감탄문은 'What+명사' 또는 'How+형용사'의 형태로 말할 수 있다.
- **What** a beautiful **castle** it is! 정말 아름다운 성이야!
- **How wonderful** life is! 인생은 정말 멋지군요!

2 다음의 부사들을 써서 '정도(degree)'를 나타낼 수 있다.

strong
- extremely, terribly
- really
- very, pretty
- quite, rather, fairly
- a bit

weak

I tried the new restaurant on Maple. 난 어제 메이플 가의 새 식당에 가봤다.
- The food was **extremely** good. 음식은 엄청나게 훌륭했다.
- The food was **really** good. 음식이 정말 좋았다.
- The food was **very** good. 음식이 아주 좋았다.
- The food was **quite** good. 음식이 꽤 좋았다.
- The food was **a bit** good, but… 음식이 조금은 좋았지만…

3 다음과 같이 이미 '매우 그러함'의 의미가 포함된 형용사들은 very와 함께 쓰지 않는다.

freezing	excellent, fantastic	awful, terrible	gorgeous	enormous
= very cold	= very good	= very bad	= very beautiful	= very big

- It was **freezing** yesterday. 어제 엄청 추웠어. *It was very freezing.* (X)
- The traffic was **terrible**. 교통 상황이 아주 끔찍했어. *It was very terrible.* (X)

4 ever는 문장에서 '어느 때이건/언제든/한 번이라도' 등의 뉘앙스를 더한다.
- Does it **ever** snow in Florida? 플로리다에도 눈이 오긴 **하나요**?
- It's the best fantasy film **ever**! 그건 역대 최고의 판타지 영화예요. *See Unit 076▶*

who, what, which, when, where, how+ever: 누구/무엇/언제/어디서/어떻게+든지
- **Whatever** happens, I'll stand by you. 무슨 일이 벌어지든지 난 너를 지지할 거야.

5 even이 앞에 더해지면 해당 표현에 듣는 이가 예상하지 못한 놀라움 또는 '심지어' 등의 뉘앙스를 나타낸다.
- **Even** my best friend didn't support me. 심지어 내 절친마저도 내 편을 안 들더라.

not은 even 앞에 온다. 심지어 ~조차도 아니라는 뉘앙스
- Amy was really angry. She **didn't even** text me. Amy는 정말로 화가 났어. 나한테 문자**조차** 안 보냈다니까.

비교급을 더욱 강조하기 위해 even이 앞에 올 수 있다. '훨씬'의 의미
- A: I think the Crown Hotel is quite expensive. How about the Sheraton?
  크라운 호텔은 좀 비싼 것 같아. 쉐라톤은 어때?
- B: The Sheraton? It's **even more expensive**. 쉐라톤? 거긴 **훨씬 더 비싸**.

even+when/if/though 접속사 앞에도 even이 올 수 있다.
- With this technology, you can control the air conditioner **even when** you're not at home.
  이 기술로 당신은 심지어 집에 없을 때에도 에어컨을 제어할 수 있습니다.
- **Even if** we leave now, we won't be able to catch the plane. It's too late.
  지금 출발**한다고 해도** 비행기를 탈 수 없을 거야. 너무 늦었어.
- **Even though** he's a millionaire, he takes the subway to work. 그는 백만장자**임에도 불구하고** 전철로 출근한다.

Exercises

1. What 또는 How를 넣어 감탄문을 완성하세요.

1. _How_ nice!
2. _____ a surprise!
3. _____ fabulous wine it is!
4. _____ lovely to see you!

2. 주어진 내용을 읽고 질문에 답하세요.

1. Arizona is extremely hot in summer. | Hong Kong is quite hot in summer.
   Q: Which place is hotter in summer?   A: _Arizona_

2. Naples is a bit cold in winter. | Moscow is freezing in winter.
   Q: Which place is colder in winter?   A: _____

3. I think the food in the restaurant is fantastic. | I think their service is fairly good.
   Q: Which one does the speaker think is better – the food or the service?   A: _____

3. 보기 중 빈칸에 들어갈 가장 적합한 표현을 골라 넣어 문장을 완성하세요.

   ever   however   whatever   whenever   wherever   whichever   ~~whoever~~

1. _Whoever_ you are, I want to thank you.
2. If you're _____ in Seoul, come and see me.
3. A: What time shall I call you? / B: _____.
4. I'm going to buy the new S-phone, _____ much it costs.

4. even을 더해 밑줄 친 부분을 강조하는 문장으로 다시 쓰세요.

1. <u>Little kids</u> know the difference between right and wrong.
   → _Even little kids know the difference between right and wrong._
2. They <u>didn't have enough money</u> for food.
   → _____
3. The band is <u>more popular</u> abroad.
   → _____

🔊 Dialogue

5. 주어진 표현을 더해 밑줄 친 문장을 다시 쓰세요.

David and Nicole are at a party. David과 Nicole은 파티에 있습니다.

David Do you know who that guy is?
Nicole Come on, Mike. That's Patrick. He is one of Mrs. Watson's two sons.
David Now I remember. <u>I thought he looked familiar.</u> (quite)
Nicole <u>You've took photos with him.</u> (even)
David <u>You know that I can remember people's faces.</u> (never)
Nicole And names.

Unit 073

so, such

It's such a brilliant idea!
그건 정말 멋진 생각이에요!

1 **very는 형용사나 부사를 강조해 준다.**
- I think Rihanna sings **very** well. 저는 Rihanna가 노래를 아주 잘한다고 생각해요.

very는 a 뒤에 온다: a+very+형용사+명사 관사나 한정사 뒤에 위치
- It was **a very** hot day. 매우 더운 날이었다.

---

2 **so는 형용사나 부사를 강조하며, 문맥에서 말하는 사람이 생각하는 '정도(degree)'가 암시되거나 함께 표현되는 경우가 많다.**
- The music from next door is **so** loud. I wish they would turn it down.
  옆집에서 들리는 음악소리가 너무 시끄럽네요. 저 사람들이 소리 좀 줄여 줬음 좋겠어요. 소리를 줄였으면 하고 바랄 정도로 시끄러움

'so+형용사/부사+that S+V'는 '매우 ~(형용사/부사)하여 S+V하다'라는 의미이다.
that S+V는 '형용사/부사'의 정도가 심하여 생긴 결과에 해당. that은 종종 생략될 수 있다.
- The music is **so** loud **that** we can't sleep.
  음악 소리가 너무 시끄러워서 우리가 잘 수가 없어요.
- The problem was **so** difficult **that** nobody could solve it.
  그 문제는 매우 어려워서 아무도 그걸 풀지 못했다.
- The thief walked in **so** quietly **that** the guard didn't even notice him.
  도둑이 너무 조용히 들어와서 경비원은 그를 알아채지도 못했다.

so는 many/few/much/little 등 수량 표현을 강조하기도 한다.
- Ben has **so many** action figures. Ben은 정말 많은 액션 피규어를 갖고 있어요.
- Mars has **so little** air. 화성은 공기가 매우 적다.

---

3 **such는 명사의 '어떠한 정도'를 강조할 수 있다.**
- She has **such beautiful eyes**. 그녀는 정말 아름다운 눈을 가졌어요.

a나 an은 such 뒤에 온다: such+a/an+(형용사)+명사
- It's **such a brilliant idea**! 그건 정말 멋진 생각이에요!

형용사 없이 'such+(a/an)+명사'로도 쓰일 수 있다. 문맥으로 충분히 연상되는 형용사의 내용으로 강조
- Erika is **such a genius**! Erika는 대단한 천재야!

'such+명사+that S+V'는 보통 명사가 '매우 ~(형용사)하여 S+V하다'라는 의미이다.
'어느 정도'로 그러한지를 뒤의 that S+V로 나타낼 수 있다.
- Erika is **such** a smart student **that** she gets straight As all the time.
  Erika는 어찌나 똑똑한 학생인지 항상 올 A를 받는다.

명사의 수량을 강조하기 위해 such 뒤에는 a lot (of)가 올 수 있다. many, few 등 다른 수량 표현은 such와 쓰지 않음
- We had **such a lot of** fun in Las Vegas. 우리는 라스베가스에서 정말 재미있었다.

때로 such는 '이러한' 또는 '그러한'의 의미로도 쓰인다.
- I've never made **such** mistakes before. 나는 이러한 실수는 전에 한 적이 없어.

Exercises

1. 주어진 단어를 맞는 순서대로 배열하여 문장을 완성하세요.

1. (Ms. Watson, a, very, patient, person, is) → _Ms. Watson is a very patient person._
2. (are, stars, in the sky, There, many, so, tonight) → _____
3. (mistake, a, terrible, It, was, such) → _____
4. (How, did, such, he, money, earn, a lot of, ?) → _____
5. (in, I'm, situation, very, a, difficult) → _____

2. so나 such를 넣어 강조하는 문장을 완성하세요.

1. You're ___such___ a good friend.
2. I've never seen _____ a dirty bathroom.
3. I've never seen _____ many people at a concert.
4. They moved _____ quickly.
5. He's _____ a liar. I'll never believe him again.
6. Thank you _____ much.

3. 주어진 표현들을 문맥에 맞게 연결하여 문장을 완성하세요.

1. The problems were so easy • • a. she was put into the advanced level.
2. The T-shirt was so big • • b. I can't help recommending it.
3. It was so cold • • c. I could hardly breathe.
4. It was such a hot day • • d. we canceled the trip.
5. Erika was such an intelligent student • (that) • e. everybody thought she was American.
6. There was so much smoke in the room • • f. I got them all correct.
7. Nicole speaks English so fluently • • g. my hands turned blue.
8. The movie Logan is so touching. • • h. it touched her knees.
9. There was such a lack of interest • • i. everyone stayed indoors.

🔊 Dialogue

4. 주어진 단어를 맞는 순서대로 배열하여 문장을 완성하세요.

Erika has recently moved into a new apartment. Patrick is asking about it.
Erika는 최근 새 아파트로 이사했습니다. Patrick은 그에 대해 묻고 있습니다.

Patrick How's your new apartment?

Erika Terrible.

Patrick What's wrong?

Erika _____ (I, almost everything, so, The ceiling, can, is, thin, that, hear) my upstairs neighbors do.

Patrick That's too bad.

Erika And the worst thing is that I am woken up by their alarm clock going off at 4 a.m. every morning.

Unit 074

enough, too

The house isn't big enough for 4 people to live in.
그 집은 4명이 살기에 충분히 크지 않다.

1
enough는 어떤 기준에 '충분한' 또는 '충분히'의 의미로 명사 앞 또는 형용사나 부사 뒤에 올 수 있다.

- Have we got **enough time**? enough+명사 우리 시간이 충분한가?
- You're working **hard enough**. 부사+enough 넌 충분히 열심히 일하고 있어.
- The service was **good enough**. 형용사+enough 서비스는 충분히 괜찮았다.

not ~ enough는 어떤 기준을 충족시키지 못한다는 의미이다.

- We **don't** have **enough** time. 우리에겐 충분한 시간이 없어요.
- You were **not** careful **enough**. 넌 충분히 주의 깊지 못했다.

enough 뒤에 명사 없이 쓰일 수도 있다.

- Stop telling me what to do. That's **enough**. 내게 이래라 저래라 그만해. 그만하면 됐어.
- A: Would you like some more cake? 케이크 좀 더 드시겠어요?
  B: No, thank you. I've had **enough**. 아뇨, 고맙습니다만 충분히 먹었습니다.
  I've had enough는 '이제 그만 하면 됐다', '이제 지긋지긋하다' 등의 의미로도 쓰일 수 있다.

2
too는 어떤 기준을 과도하게 넘어서 좋지 않다는 의미로, 형용사나 부사 앞에 온다.

- The restaurant was **too crowded**. We couldn't get a table. 그 식당은 너무 붐볐다. 우리는 자리를 얻을 수가 없었다.
- You're driving **too fast**. It's dangerous. 너 지금 과속하고 있어. 위험하잖아.
- There is **too much** traffic on 11th Avenue today. 오늘 11번가에 교통량이 너무 많아요.

긍정적인 의미로는 **too**를 쓰지 않는다.

- She is **very** beautiful. 그녀는 무척 아름답다.
  She is **too** beautiful. (X)

3
enough와 **too**의 기준을 다음과 같이 말할 수 있다.

❶ for+명사

- We have **enough** food **for everyone**. 우리는 모두에게 충분한 식량이 있습니다.
- It's **too** difficult **for me**. 그건 제게 너무 어려워요.

❷ to+동사

- He is fit **enough to run** a marathon. 그는 마라톤을 뛸 정도로 충분히 건강하다.
- It's **too** cold **to go** outside. 밖에 나가기엔 너무 춥다.

❸ for+명사+to+동사

- The house isn't big **enough for 4 people to live** in. 그 집은 4명이 살기에 충분히 크지 않다.
- The math problem was **too** difficult **for 7th graders to solve**. 그 수학문제는 7학년들이 풀기에는 너무 어려웠다.

4
not ~ enough와 **too**가 각각 같은 의미를 나타낼 수 있다. 각각 반대되는 의미의 형용사 사용

- These shoes are **not big enough for me**. = These shoes are **too small for me**.
  이 신발은 내게 크기가 충분치 않다. = 이 신발은 내게 너무 작다.
- The train is **not fast enough**. = The train is **too slow**.
  그 열차는 충분히 빠르지 않다. = 그 열차는 너무 느리다.

Exercises

1. enough, too 또는 very를 넣어 문장을 완성하세요.

1. Is there _enough_ food for all of us?
2. Take your time and try not to make _____ many mistakes.
3. No thanks. I've had more than _____ to eat.
4. The test was _____ difficult, but I think I did quite OK.
5. The coffee was _____ hot, so I left it for a while to cool down.
6. My house is _____ close to the subway station.
7. The photograph didn't come out very well because it was _____ dark.
8. Everybody says Erika is a _____ intelligent student.

2. 주어진 표현을 사용하여 문장을 완성하세요.

1. (too, You, to, are, young, drive)
   → _You're too young to drive._
2. (wasn't, everyone, room, There, enough, for, in the car)
   → _____
3. (experienced, the job, He, isn't, enough, get, to)
   → _____
4. (me, speaks, She, quickly, for, to, understand, too)
   → _____

3. 주어진 표현을 사용하여 같거나 비슷한 의미의 문장으로 다시 쓰세요. 가능하면 축약형을 쓰세요.

1. My room is too small. (enough, big)
   → _My room isn't big enough._
2. She hasn't got enough time to prepare for the presentation. (too, little)
   → _____
3. The weather is too bad for a BBQ party. (enough, good)
   → _____
4. You're walking too slowly. Hurry up! (enough, fast)
   → _____

🔊 Dialogue

4. 주어진 단어를 맞는 순서대로 배열하여 문장을 완성하세요. 가능하면 축약형을 쓰세요.

Amy and Sarah are watching a talent show on TV. Amy와 Sarah는 TV로 탤런트 쇼를 보고 있습니다.

Amy Who are you voting for?
Sarah Well, I'm definitely not voting for the third guy.
Amy Why not?
Sarah _____. (do, I, talented, think, not, enough, is, he) He's just all looks.
Amy Well, whoever wins, I'm looking forward to the final.

Unit 075

비교급과 최상급(1)

I'd like to have a more powerful computer.
저는 좀 더 성능이 좋은 컴퓨터를 갖고 싶어요.

1
둘이나 두 묶음의 대상에 대해서는 비교급, 셋이나 그 이상의 대상에 대해서는 최상급을 써서 말할 수 있다.

- Today is **colder** than yesterday. 오늘이 어제보다 **더 춥다**.
- Yesterday was **the coldest** day of the year. 어제는 일 년 중 **가장 추운** 날이었다.

2
비교급과 최상급의 형태는 다음과 같다.

	형용사 or 부사	비교급	최상급: the +
1음절	cheap fast	cheaper faster	cheapest fastest
2음절 이상	modern expensive	more modern more expensive	most modern most expensive
-y	happy early	happier earlier	happiest earliest
예외	good/well bad/badly far	better worse farther/further	best worst farthest/furthest
수량	many/much few little	more fewer less	most fewest least

- Which train is **faster** – TGV or KTX? 어떤 기차가 **더 빠른가요**? TGV 아니면 KTX?
- His house is **the largest** one in our neighborhood. 그의 집은 우리 동네에서 **제일 크다**.
- I'd like to have a **more powerful** computer. 저는 좀 더 **성능이 좋은** 컴퓨터를 갖고 싶어요.
- I think we should spend **less** this month. 우리 이달에 돈을 **덜** 써야 할 것 같아요.

simple, slow, narrow, common, quick, polite, quiet, clever, loud(ly) 등 두 가지 비교급/최상급 형태가 모두 가능한 표현들이 여럿 있다. 3음절이 넘는 경우는 대부분이 more ~와 the most ~ 형태를 취한다.

- Could you please be **quieter**? = Could you please be **more quiet**? 좀 더 조용히 해 주시겠어요?

- A: Am I speaking loud enough? 제 목소리가 충분히 큰가요?
  B: Actually, you should speak **louder**.
  = Actually, you should speak **more loudly**.
  실은 좀 더 크게 말하셔야겠어요.

3
'~보다'의 의미로 **than**을 비교급과 함께 쓸 수 있다.

- Canada is larger **than** the U.S. 캐나다가 미국**보다** 크다.
- Is Spanish more difficult **than** French? 스페인어가 불어**보다** 어려운가요?
- There are fewer customers in the store today **than** yesterday. 오늘은 어제**보다** 매장에 손님이 더 적습니다.
- The IT job market is better **than** ever. IT 인력 시장이 그 어느 때보다도 좋다. than ever는 '그 어느 때보다도'라는 의미

4
최상급 앞에는 **the**나 **my/your/his/her** 등이 온다.

- Burj Khalifa was once **the highest** building in the world. 버즈 칼리파는 한때 세계에서 **가장 높은** 빌딩이었다.
- He's **my best** friend. 그는 나의 가장 친한 친구이다.

간혹 대화체 등에서 the가 생략되는 경우도 있다.

- Who can run **fastest**? 누가 제일 빠르게 달릴 수 있니?

Exercises

1. 주어진 표현을 비교급 또는 최상급 형태로 만들어 문장을 완성하세요.

1. Yesterday wasn't so cold. Today is __colder__ (cold).
2. Your English is getting _____ (good).
3. The cheetah is _____ (fast) land animal in the world.
4. Pessimists believe the world is getting _____ (bad).
5. Indoor air pollution is probably _____ (dangerous) to your health.
6. _____ (far) research would be necessary to answer those questions.

2. 보기에서 빈칸에 들어갈 가장 적절한 단어를 골라 넣어 문장을 완성하세요.

| more |
| fewer |
| ~~less~~ |
| most |
| fewest |
| least |

1. Children usually have __less__ money but _____ time than adults.
2. She had the _____ experience of all but showed the best performance.
3. The player who gets the _____ points wins.
4. Everybody has more than three candy bars except for me. I have the _____ ones.
5. There are _____ than 7,000 cheetahs in the wild today.

3. 주어진 표현에서 적절한 표현을 하나씩 골라 변형하여 문장을 완성하세요.

high mountain	a violin
far away from the Sun	in the solar system
hot planet	in the world
~~large~~	Mars
strings	~~the Atlantic Ocean~~

1. The Pacific Ocean is _larger than the Atlantic Ocean_.
2. Everest is _____.
3. Neptune is _____.
4. A guitar has _____.
5. Mercury is _____.

★ Dialogue

4. 주어진 표현을 적합한 형태로 바꾸어 문장을 완성하세요.

Mr. Harris is making a phone call to his client. Mr. Harris는 고객에게 전화를 하고 있습니다.

Secretary Henderson's office. How may I help you?

Mr. Harris Hello? This is Tim Harris from Harris Law Firm. May I speak to Mr. Henderson, please?

Secretary The line is bad. Could you speak _____ (loud) please?

Mr. Harris Oh. I'd like to speak to Mr. Henderson.

Secretary May I ask who's calling again?

Mr. Harris Tim Harris.

Secretary Oh, hello, Mr. Harris. I'll put you through to Mr. Henderson.

Unit 076

비교급과 최상급(2)

Busan is the second largest city in Korea.
부산은 한국에서 두 번째로 큰 도시입니다.

1 다음의 비교의 정도를 보다 구체적으로 나타내는 표현이다.

much, far, a lot, even 훨씬, 더욱	▶ His computer is **much more powerful** than mine. **Far better!** 그의 컴퓨터가 내 것보다 훨씬 더 성능이 좋다. 훨씬 낫지!
a little, a bit, slightly 약간, 조금	▶ Would you speak **a little louder**, please? 조금만 더 크게 말씀해 주시겠어요? ▶ His score is **slightly higher** than mine. 그의 점수가 내 점수보다 조금 더 높다.

2 'less+형용사/부사'는 '덜 ~한/하게'라는 의미이다.

▶ Measles is **less common** today than 50 years ago. 오늘날 홍역은 50년 전보다 덜 흔하다.
▶ He was driving **less carefully** then. 그때 그는 덜 조심스럽게 운전하고 있었다.

3 '비교급 and 비교급'은 '점점 더 ~한/하게'의 의미로 이해할 수 있다.

▶ Our market is becoming **bigger and bigger**. 우리의 시장이 점점 더 커지고 있습니다.
▶ Social media is getting **more and more popular**. 소셜미디어(SNS)는 갈수록 인기를 더해가고 있습니다.

4 'the 비교급 ~, the 비교급 ~'는 '~할수록 더욱 ~하다'라는 의미이다.

▶ **The more** you exercise, **the healthier** you are. 운동을 많이 할수록 더 건강해 진다.

5 'the least+형용사/부사'는 '가장 ~하지 않은/덜 ~하게'라는 의미이다.

▶ It's **the least expensive** option. 그것이 가장 덜 비싼 선택사항입니다.

6 최상급 표현에는 종종 뒤에 다음과 같은 표현이 온다. '가장 ~한 것'의 범위를 나타냄. 보통 '~ 중에서'로 해석

in+town, the world, my life 등	▶ It's the oldest shop **in town**. 도시에서 가장 오래된 가게이다.
of+the year, all time 등	▶ She was awarded the Best Writer **of the Year** in 1998. 그녀는 1998년에 그 해의 최고 작가상을 수상했습니다.
ever	▶ Michael Jordan was the best basketball player **ever**. 마이클 조던은 역대 최고의 농구선수였습니다.
I know, I've ever p.p. 등	▶ It's the worst thing **I've ever done**. 그건 내가 한 일 중에서도 최악이었어요.

7 최상급 앞에 다음과 같은 표현들이 잘 쓰인다.

The second/third/fourth...	▶ Busan is **the second largest** city in Korea. 부산은 한국에서 두 번째로 큰 도시입니다.
One of the...	▶ Daegu is **one of the largest cities** in Korea. of 뒤에 복수가 쓰임에 유의 대구는 한국에서 가장 큰 도시 중 하나입니다.
By far the...	▶ Seoul is **by far the largest city** in Korea. 서울은 단연코 한국에서 가장 큰 도시이다.

8 비교급으로 최상급의 의미를 나타낼 수 있다.

▶ Seoul is **larger than any other** cities in Korea. 서울은 한국의 그 어느 도시보다도 크다.
= Seoul is **the largest** city in Korea. 서울은 한국에서 가장 큰 도시이다.
▶ Things **couldn't be better**. 상황이 더 이상 좋아질 수가 없다(=최고이다).

Exercises

1. 본인의 의견을 반영하여 두 대상을 비교하는 문장을 완성하세요. 주어진 표현을 사용하세요.

1. London / Paris (attractive)
   → London *is much/far/a lot/even/a little/a bit/slightly more/less attractive than Paris* .
2. dogs / cats (smart)
   → Dogs _____ .
3. math / history (difficult)
   → Math _____ .
4. hiking / playing video games (fun)
   → Hiking _____ .
5. the Harry Potter series / the Greek myth (interesting)
   → The Harry Potter series _____ .

2. 주어진 표현을 이용하여 보기와 같이 문장을 완성하세요.

1. Social media is getting *more and more popular* (popular).
2. Warren Buffett got _____ (rich).
3. Every time I see her, she looks _____ (beautiful).
4. There will be _____ (many) electric cars.
5. The train ran _____ (faster).

3. 주어진 표현을 문맥에 맞게 연결하여 문장을 완성하세요.

1. She's the most beautiful woman   •   • a. favorite subject.
2. Malala is by far   •   • b. the angrier I got.
3. Jupiter is the largest planet   •   • c. in the solar system.
4. The longer I waited   •   • d. the youngest winner of the Nobel Peace Prize.
5. Math is my least   •   • e. of all time.
6. Vote for the greatest invention   •   • f. I've ever seen.

Dialogue

4. 문맥에 맞는 적절한 단어를 채워 문장을 완성하세요.

Naomi and Suzi are talking together. Naomi와 Suzi가 함께 이야기하고 있습니다.

Suzi How about grabbing a bite to eat after class gets out?

Naomi Can I take a rain check on that? Actually I've got to watch my favorite soap tonight.

Suzi You mean "Stranger"? Everybody's talking about it these days. Is it that good?

Naomi Yeah. It's getting _____ and _____ thrilling with each episode. I just can't miss it.

정답 p.271 ▶

Unit 077

비교급과 최상급(3)

The car is twice as expensive as this one.
그 차는 이것보다 두 배 더 비싸다.

1 'as 형용사/부사 as ~'는 '~만큼 (형용사/부사)하다'라는 의미로, 두 대상을 비교하는 표현이다.
- Your computer is **as powerful as** mine. 네 컴퓨터는 내 것만큼이나 성능이 좋다.

'not as 형용사/부사 as ~'는 비교급으로 비슷하게 의미를 나타낼 수 있다.
- My computer is **not as powerful as** his. 내 컴퓨터는 그의 컴퓨터만큼 성능이 좋지는 않다.
= His computer is **more powerful than** mine. 그의 컴퓨터는 내 것보다 성능이 더 좋다.
= My computer is **less powerful than** his. 내 컴퓨터는 그의 컴퓨터보다 성능이 떨어진다.

2 as나 than 뒤에는 him, her 등의 목적격뿐 아니라 S+V 형태도 올 수 있다.
- You can run <u>as fast as</u> **he can**. (= … as fast as him.) 넌 그 사람만큼 빨리 뛸 수 있어.
- She's done <u>more</u> work <u>than</u> **I have**. (= … than me.) 그녀는 내가 한 것보다 많은 일을 했다.

3 'as 형용사/부사 as ~' 앞에 다음과 같은 표현들이 올 수 있다.

just (딱 ...만큼 ...한/하게)	▶ The salad was **just** as good as the pizza. 샐러드가 피자만큼이나 좋았다.
almost, nearly (거의 ...만큼 ...한/하게)	▶ Venus is **almost** as big as the Earth. 금성은 거의 지구만큼 크다.

4 as ~ as 앞에 twice, three times 등을 써서 배수를 나타낼 수 있다.
- The car is **twice** as expensive as this one. 그 차는 이것보다 두 배 더 비싸다.
- Platinum is **three times** as heavy as gold. 백금은 금보다 세 배 더 무겁다.

5 as ~ as ~ 형태의 고정적인 표현들이 쓰인다.
- Call me **as soon as possible**. 가능한 빨리 제게 전화 주세요.
- **As far as I remember**, the bakery was around the corner over there.
제가 기억하기로는 그 제과점이 저기 모퉁이 돌아서 있었어요.

6 비교급과 최상급 외에 다음 표현들을 사용하여 두 대상을 비교할 수 있다.

exactly, just, almost, early 등	the same ~ as ~	quite, completely, slightly 등	different from ~
exactly, more, quite, a bit, a little 등	like ~	quite, very	similar to ~

- You look **almost the same as** you did five years ago. 넌 5년 전에 그랬던 것과 거의 똑같아 보여.
- The movie was **exactly like** the book. 그 영화는 딱 책이랑 같아.
- Today's lifestyle is **completely different from** the way people lived in the past.
오늘날의 생활 양식은 과거 사람들의 방식과는 완전히 다르다.
- It tastes **very similar to** coffee. 그것은 커피와 아주 비슷한 맛이 난다.

7 비교 대상의 분류나 속성이 일치하도록 주의하자.
- **He ate** more dumplings than **his sister did**. (O) 그는 누나보다 만두를 더 많이 먹었다. 먹은 행위를 비교
He ate more dumplings than **his sister**. (X) 만두와 누나의 비교로 오해될 여지가 있음
- **The weather in Cuba** is similar to **that of Florida**. (O) 쿠바의 날씨는 플로리다의 날씨와 비슷하다.
The weather in Cuba is similar to **Florida**. (X) 쿠바의 날씨와 플로리다 자체 비교로 오해될 수 있음

Exercises

1. 같거나 비슷한 의미가 될 수 있도록 as ~ as를 써서 문장을 완성하세요.

1. Andy can run faster than Ben. → Ben can't _run as fast as Andy_.
2. Amy ate less than Sarah. → Amy didn't _____.
3. His new movie is more interesting than the last one. → His last movie wasn't _____.
4. I expected the battery to last longer. → The battery didn't _____.

2. 그림을 보고 주어진 표현을 사용하여 문장을 완성하세요.

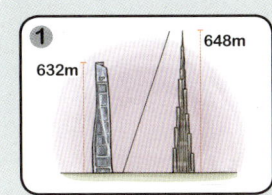   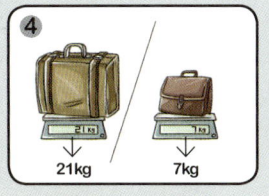

1. The Shanghai Tower is _almost as high as_ (almost, high) The Burj Khalifa.
2. Chang-tzu Mountain is _____ (twice, high) Mount Fuji.
3. Andy is _____ (just, old) Sarah.
4. The suitcase is _____ (three times, heavy) the briefcase.

3. 빈칸에 들어갈 가장 적절한 표현을 보기에서 골라 넣어 문장을 완성하세요.

> different   far   ~~possible~~   same   similar

1. I need to talk to you as soon as _possible_.
2. The movie is totally _____ from the book.
3. As _____ as I know, he is very reliable.
4. The weather here is very _____ to our winter in the west.
5. 'Whereas' means the _____ as 'while' in sentences expressing contrasts.

✦ Dialogue

4. 주어진 단어를 이용하여 문맥에 맞게 문장을 완성하세요. 가능하면 축약형을 쓰세요.

Erika is talking to her friend Anna, who is getting married soon.
Erika는 곧 결혼하는 친구 Anna와 이야기하고 있습니다.

Anna Henry and I have decided to go to Hawaii.

Erika Great. So, did you decide on a hotel?

Anna Well… I don't know. The Kahala looks wonderful but it's quite expensive. The Royal is cheap but _____ (as, look, not, it, as, does, nice) the Kahala.

Erika I would choose the Kahala because it's a honeymoon, not a backpacking trip.

Unit 078

관계대명사(1)

I think I deleted the email you sent me by accident.
당신이 보낸 이메일을 실수로 지워버린 것 같아요.

1 명사가 어떤 것인지를 말해 주는 문장을 다음과 같이 **who, that, which**를 써서 연결할 수 있다.

❶ 명사가 사람일 때: **who** 또는 **that**   who가 좀 더 많이 쓰임

We're looking for a secretary.   ~~The secretary~~ can speak English and Korean.
—— who/that ——

→ We're looking for a secretary **who/that** can speak English and Korean.
우리는 영어와 한국어를 할 수 **있는** 비서를 찾고 있습니다.

❷ 명사가 사람이 아닌 사물일 때: **that** 또는 **which**   that이 좀 더 많이 쓰임

The train doesn't stop at Daegu.   ~~The train~~ leaves at 9:30 a.m.
—— that/which ——

→ The train **that/which** leaves at 9:30 a.m. doesn't stop at Daegu.
오전 9시 30분에 출발**하는** 기차는 대구에 정차하지 않습니다.

다음과 같은 경우 연결표현이 생략될 수 있다.   that/who/which 뒤에 S+V가 오는 경우(목적격관계대명사)

What did you think of the man?   You interviewed ~~the man~~ yesterday.
—— who/that ——
이 경우 whom도 쓰일 수 있으나 구어체에서는 거의 쓰이지 않는다.

→ What did you think of the man **(who/that)** you interviewed yesterday?
어제 면접 **본** 사람에 대해 어떻게 생각하셨나요?

I think I deleted the email by accident.   You sent me ~~the email~~.
—— that/which ——

→ I think I deleted the email **(that/which)** you sent me by accident.
당신이 보**낸** 이메일을 실수로 지워버린 것 같아요.

2 전치사가 누락되지 않도록 주의한다.

▶ Do you remember the name of customer you talked **with**? 함께 이야기했던 고객의 성함이 기억나시나요?
▶ I liked the music we were listening **to** the other day. 우리가 일전에 들었**던** 노래 좋더라.

3 전치사를 관계대명사 앞으로 이동할 수 있다. 단, 이때에는 **that**을 쓸 수 없고, **who**는 **whom**으로 쓸 수 있다.
대화체보다는 주로 글에서 더 많이 볼 수 있다.

▶ The sales clerk who I complained **to** was not very kind. 내가 불평을 **했던** 판매 점원은 썩 친절하지 않았다.
　= The sales clerk **to whom** I complained was not very kind.
▶ Tonight, we're going to the restaurant that I read **about** on a blog.
오늘 밤에 우리는 블로그에서 내가 읽었**던** 식당에 갈 거야.
　= Tonight, we're going to the restaurant **about which** I read on a bog.

Exercises

1. **who를 넣을 수 있는 곳에는 who를 넣고, 그렇지 않은 곳에는 that을 넣어 문장을 완성하세요.**
   1. Do you know anything about the accident __that__ happened last night?
   2. Tom Hiddleston is an actor _____ has appeared in many movies.
   3. I'm looking for a laptop _____ can be used for gaming.
   4. Police identified the man _____ was arrested on Monday.
   5. The mistake _____ you made is a common one.

2. **문장에 쓰인 that, who, which가 생략 가능하면 괄호로 표시하세요. 생략할 수 없다면 그대로 두세요.**
   1. The man **(who)** I was talking to is a journalist from the Los Angeles Times.
   2. The book that you lent me about planets is really interesting.
   3. The people who attended the seminar found it very useful.
   4. Zaha Hadid is the architect who designed the Dongdaemun Design Plaza in Seoul.
   5. I really liked the salad that came with the steak.
   6. *The Guardian* is the British newspaper that I read most often.

3. **전치사를 관계대명사 앞으로 옮겨 문장을 다시 쓰세요.**
   1. The hotel that we stayed at had more than 800 rooms.
      → _The hotel at which we stayed had more than 800 rooms._
   2. What's the name of the client who you had lunch with?
      → _____
   3. The exact shipping rates depend on the country which your order is being delivered to.
      → _____
   4. This is the breakthrough that we have been waiting for.
      → _____
   5. The world that we are living in is changing very fast.
      → _____

🔊 Dialogue

4. **대화 속 빈칸에 공통으로 들어갈 수 있는 표현을 넣어 문장을 완성하세요.**

   Ms. Watson would like to buy a refrigerator.
   Watson 부인은 냉장고를 사고 싶어 합니다.

   Clerk   How may I help you?
   Ms. Watson Hi. I'd like to buy a fridge.
   Clerk   What type fridge would you like?
   Ms. Watson I'm looking for one _____ can dispense water and ice.
   Clerk   Right this way. We have a nice one on sale _____ has a water and ice dispenser.

Unit 079

관계대명사(2)

He has three sisters, two of whom are nurses.
그에겐 여자형제가 셋 있는데, 그 중 둘이 간호사예요.

1 'comma(,)+which/who'는 문장 구성에 필수는 아니지만 추가적인 정보를 더하고자 할 때 쓸 수 있다.
문장이 완전해지는 데에 꼭 필요한 내용은 comma 없이 관계사로 연결

comma(,)가 없는 경우	comma(,)가 있는 경우
▶ Most of the people **who** live in Washington come from other places. 워싱턴에 사는 사람 대부분은 다른 곳 출신이다.	▶ My parents, **who** live in Washington, are visiting me tomorrow. 워싱턴에 살고 있는 우리 부모님이 내일 나를 보러 오신다.

- ▶ I've just read Rowling's Harry Potter series, **which** is one of the most popular books of the 21st century. 나는 21세기에 가장 인기 있는 책들 중 하나인 Rolling의 해리포터 시리즈를 방금 읽었다.
- ▶ My favorite actor is Eddie Redmayne, **who** I saw in *"The Theory of Everything."*
  내가 제일 좋아하는 배우는 '모든 것의 이론'에서 봤던 에디 레드메인이다.

2 'comma(,)+which'는 명사가 아닌 문장 전체에 대해서 추가로 덧붙이는 내용을 더할 때에도 쓸 수 있다.

- ▶ I've just missed the last bus, **which** means I have to take a taxi.
  방금 마지막 버스를 놓쳤는데, **그건** 내가 택시를 탈 수 밖에 없다는 얘기지.
- ▶ He forgot his wife's birthday a couple of times, **which** disappointed her a lot.
  그는 그의 아내의 생일을 두어 번 까먹었는데, **이는** 그녀를 무척 실망시켰다.

3 명사의 부분만을 설명할 때 다음과 같이 말할 수 있다.

He has three sisters. + Two of them are nurses.
= He has three sisters, **two of whom** are nurses.
그에겐 여자형제가 셋 있는데, **그 중 둘이** 간호사예요.

- ▶ He answered all the questions. + Some of them were very difficult.
  = He answered all the questions, **some of which** were very difficult.
  그는 모든 문제에 답을 했는데, **그 중에 일부는** 아주 어려웠다.
- ▶ She taught 100 students last year, **most of whom** were from Asia.
  그녀는 작년에 100명의 학생을 가르쳤는데, **그 중 대부분은** 아시아에서 왔다.
- ▶ There were many shops on Kensington Road, **none of which** I visited.
  켄싱턴 길에 가게가 많은데, 나는 **이 중 어느 한 곳도** 가 본 적이 없다.

4 **speaking of which**는 '말이 나온 김에', '얘기가 나왔으니 말인데'의 의미로 쓸 수 있는 표현이다.

- ▶ I won't be home when you get home tonight. **Speaking of which**, don't forget your keys.
  오늘 밤에 당신이 집에 왔을 땐 제가 없을 거예요. 얘기가 나와서 말인데, 열쇠 잊지 말아요.

5 다음과 같은 경우에 that이 아닌 which나 who/whom만 쓸 수 있다.

- ● comma(,) 뒤
  - ▶ Yesterday I called my cousin Sia, **who** lives in London. 어제 나는 런던에 사는 사촌 Sia에게 전화를 했다.
    Yesterday I called my cousin Sia, that lives in London. (X)

- ● 전치사 뒤
  - ▶ I'm going to visit the city **from which** Jay comes. 나는 Jay가 온 도시를 방문할 거야.
    I'm going to visit the city from that Jay comes. (X)

Exercises

1. 문장의 문맥에 가장 적합한 표현을 골라 문장을 완성하세요.
   1. I've lost the book (that I was reading / , which I was reading).
   2. Andy did really well on his math test (which surprised everyone / , which surprised everyone).
   3. Is that the man (who you were talking about / , who you were talking about)?
   4. There was a lot of rain (which was unusual for that time of year / , which was unusual for that time of year).
   5. My favorite drink is coffee. (Speaking of what / Speaking of which), I think I need some.
   6. Yesterday we bought a TV (that was half price / , which was half price).

2. 두 문장을 보기처럼 같은 의미의 한 문장으로 다시 쓰세요.
   1. I read four books during the summer. I really enjoyed one of them.
      → *I read four books during the summer, one of which I really enjoyed.*
   2. The box contains 10 light bulbs. Half of them are broken.
      → _____
   3. I have eight nieces and nephews. All of them are so adorable.
      → _____
   4. There were a lot of people at the party. I had known many of them for a long time.
      → _____

3. that, who 또는 which를 넣어 문장을 완성하세요. 여러 개가 가능한 경우, 모두 쓰세요.
   1. My grandmother, __who__ lives in Vancouver, has 6 cats.
   2. The steak _____ you ordered is much bigger than mine.
   3. The Kleins live in an apartment, _____ is twice as big as their old one.
   4. The people _____ live next door really love to party.
   5. Sia lives in a suburb of London, _____ is the capital of the United Kingdom.
   6. Mr. Branson, _____ he's worked for before, wants to hire him again.

🔊 Dialogue

4. 주어진 표현 중 가장 적절한 표현을 보기에서 골라 문장을 완성하세요.

Sarah is a reporter of the school newspaper. She is interviewing Rachel.
Sarah는 학교 신문의 기자입니다. 그녀는 Rachel을 인터뷰하고 있습니다.

Sarah What do you do, Ms. Cruz?
Rachel I'm a travel writer.
Sarah Wow! Are you a freelancer or employed?
Rachel I work for a couple of magazines as a contracted writer.
Sarah I see. Where do you work? I mean, do you have to go to work every day?
Rachel No. I work from home, (that / which) is a big advantage.

Unit 080

관계사절(1)

Tell me how you practice English.
영어를 어떻게 연습하는지 알려 주세요.

1. what은 'the thing that ~'과 같은 의미이다.

- Is this **what** you're looking for? 찾고 계시는 **것이** 이건가요?
- **What** you did was completely unacceptable. 네가 한 **일**은 절대 용인될 수 없는 것이었어.

what 앞에 명사가 오지 않는 것에 유의한다.

- Is this the book **(that)** you're looking for? 이 책이 당신이 찾고 있는 **건가요**?
  Is this the book **what** you're looking for? (X)

2. who, that, which 외에도 다른 연결 표현이 쓰일 수 있다.

❶ the reason+why/that `why/that 생략 가능`

- That's not the reason **(why/that)** I was angry. 그건 내가 화난 **이유가** 아니에요.
- Can you tell me the reason **(why/that)** my flight has been canceled?
  제 항공편이 왜 취소된 건지 **이유**를 말해 주시겠어요?

❷ 명사의 소유에 대해 설명할 때 – whose를 사용

> I met [a guy] yesterday. ← His sister works in your department.
> — whose —
>
> → I met a guy **whose** sister works in your department yesterday.
> 나 어제 너네 부서에 **자기** 누나가 일한다는 남자를 만났어.

- I would like to buy a house **whose** yard is big enough for my children to play in.
  저는 제 아이들이 안에서 놀기에 충분히 큰 마당을 가진 집을 사고자 합니다. `주로 사람에 대해 쓰이지만, 사람이 아닌 경우에도 가능하다.`

❸ 장소+where `where에는 장소 전치사 in, at 등이 포함되었다고 볼 수 있다.`

- **The hotel where** they stayed was quite expensive. 그들이 묵었던 **호텔은** 꽤 비쌌다.
- **The coffee shop where** I first met my husband is not there anymore.
  내가 남편을 처음 만**난 커피숍**이 이제 더 이상 거기에 없어요.

다음과 같이 말할 수도 있다.

- The hotel **which/that** they stayed **in** was quite expensive.
- The hotel **in which** they stayed was quite expensive.

- The coffee shop **which/that** I first met my husband **in** is not there anymore.
- The coffee shop **in which** I first met my husband is not there anymore.

❹ 시간/때+when/that `when/that 생략 가능`

- Do you remember **the day (when/that)** you started working here? 여기서 근무 시작했**던 날** 기억나요?
- **The summer (when/that)** I went camping to the Rockies was very hot.
  내가 로키산맥으로 캠핑 갔**던 여름**은 무척 더웠다.

❺ how = the way (that) `the way how라고 하지는 않음`

- Tell me **how** you practice English. (= Tell me **the way (that)** you practice English.)
  영어를 **어떻게** 연습하**는지** 알려 주세요.

Exercises

1. **that 또는 what을 넣어 문장을 완성하세요.**

    1. Everything _that_ glitters is not gold.
    2. _____ I saw there was absolutely shocking.
    3. I don't believe _____ he told me.
    4. Sweet champagne gives me a headache. Are there any ones _____ are not sweet?

2. **who 또는 whose를 넣어 문장을 완성하세요.**

    1. Suzi's brother _who_ I met at the party was very sociable.
    2. The candidate _____ resume I've just looked at is very well qualified.
    3. Do you know _____ Marisa works for?
    4. The lawyer _____ office you visited yesterday is on the line waiting.

3. **빈칸에 들어갈 가장 적절한 표현을 보기에서 골라 넣어 문장을 완성하세요.**

    > what   where   when   how   why   who

    1. Do you remember the day _when_ you first met your wife?
    2. That's not the reason _____ I decided to resign.
    3. Learn _____ you can perform better by following tips.
    4. This is the picture of the park _____ I used to play as a child.
    5. The calendar we use today started with the year _____ Jesus Christ was born.

    ▶ 위 완성된 문장 중 연결 표현을 that으로 바꾸어 쓸 수 있는 문장을 골라 다시 쓰세요.
    1. _Do you remember the day that you first met your wife?_
    2. _____
    3. _____

Dialogue

4. **보기 중 빈칸에 들어갈 가장 적합한 표현을 골라 넣어 문장을 완성하세요.**

    > when   where   which   who   why

    Patrick, Andy, and Amy are talking together.
    Patrick, Andy, Amy는 대화를 하고 있습니다.

    Patrick Remember the time _____ we were in Morocco?
    Andy How can I forget the day?
    Amy Why? What happened?
    Andy He made me ride on the camel, and it was trying to bite my ass.
    Patrick Come on, Andy. The camel wasn't trying to bite your ass. It just wanted to eat the carrot in your back pocket.
    Andy And you were the one _____ put that carrot in my pocket!

Unit 081

관계사절(2)

He works for a factory making smartphones.
그는 스마트폰을 만드는 공장에서 일한다.

1. 관계사 표현은 보다 간결하게 표현될 수 있다. `관계사+Be동사`는 종종 생략될 수 있다.

❶ that/which/who+be+위치 전치사(in, on, at 등) = 전치사
- He painted the picture <u>that is on the wall</u>.
  = He painted the picture **on the wall**. 그는 **벽에 걸린** 그 그림을 그렸다.

❷ that/which/who+be = 동격
- Mark Zuckerberg, <u>who is the inventor of Facebook</u>, is an atheist.
  = Mark Zuckerberg, **the inventor of Facebook**, is an atheist.
  페이스북을 발명한 마크 저커버그는 무신론자이다.
- Andy, <u>who is Patrick's little brother</u>, is going to graduate high school next month.
  = Andy, **Patrick's little brother**, is going to graduate high school next month.
  Patrick의 남동생인 Andy는 다음 달에 고등학교를 졸업한다.

❸ that/which/who+be+p.p. = p.p.
- I'm going to meet a client <u>who is called</u> Mr. Branson.
  = I'm going to meet a client **called** Mr. Branson.
  저는 Branson 씨라고 하는 고객님을 만날 예정입니다.
- I've read most of the books <u>that were written</u> by Philip K. Dick.
  = I've read most of the books **written** by Philip K. Dick.
  나는 Philip K. Dick에 의해 **쓰여진** 책 대부분을 읽어 봤다.

❹ 'that/which/who+동사' 또는 'that/which/who+be -ing' = -ing
- Yesterday, I talked to the couple <u>who live</u> next door.
  = Yesterday, I talked to the couple **living** next door. 어제 옆집에 **사는** 부부와 이야기를 했어.
- He works for a factory <u>that makes</u> smartphones.
  = He works for a factory **making** smartphones. 그는 스마트폰을 **만드는** 공장에서 일한다.
- The train <u>that leaves</u> at 9:30 a.m. doesn't stop at Daegu.
  = The train **leaving** at 9:30 a.m. doesn't stop at Daegu. 오전 9시 30분에 **출발하는** 기차는 대구에 정차하지 않습니다.
- The man <u>who was driving</u> the car was not injured.
  = The man **driving** the car was not injured. 차를 운전하고 있던 남자는 부상당하지 않았다.

2. that/which/who 등으로 이어진 표현을 달리 말할 수도 있다.

❶ that/which/who+have = with
- A sociopath is a person <u>who has</u> an antisocial personality disorder.
  소시오패스는 반사회적 성격 장애를 **가진** 사람이다.
  = A sociopath is a person **with** an antisocial personality disorder.

❷ (which/what was) written/composed/sung/···+by = by   `p.p.의 생략`
- I've just read a book <u>(that was) written by</u> Ray Bradbury.
  = I've just read a book **by** Ray Bradbury. 저는 방금 Ray Bradbury의 책을 한 권 읽었어요.
- *Hero* <u>(that was) sung by</u> Mariah Carey is my favorite.
  = *Hero* **by** Mariah Carey is my favorite. 머라이어 캐리가 **부른** 'Hero'는 내가 제일 좋아하는 곡이다.

Exercises

1. 밑줄 친 부분을 전치사를 사용한 표현으로 바꾸어 문장을 다시 쓰세요.

1. He painted the picture that is on the wall.
   → He painted the picture __on the wall__.
2. I like the black phone which is next to the silver one.
   → I like the black phone _____.
3. The books that are on the table are mine.
   → The books _____ are mine.
4. She's from London which is in Ontario, Canada.
   → She's from London _____.
5. Eugene bought a new car, which has two doors.
   → Eugene bought a new car _____.

2. 밑줄 친 부분을 –ing 또는 p.p. 형태로 바꾸어 문장을 다시 쓰세요.

1. He works for a factory that makes smartphones.
   → He works for a factory __making smartphones__.
2. Do you know anything about the accident that happened last night?
   → Do you know anything about the accident _____?
3. Nearly 5 percent of all the food that is sold in the U.S. in 2015 was organic.
   → Nearly 5 percent of all the food _____ was organic.
4. Anybody who is found damaging museum property will be prosecuted.
   → Anybody _____ will be prosecuted.
5. The airport has a VIP lounge for the passengers who are waiting for their flight.
   → The airport has a VIP lounge for the passengers _____.

3. 주어진 문장에서 생략이 가능한 표현을 괄호로 표시하세요.

1. Mark Zuckerberg, **(who is)** the inventor of Facebook, is an atheist.
2. What is your favorite book that was written by Stephen King?
3. The car which had been parked in front of the fire station was towed away immediately.
4. Paintings that were painted by Van Gogh are rarely sold at auction.
5. Eugene's new car, which is a black convertible, is really cool.

Dialogue

4. 밑줄 친 부분을 전치사를 사용해서 다시 쓰세요.

Ms. Watson is talking about the refrigerator she bought last week.
Watson 씨가 지난 주에 산 냉장고에 대해 이야기하고 있습니다.

Jessica Have you bought a new fridge?

Ms. Watson Yes. I found a good one on sale last week.

Jessica Good for you. What kind of fridge did you buy?

Ms. Watson Exactly what I was looking for. The one that has a water and ice dispenser.

Big Picture

전치사

09

1 명사 연결

전치사는 한마디로 명사를 덧붙여 주는 접착제(연결표현)입니다. 전치사는 여러 가지가 있습니다. 명사가 더해질 문장이나 표현과 더할 명사와의 관계에 따라 다른 전치사가 쓰일 수 있습니다.

There is a clock <u>on</u> <u>the wall</u>. 벽에 시계가 걸려 있다.
└ 표면과 표면의 맞닿음, 연결의 의미를 가진 전치사

Cut this paper <u>with</u> <u>scissors</u>. 가위로 이 종이를 자르시오.
└ 동반, 도구 등의 의미를 가진 전치사

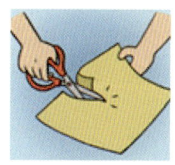

2 부사 역할

많은 전치사들은 또한 부사로도 쓰입니다. 특히 동사와 결합하여 하나의 표현, 구동사(phrasal verbs)를 이룰 수 있습니다. 이럴 때 구동사가 자동사인 경우, 뒤에 명사가 오지 않아도 됩니다. 전치사가 갖고 있는 의미대로 명사를 잇는 것이 아닌 부사로서 동사나 문장에 해당 의미를 더해 줍니다.

- A: Can I talk to Lisa, please? Lisa와 통화할 수 있을까요?
  B: Hold <u>on</u> please. 잠시만 기다려 주세요.
  └ 끊어지지 않고 계속 이어짐, 지속 등의 의미하는 부사

- Take your shoes <u>off</u>, please. 신발을 벗어 주세요.
  └ 분리, 단절 등의 의미하는 부사

Unit 082

시간 전치사(1)

The singer became famous in her early twenties.
그 가수는 20대 초반에 유명해졌다.

1. 다음과 같은 시간표현에는 in을 쓴다.

연도, 시대 등	in 1999/2017…	in the 21st century / the Middle Ages…
계절, 시기 등	in (the) spring/summer… in the past/future	in one's (early/mid/late) teens/twenties/thirties… in one's youth
달	in January/February/March…	
오전, 오후, 저녁	in the morning/afternoon/evening	
기타 표현	in time(제시간 안에), in advance(미리), in the meantime(한편 그 동안/사이에는), in the end(마침내)	

- ▶ Jason Statham was a talented soccer player **in** his youth. 제이슨 스타뎀은 젊은 시절에 재능 있는 축구선수였다.
- ▶ The singer became famous **in** her early twenties. 그 가수는 20대 초반에 유명해졌다.
- ▶ Make sure you arrive at the airport **in time**. 반드시 제시간에 공항에 도착하세요.

in은 '(얼마) 후에' 또는 '(얼마) 만에'의 의미로도 쓰인다. *See Unit 083▶*

- ▶ I'll be back **in** a week. 저는 일주일 후에 돌아 올 겁니다.

2. 다음과 같은 시간표현에는 on을 쓴다.

날짜, 요일, 주말 등 '날'	on April 3rd/the Fourth of July… on Monday/Tuesday…	on the weekend/weekends/weekdays/weeknights… on Christmas (day)/my birthday/our anniversary…
요일+오전/오후/저녁	on Monday morning/Friday afternoon/Saturday night…	
기타 표현: 순간	on time(제시간에 딱 맞춰, 정각/정시에), on arrival(도착하자마자)	

- ▶ My office is closed **on** the weekend. 제 사무실은 주말에는 문을 닫습니다. *영국 영어는 at the weekend라고 함*
- ▶ Disneyland is very crowded **on** Christmas. 디즈니랜드는 크리스마스에 매우 붐빈다.
- ▶ The train arrived **on time**. 열차는 제시간에 도착했다.

날짜나 요일 앞의 on은 종종 생략될 수 있다.

- ▶ We're leaving **(on) Monday morning**. 우리는 월요일 아침에 떠납니다.

today/yesterday/tomorrow/the day before yesterday 등 앞에는 on을 쓰지 않는다.

- ▶ She came back **the day before yesterday**. 그녀는 그저께 돌아왔어요.

3. 다음과 같은 시간표현에는 at을 쓴다.

시각	at 2 o'clock/9:30/noon/midnight/a half past four…
시간, 때 (하루나 어느 시기의 일부, 한 때)	at breakfast(time)/lunch(time)/dinner(time)/bedtime/Christmas ㄴ 성탄절 즈음을 의미 at night
시작 또는 끝 무렵	at the end of January/the year…
기타 표현	at first(처음에는), at last(드디어, 마침내), at the moment(현재, 지금은), at that time(그 때에는)

- ▶ Do you read books **at** bedtime? 잘 때 책 읽으시나요?
- ▶ The actor says he's quitting the lead role in the TV series **at the end** of the year.
  그 배우는 연말에 그 TV 시리즈물의 주역을 그만둘 것이라고 한다.

4. 'last/next/this/that/every+시간표현' 앞에도 in/on/at 등을 쓰지 않는다.

- ▶ I sold my car **last week**. 나는 지난 주에 차를 팔았다.
- ▶ My mother grows vegetables **every year**. 우리 엄마는 매년 채소를 기르신다.

Exercises

1. 빈칸에 in, on 또는 at을 넣어 문장을 완성하세요.

1. The movie starts __at__ a half past eight.
2. I first met my fiancé _____ a rainy day in April.
3. I'll be there _____ 10 minutes.
4. See you _____ noon.
5. I have lessons _____ Mondays and Wednesdays.
6. More people have heart attacks _____ Monday morning than _____ any other time of the week.
7. He'll be here _____ a moment.
8. _____ the Middle Ages, chimneys were a luxury.
9. Erika always gets up early _____ the morning so she can make it to class _____ time.
10. In San Bernardino, you can hear coyotes howling in the distance late _____ night.
11. _____ the first of the course, the professor said that there would be a final test _____ the end of the semester.
12. _____ the end, he decided to quit his job.

2. 문장 중 틀린 부분을 맞게 고치세요. 고칠 부분이 없다면 X를 쓰세요.

1. I'll be away in next week.   __next week__
2. She was born on Christmas Eve.   _____
3. They arrived on the day before yesterday.   _____
4. He takes pictures of the moon every night.   _____
5. I've finished my report at last!   _____
6. You don't have to pay at advance.   _____

🔊 Dialogue

3. 빈칸에 in, on 또는 at을 넣어 문장을 완성하세요. 전치사가 필요 없는 경우 그대로 두세요.

Alice and Julia are talking on the phone.
Alice와 Julia는 통화를 하고 있습니다.

Alice I'm sorry I was out when you called yesterday afternoon. Look, I'm free _____ the 28th. Shall we have dinner at Thai Dreams? You've wanted to eat there.

Julia I'm pretty busy _____ next week, I'm afraid. I'm working nights.

Alice Then… shall we meet the week after? Say… _____ the 2nd? That's a Tuesday.

Julia Tuesday the 2nd sounds fine.

Alice OK. Let's meet _____ Tuesday evening. Is 7 o'clock OK with you?

Julia Yep. I'll see you _____ 7 at Thai Dreams.

Unit 083

시간 전치사(2)

I couldn't get up until 9:30 this morning.
나는 오늘 아침 9시 30분이 되어서야 일어났다.

1. '~ 동안에'의 의미로 다음 표현을 쓸 수 있다.

❶ **for**: 2 hours/9 days/5 years/a long time/a while… `숫자나 길고 짧음으로 나타난 기간`
  ▶ I've wanted to become a writer **for** a long time. 저는 오랫**동안** 작가가 되고팠어요.

❷ **during**: the night/weekend/vacation/summer/class/meeting… `자체가 '기간'이 될 수 있는 단어`
  ▶ Could you please turn your cell phone off **during** the meeting? 회의 **동안에** 휴대폰을 꺼 주시겠습니까?

❸ **while**+S+V 또는 -ing `while은 접속사로, 뒤에 명사가 올 수 없다.` *See Unit 091 ▶*
  ▶ Many people check social media **while** (they are) waiting in line. 많은 사람들이 줄 서서 기다릴 **때** SNS를 한다.

2. '~까지'의 의미로 다음 표현을 쓸 수 있다.

until	by
'~까지' 계속/지속. 해당 시점에 종료	늦어도 '~까지'의 의미. 해당 시점 또는 그 이전에 종료
▶ She'll be here **until** 6 o'clock. 그녀는 6시**까지** 여기에 있을 겁니다.	▶ She'll be back **by** 6 o'clock. 그녀는 6시**까지는** 돌아올 겁니다.

not ~ until…은 '…때가 되어서야 ~하다'는 의미로 쓸 수 있다.
  ▶ I could**n't** get up **until** 9:30 this morning. 나는 오늘 아침 9시 30분이 **되어서야** 일어났다.

3. '~부터'의 의미로 다음 표현을 쓸 수 있다.

from	since
단독으로 쓰이거나, to나 until과 함께 '~부터 …까지'의 의미로 쓰일 수 있다. `이 경우 to는 단독으로는 쓰지 않음`	'~부터 완료시제의 기준시간까지'의 의미
▶ He had to work **from** early morning **to/until** late night. 그는 이른 아침**부터** 늦은 밤**까지** 일해야만 했다.	▶ I've been working here **since** 2009. 저는 2009년**부터** (지금**까지**) 여기서 일해 왔습니다.

4. 'last/next/this/that/every+시간표현' 앞에도 in/on/at 등을 쓰지 않는다.

❶ **before**+명사 `접속사로도 쓰일 수 있으며, 이때 뒤에 S+V나 -ing가 올 수도 있다.`
  ▶ I need to talk to you **before** lunch. 점심시간 **전에** 당신하고 얘기를 좀 해야 해요.

❷ 기간+**ago** `부사로서 기간 표현 뒤에 온다.`
  ▶ The meeting finished an hour **ago**. 회의는 한 시간 **전에** 끝났습니다.

5. '~ 후/뒤에'의 의미로 다음 표현을 쓸 수 있다.

❶ **after**+명사 `접속사로도 쓰일 수 있으며, 이때 뒤에 S+V나 -ing가 올 수도 있다.`
  ▶ What do you usually do **after** breakfast? 아침 식사 **후엔** 보통 무엇을 하시나요?

❷ **in**+기간 *See Unit 082 ▶*
  ▶ I'll be back **in** a minute. 금방 돌아올게요.

❸ 기간+**later** `부사로서 기간표현 뒤에 온다.`
  ▶ They met each other again nine years **later**. 그들은 9년 **뒤에** 서로 다시 만났다.

Exercises

1. 빈칸에 for, during 또는 while을 넣어 문장을 완성하세요.

1. Don't speak __while__ you're eating.
2. His phone rang _____ the meeting.
3. I stayed in Madrid _____ three days.
4. Did you visit the Empire State Building _____ your stay in New York?
5. My brother talks _____ sleeping.
6. I'll be out _____ a while.

2. 주어진 표현을 문맥에 맞게 연결하여 문장을 완성하세요.

1. Can you deliver the washing machine •   • a. since 2011.
2. He said he would be here •   • b. by the end of next week?
3. I waited for him •   • c. until four, but he didn't come.
4. They lived in Toronto •   • d. until the end of this month.
5. I haven't heard from her •   • e. by four but he hasn't come yet.
6. I'll be back •   • f. from 2011 until 2014.
7. My cousins are going to stay with me •   • g. in a moment.

3. 문장의 문맥에 가장 적합한 표현을 골라 문장을 완성하세요.

1. I'll call you (after dinner / dinner later).
2. I met his father once, (ago a long time / a long time ago).
3. He went to bed late and slept (to noon / until noon) the next day.
4. Where do you think you will live (in ten years' time / ten years' time after)?
5. Could you post the agenda (before the meeting / the meeting ago)?
6. He left on Monday and returned (later a week / a week later).

🔊 Dialogue

4. 문장의 문맥에 가장 적합한 표현을 골라 문장을 완성하세요.

Mike and Trish are talking at a canteen.
Mike와 Trish는 구내식당에서 대화 중입니다.

Mike I'm thinking of moving into an apartment near here.

Trish Why? You don't like your current place?

Mike No. It's too far from work. I spend three hours on the road every day.

Trish Three hours? That's too much.

Mike I arrive home at about 7:30, and (by / to / until) then, I'm too tired to even eat.

Unit 084

장소 전치사(1)

My old car is still in good condition.
내 오래된 차는 여전히 상태가 좋다.

1. in은 다음과 같은 경우에 쓸 수 있다.

경계선, 범위 안이나 내부	**in** the bag/one's hand/the water/the car/the classroom/the park/Korea…
환경	**in the** rain/sun/dark/sky/sea/forest/world…
형태, 형식	**in (a/the)** line/row/circle…　**in a/the** book/newspaper/picture/photograph… **in** English/writing/capital letters/a loud voice/black (ink)/cash…
상태	**in** bed/good condition/flight/the hospital…
소속, 분야, 범주 등	**in** business/education/high school/college/the army…

▶ My old car is still **in good condition**. 내 오래된 차는 여전히 **상태가 좋다**.

2. on은 다음과 같은 경우에 쓸 수 있다.

표면, 접촉, 디딤, 통신, 접속 등	**on the** table/wall/floor/balcony/screen/road/way/page/list/Internet/line/TV…
탑승, 승차, 방향, 입장	**on a/the** bike/bus/train/plane/the left…　**on** the right/one's side…
목적, 의도, 일정(여행)	**on** business/vacation/purpose/a trip/strike/sale/a diet…

▶ Are you in Boston **on business**? 보스톤에는 **사업 차** 오셨나요?

3. at은 다음과 같은 경우에 쓸 수 있다.

모호한 경계, 내/외부 구분 안 함	**at a/the** bus stop/the traffic light/the door/one's desk…
위, 아래, 끝 등	**at the** bottom/top/end of…
행사나 활동의 장소 (집, 학교, 직장)	**at a/the** concert/baseball game/party/conference… **at** home/school/work

▶ Please, sign **at the bottom of the application**. 지원서의 맨 밑에 서명을 해 주세요.

4. 전치사에 따라 의미가 달라질 수 있다. in은 명사와 관련된 상태나 지위 등을, at은 명사와 관련된 활동을 암시한다.

❶ in school/college — at school/college
- ▶ My elder brother is still **in school**. 우리 형은 아직 **학생이다**.
- ▶ My children aren't home yet. They're still **at school**. 아이들은 아직 집에 안 왔어요. 아직 **학교에 있어요**.

❷ in the hospital — at the hospital
- ▶ Yesterday, I was **at the hospital** to see my grandfather. He's been **in the hospital** for a week.
  어제 난 할아버지를 문병하려 **병원에 가** 있었어요. 할아버지께서 일주일 째 병원에 **입원해 계시거든요**. 영국 영어에서는 in hospital로 말한다.

❸ in the restaurant/supermarket/airport… — at the restaurant/supermarket/airport…
- ▶ All the shops **in the airport** are open on Sundays. 공항 내 모든 상점은 일요일에 영업합니다.
- ▶ Will you meet me **at the airport**? 공항으로 나 마중 나와 줄래?

❹ on my desk — at my desk
- ▶ I always have a coffee mug **on my desk**. 난 항상 **책상 위에** 커피 머그잔을 두고 있어요.
- ▶ I'm not **at my desk** at the moment. 지금 전 **제자리에** 있지 않아요.

❺ church는 '예배 중'의 의미일 때 in church와 at church 모두 쓰일 수 있다.
- ▶ The Watsons are **at/in church** now. Watson 씨 가족은 지금 **교회에 있다**(예배 중이다).

Exercises

1. 빈칸에 in, on 또는 at을 넣어 문장을 완성하세요.

1. What's the best way to sleep __in__ flight?
2. What's _____ TV tonight?
3. There's no need to fight. I'm _____ your side.
4. Naomi is waiting for the bus _____ the bus stop.
5. The ladies' restroom is _____ the second floor.
6. I saw him standing _____ the corner of the street.
7. We'll send someone to meet you _____ the airport.
8. Do you like walking _____ the rain?
9. The miners have been _____ strike since May.
10. Please write legibly _____ black ink.
11. A: Would you like some cake?
    B: No, thanks. I'm _____ a diet.
12. She's been _____ education for 20 years.
13. Turn left _____ the traffic light.
14. The coffee shop is _____ the right of the station.
15. He started reading the letter _____ a loud voice.
16. Guests shouldn't wear white _____ a wedding.

2. 문장의 문맥에 가장 적합한 표현을 골라 문장을 완성하세요.

1. There are only eight tables (at /(in)) the restaurant.
2. A: Is Trish back in the office?
   B: Yes. She's (at / on) her desk.
3. Doctor Grey isn't (at / in) the hospital now. He's on vacation.
4. Do not sit or stand (at / on) the desk.
5. Is your child old enough to be (at / in) kindergarten?
6. I'll do the shopping while the kids are (at / in) school.

🔊 Dialogue

3. 빈칸에 적절한 전치사를 넣어 문장을 완성하세요.

Eugene is apologizing to Jay. Eugene은 Jay에게 사과를 하고 있습니다.

Eugene I'm sorry I broke your cell phone, but I didn't do it _____ purpose.

Jay That's all right. I know it was an accident, Eugene.

Eugene Listen. I'll pay for it.

Jay No, you don't have to. It was insured. And I was going to buy a new one anyway.

Eugene Really? That's good. Hey, I think I owe you a meal. Just choose a day and a place.

Unit 085

장소 전치사(2)

Does this bus go downtown?
이 버스 시내 가나요?

1. 그 외의 위치나 장소 표현에 대해 다음과 같은 전치사를 쓸 수 있다.

The rabbit is...

- **near/by/close to** the window. 토끼가 창가에 있다. 멀지 않은 정도
- **next to/beside** the box. 토끼가 상자 옆에 있다. 바짝, 나란히 붙어서
- **between** the boxes. 토끼가 상자 사이에 있다. 두 개의 상자 사이에
- **among** the boxes. 토끼가 상자들 가운데에 있다. 여러 개 상자에 둘러 싸인
- **under** the table. 토끼가 탁자 밑에 있다.
- **in front of** the box. 토끼가 상자 앞에 있다.
- **behind** the box. 토끼가 상자 뒤에 있다.
- **across from** the street. 토끼가 길 건너에 있다.

2. 이동 방향이나 움직임에 대해 말할 경우 전치사가 달라질 수 있다.

The rabbit goes...

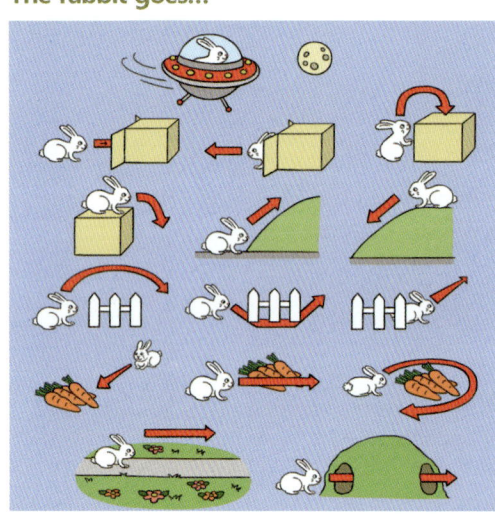

- **to** the moon. 토끼가 달로 간다. 우주선 타고
- **in/into** the box. 토끼가 상자 속으로 들어간다.
- **out of** the box. 토끼가 상자 밖으로 나온다.
- **on/onto** the box. 토끼가 상자 위로 올라간다.
- **off** the box. 토끼가 상자에서 내려 간다.
- **up** the hill. 토끼가 언덕 위로 간다.
- **down** the hill. 토끼가 언덕 아래로 간다.
- **over** the fence. 토끼가 울타리 위로 넘어간다.
- **under** the fence. 토끼가 울타리 밑으로 간다.
- **away from** the fence. 토끼가 울타리로부터 멀리 간다.
- **toward** the carrots. 토끼가 당근들을 향해 온다.
- **past** the carrots. 토끼가 당근들을 지나쳐 간다.
- **around** the carrots. 토끼가 당근들을 돌아서 간다.
- **across** the yard. 토끼가 마당을 가로질러 간다.
- **through** the hole. 토끼가 굴을 통과한다.

3. 다음 표현들 앞에는 전치사를 쓰지 않는다. '~로'의 의미로 쓰일 수 있음(부사)

here   there   upstairs   downstairs   downtown

▶ Please come and sit **here**. 와서 여기 앉으세요.
▶ I can hear noises from the people living **upstairs**. 위층에 사는 사람들이 내는 소음이 들려요.
▶ Does this bus go **downtown**? 이 버스 시내로 가나요?

home 앞에는 to를 쓰지 않는다. Be동사나 stay와 함께 쓰일 때 at이 생략될 수 있다.

▶ Are you going **home** now? 이제 집에 가니?
▶ I might stay **(at) home** all day tomorrow. 나는 내일 하루 종일 집에 있을지도 몰라.

Exercises

1. 빈칸에 적절한 전치사를 넣어 문장을 완성하세요.
   1. Please, close the door __behind__ you.
   2. The town is located 119 meters _____ sea level.
   3. How many bridges are there _____ the River Thames in London?
   4. Go _____ the table when an earthquake strikes.
   5. Mom used to sit _____ my bed and read to me.
   6. Ulsan is _____ Daegu and Busan.
   7. He disappeared _____ the crowd.

2. 문장의 문맥에 가장 적합한 표현을 골라 문장을 완성하세요.
   1. They sailed (along / past) the river.
   2. The hot water runs (over / through) the pipes to the heat the floor.
   3. The drone was circling (across / around), looking for a place to land.
   4. The kid climbed (up / toward) the tree to get a better view.
   5. The parking lot is just (onto / past) the building over there.
   6. He fell (off / to) the ladder and broke his arm.
   7. The car came (out of / under) the garage.

3. 문장의 틀린 부분이 있다면 고쳐서 다시 쓰세요. 틀린 부분이 없다면 X를 쓰세요.
   1. They live somewhere near to San Francisco.   *They live somewhere near San Francisco.*
   2. Go to upstairs and get dressed for school.   _____
   3. Are your parents at home now?   _____
   4. Our hotel was very close the beach.   _____

🌟 Dialogue

4. 빈칸에 들어갈 가장 적합한 표현을 골라 넣어 문장을 완성하세요.

| around   over   under |

Ben is having dinner with his grandma Ms. Diaz. Ben은 그의 할머니인 Ms. Diaz와 저녁을 먹고 있습니다.

Ms. Diaz Could you pass the salt?
Ben Sure. Whoops! I've spilt some.
Ms. Diaz That's OK, but throw a pinch of it _____ your shoulder.
Ben Grandma, do you believe in all that superstitious stuff?
Ms. Diaz I do. I always do so if I ever spill it.
Ben Really? Then you must walk _____ a ladder?
Ms. Diaz Sure. I never walk _____ a ladder. Wouldn't you?
Ben No, but that's so nothing falls on my head!

207

Unit 086

기타 전치사(1)

You can pay by credit card or in cash.
신용카드로 지불하시거나 현금으로 지불하실 수 있습니다.

1 by는 힘의 영향을 받거나 그 범위에 있음 등을 암시한다.

(주로 수동태에서) 주체	**by** Adele/Beethoven/Michelangelo/myself…
교통/통신/지불 수단	**by** bus/subway/plane/phone/e-mail/check/credit card… on foot(도보로), in cash(현금으로) **by** -ing ~함으로써
~에 의하면/따르면, ~로 보아	**by** name/law/my watch
실수, 우발적으로	**by** mistake/accident/chance
부근, 주변에 See unit 085▶	**by** the window/the sea/ones' side…
~까지 See unit 083▶	**by** 5 o'clock/noon…
폭, 마진, 간격	**by** 50%/100 dollars/the hour/a nose…

▶ You can pay **by** credit card or in cash. 신용카드로 지불하시거나 현금으로 지불하실 수 있습니다.
▶ A: Hello. Can I speak to Mr. Branson, please? 여보세요. Branson 씨 좀 부탁합니다.
  B: Mr. Branson? Sorry. There is no one here **by** that name.
  Branson 씨요? 죄송하지만, 그런 이름**의** 사람은 여기 없는데요.
▶ The price went up **by** 30% last year. 작년에 가격이 30% 인상되었다.

2 with는 동반, 보조 등의 의미를 암시한다.

동반, 동행, 연관, 지지	**with** you/my family/me/each other…
부속, 추가	**with** buttons/a handle/a view/an accent/a little luck/French fries…
외모	**with** long hair/blue eyes/glasses…
감정, 질병	**with** fear/excitement/joy/fear/anger/a cold…
도구	**with** a knife/some scissors/the key/care…

▶ Are you coming **with** me? 너도 나랑 가는 거니?
▶ I'd like a cheeseburger **with** french fries, please. 감자프라이가 **곁들여진** 치즈버거 하나 주세요.
▶ Everybody jumped **with** joy. 모두가 기쁨에 펄쩍 뛰었다.
▶ Open the door **with** the key. 그 열쇠로 문을 여시오.

'~ 없이'의 의미로 **without**이 쓰일 수 있다.

▶ I can't live **without** you. 난 당신 **없이는** 못 살아요.
▶ He walked past me **without** saying hello. 그는 인사도 **안** 하고 내 앞을 지나갔다.

다음 표현들 뒤에 **with**가 쓰인다.

a relationship/connection/contact	**with**	~
happy/satisfied/pleased/disappointed/fed up/bored/impressed/crowded/filled…		
provide/supply…+somebody		

▶ I've had a good **relationship with** my boss. 나는 사장님**과** 좋은 **관계**를 유지해 왔어요.
▶ I'm very **impressed with** his Korean. 나는 그의 한국어에 무척 **인상**이 깊었다. impressed by로도 말할 수 있다.
▶ This course **provides students with** a basic foundation in international trade.
  이 과정은 **학생들에게** 국제 무역의 기본기**를 제공합니다**.

Exercises

1. 주어진 표현에서 적절한 표현을 골라 문장을 완성하세요.

	by	
1. ~~She was standing~~		law.
2. We were overcharged		email.
3. I'll be there		seven.
4. You can contact me		mistake.
5. I deleted the file		$15.
6. Domestic violence is prohibited		~~the door.~~

1. _She was standing by the door._
2. _____
3. _____
4. _____
5. _____
6. _____

2. 주어진 표현에서 적절한 표현을 골라 문장을 완성하세요.

	with	
1. ~~The kid was frozen~~		many pockets.
2. I'm looking for a bag		curly hair.
3. Don't go. Just stay		me.
4. I haven't decided what to buy		this money.
5. Eva is a cute little girl		a garden salad.
6. I'll have a veggie burger		~~fear.~~

1. _The kid was frozen with fear._
2. _____
3. _____
4. _____
5. _____
6. _____

3. by, with 또는 without을 넣어 문장을 완성하세요.

1. The witness provided the police __with__ some information.
2. I chose a room _____ a shower because it's cheaper.
3. She met him again _____ chance on a plane.
4. The speaker knew how to build a connection _____ his audience.
5. _____ working faithfully eight hours a day, you may eventually get to be boss and work twelve hours a day. -by Robert Frost

◀ Dialogue

4. 빈칸에 들어갈 가장 적합한 표현을 골라 넣어 문장을 완성하세요.

by   for   in   on   with

Kate is shopping for clothes. Kate는 지금 옷 쇼핑 중입니다.

Kate I'm looking for a white shirt - in a size medium.

Clerk Let's see. Here's a nice one. Would you like to try it on?

Kate OK… yes. I love it. It fits perfectly. How much is it?

Clerk It's $38 _____ tax.

Kate Perfect! I'll take it.

Unit 087

기타 전치사(2)

Their parents don't approve of their marriage.
그들의 부모님은 그들의 결혼에 대해 찬성하지 않습니다.

1. of는 해당 명사가 근본 중심(주체)이거나 그로부터 비롯되거나 관련된 것, 집중 등의 의미를 암시한다.

- **~의, ~에 관련된**
  - The <u>title</u> **of** the song is *Hello*. 그 노래의 제목은 'Hello'입니다.
  - What's the <u>advantage</u> **of** living in the country? 시골에서 사는 이점이 무엇일까요?

- **자동사, 형용사, 명사 등의 대상(목적어, ~를) 연결** 『실질적인 주체 또는 근본 원인』

afraid/frightened/terrified/scared/tired/sick/fond/proud/ashamed/jealous/suspicious/critical/aware/capable/full/short/typical/certain/sure…	**of**	…
consist/approve/disapprove/think/dream/take care/complain/die…		

  - My sister is <u>afraid</u> **of** birds. 우리 언니는 새를 두려워 합니다. 『두려움의 원인』
  - The meal <u>consisted</u> **of** smoked salmon and a small salad.
    그 식사는 훈제 연어와 작은 샐러드로 구성되어 있었다. 『훈제 연어와 샐러드가 식사를 구성하였음』
  - Their parents don't <u>approve</u> **of** their marriage.
    그들의 부모님은 그들의 결혼에 대해 찬성하지 않습니다. 『자동사 approve 뒤의 대상 연결』
  - She has to <u>take care</u> **of** her little brother after school.
    그녀는 방과 후에 어린 남동생을 돌봐야 한다. 『(take) care의 대상 연결』

타동사의 경우에도 of가 원인 등을 나타낼 수 있다.

remind/warn/accuse/suspect…+somebody	**of**	…

  - You can't <u>accuse</u> me **of** lying. 넌 거짓말했다고 나를 비난할 수는 없어.
  - He is <u>suspected</u> **of** animal abuse. 그는 동물 학대로 의심받고 있다.

- **It's kind/nice/polite/silly…(형용사)+of+사람+…** 『of 뒤의 사람이 실질적인 주어(중심 대상)임』
  - It's <u>nice</u> **of** him to help me. (= He is nice.) 나를 도와주다니 그는 정말 사람 좋아요.

---

2. for는 대상, 목적(지), 이유, 자격 등을 의미한다.
  - Is it a book **for** children? 그거 어린이용 책인가요?
  - I'm here **for** sightseeing. 전 여기에 관광하러 왔습니다.
  - I'd like to reserve a table **for** three, please. 세 사람 자리를 예약하고자 합니다.

다음 표현들 뒤에서 for가 쓰인다.

a check/demand/need/reason…		
sorry/famous/responsible…	**for**	목적(지), 원인, 이유 등
look/search/care/wait/ask/apply/leave…		

  - What's the <u>reason</u> **for** the delay? 지연의 이유가 뭔가요?
  - Seattle is <u>famous</u> **for** coffee. 시애틀은 커피로 유명하다.
  - Would you <u>care</u> **for** a cup of tea? 차 한 잔 하시겠어요?

---

3. 'because of/thanks to/due to+명사'도 원인을 말할 때 쓸 수 있다.
원인/이유의 내용으로 S+V(절, 문장)을 연결하고자 할 때에는 because/since/as 등을 쓸 수 있다.

  - My flight was delayed **because of** heavy snow. 내 비행편이 폭설로 지연되었다.
  - We've raised over $70,000 **thanks to** your help. 여러분의 도움으로 우리가 7만 달러가 넘는 돈을 모았습니다.
  - **Due to** the severe weather conditions, we will be closed for today.
    악천후로 인해 우리는 오늘 영업하지 않을 것입니다.

Exercises

1. 빈칸에 들어갈 가장 적절한 표현을 보기에서 골라 넣어 문장을 완성하세요.

> afraid   approve   consist(s)   die   full   proud   take care

1. Many children are __afraid__ of the dark.
2. Don't worry. I'm old enough to _____ of myself.
3. The room was _____ of people.
4. Wild animals _____ of cancer at about the same rate that humans do.
5. You should be _____ of yourself.
6. My family _____ of five people: my father, my mother, my twin brothers, and me.
7. My parents don't _____ of plastic surgery.

2. for나 of를 넣어 문장을 완성하세요.

1. This song reminds me __of__ my childhood.
2. A: What's the purpose _____ your visit?
   B: Business. I'm here _____ a conference.
3. There's no need _____ violence to be in this situation.
4. Are you going to apply _____ the position?
5. It's silly _____ you to believe what he said.
6. She is responsible _____ training new staff.

3. 빈칸에 적합한 전치사를 넣어 문장을 완성하세요.

1. The reason __for__ the blackout is unknown yet.
2. She missed her flight yesterday because _____ the storm.
3. I was able to finish the project thanks _____ his help.
4. His business failed due _____ cash-flow problems.

🔸 Dialogue

4. 주어진 전치사 중 가장 적합한 전치사를 골라 문장을 완성하세요.

Erika went to the movies last Sunday. Suzi is asking about the movie.
Erika는 지난 일요일에 영화를 보러 갔습니다. Suzi가 영화에 대해 묻고 있습니다.

Suzi   Did you like the film?

Erika   Yeah, it's not a masterpiece but quite good (for / of) killing time.

Suzi   What was it like?

Erika   It's a typical Christmas movie. A man and a woman fell in love, but they had a hard time because neither of their parents approved (for / of) their marriage.

Suzi   Does it have a happy ending?

Erika   Yes. Finally they were able to smooth things over with their parents.

Unit 088

기타 전치사(3)

I apologized to her for what I said.
나는 내가 말한 것에 대해 그녀에게 사과했다.

1 to는 방향, 도달점이나 직전, 정도나 범위의 끝 등을 의미한다.

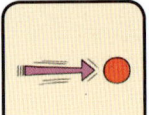

- I'm on my way **to** school now. 저는 지금 학교**에** 가는 길이에요.
- A: What time is it? 몇 시지?
  B: It's ten **to** nine. 9시 10분 **전**이야.
- This morning I had dark circles down **to** my knees. 오늘 아침에 난 다크서클이 무릎**까지** 내려왔어.

다음 표현들 위에서 to가 쓰인다.

damage/an invitation/one's visit/a solution/a reply/a key/an answer...	**to**	...
similar/married/engaged...		
talk/speak/listen/apologize...		
explain/describe...+something		

- It will be my first <u>visit</u> **to** Norway. 제 첫 노르웨이 방문이 될 것입니다.
- Is Spanish <u>similar</u> **to** Portuguese? 스페인어가 포르투갈어**랑** 비슷한가요?
- I <u>apologized</u> **to** her for what I said. 나는 내가 말한 것에 대해 그녀**에게** 사과했다.
- Can you <u>explain</u> it **to** me? 제게 그것을 설명해 주시겠어요?

call, answer, ask, thank 등의 동사 뒤에는 to를 쓰지 않는다.

- Are you ready to **answer** my questions? 제 질문에 **답하실** 준비가 되셨나요?
- Everyone **thanked** Mr. Cruz for all his hard work. 모두가 Cruz 씨의 모든 노고에 **감사했습니다**.

움직이는 방향과 태도에 대해 toward를 쓰기도 한다. 영국 영어에서는 towards를 쓰기도 한다.

- They sailed **toward** the horizon. 그들은 수평선을 **향해** 항해했다.
- His attitude **toward** women is biased. 그의 여성에 **대한** 태도는 편향되어 있다.

2 at은 지점, 방향, 표적, 상황/상태, 반응 등의 의미를 암시하고, 숫자 앞에 자주 쓰인다.

- It's a stopping train. It stops **at** all the intermediate stations. 그건 완행열차입니다. 모든 중간 역**에** 다 섭니다.
- The two countries were **at** war for two years. 그 두 나라는 2년간 전쟁 **중**이었다.
- He got married **at** the age of 19. 그는 19세의 나이**에** 결혼했다.

angry/mad/furious/surprised/shocked/amazed/astonished 등	**at**	...
look/stare/glance/take a look/have a look/laugh/aim/point/shoot/fire 등		

- My brother was mad **at** me for using his smartphone. 자기 스마트폰을 썼다고 형이 내게 화를 냈다.
- What are you looking **at**? 무엇을 보고 있니?
- Everyone would laugh **at** me if I sang. 내가 노래를 불렀다간 모두가 나를 비웃을 거야.

3 같은 표현이라도 뒤에 to와 at의 사용에 따라 의미가 달라진다.

- The music was so loud that I had to <u>shout</u> **to** him. 음악이 너무 커서 나는 그에게 큰 소리로 말해야 했다.
- The angry crowd <u>shouted</u> **at** the politician. 화가 난 군중들이 그 정치인에게 소리를 질렀다.

- If you <u>throw</u> bread **to** the ducks, they'll eat it. 오리들에게 빵을 던져주면 먹을 거야.
- Don't <u>throw</u> stones **at** the ducks. 오리들에게 돌을 던지지 마시오.

Exercises

1. 빈칸에 들어갈 가장 적절한 표현을 보기에서 골라 문장을 완성하세요.

> apologize   ~~damage~~   invitation   key   married   similar   solution

1. Acid rain causes _damage_ to buildings, soil, trees and water.
2. Anna sent me an _____ to her wedding.
3. Is there a _____ to the problem?
4. He is _____ to my cousin.
5. It's not too late to _____ to her.
6. Do you have anything _____ to this design?
7. Here's the _____ to your room.

2. 주어진 표현을 문맥에 맞게 연결하여 문장을 완성하세요.

1. He's still angry   a. toward environmental issues these day.
2. I was surprised   b. at me.
3. She described everything   c. to Laguna Beach?
4. Which is the road   d. at the news.
5. More people are sympathetic   e. to me in detail.
6. He started skating   f. at the age of five.

3. 문장의 문맥에 가장 적합한 표현을 골라 문장을 완성하세요.

1. If I wear this, everybody will laugh ((at) / to) me.
2. The pitcher threw the ball (at / to) the catcher.
3. He shouted (at / to) the dog to stop.
4. Nobody answered (my question / to my question).
5. That's not an answer (the question / to the question).
6. Angry people threw eggs (at / to) the politician.

✦ Dialogue

4. 빈칸에 알맞은 전치사를 채워서 문장을 완성하세요.

Rachel wants to call a taxi. Rachel은 택시를 부르고 싶어 합니다.

Rachel   Hello? Can I get a taxi _____ the airport?
Operator Sure. Where are you located now?
Rachel   I'm _____ the Milton Hotel.
Operator What time do you want your taxi?
Rachel   As soon as possible.
Operator OK. We have one available around the Milton Hotel now.
           I'll send it _____ you right away.

Unit 089

기타 전치사(4)

Why don't we talk about it over lunch?
그거에 대해 점심 먹으면서 얘기하는 거 어때?

1 전치사는 부사, 접속사 등으로도 다양하게 쓰일 수 있다.
- I look nothing **like** my brother. 나는 오빠와 조금도 비슷하게 생기지 않았어요. `전치사`
- The building is more **like** 20 years old. 그 건물은 대략 20년 정도 된다. `부사`
- He acted **like** I wasn't there. 그는 내가 마치 거기 없었던 것처럼 행동했다. `접속사`

2 **as**는 비교의 기준, 자격, 동시/동반, 이유 등의 의미를 나타낼 수 있다. `See Unit 077▶`
- I'm not **as** tall **as** my brother. 나는 오빠만큼 키가 크지는 않아요.

like도 '~와 비슷한', '~처럼' 등의 의미로 쓰일 수 있다. `대화체에서 like 뒤에는 명사와 S+V가 모두 온다.`
- He drinks **like** a fish. 그는 술고래야(그는 물고기처럼 술을 마셔).

3 **about**은 중심 대상에 대한 관련성, 주변 등을 암시한다.
- There's nothing you can do **about** it. 그것에 대해 네가 할 수 있는 건 없어.

on도 '~에 대해서'라는 의미로 쓸 수 있으나, about보다 전문적이거나 주제에 집중한 뉘앙스를 줄 수 있다.
- It's a documentary **on** earthquakes. 그것은 지진에 대한 다큐멘터리입니다.

about과 **around** 모두 '대략'의 의미의 부사로 쓰일 수 있다.
- She's **about/around** 30 years old. 그녀는 대략 서른 살 쯤 돼요.

around는 '~의 둘레에/주위에', '~로 돌아', '여기저기' 등의 의미로도 쓰인다. `See Unit 085▶`
- Everyone sat **around** the table. 모두가 테이블에 둘러 앉았다.

4 **over**는 대상의 위를 덮거나 가로지르거나 넘어감, 시간이 걸쳐짐 등의 의미를 암시한다.

- The thief climbed **over** the wall. 그 도둑은 벽을 타고 넘어 갔다.
- An adult under British law is someone **over** 18 years old. 영국 법에서 성인은 18세 이상의 사람이다.
- Why don't we talk about it **over** lunch? 그거에 대해 점심 먹으면서 얘기하는 거 어때?

over는 종료, 다시, 뒤집음 등의 의미를 나타내기도 한다. `부사`
- The exam's **over**! 시험 끝났다!
- I had to write the report **over** again. 나는 그 보고서를 다시 써야 했다.
- Turn the pancake **over** when it starts to bubble. 거품이 나기 시작하면 팬케익을 뒤집으세요.

over는 위치와 움직임 모두에 대해 쓸 수 있으나, **above**는 위치에 대해서만 쓴다.
- The thief climbed **over** the wall. 그 도둑은 벽을 타고 넘어 갔다. *The thief climbed **above** the wall.* (X)

5 **across**는 한쪽에서 다른 한쪽으로 가로지르는 평면적 개념이다. `over는 보다 입체적`
- They walked **across** to the shop. = They walked **over** to the shop. 그들은 길을 건너 가게로 갔다.

through는 내부를 통과하거나 어떤 상황이나 시기의 처음부터 끝까지를 의미한다.

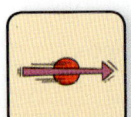

- The Han River flows **through** Seoul. 한강은 서울을 관통하여 흐른다.
- I'm halfway **through** the book. 난 그 책을 절반 정도 읽었다.

Exercises

1. 밑줄 친 부분이 틀렸다면 맞게 고치세요. 고칠 부분이 없다면 X를 쓰세요.

1. I like looking <u>around</u> bookshops.　　　　X
2. When in Rome, do <u>about</u> the Romans do.　　_____
3. Is there a park <u>around</u> here?　　_____
4. She tied a pink ribbon <u>about</u> the cake.　　_____
5. Toledo was known <u>like</u> the city of glass.　　_____
6. What did you like best <u>around</u> the movie?　　_____
7. <u>Like</u> I said before, I'm here to win.　　_____
8. Social media is getting common all <u>around</u> the world.　　_____

2. 문장의 문맥에 가장 적합한 표현을 골라 문장을 완성하세요.

1. The boy climbed (above /(over)) the fence.
2. Put the blanket (above / over) the bed.
3. The village is 800 meters (above / over) sea level.
4. The plane flew (above / over) the island.
5. Who lives (above / over) you on the fifth floor?
6. You have to be (above / over) 18 to see this movie.
7. The baby cried all (across / through) the night.
8. Amelia Earhart was the first woman pilot to fly (across / through) the Atlantic.
9. He ran (across / through) the street and disappeared in the crowd.
10. Is there a bridge (across / through) the river?
11. Up to 400 trains pass (across / through) the Channel Tunnel each day.
12. The guard at the gate didn't let him (across / through).
13. I want to toast marshmallows (across / over) the fire.
14. The children were running (across / around).

✦ Dialogue

3. 보기 중 빈칸에 들어갈 가장 적합한 표현을 골라 넣어 문장을 완성하세요.

| around　　as　　like　　over |

Patrick, Naomi, and Suzi are on the subway. Patrick, Naomi, Suzi는 지하철을 타고 있습니다.

Patrick Hey. That guy almost knocked you _____ getting off the subway.
Naomi Did you notice his facial expression? He acted as if we were in his way.
Suzi I get so annoyed with people _____ that.
Naomi Me too. Those rude people hardly ever say sorry.
Patrick These days, Very few people apologize for their offences.

Unit 090

구동사

Did you look it up on the Internet?
그거 인터넷에서 찾아 본 거니?

1
'구동사(phrasal verbs)'는 동사와 in, out, up 등이 더해져 만들어진 하나의 덩어리 표현이다.

> 구동사(phrasal verbs) = 동사+in/out/up/down/on/off/back/away...

- We'd like to **get away** for a few days. 우리는 며칠간 **휴가를 가고** 싶어요.
- His car **broke down** on the highway. 그의 차가 고속도로에서 **고장 났다**.

동사 뒤에 더해지는 표현(particle)에 따라 구동사의 의미가 달라진다.

- His grandfather **passed away** fifteen years ago. 그의 할아버지는 15년 전에 **돌아가셨다**.
- He was hit on the head and **passed out**. 그는 머리를 맞고 **기절했다**.

2
구동사에도 대상(목적어)이 필요 없는 자동사와 반드시 필요한 타동사가 있다.

- I'm an early riser. I always **get up** before 6:00. [자동사]
  저는 일찍 일어나는 사람이에요. 항상 6시 전에 **일어나지요**.
- Eva **takes after** her mother. Eva는 엄마를 닮았어요. [타동사]

같은 구동사라도 의미에 따라 자동사와 타동사로 나뉠 수 있다.

- The airplane **took off** on time. 비행기는 제시간에 **이륙했다**.
- Please **take off** your shoes before you enter the house. 집에 들어오기 전에 신발을 **벗어 주세요**.

3
타동사 구동사의 경우, 대상(목적어)이 구동사 표현 중간에 올 수 있다.

> He turned on the light. = He turned the light on. 그는 불을 켰다.

- Please, **bring** all the books **back** to the library.
  (= Please, **bring back** all the books to the library.) 모든 책을 도서관에 돌려 주세요.
- She **held** her tears **back**. (=She **held back** her tears.) 그녀는 눈물을 참았다.

대상(목적어)이 it이나 them처럼 대명사인 경우에는 반드시 구동사 중간에 온다.

- Did you **look** it **up** on the Internet? 그거 인터넷에서 찾아 본 거니? *Did you look up it on the Internet?* (X)
- Wash your dishes and **put** them **away**. 설거지를 하고 그릇을 치워 주세요.
- I'll **pick** you **up** at the airport. 내가 공항에서 널 **픽업할게**. *I'll pick up you at the airport.* (X)

대상이 중간에 올 수 없는 구동사도 있다.

- UN **stands for** United Nations. UN은 United Nations의 약자입니다. *UN stands United Nations for.* (X)
- Somebody has **broken into** the house! 누가 집에 **침입했어요**!
  Somebody has broken the house into. (X)

4
구동사는 해당 의미의 명사나 형용사 표현이 되기도 한다.

- The billionaire **gave away** most of her money to charity. [구동사]
  그 백만장자는 자신의 돈의 대부분을 자선단체에 **기부했다**.
- We're offering a headset as a **giveaway**. [명사]
  사은품으로 헤드폰을 드리고 있어요.
- I bought a new S-phone at a **giveaway** price. [형용사]
  그는 새 S-phone을 공짜나 다름없는 가격에 샀다.

구동사가 명사나 형용사로 쓰일 때에는 통으로 붙여 쓰거나 -(hyphen)으로 연결한다.

Exercises

1. 각 영역에서 적합한 표현을 골라 넣어 문장을 완성하세요. 문장에 맞게 동사의 형태를 바꾸세요.

give	after
hold	away
look	back
pass	for
take	out

   1. He __gave__ his textbooks __away__ when he left school.
   2. Who do you _____, your mother or your father?
   3. I tried to _____ my feelings _____.
   4. Police are _____ a suspect after a 78-year-old woman was robbed.
   5. I almost _____ when I saw the blood.

2. 주어진 단어를 맞는 순서대로 배열하여 문장을 완성하세요.

   1. Why are you wearing a coat in this warm weather? __Take it off__ (it / off / Take).
   2. Excuse me, _____ (I / try / can / this / on)?
   3. When you have completed the form, please _____ (it / hand / in).
   4. I can't hear the TV. _____ (turn / you / up / it / Will)?
   5. _____ (down / Rain / me / gets).

3. 문장의 문맥에 가장 적합한 표현을 골라 문장을 완성하세요.

   1. Everybody (got off the bus / got the bus off).
   2. He (looks after his brother / looks his brother after).
   3. They made a major (break through / breakthrough) in the treatment of AIDS.
   4. MVP (stands for Most Valuable Player / Stands Most Valuable Player for).
   5. Laguna Beach is a popular weekend (get away / getaway).

🔊 Dialogue

4. 보기 중 빈칸에 들어갈 가장 적합한 표현을 골라 넣어 문장을 완성하세요. 문장에 맞게 동사의 형태를 바꾸세요.

   go on   leave out   make up   print out   put off   throw away

   Andy and Amy are talking together. Andy와 Amy는 대화를 하고 있습니다.

   Andy   Have you heard? The exam has been postponed to next week.
   Amy   Really? Why?
   Andy   Mr. Platt _____ a page when he _____ the papers. So, he had to _____ all the papers _____ and _____ the exam.
   Amy   You haven't _____ this story, have you?
   Andy   It's true, Amy. Don't you think it's good news?
   Amy   I don't know. It means we'll have to _____ revising until next week.

Unit 091

접속사(1)

I wear long sleeves when working in the garden.
나는 정원에서 일할 때 긴 소매를 입는다.

1 when, after, until 등의 접속사를 써서 구체적인 때를 나타낼 수 있다.

when	▸ I hate it **when** there's no one in the house. 집에 아무도 없으면 정말 싫어. ▸ Mozart was five years old **when** he wrote his first piece. 　모짜르트는 첫 곡을 썼을 **때** 5살이었다.
whenever (=every/any/each time)	▸ Just let me know **whenever** you need help. 　도움이 필요하면 **언제든지** 내게 알려줘요. ▸ **Each time** you feel an earthquake, drop, cover, and hold on. 　지진을 느낄 **때마다** 몸을 숙이고 머리를 감싸고 그대로 있으세요.
once	▸ **Once** I've found a place to live, I'll text you my address. 　살 데를 찾는 **대로** 너에게 문자로 주소를 보내 줄게.
as	▸ He tripped **as** he got off the bus. 그는 버스에서 내리**면서** 발을 헛디뎠다.
if	▸ I won't go out **if** it rains this afternoon. 오후에 비가 **오면** 난 안 나갈래.
before	▸ Think twice **before** you speak. 말하기 **전에** 두 번 생각하라.
after	▸ I got a job soon **after** I graduated from high school. 　나는 고등학교를 졸업하**고 나서** 곧 취직했다.
while	▸ She's acting as deputy **while** the boss is away. 　사장님이 안 계시는 **동안** 그녀가 대행을 하고 있어요.
as soon as	▸ I knew there was something wrong **as soon as** I saw him. 　나는 그를 보**자마자** 뭔가 잘못되었다는 것을 알았다.
since	▸ Many years have passed **since** we last met. 　우리가 마지막으로 만난 **이후로** 수년이 흘렀다.
until	▸ They all lived happily ever after **until** they died. 　그들은 죽을 **때까지** 모두 행복하게 살았습니다.
by the time	▸ I'll be long gone **by the time** you read this. 　네가 이걸 읽을 **무렵이면** 난 이미 오래 전에 떠나있을 거야.

전치사나 부사 등으로도 쓰이는 접속사도 있다. See Unit 089▶

- ▸ Nicole lived in the country **as** a child. Nicole은 어릴 **때** 시골에서 살았었다.
- ▸ They didn't arrive at the hotel **until after** midnight. 그들은 자정 **넘어서까지** 호텔에 도착하지 않았다.
- ▸ I've never seen a whale **before**. 나는 **전에** 한 번도 고래를 본 적이 없어요.

2 when, after, until 등의 접속사 뒤에 오는 S+V의 시간표현

❶ S+V에는 미래 내용이라도 will을 쓰지 않는다. See Unit 016▶

- ▸ I'll wait here until you **finish** the work. 네가 그 일을 **마칠 때까지** 여기서 기다릴게.
　I'll wait here until you **will finish** the work. (X)

❷ when, after, until… S+V의 have p.p.는 그 일이 마쳐지는 시점에 초점이 있다.

- ▸ Can I borrow that book when you**'ve read** it? 그 책 다 **읽으면** 내가 빌려도 돼?

3 주어가 일치하는 경우 '접속사 S+V'의 S+V를 –ing로 말할 수 있다.

- ▸ I wear long sleeves **when working** in the garden. (= …when **I'm working** in the garden.)
　나는 정원에서 **일할 때** 긴 소매를 입는다.
- ▸ Review and spell-check every message **before clicking** 'Send.' (= …**before you click** 'Send.')
　'보내기'를 **클릭하기 전에** 모든 메시지를 검토하고 철자를 확인하세요.

Exercises

1. 주어진 표현을 문맥에 맞게 연결하여 문장을 완성하세요.

1. You must look both ways	a. as soon as I get my driver's license.
2. I listen to music	b. after you eat something sugary.
3. Mr. Platt was smiling	c. whenever you need me.
4. We've been friends	d. until you read her a fairy-tale.
5. Eva won't sleep	e. since we were in elementary school.
6. Please feel free to call me	f. as he walked into the class.
7. I'll buy a car	g. before you cross the street.
8. Your blood sugar begins to rise around 15~30 minutes	h. while I'm doing the housework.

(1 connected to g.)

2. 문장의 문맥에 가장 적합한 표현을 골라 문장을 완성하세요.

1. The sun will have set (by / **by the time**) we arrive there.
2. It will be easy (once / until) you understand how it works.
3. I didn't like meat (as / when) a child.
4. My sister has lived in San Francisco (from / since) she left school.
5. The moon didn't rise until (after / later) sunset.

3. 문장의 틀린 부분이 있다면 고쳐서 다시 쓰세요. 고칠 부분이 없다면 X를 쓰세요.

1. If he won't change his attitude, he'll be fired.   _If he doesn't change his attitude, ..._
2. I exercise when I've eaten too much.   _____
3. Haven't we met before somewhere?   _____
4. We'll go out as soon as it'll stop raining.   _____
5. My heart beats fast when talking to girls.   _____

🔊 Dialogue

4. 문장의 문맥에 가장 적합한 표현을 골라 문장을 완성하세요.

Suzi has invited friends to dinner. Patrick is wondering if the food is ready.
Suzi는 친구들을 저녁식사에 초대했습니다. Patrick이 음식이 준비되었는지 궁금해 합니다.

Patrick Isn't the rice ready yet?

Suzi No. Not yet.

Patrick Don't you think you should check it out?

Suzi I don't have to. It will say it's done (**by the time** / when) it's done.

Patrick What? You mean the rice cooker talks?

Suzi Yes. The rice cooker is controlled by a computer that talks.

Patrick Wow. That's amazing. I think most machines will be able to talk (before / until) long.

Unit 092

접속사(2)

The car was too expensive. Besides, I didn't like the color.
그 차는 너무 비쌌다. 게다가, 색깔도 맘에 들지 않았다.

1　and는 단어나 내용을 '추가'할 때 쓸 수 있는 연결 표현이다.

여러 개를 열거할 때	▶ Last winter was long **and** cold. 지난 겨울은 길**고도** 추웠다. ▶ In Switzerland, they speak German, French, **and** Italian. 　스위스에서는 독일어, 프랑스어 **그리고** 이태리어를 쓴다. 　보통 마지막 것을 말하기 전에 쓰지만 대화체에는 여러 번 반복해 쓰기도 한다.
시간 순서상 다음에 일어난 일을 이어 말할 때	▶ He sat down **and** turned on the computer. 그는 앉아서 컴퓨터를 켰다.
추가 정보를 제시할 때	▶ English is spoken all over the world **and** is often a top choice for those who wish to learn a second language. 영어는 전 세계적으로 사용되고 있으며, 제 2 외국어를 배우고자 하는 사람들에게 종종 1순위 선택이 되곤 한다.

2　앞서 나온 내용에 추가, 심화되는 내용이 이어질 때에 다음과 같은 표현을 쓸 수 있다.
접속부사로서 문장과 문장을 하나로 이어주지는 않고 내용적 흐름만 살려 준다.

❶ **in addition / in addition to+명사**
- ▶ The hotel is modern and clean. **In addition**, it has an awesome spa.
  그 호텔은 현대적이고 깨끗하다. **게다가** 끝내주는 스파가 있다.
- ▶ **In addition to** the registration fee, you will also have to pay sales tax.
  등록 요금에 **추가하여** 판매세를 내야만 할 것입니다.

❷ **besides**
- ▶ The car was too expensive. **Besides**, I didn't like the color. 그 차는 너무 비쌌다. **게다가**, 색깔도 맘에 들지 않았다.

전치사로 '~ 외에'의 의미로도 쓰인다.　철자가 비슷한 beside는 '~옆에'라는 뜻이므로 주의
- ▶ What other types of music do you like **besides** hip hop? 힙합 **외에** 좋아하는 다른 타입의 음악은 무엇인가요?

3　'~도 그러하다'라는 의미로 다음과 같이 말할 수 있다.

❶ **too / either**
- ▶ You like baseball? I'm a big fan of baseball, **too**! 야구 좋아한다고? 나**도** 야구 열혈 팬이야!
- ▶ My mother isn't tall. I'm not, **either**. 우리 엄마는 키가 안 크세요. 저**도** 아니고요.

❷ **So do I / Neither am I**
- ▶ Jay is an exchange student. **So** am I. Jay는 교환학생이에요. 저**도** 그렇고요.
- ▶ Sarah can't drive. **Neither** can I. Sarah는 운전을 못합니다. 저**도** 못하고요.

❸ **as well (as)**
- ▶ Are you coming **as well**? 너**도** 오는 거니?
- ▶ They invited Jay **as well as** Suzi. 그들은 Suzi와 함께 Jay**도** 초대했다.

4　or는 '또는', '그렇지 않으면' 등의 의미로 다음과 같이 쓸 수 있다.
- ▶ Which would you like to drink? Tea **or** coffee? 어떤 것으로 마시겠어요? 차 **아니면** 커피?
- ▶ Freeze **or** I'll shoot. 꼼짝 마. 안 그러면 쏜다.

instead / instead of+명사
- ▶ We've run out of coffee. Would you like some tea **instead**? 커피가 다 떨어졌어요. **대신에** 차를 좀 드시겠어요?
- ▶ Would you like some tea **instead of** coffee? 커피 **대신에** 차를 좀 드시겠어요?

Exercises

1. 빈칸에 들어갈 가장 적절한 표현을 보기에서 골라 넣어 문장을 완성하세요.

> and   as well   either   in addition   instead   ~~neither~~   so   too

1. They didn't believe what he said, and _neither_ did I.
2. Anna is an artist. _____, she works as a teacher.
3. I'll have the chicken please. Oh, I'd like the salad _____.
4. I can read _____ write English quite well.
5. Erika was quite disappointed, and _____ was I.
6. The food wasn't good. It wasn't cheap, _____.
7. Andy is a funny _____ outgoing teenager.
8. A: I'm a little tired.
   B: Me _____.

2. 문장의 문맥에 가장 적합한 표현을 골라 문장을 완성하세요.

1. Would you like noodles (instead /(or)) rice for lunch?
2. If Trish can't go to the conference, Mike could go (in addition / instead).
3. Why don't you talk to the boss about it (instead of / or) just complaining to me?
4. You can save your money (as well as / instead of) your time by shopping online.

3. beside 또는 besides를 넣어 문장을 완성하세요.

1. _Besides_ money, what else should I consider?
2. I'm too tired to go skating. _____, it's too cold today.
3. _____ being smart, he's very good looking.
4. Let's go home now. It's late, and _____ I'm very tired.
5. There is a small house _____ the lake.

🔊 Dialogue

4. 문장의 문맥에 가장 적합한 표현을 골라 문장을 완성하세요.

Eugene and Mr. Cruz are talking about music.
Eugene과 Cruz 씨는 음악에 대해 얘기하고 있습니다.

Eugene   Mr. Cruz. I guess you like classical music?

Mr. Cruz   Well, classical music is fine, but to be honest, I'm a big fan of rock music.

Eugene   Really? What band do you like?

Mr. Cruz   I still like old bands like Led Zeppelin (and / besides) Deep Purple.

Eugene   Wow, I'm quite impressed.

Mr. Cruz   Believe it (instead of / or) not, I did play the guitar in a band.

Eugene   You're amazing, Mr. Cruz.

Unit 093

접속사(3)

My brother likes dogs while I prefer cats.
우리 오빠는 개를 좋아하는 반면 나는 고양이를 더 좋아한다.

1. 상반, 반전되는 내용을 한 문장 안에서 연결할 때 but을 쓸 수 있다.
등위접속사. 문장 처음에는 쓸 수 없으나, 대화체에서는 종종 가능하다.

- I like fruit, **but** I'm allergic to peaches. 저는 과일을 좋아하**지만**, 복숭아에 알레르기가 있어요.
- There were dark clouds in the sky, **but** it didn't rain. 하늘에 먹구름이 끼었**지만**, 비가 오지는 않았습니다.

but은 '~을 제외한'의 의미로 다음과 같이 쓸 수도 있다.
- I had no choice **but** to tell her the truth. 나는 그녀에게 진실을 말하는 것 **외에** 달리 선택의 여지가 없었다.
- Age is nothing **but** a number. 나이는 단지 숫자**일** 뿐이다. *nothing but ~는 '~ 외에 아무 것도 없는', 즉 only의 의미로 쓰인다.*
- Everyone **but** me has a cat. 나 빼고 다 고양이가 있어.

2. 상반 또는 반전되는 내용이 이어질 때 다음과 같은 표현을 쓸 수 있다.
접속부사로서, 문장과 문장을 하나로 이어주지는 않고 내용적 흐름만 살려 준다.

① however: 하지만, 그러나
- I was still hungry. **However**, I didn't eat. 나는 여전히 배가 고팠다. **하지만** 먹지는 않았다.

however는 '아무리 ~해도'의 의미로도 쓰인다.
- **However** hard she tried, it was impossible to forget him.
  그녀가 **아무리 힘들게 애를 써도** 그를 잊는 것이 불가능했다.

② nevertheless, even so, still: 그렇기는 하지만, 그럼에도 불구하고
- It was cold and windy. **Nevertheless/Even so/Still**, we had a great time camping.
  날씨가 춥고 바람이 불었다. **그럼에도** 우리는 즐겁게 캠핑을 했다.

3. 문장에 상반 또는 반전되는 내용을 더해 줄 때 다음과 같은 표현을 쓸 수 있다. 종속접속사

① although, though, even though: ~임에도 불구하고
even though는 반전의 뉘앙스가 although보다 크다. though는 대화체에서 많이 쓰인다.

- The staff was very friendly and helpful **although/though** they didn't speak English very well.
  직원들이 영어를 잘 하지는 못했**음에도 불구하고**, 아주 친절하고 도움을 많이 주었습니다.
- **Even though** he's a millionaire, he goes to work by subway. 그는 백만장자**임에도 불구하고** 전철로 출근한다.

though는 대화체에서 '그렇지만' 또는 '그럼에도' 등의 의미로 자주 쓰인다. 문장의 뒤에 위치
- A: Have you checked out the new S-phone? It's very expensive. 새 S-phone 봤니? 되게 비싸더라.
  B: It's nice, **though**. 근데 좋긴 하지.

despite는 전치사로 뒤에 명사가 오며, despite the fact (that)로 말하면 S+V가 뒤에 올 수 있다.
in spite of를 쓸 수도 있다.
- We decided to go out **despite** the heavy snow. 폭설**에도 불구하고** 우리는 나가기로 결심했다.
- We decided to go out **despite the fact (that)** it was snowing heavily.
  눈이 펑펑 내리고 있었다는 **사실에도 불구하고** 우리는 나가기로 결심했다.

② while: ~인데 반하여, 반면
- My brother likes dogs **while** I prefer cats. 우리 오빠는 개를 좋아하는 **반면** 나는 고양이를 더 좋아한다.

whereas는 두 가지 사실이나 생각을 비교하거나 대조할 때 쓴다.
- Dogs need to be cared for, **whereas** cats are independent animals.
  고양이는 독립적인 동물인 **반면**, 개는 돌봄을 필요로 한다.

Exercises

1. 문맥에 맞게 but 또는 however를 넣어 문장을 완성하세요.
   1. I wanted to fly to Seattle, ___but___ my husband insisted that we drive.
   2. He was born in New York. _____, he doesn't speak English.
   3. I waited for the bus for ages, _____ it never came.
   4. There was nothing we could do _____ wait.
   5. Do wear underwear _____ hot it is.

2. 문장의 문맥에 가장 적합한 표현을 골라 문장을 완성하세요.
   1. I loved her (even so / (in spite of)) everything.
   2. I really enjoyed my stay in Cancun, but (even so / even though) I missed my family a lot.
   3. (Despite / Even though) the financial problems, the company has been successful.
   4. She did all the house work (nevertheless / while) he just enjoyed his nap.
   5. She was extremely busy. (Still / While), she offered to help us.
   6. He's fun and kind. Well, a bit too talkative, (despite / though).
   7. (Although / Despite) they had planned everything very carefully, a lot of things went wrong.

3. 주어진 표현을 문맥에 맞게 연결하여 문장을 완성하세요.
   1. The new S-phone is $120,   •   • a. although we can't feel it.
   2. It's the last test   •   • b. however much it costs.
   3. The earth is spinning   •   • c. whereas the old model costs only $45.
   4. It doesn't matter   •   • d. despite the noise.
   5. Eva didn't wake up   •   • e. but one.

★ Dialogue

4. 보기 중 빈칸에 들어갈 가장 적합한 표현을 골라 넣어 문장을 완성하세요.

   although   despite   however

   Naomi is asking Suzi where to visit in Seoul.
   Naomi는 Suzi에게 서울의 어디를 방문할지를 묻고 있습니다.
   Naomi My parents and I are visiting Seoul this summer.
   Suzi   Really? That's great.
   Naomi So, can you tell me where to go in Seoul?
   Suzi   _____ the traffic, there are some reasons to visit downtown. The palaces are a huge draw. The gardens are very pretty and you could spend hours walking around.
   Naomi Sounds like my type of place.

Unit 094

접속사(4)

I left home early so that I could catch the first bus.
첫 버스를 타기 위해 집을 일찍 나섰습니다.

1. 원인을 말할 때 다음 표현을 쓸 수 있다.

❶ because

- I'm calling to complain **because** the goods are damaged. 상품이 손상되**어서** 불만을 제기하려고 전화했습니다.
- **Because** Mike had done a good job, his boss gave him a 20% bonus.
  Mike가 일을 아주 잘 해줬기 **때문에** 사장님께서 그에게 20% 보너스를 주었다.

대화체에서는 종종 cos 또는 'cause로도 쓰인다.

- I didn't go to the pool **cos** it was cold outside. 밖에 추웠기 **때문에** 나는 풀장에 가지 않았다.
- Jessica couldn't come **'cause** he had to work. Jessica는 일을 해야 했기 **때문에** 오지 못했습니다.

'because S+V'는 주절(S+V)과 함께 쓰여야 하지만, 대화체에서는 종종 단독으로 쓰인다.

- A: Why did you buy an S-phone? I thought you liked the K-phone better.
  왜 S-phone을 샀니? 난 네가 K-phone을 더 맘에 들어했다고 생각했는데.
  B: **Because it was cheaper**. 그게 더 쌌으니까.

'because of+명사'로 말할 수도 있다.

- I'm calling to complain **because of** the damaged goods. 손상된 상품 **때문에** 불만을 제기하려고 전화했습니다.

좀 더 격식 있는(formal) 말이나 글에서는 due to나 owing to 가 쓰일 수 있다.

- The parade was canceled **due to / owing to** bad weather. 안 좋은 날씨 **때문에** 퍼레이드가 취소되었다.

'~ 덕분에'의 의미로 thanks to가 쓰인다. 누군가의 존재나 노력 때문에 어떤 좋은 일이 생긴 경우

- The campaign was successful **thanks to** you. 여러분 **덕분에** 캠페인이 성공적이었습니다.

❷ since / as
because보다 다소 격식 있는 뉘앙스. 문장의 앞에 자주 오며, 이미 듣는 사람이 알고 있는 이유를 말할 때 쓰인다. 이유보다는 결과에 보다 초점이 있음

- **Since** it is Saturday tomorrow, I won't have to get up early. 내일은 토요일**이므로** 난 일찍 일어날 필요가 없다.
- **As** everyone already knows each other, I don't think we need introductions.
  모두 서로를 이미 알고 있**으므로** 소개는 필요가 없을 것 같군요.

2. 결과를 말할 때 다음 표현을 쓸 수 있다.

❶ so

- It's cold outside, **so** I'm not going out today. 밖이 추워서 오늘은 안 나갈 거야.

❷ as a result 접속부사로서 두 절(S+V)을 한 문장으로 이을 수 없고, 새 문장을 시작할 때만 쓸 수 있다.

- He got another speeding ticket. **As a result**, he had his license suspended for a year.
  그는 속도위반 딱지를 추가로 받았다. 그 **결과** 그는 1년간 면허가 정지되었다.

3. 목적에 대해 말할 때 다음 표현을 쓸 수 있다.

❶ (in order) to+동사 in order to로 말하면 보다 격식 있는 뉘앙스

- I'm going to the airport **to** meet a buyer from Japan. 일본에서 오는 바이어를 마중**하러** 공항에 갑니다.

❷ for+명사

- I'm going out **for** lunch. 전 점심 먹**으러** 나가요.

❸ so that+S+V

- I left home early **so that** I could catch the first bus. 첫 버스를 타기 **위해** 집을 일찍 나섰습니다.

Exercises

1. 문맥에 맞게 이어질 수 있는 부분을 보기에서 골라 문장을 완성하세요.

   > · because he speaks very fast.
   > · so he may not be able to go to work tomorrow.
   > · 'cause the oven was broken.
   > · since you paid for mine yesterday.

   > · as he had a lot of homework.
   > · cos I have to work late.
   > · ~~so I take the bus everywhere.~~
   > · because there were no more buses.

   1. I don't like to drive, _so I take the bus everywhere_.
   2. Andy didn't hang out with friends _____.
   3. I'll be home late tonight _____.
   4. I walked home last night _____.
   5. It's not easy to follow him _____.
   6. Mike isn't feeling well today, _____.
   7. Mom couldn't bake cookies _____.
   8. I'll pay for your lunch _____.

2. 문장의 문맥에 가장 적합한 표현을 골라 문장을 완성하세요.

   1. The soccer player had to miss several games (because /(because of)) the injury.
   2. Mr. Harris's return flight was canceled. (As a result / So that), the meeting was postponed.
   3. Shall we stop by the supermarket (in order to / so that) we can buy some food?
   4. Our website is down temporarily (because / due to) technical server issues.
   5. He worked in the garden all day long yesterday. (As a result / Since), his back hurts.
   6. I study grammar and vocabulary every day (in order to / so that) improve my English.
   7. (Thank / Thanks) to his excellent instruction, I passed my driving test.
   8. (In order / Due) to achieve anything, you must be brave enough to fail.
   9. I missed the last bus, (so / so that) I had to take a taxi home.
   10. A corkscrew is used (because of / for) opening bottles.

🔊 Dialogue

3. 문맥에 맞게 가장 적합한 표현을 골라 문장을 완성하세요.

Naomi is making a phone call to Jay.
Naomi는 Jay에게 전화를 걸고 있습니다.

Naomi Hi, Jay, It's Naomi. Is this a good time to talk?

Jay Uhm, not really. I'm late for class. I'm going to have to run.

Naomi OK. I just wanted to ask about this weekend (as a result / since / so that) we can make plans.

Jay Well, can I call you back tonight? I've got to get going.

Naomi Sure. Talk to you later.

Unit 095

접속사(5)

Above all, I value honesty and social justice.
무엇보다도 나는 진실함과 사회 정의에 가치를 둔다.

1 예를 들 때에는 다음과 같은 표현을 쓸 수 있다.

❶ for example 문장의 맨 앞이나 중간 모두에 올 수 있다.
- We can make our office more environmentally-friendly by, **for example**, using recycled paper.
  우리의 사무실을 보다 친환경적으로 만들 수 있어요. **예를 들면** 재활용지를 사용함으로써 말이죠.

❷ such as 문장의 맨 앞에는 오지 않음
- I like tropical fruits, **such as** pineapples, mangoes and papayas.
  나는 파인애플, 망고, 파파야 **같은** 열대과일을 좋아해요.

대화체에서는 like가 자주 쓰인다. *See Unit 089▶*
- I like tropical fruits, **like** pineapples, mangoes and papayas.
  나는 파인애플, 망고, 파파야 **같은** 열대과일을 좋아해요.

2 보다 구체적인 내용을 더하거나 상대방이 예상 못한 사실을 말할 때 **in fact, as a matter of fact, actually**를 쓸 수 있다.

- I really enjoyed the new Star Wars movie. **In fact/Actually**, it's one of the best Star Wars movies I've ever watched. 나는 새 스타워즈 영화를 정말 재미있게 봤어. **사실**, 내가 지금껏 본 스타워즈 영화 중 최고였다.

3 보다 간략하게 요약해서 말하고자 할 때, 다음 표현들을 쓸 수 있다.

| so | in short | to put it simply | simply put | to sum up | in summary |

- **So/To sum up**, there are many benefits of online education that may replace traditional education. 요약하자면, 전통 교육을 대체할 수 있는 온라인 교육의 이점이 많습니다.
- This app is more convenient. **Simply put**, you don't need to login.
  이 앱은 더 편리합니다. **간단히 말하자면**, 로그인을 할 필요가 없어요.

in short는 문장의 중간에 쓰일 수도 있다.
- I didn't like the dresses. They were, **in short**, tacky. 난 그 옷들이 맘에 들지 않았다. 그것들은, **한마디로**, 구렸다.

4 다음은 그 외에 대화에서 자주 쓰이는 표현들이다.

그건 그렇고, 그런데(주제 전환)	By the way, Anyway, So
제 생각으로는, 개인적으로는	From my point of view, In my opinion, Personally
분명히	Clearly, Of course, Obviously
운 좋게도	Luckily, Fortunately
안타깝게도	Unfortunately, Sadly
솔직하게 말하자면	To be honest, Actually
특히, 무엇보다도	Especially, In particular, Above all
(예상과 달리) 결국은, 어쨌든	After all
~에 관한 한	As far as ~ (is/are concerned)

- **Obviously** she's out of my league. **분명히** 그녀는 나에겐 넘사벽이에요.
- **Above all**, I value honesty and social justice. **무엇보다도** 나는 진실함과 사회 정의에 가치를 둔다.
- I like him. **After all**, he's my husband. 난 그를 좋아해요. **어쨌든** 내 남편이잖아요.
- A: What's the weather like in Hong Kong? 홍콩은 날씨가 어때요?
  B: **As far as** the climate**'s concerned**, it reaches 34 degrees Celsius in the summer.
  기후에 대해 말하자면, 여름에는 34도에 달합니다.

Exercises

Dialogue

1. 각 대화문의 빈칸에 들어갈 표현을 보기에서 골라 넣으세요.

> for example   fortunately   in fact   in my opinion   so   to be honest

1. **Jay** I think my wallet was stolen.
   Patrick Did you have a lot of money in there?
   Jay _____, there was only a little change.

2. **Immigration officer** Are you here on business?
   James Yes, I am.
   Immigration officer How many days are you here for?
   James Just five.
   Immigration officer And how much money do you have with you?
   James _____, I don't carry much money. Mostly I use credit cards.
   Immigration officer OK, thank you. Enjoy your stay.

3. **Mike** I was wondering if I could talk to you for a second.
   Supervisor Sure. Let me just send this email. All right. _____, what can I do for you?
   Mike Um… Would it be alright with you if I took this Thursday off?
   Supervisor You mean the 13th?
   Mike Yes. My grandfather passed away last week, and his funeral is on Thursday.

4. **Patrick** What do you think is the biggest energy problem?
   Erika _____, most people aren't doing enough to save energy.
   Patrick Right. They also use too much water and electricity.

5. **Andy** Have you heard? Mr. Cruz is running a marathon next month.
   Ben Yes. He's quite fit for his age.
   Andy _____, I think he's healthier than we are.

6. **Patrick** What's it like to live in Tokyo?
   Naomi Well, Tokyo is very expensive and crowded like other metropolitan cities around the world.
   Patrick Is it more expensive than L.A.?
   Naomi I think so. _____, limes are only a couple of dollars a pound here, but in Tokyo they're more than a dollar each.

227

Big Picture

문장의 종류와 어순

10

1 문장의 다양한 종류

영어 문장은 보통 평서문(긍정문), 부정문, 의문문 이렇게 세 가지가 대표적입니다. 그리고 이외에도 지시나 권유를 나타내는 명령문, 놀라움이나 감정을 강조하는 감탄문, 축복과 바람을 나타내는 기원문 등이 있지요.

부정문은 평서문(긍정문)에 부정의 의미를 담은 not이 더해집니다. 동사의 종류에 따라 not이 더해지는 형태가 다릅니다. 의문문도 동사의 종류에 따라 방법이 약간 다르지만, 공통적으로 동사가 주어 앞으로 오는 형태로 어순이 바뀐다고 볼 수 있습니다.

	BE type 동사	DO type 동사
O 일반문장	am, are, is ex I am hungry.	like, eat, run, fly… ex I like chocolate.
X 부정문	+ not ex I am not hungry.	do + not… ex I don't like chocolate.
? 의문문	V + S ? ex Are you hungry?	Do…? ex Do you like chocolate?

2 어순에 따른 문장의 변화

명령문은 일반적으로 주어를 생략하여 동사가 제일 먼저 문장 앞에 보입니다. 기원문은 보통 May로 시작합니다. 이렇게 문장의 종류를 보면 영어 문장에서는 단어의 순서, 즉 '어순'이 매우 중요한 역할을 합니다. 어느 자리에 오느냐에 따라 단어의 역할이 달라지고, 강조의 여부가 달라지죠. 예를 들어 water는 주로 '물'이라는 의미의 명사로 쓰이는데, 동사의 자리에 위치하면 '물을 주다'라는 의미로 쓰일 수 있습니다.

- He's very kind. 그는 매우 친절합니다.
- It's very kind of him. 그는 참 친절하기도 하지!

위 두 문장은 기본적으로는 '그가 친절하다'라는 내용을 전달하지만, 뉘앙스가 사뭇 다릅니다. 첫 번째 문장은 He가 먼저 나오는 반면, 두 번째 문장은 별다른 의미가 없는 It을 주어에 내세워 실질적으로 뚜렷한 의미를 갖는 첫 번째 단어는 kind가 됩니다. 그래서 '친절하기도 하지'라는 '친절'을 보다 강조한 뉘앙스로 이해되지요.

이 외에도 영어 문장은 어순의 변화를 통해 의미를 가진 표현 간의 논리적인 연결을 이루기도 하고, 뉘앙스를 달리하기도 합니다. 때문에 문장 구조를 파악한다는 것은 문장이 말하는 바를 파악한다는 의미이고, 문장 구조에 맞게 말한다는 것은 정확하게 의미를 전달할 수 있다는 의미입니다.

Unit 096

That S+V / It ...to/that

There is one key fact (that) you have overlooked.
네가 간과한 한 가지 중요한 사실이 있어.

1. that은 '~라는/라고'의 의미로, S+V(절, 문장)을 이어 주는 역할을 한다. 생략 가능

- **think, believe, guess, know, remember, hear, hope, agree, suggest, insist 등의 동사 뒤**
  - ▸ Did you know (**that**) giraffes can't cough? 기린이 기침을 못한**다는 사실을** 아셨나요?
  - ▸ I hear (**that**) the old house is haunted. 그 오래된 집에 귀신이 나온**다고** 들었어.
  - ▸ I hope (**that**) you like the flowers. 당신이 그 꽃을 맘에 들어 **하기를** 바라요. *See Unit 017▶*
  - ▸ I agree (**that**) there should be more information. 정보가 더 있어야 한**다는 것에** 동의합니다.
  - ▸ The manager suggested (**that**) we develop a training program.
    매니저는 우리가 연수 프로그램을 개발할 **것을** 제안했습니다.

- **Be동사 뒤**
  - ▸ I'm a little bored with my job. **The thing is** (**that**) I'm not learning anything new.
    난 내 일이 좀 지겨워. **문제는** 내가 새로운 걸 전혀 배우고 있지 않**다는 거야**.
  - ▸ **The trouble is** (**that**) it's going to be very expensive. 문제는 그것이 매우 비싸질 **거란 거지**.
  - ▸ **The truth is** (**that**) everybody lies. 진실은 모든 사람들이 거짓말을 한**다는 것이다**.

- **sorry, sure, certain 등의 형용사 뒤**
  - ▸ I'm sorry (**that**) you had the flu. 네가 독감에 걸렸**다니** 안타깝구나.
  - ▸ I'm sure (**that**) they'll like it. 그들이 분명 마음에 들어 **할 것이라고** 확신해요.
  - ▸ She is certain (**that**) her phone is tapped. 그녀는 자신의 전화기가 도청**되었다고** 확신합니다.

- **fact, idea, story 등의 명사 뒤**
  - ▸ There is one key fact (**that**) you have overlooked. 네가 간과**한** 한 가지 중요한 사실이 있어.
  - ▸ I agree with the idea (**that**) animals should have the same rights as people.
    나는 동물이 사람과 같은 권리를 가져야 **한다는** 생각에 동의합니다.

- **'~라는 것'의 의미로 주어 자리**
  - ▸ **That** we need more programmers is clear to everyone.
    우리에게 프로그래머가 더 필요하**다는 것은** 모두에게 명백하다.
  - ▸ **That** the banks are closed on Saturday is a problem. 은행이 토요일엔 문을 닫는다는 것이 문제지.

2. 동사나 절(S+V)로 된 주어는 it을 써서 말할 수 있다.

- **동사로 시작되는 긴 주어: It … to ~** *See Unit 046▶*
  - ▸ **It**'s great **to be** back. 다시 돌아오니 좋군요.
    └ 실질적인 주어
  - ▸ How long does **it** take **to learn** a language? 언어를 하나 배우는 데에는 시간이 얼마나 걸리나요?
  - ▸ **It**'s dangerous **to dive** in shallow water. 얕은 물에서 다이빙하는 것은 위험하다.

- **S+V 형태의 긴 주어: It … that S+V**
  - ▸ **It**'s true (**that**) the Internet creates many positive opportunities.
    인터넷이 많은 긍정적인 기회를 창출한다는 것은 사실입니다. └ 실질적인 주어
  - ▸ **It**'s good (**that**) you are exercising again. 네가 다시 운동을 하고 있다니 좋은 일이구나.
  - ▸ **It** is said (**that**) the tree is 500 years old. 그 나무가 500년 되었다고들 말한다. 간접화법 *See Unit 099▶*

- **강조의 It … who/that S+V** *See Unit 068▶*
  - ▸ Was **it** his phone **that** kept ringing? 계속 울려댔던 게 그의 전화기였어?

Exercises

1. 빈칸에 들어갈 가장 적절한 표현을 보기에서 골라 넣어 문장을 완성하세요.

   > certain   hear   recommended   ~~sorry~~

   1. I'm _sorry_ that I forgot our anniversary.
   2. The doctor _____ that I stay in bed for a few days.
   3. It is _____ that Erika will pass the exam.
   4. I _____ that there is a secret room in the old mansion.

2. 문맥에 맞게 이어질 수 있는 부분을 보기에서 골라 문장을 완성하세요.

   > a. ~~you get better soon~~
   > b. you'll get the job
   > c. it costs too much
   > d. you missed it
   > e. two people were killed in the fire
   > f. watching TV is a waste of time

   1. I hope (that) _you get better soon_.
   2. I disagree with the idea (that) _____.
   3. The party was pretty exciting. I'm sorry (that) _____.
   4. Don't worry. I'm sure (that) _____.
   5. It is reported (that) _____.
   6. Everybody says it's a good idea. The problem is (that) _____.

3. that 또는 to를 넣어 문장을 완성하세요.

   1. It takes a long time _to_ become successful.
   2. _____ he is a liar is a rumor.
   3. It turned out _____ his reference was fake.
   4. It's good _____ know how to read a map.
   5. My parents were very strict with the fact _____ sleeping and eating schedules had to be in a regular pattern.

🔊 Dialogue

4. 보기 중 빈칸에 들어갈 가장 적합한 표현을 골라 넣어 문장을 완성하세요.

   > The fact that   The thing is that   There is a story that

   Jessica is asking Naomi for a favor. Jessica는 Naomi에게 부탁을 하고 있습니다.

   Jessica Naomi, will you be at home this morning?
   Naomi   Yes, I don't have any classes today.
   Jessica Well, a man is delivering a washingmachine this morning. _____ I have to go to work. Could you please let him in for me unless you're busy?
   Naomi   OK, that's no problem.
   Jessica Oh, thanks.

Unit 097

간접의문문

How often does the app update?
그 앱은 얼마나 자주 업데이트 하나요?

1 Yes/No로 답할 수 있는 질문은 다음과 같이 답할 수 있다.

Be type 동사	**Are** you staying at the Crown Hotel?	Yes, I am.	No, I'm not.
	Have you finished your report?	Yes, I have.	No, I haven't.
	Will you be back before lunch?	Yes, I will.	No, I won't.
	Can you type more than 60 words per minute?	Yes, I can.	No, I can't.
Do type 동사	**Do** you drive to work?	Yes, I do.	No, I don't.
	Did you check the invoice?	Yes, I did.	No, I didn't.

의문문에 not이 들어가도(부정의문문) 응답이 달라지지 않는다. _{no가 답으로 예상되거나 놀라움을 나타낼 때 쓰임}

▶ A: Don't you drive to work? 운전해서 출근하지 않으시나요?
  B: **No, not really**. I walk to work. I live near my office. 아뇨. 걸어서 출근합니다. 사무실 근처에 살거든요.
▶ A: Weren't you surprised? 넌 안 놀랐니?
  B: **Yes, I was**. I just didn't show it. 놀랐지. 다만 드러내지 않았을 뿐이야.

2 'What/Which+명사'로 '무슨/어떤 ~'에 대해 물을 수 있다.

▶ **What time** is he arriving? 그가 몇 시에 도착하나요?
▶ **What language** do they speak in Belgium? 벨기에에서는 어떤 언어를 쓰죠?
▶ **Which way** is it? 어느 길이죠? ⎫
▶ **Which car** do you prefer? Sedan or SUV? 어떤 차가 더 좋아요? 세단형 승용차 아니면 SUV? ⎬ 범위가 좁은 경우
▶ **What** was the new cafe **like**? 새 카페는 어땠어?

'How+형용사'로 '얼마나 ~한지'에 대해 물을 수 있다.

▶ **How often** does the app update? 그 앱은 얼마나 자주 업데이트 하나요?
▶ **How long** will the meeting last? 회의가 얼마나 오래 진행될까요?

3 What(무엇)이나 Who(누구)가 주어인 질문은 do/does/did를 사용하지 않는다.

⎡ What did you buy? 무엇을 샀나요?
⎣ **What happened**? 무슨 일이 일어났나요?

⎡ Who did you meet? 누구를 만났나요?
⎣ **Who met** you at the station? 역에서 누가 당신을 마중했나요?

4 다음 표현들로 시작하는 간접의문문은 일반 문장과 같은 어순이다. _{좀 더 예의 바른 뉘앙스}

> Do you know   Could you tell me   Could I ask you   I was wondering

▶ When will he be back? → Do you know **when he will be back**? 그가 언제 돌아올지 아시나요?
▶ Where did the conference take place? → I was wondering **where the conference took place**.
  그 컨퍼런스가 어디서 개최되었는지 궁금했습니다.

Yes/No 질문의 경우 if를 쓴다.

▶ Does he still work here? → Could you tell me **if** he still works here?
  그가 아직도 여기서 일하는지 아닌지 말씀해 주실 수 있나요?
▶ Have you checked the invoice? → Could I ask **if** you have checked the invoice?
  그 인보이스를 확인하셨는지 여쭤봐도 될까요?

Exercises

1. 문장의 문맥에 가장 적합한 표현을 골라 문장을 완성하세요.

    1. A: Aren't you coming?
       B: (Yes, I am. / **No, I'm not.**) I just want to stay home tonight.
    2. A: Hasn't the pizza arrived yet?
       B: (Yes, it has. / No, not really.) It's on the table.
    3. A: Didn't you have lunch? Why not?
       B: (I did. / No, not really.) I wasn't hungry.
    4. A: Don't you love me?
       B: (I do. / I don't.) How can I not love you? You're my son.

2. 빈칸에 들어갈 가장 적절한 표현을 보기에서 골라 넣어 문장을 완성하세요.

    > How far   How long   What   ~~What kind of~~   What time   Who

    1. So, tell me about your new job. ___What kind of___ work is it?
    2. _____ is your office from your home?
    3. _____ told you about it?
    4. _____ 's going on?
    5. _____ do you start work in the morning?
    6. _____ did it take you to be fluent in speaking English?

3. 주어진 표현을 사용하여 간접의문문으로 문장을 다시 쓰세요.

    1. Where do you come from? (Could you tell me)
       → ___Could you tell me where you come from___ ?
    2. Could you call me a taxi? (Do you think)
       → _____ ?
    3. Why did you leave your last job? (Could I ask)
       → _____ ?
    4. Could you send me the information by email? (I was wondering)
       → _____ .

🔊 Dialogue

4. 주어진 단어를 맞는 순서대로 배열하여 문장을 완성하세요.

A man is getting on the elevator. 한 남자가 엘리베이터에 타고 있습니다.

Man   Hold it, please.
Suzi   It's all right. I have the door-hold button.
Man   Thank you.
Suzi   _____ (down, Are, going, you)? Which floor?
Man   I'm going down to the parking lot. _____ (you, hit, basement level 4, Could) please?
Suzi   Sure. No problem.

Unit 098

부가의문문

You two have met before, haven't you?
두 분 서로 전에 만난 적 있죠, 그렇죠?

1 대화에서 상대방 문장의 S+V만 남겨 질문처럼 대꾸함으로써 놀라움, 흥미, 확인 등의 반응을 보일 수 있다. Really? Is that true? 등과 비슷

❶ Be type 동사(be, will, can…)는 그대로 쓴다.
- A: I think he's arriving late. 그가 늦을 것 같아요.
  B: **He is**? 그런가요? 영국 영어에서는 Is he?로 말한다.
- A: I can't download this app. 이 앱 다운로드가 안 되는데요.
  B: **You can't**? 안 된다고요? 영국 영어에서는 Can't you?로 말한다.

❷ Do type 동사(do, go, get…)는 do/does/did로 대신한다.
- A: We visited Google. 우린 구글을 방문했어요.
  B: **You did**? 정말요? 영국 영어에서는 Did you?로 말한다.

2 문장의 끝에 짧은 질문(Tag Question)을 덧붙여 상대방에게 반응을 끌어낼 수 있다. 부가의문문

❶ 문장이 긍정문이면, 부가의문문은 부정문 형태로 말한다.
- Naomi **is** Japanese, **isn't she**? Naomi는 일본인이에요, 그렇죠?
- You two **have met** before, **haven't you**? 두 분 서로 전에 만난 적 있죠, 그렇죠?
- You **speak** Chinese, **don't you**? 중국어 하시죠, 그렇죠?
- They **agreed**, **didn't they**? 그들은 동의했어요, 그렇죠?

❷ 문장이 부정문이면, 부가의문문은 긍정문 형태로 말한다.
- Erika **isn't** Japanese, **is she**? Erika는 일본인이 아니에요, 그렇죠?
- You **haven't met** Mr. Harris, **have you**? Harris 씨를 만난 적은 없으시죠, 그렇죠?
- You **don't speak** Chinese, **do you**? 중국어는 못 하시죠, 그렇죠?
- They **didn't sign** the contract, **did they**? 그들은 계약서에 서명하지 않은 거죠, 그렇죠?

❸ 일부 조동사 및 명령문에 대한 부가 의문문은 다음과 같다.
- **I'm** such a klutz, **aren't I**? 난 정말 어설퍼, 그렇지 않니?
- **Nothing** happened, **did it**? 아무 일도 없었어, 그렇지? nothing, nobody 등이 주어인 문장은 부정문으로 본다.
- **Let's** have a break, **shall we**? 잠깐 쉽시다, 네?
- **You must** like chocolate, **mustn't you**? 분명 초콜릿 좋아하지, 그렇지?
- **He'd better** do it, **hadn't he**? 그는 그것을 해야 해, 그렇지?
- **Have** a seat, **will you**? 앉으세요, 네?
- **Give** me a call tonight, **won't you**? 오늘 밤 전화해 주세요, 네? 명령문에는 Will you?와 Won't you?가 모두 부가의문문으로 쓰일 수 있다. 단, 부정명령문에는 Will you?만 가능하다.
- **Don't** tell him about it, **will you**? 그에게는 그것에 대해 말하지 마, 응?
- **Hold** the elevator for me, **can you**? 엘리베이터 좀 잡고 계세요, 네? 명령문이 요청의 의미라면 can you?나 could you?를 쓸 수도 있다.
- **Pass** me that file, **could you**? 거기 파일 좀 건네 주세요, 네?

3 부가의문문의 억양은 말하는 사람의 의도에 따라 달라진다.

❶ 확신을 갖고 상대방에게 동의를 구하는 경우
- It's a nice day, **isn't it**? 날씨가 참 좋아요, 그렇죠?

❷ 내용을 확신하지 않아서 상대방에게 확인을 구하는 경우
- He's not your boyfriend, **is he**? 그 사람 당신 남자 친구 아니죠, 그렇죠?

Exercises

1. 보기처럼 A의 말에 적절하게 대꾸해 보세요.

1. A: He's from Russia.
   B: _He is_ ? I thought he was American.
2. A: I passed the exam!
   B: _____? Congratulations!
3. A: I've never driven a car. I don't even have my driver's license yet.
   B: _____? Really?
4. A: My mother baked some cookies for you.
   B: _____? How sweet of her.
5. A: It's not bad to make mistakes.
   B: _____? That's good news.
6. A: Eating cheese is good for your health.
   B: _____? I didn't know that.

2. 주어진 문장에 적합한 부가의문문을 덧붙여 보세요. 여러 개가 가능하다면 다 적어 보세요.

1. Jay is Korean, _isn't he_ ?
2. We're nearly there, _____?
3. Pass me the salt over there, _____?
4. I'm not late, _____?
5. I'm late, _____?
6. You have to go, _____?
7. You know my brother Andy, _____?
8. She didn't call you, _____?
9. Don't forget to bring my book back, _____?
10. Let's go somewhere else for lunch, _____?
11. They won't help us, _____?
12. You haven't sent the email yet, _____?

🔊 Dialogue

3. 빈칸에 적절한 부가의문문을 써 넣어 문장을 완성하세요.

Jay and Erika are talking about their friends Patrick and Andy's vacation.
Jay와 Erika는 친구 Patrick과 Andy의 휴가에 대해 얘기하고 있습니다.

Jay Have you heard about Patrick and Andy?

Erika No. Is there anything wrong with them?

Jay They had the flu all through their vacation in Colorado.

Erika Really? That's too bad. They were so excited to go to Colorado.

Jay What bad luck they had, _____?

Unit 099

간접화법

May both of you live a long and happy life together!
두 분이 오랫동안 행복하게 함께 사시길!

1 say나 tell 등을 써서 다른 사람의 말을 간접적으로 인용할 수 있다.

① 인용한 문장(S+V)의 시제가 한 단계 과거로 물러난다.
- I said, "I've never been abroad before."
  → I **told** you (that) I **had** never **been** abroad before. Remember?
  내가 전에 한 번도 해외에 **가 본 적 없었다**고 너한테 **말했어**. 기억해?

② 주어가 말하는 사람의 입장에 맞춰 달라질 수 있다.
- My boss said, "I will give you a raise." 〔직접 인용문. Comma(,)와 " "를 사용〕
  → My boss **said** (that) **he** would give me a raise.
  사장님이 내게 월급을 인상해 주시겠**다고 했어**.

③ 현재에도 바뀌지 않은 사실인 경우 동사의 시제가 변하지 않을 수 있다.
- My boss said (**that**) he **wants** me to finish the project by next month. So, I'll be busy working on it for a while. 사장님이 내가 프로젝트를 다음달까지 마치기를 **바라신다고** 말했어. 그래서 난 한동안 그 작업으로 바쁠 것 같아. 〔사장님의 요구사항이 말하는 지금도 유효함〕
- The professor said (**that**) the Sun **is** the largest object in the solar system.
  교수님은 태양이 태양계에서 가장 큰 물체**라고** 말했어. 〔누구나 아는 변함없는 사실은 시제를 바꾸지 않음〕

동사의 시제를 바꿈으로써 현재 상황이 바뀌었거나, 당시에만 해당함을 강조할 수 있다.
- You told me I **was** wrong, but I wasn't. 넌 내가 틀렸**다고** 말했지만, 그렇지 않았어. 〔내가 틀리지 않았음〕

현재에도 유효한지 아닌지 확실하지 않은 경우에는 보통 시제를 바꾼다.
- A: Do you know where Andy is now? Andy가 지금 어디 있는지 아니?
  B: Amy said that he **was studying** in the library.
  Amy가 그러는데, 도서관에서 **공부하고 있다고** 했어. 〔지금도 도서관에서 공부하고 있는지 아닌지 확실하지 않음〕

④ 인용하는 내용이 명령문인 경우에는 that이 아닌 to를 쓴다.
- My boss told him **to** leave the company after the scandal.
  그 스캔들 이후에 사장님이 그에게 회사를 떠나**라고** 했어.
- I asked my boss not **to** assign me to his team.
  나는 사장님께 나를 그의 팀에 배정하지 말아 **달라고** 부탁했다.

2 may를 써서 바람이나 기원을 표현하는 문장을 말할 수 있다. 〔의문문의 어순을 따름〕 See Unit 100▶

- **May** both of you live a long and happy life together! 두 분이 오랫동안 행복하게 함께 사시길!
- **May** your days be merry and bright. 당신의 나날이 즐겁고 밝기를!
- **May** the Force be with you. *(from the movie 'Star Wars')* Force가 그대와 함께 하기를.

wish나 hope를 사용해서 바람을 표현할 수도 있다. See Unit 034▶

- I **hope** you get better soon. 네가 곧 낫기를 바라.
- I **wish** you a merry Christmas. 즐거운 크리스마스 되길 바라.

이외에도 다음과 같은 감탄문 등이 있다. 〔맨 앞의 may가 생략된 듯한 유형〕

- God save the Queen. 신이여, 여왕을 보호하소서.
- Peace be upon him. 그에게 평화가 함께 하길.

236

Exercises

1. 주어진 문장을 보기처럼 간접적으로 인용한 문장으로 바꾸어 보세요.

    1. Trish said, "I'll be back after lunch."
        → _Trish said (that) she would be back after lunch._
    2. The man said, "I work for Microsoft."
        → _____
    3. Mom said, "You can help yourself to anything in the fridge."
        → _____
    4. My biology teacher said, "A red blood cell takes 20 seconds to circulate around the human body."
        → _____
    5. Mike said, "I have to be back in the office by three."
        → _____
    6. The boss told me, "Send the email immediately."
        → _____
    7. Amy asked Sarah, "Please don't tell others about it."
        → _____

2. May와 주어진 표현을 사용하며 그림이 말하는 상황에 맞는 문장을 만드세요.

    1. (both of you / live a long and happy life together)   _May both of you live a long and happy life together!_
    2. (he / rest in peace)
    3. (all your wishes / come true)
    4. (the new year / bring you happiness and success)

🔊 Dialogue

3. 밑줄 친 문장을 간접의문문과 인용문으로 바꾸세요.

Andy is late for a date again. Andy는 데이트에 또 늦었습니다.

Amy   You're late, Andy!
Andy Sorry. I was stopped by one of those people on the way again.
Amy   What people?
Andy You know, those who <u>ask you, "Are you interested in spiritual stuff?"</u>
          <u>They told me, "You have some aura."</u>
Amy   They're right this time. You have an aura of tardiness.

* tardiness 느림, 지각

Unit 100

도치법

Little did she realize what was about to happen.
무슨 일이 벌어질지 그녀는 조금도 깨닫지 못했다.

1 문장의 어순을 의문문의 어순처럼 바꾸어 다양한 문장을 표현할 수 있다.

❶ 의문문
- **Are you** a member here? 여기 회원**이신가요**?
- **Do you** like pizza? 피자 좋아하세요?

❷ 감탄 명사나 형용사를 강조하는 What이나 How로 시작하는 감탄문도 있다. *See Unit 072 ▶*
- **Isn't she** lovely! (=She is so lovely!) 그녀는 너무 사랑스러워!
- Oh, my. **Am I** hungry! (=I'm so hungry.) 아아, 정말 허기지누나!

❸ 바람, 기원
- **May all your wishes come** true! 당신의 모든 소망이 이루어지길!

❹ 가정법
- **Should you have** any questions, please let me know. 질문이 **있으시다면** 알려 주세요.
- **Had I known**, I would have come sooner. (= If I had known, …) 내가 **알았었더라면** 더 일찍 왔을 것을.
- **Were it not** for your help, I would never be able to do this. 너의 도움이 **없다면** 난 결코 이것을 해내지 못할 거야.

❺ 비교
- Research shows that parents watch more TV **than do their children**.
(=… than their children do.) 연구에 의하면, 부모들이 **아이들보다** TV를 더 많이 시청한다.
- The cake was excellent, <u>as was the tea</u>. 그 케이크는 **차만큼이나** 훌륭했다.

---

2 강조하고자 하는 부분을 앞으로 보내면서 뒤의 어순이 바뀔 수 있다: S+V+■ → ■+V+S

❶ 직접 인용문에서 소설 등에서 자주 볼 수 있음
- "**I've just finished**," <u>said Tom</u>.
(= Tom said, "I've just finished.")
"방금 마쳤어요."라고 Tom이 말했다.

❷ never, rarely, little 등 부정적인 의미의 표현이나 only 등을 강조할 때
- **Never** <u>had I seen</u> so many people in one room.
그렇게 많은 사람이 한 방에 있는 건 **한 번도** 본 적이 **없었다**.
- **Little** <u>did she realize</u> what was about to happen.
무슨 일이 벌어질지 그녀는 **조금도** 깨닫지 **못했다**.

❸ so나 such를 강조할 때
- **So quickly** <u>did she run</u> that the others couldn't catch up with her.
그녀는 **얼마나 재빨리** 달렸**는지** 다른 사람들이 그녀를 따라잡을 수가 없었다.

❹ 동감의 표현
- I like sports, and **so** <u>does my boyfriend</u>. 나는 운동을 좋아하고, 내 남자친구도 그렇다.
- He can't drive, and **neither** <u>can I</u>. 그는 운전을 못하고, 나도 못해.

❺ 장소, 위치 소설 등에서 자주 볼 수 있음
- **On the hill** <u>stood an old church</u>. 언덕 위에 오래된 교회가 하나 있었다.
- **Here**'s <u>my number</u>. (= My number is here.) 여기 제 번호요.

> **TIP** 단, 대명사가 주어인 경우에는 어순이 달라진다.
> 예) **Here it is!** / **Off we go.**

Exercises

1. 보기처럼 밑줄 친 부분을 강조하는 문장으로 다시 써 보세요.

    1. I rarely drive to work.
       → Rarely _____do I drive to work_____.
    2. We have never seen such a beautiful view.
       → Never _____.
    3. I will not speak to him again until he apologized for what he said.
       → Not until he apologizes for what he said _____.
    4. I will not give up under any circumstances.
       → Under no circumstance _____!
    5. She is not only attractive, but she is also very smart.
       → Not only _____.
    6. We washed the dishes only after all the guests had left.
       → Only after all the guests had left _____.
    7. I had no sooner arrived at the airport than I realized that I had forgotten my passport.
       → No sooner _____.
    8. The coffee was so strong that I couldn't drink it.
       → So strong _____.

2. 주어진 문장 중 틀린 부분을 맞게 고치세요. 고칠 부분이 없다면 X를 쓰세요.

    1. Wow! Look at that! Isn't it great!   _____X_____
    2. My father is a teacher, and so my mother is.   _____
    3. "Come here," said Noah.   _____
    4. Here the winner comes!   _____
    5. May your new home is filled with happiness!   _____
    6. She is gorgeous, as is her mother.   _____
    7. If had the phone been cheaper, I would have bought it. _____

🔊 Dialogue

3. 밑줄 친 부분을 If를 사용하지 않은 형태로 바꾸세요.

James and Marisa are talking together in the office canteen.
James와 Marisa는 구내 식당에서 함께 이야기하고 있습니다.

James What a disaster! Sales are down this quarter in Asia.

Marisa In Europe, too.

James Since last year, nothing has gone right.

Marisa If we had done anything differently last year, would it be better now?

James I don't know. It's hard to tell what we should have done.

부록

부록 01
Be 동사 문장 구조

	긍정문	부정문	의문문
현재 (Present)	I **am** late. You/We/They **are** late. He/She/It **is** late.	I **am not** late. You/We/They **are not** late. He/She/It **is not** late.	**Am** I late? **Are** you/we/they late? **Is** he/she/it late?
과거 (Past)	I/He/She/It **was** late. You/We/They **were** late.	I/He/She/It **was not** late. You/We/They **were not** late.	**Was** I/he/she/it late? **Were** you/we/they late?
완료 (Perfect)	I/You/We/They **have been** late. He/She/It **has been** late.	I/You/We/They **haven't been** late. He/She/It **hasn't been** late.	**Have** I/You/We/They **been** late? **Has** he/she/it **been** late?

Be 동사 문장의 축약 형태(주로 대화체에서)

긍정문	I am…	You/We/They are…	He/She/It…
	I'm…	You're/We're/They're…	He's/She's/It's…
부정문	I am not…	You/We/They are not…	He/She/It is not…
	I'm not…	You're/We're/They're not… 또는 You/We/They aren't…	He's/She's/It's not… 또는 He/She/It isn't…

부록 02
상태동사표 (Non-Action(Stative) Verbs)

생각, 이해(Thinking)	agree, believe, doubt, guess, imagine, know, realize, remember, think, understand, suppose
자연스럽게 느껴지는 감각(Senses)	hear, smell, see, taste, sound
감정(Feelings/Needs/Emotion)	appreciate, dislike, hate, like love, need, prefer, regret, want, wish
소유(Possession)	belong to, contain, have, own, possess
인식(~하게 보여짐)(Appearance)	appear, look like, seem
존재(Being)	be, exist
기타(Others)	contain, Cost, depend (on), involve, matter, mean, measure, owe, weigh, require

부록 03
단순현재와 현재진행형의 시간 개념 비교: General vs. Specific

긍정문	부정문	의문문
They **are working**. Mike **is working**.	They**'re not working**. Mike **isn't working**.	**Are** they **working**? **Is** Mike **working**?

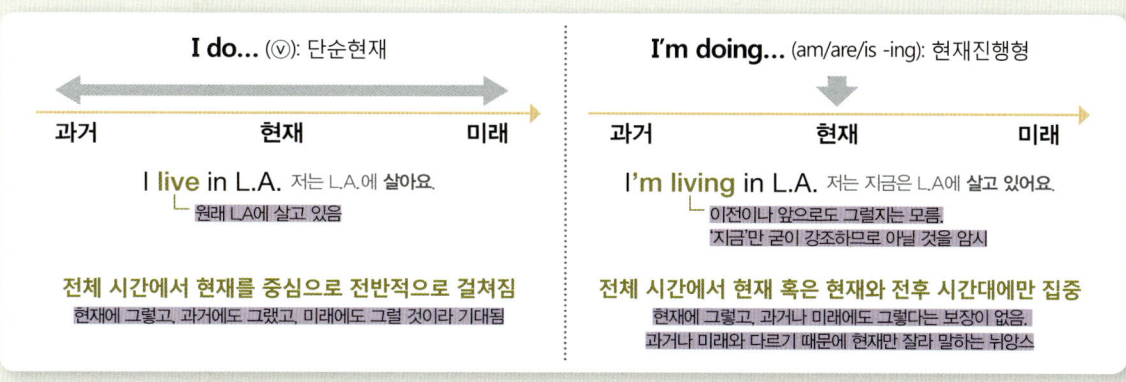

부록 04
불규칙 동사표

동사원형	과거형	과거분사형
arise	arose	arisen
be	was/were	been
bear	bore	borne
begin	began	begun
bite	bit	bitten
blow	blew	blown
break	broke	broken
bring	brought	brought
burn	burned (영 burnt)	burned (영 burnt)
buy	bought	bought
catch	caught	caught
choose	chose	chosen
come	came	come
creep	crept	crept
dive	dived/dove	dived
do	did	done

동사원형	과거형	과거분사형
draw	drew	drawn
dream	dreamed (영 dreamt)	dreamed (영 dreamt)
drink	drank	drunk
drive	drove	driven
drown	drowned	drowned
eat	ate	eaten
fall	fell	fallen
fight	fought	fought
fly	flew	flown
forget	forgot	forgotten
forgive	forgave	forgiven
freeze	froze	frozen
get	got	gotten (영 got)
give	gave	given
go	went	gone

동사원형	과거형	과거분사형	동사원형	과거형	과거분사형
grow	grew	grew	sing	sang	sung
hang	hung	hung	sink	sank	sunk
hide	hid	hid	sit	sat	sat
know	knew	known	speak	spoke	spoken
lay	laid	laid	spill	spilled (영 spilt)	spilled (영 spilt)
lead	led	led	spring	sprang	sprang
learn	learned (영 learnt)	learned (영 learnt)	steal	stole	stolen
lie	lay	lain	sting	stung	stung
light	lit	lit	strike	struck	struck
lose	lost	lost	swear	swore	sworn
prove	proved	proven (영 proved)	swim	swam	swum
read /ri:d/	read /red/	read /red/	swing	swung	swung
ride	rode	ridden	take	took	taken
ring	rang	rung	tear	tore	torn
rise	rose	risen	throw	threw	thrown
run	ran	run	uses	used	used
see	saw	seen	wake	woke	woken
seek	sought	sought	wear	wore	worn
set	set	set	win	won	won
shake	shook	shaken	write	wrote	written

부록 05

단순 과거(Past Simple)의 시간 개념

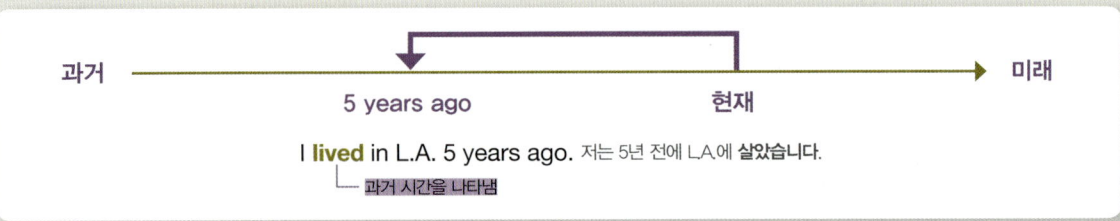

I **lived** in L.A. 5 years ago. 저는 5년 전에 L.A에 **살았습니다**.
└ 과거 시간을 나타냄

부록 06
과거 진행형(Past Continuous) 문장 구조와 시간 개념

긍정문	부정문	의문문
I was living…	I wasn't living…	Were you living…?

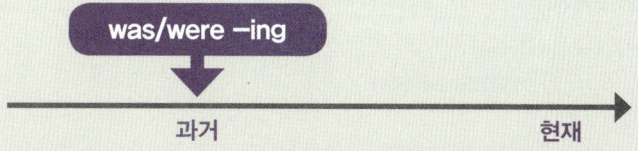

I was living in L.A. in 2016. 저는 2016년에는 L.A.에 살고 있었어요.
2016년만 해당. 아마도 그 이전과 이후는 해당되지 않을 것을 암시

부록 07
현재완료(Present Perfect)의 시간 개념

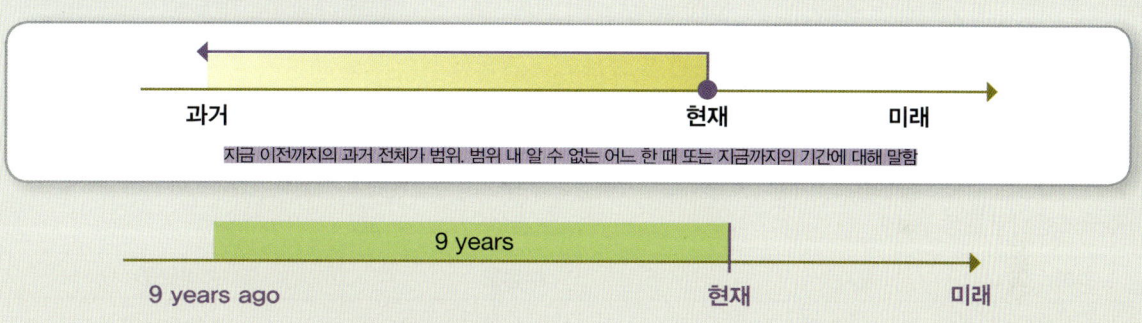

I have lived in L.A. for 9 years. 저는 9년째 L.A.에 살고 있어요.
└ 지금까지 9년간의 시간

부록 08
과거완료(Past Perfect) 문장 구조

긍정문	부정문	의문문
I had worked.	I hadn't work.	Had I worked?

```
              5 years
      ┌─────────────────────┐
      I moved to Seattle.   I moved to L.A.
```

I have lived in Seattle for 5 years when I moved to L.A.
└ L.A.에 이사 왔던(과거) 때 이전

L.A.에 이사 왔을 때, 저는 (그 때까지) 시애틀에서 5년간 살았었습니다.

부록 09
미래 진행형(Future Continuous)의 시간 개념

I **will be living** in L.A. in 2022. 저는 2022년에는 L.A.에 살고 있을 거예요.
└─ 미래인 2022년에 집중

부록 10
미래 진행형(Future Perfect Continuous)의 시간 개념

I **will have lived** in L.A. for 9 years next year. 내년이면 저는 10년째 L.A.에 살고 있게 됩니다.
└─ 내년(미래)까지 10년간의 시간

부록 11
주요 조동사와 문장 구조

의미	동사	부정문	의문문
추측	**may, might** (~일지도 모른다)	**may not / might not** (~가 아닐지도 모른다)	**May I ~?** (정중하게 허락을 구하는 표현)
	He **may/might** be American. 그는 미국인**일지도** 몰라.	He **may/might not** be American. 그는 미국인이 **아닐지도** 몰라.	**May I** sit here? 여기 앉아**도** 될까요?
	must (분명 ~일 것이다)	**must not** (틀림없이 ~가 아닐 것이다)	X
	He **must** be American. 그는 분명 미국인**일** 거야.	He **must not** be American. 그는 분명 미국인이 **아닐** 거야.	
능력, 가능성	**can, could** (~할 수 있다, ~일 수 있다)	**cannot, can't, couldn't** (~할 수 없다, 가능하지 않다, ~할 수 없었다)	**Can you ~? / Could You ~?** (능력/가능성을 묻기, 요청) **Can/Could I ~?** (허락을 구하는 표현)
	I **can** help you tomorrow. 내일은 내가 널 도울 수 있어. I **could** swim well as a child. 난 어릴 때 수영을 잘 **했다**.	I **can't** help you tomorrow. 내일은 내가 널 도울 수 **없어**. I **couldn't** swim as a child. 난 어릴 때 수영을 **못 했다**.	**Can you** help me? 나 좀 도와**줄래**? **Can I** keep this? 이거 제가 가져**도 돼요**?

의무	must (반드시 ~해야만 한다) You must stay here. 너 반드시 여기 있어야만 해.	mustn't (~해서는 안 된다) You mustn't stay here. 여기 있어서는 안 됩니다.	X
	have to (반드시 ~해야만 한다) You have to stay here. 너 반드시 여기 있어야만 해.	don't have to (~하지 않아도 된다) You don't have to stay here. 굳이 여기에 있지 않으셔도 돼요.	Do you have to ~? (~해야만 합니까?) Do you have to go now? 지금 가셔야만 합니까?
	should (~하는 것이 낫다/옳다) You should go home now. 너 집에 가는 게 좋겠다.	shouldn't (~하지 않는 것이 낫다/옳다) You shouldn't go home now. 너 집에 가지 않는 게 좋겠다.	Should I ~? (~하는 것이 좋을지 의견을 묻기) Should I go home now? 제가 집에 가는 게 나을까요?

부록 12

더해지는 표현의 종류에 따른 연결 표현 또는 형태

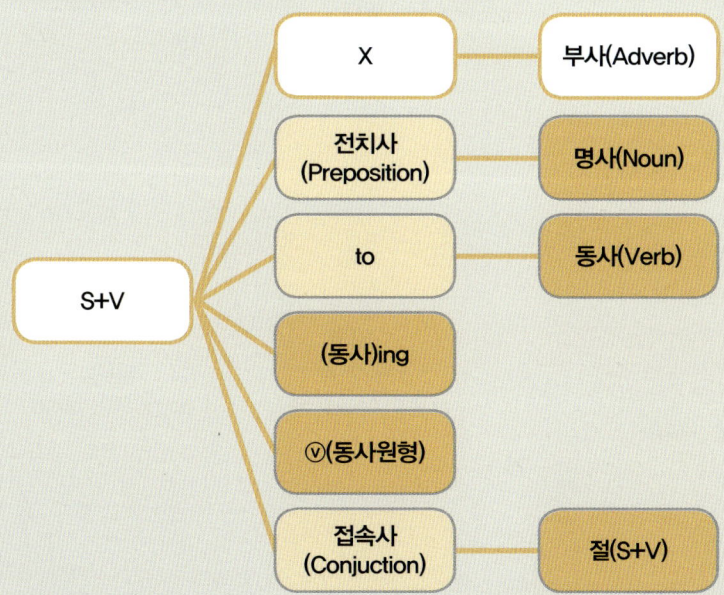

부록 13
명사 기본 개념도

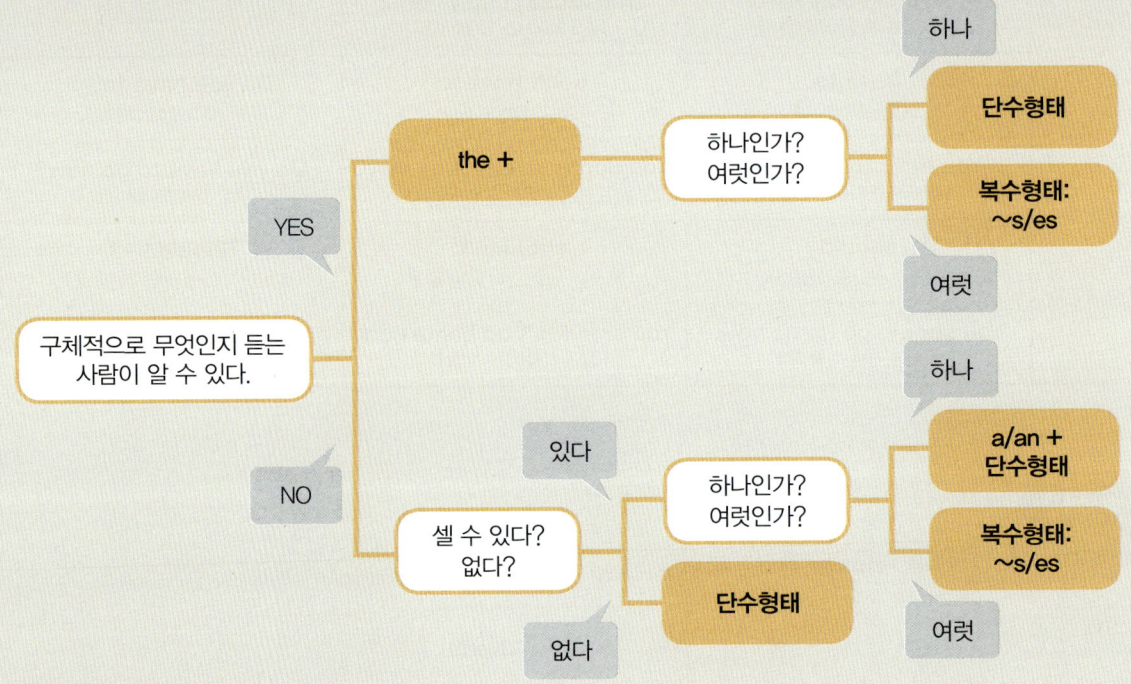

부록 14
명사가 나타내는 범위를 표현하는 한정사

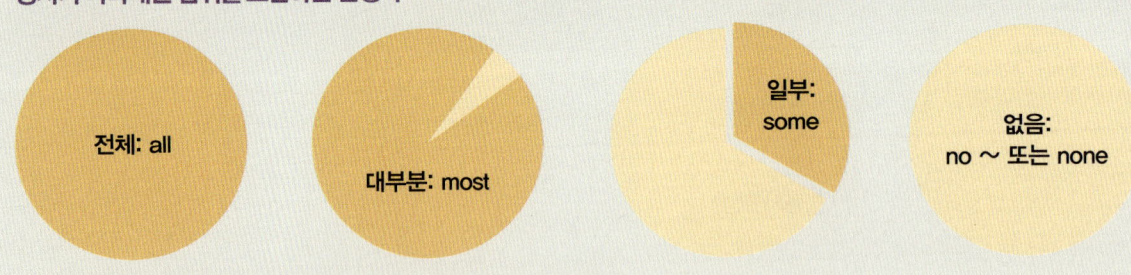

부록 15
대명사 정리표

~는	~를	~의	~의 것
I work in a bank. 나는 은행에서 일합니다.	He loves me[1]. 그는 나를 사랑해요.	Here's my phone number. 여기 제 전화번호요.	It's not your pen. It's mine[2]. 그건 네 펜이 아냐. 내 거지.
You must be excited. 너 신나겠구나.	I saw you there. 나 거기서 너를 봤어.	What's your name? 당신의 이름은 무엇인가요?	This is yours. 이건 네 것이야.
She is my sister. 그녀는 내 누이에요.	Did you talk to her? 그녀에게 말했나요?	Is this her umbrella? 이건 그녀의 우산인가요?	Is this hers? 이건 그녀의 것인가요?
He has two dogs. 그는 개 두 마리가 있어요.	I like him. 나는 그를 좋아해요.	His parents live in Paris. 그의 부모님은 파리에 살죠.	My car is older than his. 내 차는 그의 것보다 오래되었어요.
It wasn't my fault. 그건 내 잘못이 아니었어요.	Did you find it? 너 그거 찾았니?	I like its design. 난 그것의 디자인이 맘에 들어요.	X
We went to the movies. 우린 영화 보러 갔었다.	Please, help us. 부디 우리를 도와주세요.	Welcome to our office. 우리 사무실에 오신 것을 환영합니다.	Ours is a better system. 우리 것이 더 나은 시스템입니다.
[3] You two are awesome. 너희 둘 멋지구나.	These are for you. 이것들은 여러분을 위한 것이에요.	Thank you for your help. 여러분의 도움에 감사 드립니다.	It's yours now. 이제 그건 여러분의 것입니다.
[4] They love each other. 그들은 서로 사랑합니다.	I didn't eat them. 나는 그것들을 먹지 않았다.	Their son is in the army. 그들의 아들은 군대에 있다.	The books are theirs. 그 책들은 그들의 것입니다.

① 보통 '~를' 또는 '~에게'로 해석된다. 또한 전치사 뒤에 오는 대명사의 형태이다.
② 뒤에 명사가 오지 않는다. 예) It's mine. (O) / It's mine book. (X)
③ You는 '너희들, 여러분' 등 여럿(복수)의 의미로도 쓰인다.
④ they-them-their-theirs는 사람과 사물 모두에 쓸 수 있다.

특별부록

토익 빈출/비즈니스 문장 유형과 관련 학습 Units

<We Learn Grammar>에서 배운 내용을 토대로 토익/비즈니스 관련 문장을 만들 수 있습니다. 일상 대화에서 벗어나 한층 업그레이드 된 비즈니스 100 문장을 익혀 보세요. 각 문장의 의미를 정확하게 파악하기 어렵거나, 해당 문법 사항이 헷갈린다면 관련 Unit을 다시 학습하세요.

NO	문장	관련 Unit
1	New desk telephones will **be** installed this evening, so please clear a space on your desk next to your current phone.	001
2	I normally **work** 8 hours a day.	002, 004
3	I **am working** hard to meet the deadline.	003, 004
4	The customer **is always complaining** about the price or the quality.	005
5	I **stayed** at the Paradis Hotel when I **went** to Paris last month.	006
6	I **was discussing** the new catalogue with Mike at 10:30.	007
7	I'm nervous because I've never **had** an interview.	008
8	Mr. Okada **has been** with the firm **for less than two years** and **has already been** promoted to senior technical specialist.	009, 010
9	**For the past five years**, Monarch Hotel **has set** high standards in the hospitality industry.	008, 009, 010, 011
10	Sales of new cars **have increased** significantly **since last month**. = Sales of new cars **have been increasing** significantly **since last month**.	011, 012, 013
11	**For many years**, scientists **have believed** that there is a connection between severe antisocial behavior and abnormal brain development.	013
12	I **was** nervous because I **had** never **had** an interview.	014
13	**When** I **left** my last job, I **had been working** there for seven years.	015
14	Charles Ingram, the mayor of Dayton, **is addressing** the city's lack of recreational facilities on tomorrow's radio show.	016
15	Our company **is going to merge** with one of our competitors. ＊ merge 합병하다	016
16	We **expects** the price **will** go down.	017
17	Mike **was going to represent** our company at a conference in Boston next week, but unfortunately he was involved in a car accident yesterday and will have to spend at least 2 weeks in the hospital.	018
18	Mr. Walker **will be instructing** us how to access cameras that are positioned throughout the mall.	019
19	Don't forget to log out **when** you **have finished** your session.	020

20	All personnel at Lloyds **can** ask to reduce or change their contract. * personnel 인원, 직원들	021
21	Perhaps we **could** have an age limit?	022
22	Here are some coats you **might** be interested in.	023
23	The shipment **must have sent** to the wrong address.	024
24	Standard ticket holders **must** exit by 6:00 p.m.	025
25	**Should I** tell Sonia about the meeting?	026
26	I have a terrible pain in my chest. **I'd better** see a doctor.	027
27	My good friend Penny Diaz **suggested** that **I contact** you regarding the upcoming Global Culture Convention.	028, 052
28	**I wonder if I could** sign up for one of the career building workshops this Friday.	029
29	The winter weather **can cause** Main Street to be closed **if** its surface **becomes** too slippery.	030
30	**I'll give** you a ride home if you **can wait** a few more minutes. / If I **were** you, **I'd think** very carefully about it.	031
31	If we **had reduced** the price of the video game console, we **could have sold** more on its launch day.	032
32	He **will miss** the start of the seminar **unless** he **arrives** soon.	033
33	A: Which department is Mr. Stuart working in? B: **I wish I knew**.	034
34	Wild Travel Company's profits **have risen sharply** over the last ten years.	035
35	Ms. Lawler's award for business management **was** well **deserved**.	036, 037
36	The strongest tropical storms **are called** hurricanes, typhoons or tropical cyclones. The different names all mean the same thing, but **are used** in different part of the world. If these huge storms start in the Atlantic and Pacific Oceans near the Equator, they **are called** hurricanes.	038
37	The convention discounts **are offered** only **to** those on our newsletter mailing list.	039
38	Don't let anybody **use** your computer.	040
39	We have our office **cleaned** every day.	041
40	The company **is believed to be** reliable by investors.	042
41	If you have any questions, please don't **hesitate** to contact us.	043

42	Our growth in the industry this year has **allowed us to make** this much-needed improvement to our work environment.	044
43	We submitted the proposal **to build** a new library. / The goal of the department is **to increase** tourism in the area	045
44	Ms. Chan was happy **to receive** an award.	046
45	Garcia Bistro hopes to attract new customers by **updating** its menu to include healthy appetizers.	047
46	I **look forward to hearing** from you soon.	048
47	Have you **started to work** on it yet? = Have you **started working** on it yet?	049
48	My smartphone **need to be charged** again. = My smartphone **needs charging** again.	050
49	He chose to **admit that he'd made** a mistake. = He chose to **admit making** a mistake.	051
50	Everyone **noticed** the deputy chairman **enter** the room.	052
51	**Living** in Alaska, they're used to cold weather.	053
52	You need to get a lot of **information** about small business loans.	054
53	Twitter and Facebook have become a major **means** of communication and social interaction.	055
54	Do you have any **baggage** to check?	056
55	We stopped at the bank to grab **some** cash from the ATM.	057
56	Only **a few** shareholders attended last years' annual meeting.	058
57	The new manager delegated small tasks to **each** member of her staff.	059
58	A: Would you rather get tickets for Friday or Saturday night? B: **Either** day is fine.	060
59	One of the twenty items that we ordered is missing and **another** was damaged in transit.	061
60	**Dental examinations** should be included in **medical checkups** for **the elderly**, especially those with **symptoms** of **dementia**.	062, 063, 064
61	Employees are expected to arrive at **work** no later than 9:00 A.M. A detailed **company** orientation is scheduled during lunch.	065
62	Ms. Blackmore implied that **she** would place an order next week.	018, 066
63	Mr. Jones asked Ms. Sharpe whether he could hold the interviews in her office because **his** is being renovated.	066

#	Sentence	Ref
64	Ms. Lim will write the assembly instructions **herself**, but an intern will help to create the diagrams.	066
65	There was an accident on Maple Road. **That**'s why I'm late.	067
66	**It** seems that they're not coming.	068
67	If **so**, the whole town will benefit greatly from the improvements.	069
68	A dinner will be arranged to welcome the **newly appointed** managers of the Oxford branch.	070
69	Summer in Arizona is **extremely hot**.	071
70	New study says you can eat **whatever** you want and still lose weight.	072
71	**However** efficiently they worked on the project, they couldn't meet the deadline.	072
72	The movie *Logan* was **so** touching **that** I highly recommend it.	073
73	I'm worried that I may not have **enough** time to finish the project.	074
74	Mr. Coleman came to the office **earlier than** usual in order to meet an important deadline.	075
75	**The longer** he waited, **the angrier** he got.	076
76	You know, they're **the most popular** outdoor clothing brand.	077
77	Mr. Walker will be instructing us how to access cameras **that** are positioned throughout the mall.	045, 078
78	The new G-MAX movie theater, **which** will include twelve screens, is set to open in August.	079
79	They drew up a shortlist of candidates **whose** CV were very good.	080
80	Mr. Browning's multivitamins were delivered along with a leaflet **describing** their health benefits.	081
81	A: When will the new software be installed? B: **In** a week.	082
82	**Since** we have recently added two new jewelry stores, we need to protect our facilities more carefully than before.	083
83	A: Where did you see the job advertised? B: It is **on** the company Web site.	084
85	Gertrude Ederle became the first woman to swim **across** the English Channel in 1926.	085
86	We will be happy to provide you **with** a new desk at no extra cost.	086
87	I was responsible **for** Internet advertising for the company's mobile phone division.	087

No		
88	Please start making your way **toward** the exit gates.	088
89	The advertising campaign has gone **over** its budget limit.	089
90	I'm **looking after** my colleague's clients while she's away.	090
91	**By the time** the archaeologists discovered the city, it had been abandoned for hundreds of years.	091
92	**Besides** telephones, the company produces transmitters.	092
93	**While** the event is free, you should register in advance.	093
94	Please contact us immediately **so that** we can finalize the details of your trip.	094
95	Richman Language Institute's courses cover a wide range of languages **such as** Spanish, Chinese, and German.	095
96	Both strategies may be successful, but **it** is difficult **to** combine them effectively.	096
97	Who's **leading** the meeting tomorrow morning?	097
98	The computer is running slow, **isn't it**?	098
99	She **asked her boss not to** assign me to his team.	099
100	**Should you fail** the test, you can take it again next month.	100

NO	해석
1	새 탁상 전화기는 오늘 저녁에 설치될 예정이므로 책상 위의 현재 있는 전화기 옆에 공간을 비워 주십시오.
2	저는 보통 하루에 8시간 일합니다.
3	저는 마감을 맞추기 위해 열심히 일하고 있어요.
4	그 손님은 항상 가격이나 품질에 대해 불평합니다.
5	저는 지난 달 파리에 갔을 때 Paradis 호텔에 머물렀습니다.
6	저는 10:30에 Mike와 새 카탈로그에 대해 논의하고 있었습니다.
7	저는 면접을 본 적이 없기 때문에 긴장 돼요
8	Okada 씨는 그 회사에서 2년 안 되게 근무했고, 이미 고위 기술 전문가로 승진도 했습니다.
9	지난 5년 동안, Monarch 호텔은 서비스 업계에서 높은 기준을 세워 왔습니다.
10	지난 달 이후로 새 차들의 판매는 상당히 증가해 왔습니다.
11	몇 년 동안, 과학자들은 심각한 반사회적 행동과 비정상적 뇌 발달 사이에 연관성이 있다고 믿어 왔습니다.
12	저는 면접을 본 적이 없었기 때문에 긴장이 됐어요.
13	마지막 직장을 떠났을 때, 저는 7년을 일하고 있는 중이었어요.

14	Dayton 시장인 Charles Ingram은 도시의 복지시설 부족에 대해 내일 라디오 프로그램에서 연설할 예정입니다.
15	우리 회사는 우리 경쟁사 중 하나와 합병할 예정입니다.
16	우리는 가격이 내려갈 거라고 예상합니다.
17	Mike는 다음주 보스톤 컨퍼런스에서 우리 회사를 대변할 예정이었으나, 안타깝게도 어제 차 사고에 연루되어 병원에서 적어도 2주는 보내야 합니다.
18	Walker 씨는 쇼핑몰 도처에 배치된 카메라를 이용하는 법을 저희에게 알려 주고 있을 것입니다.
19	당신 차례가 끝나고 나면 로그아웃 하는 것을 잊지 마세요.
20	Lloyds의 모든 직원들은 그들의 계약 단축이나 변경을 요청할 수 있습니다.
21	아마 우리 연령 제한이 있을걸요?
22	당신이 관심 있을 만한 코트들이 여기 있습니다.
23	배송물이 잘못된 주소로 발송된 것이 분명합니다.
24	보통 티켓 소지자는 오후 6시까지는 퇴장해야 합니다.
25	회의에 대해 Sonia에게 말해야 할까요?
26	나 가슴에 심각한 통증이 있어. 병원에 가 봐야 할 것 같아.
27	내 좋은 친구인 Penny Diaz는 제가 돌아오는 국제 문화 컨벤션에 대해 당신에게 연락해 보라고 제안했습니다.
28	저는 이번 금요일에 있는 커리어 증진 워크숍 중 하나에 제가 신청할 수 있는지 궁금합니다.
29	겨울 날씨는 Main Street의 표면이 너무 미끄러울 경우 길의 폐쇄를 야기할 수 있습니다.
30	만약 당신이 몇 분만 더 기다려 줄 수 있다면 집까지 태워다 드릴게요. / 내가 너라면, 그것에 대해 매우 신중하게 생각할 텐데.
31	만약 우리가 비디오 게임 콘솔의 가격을 내렸었더라면 출시 당일 더 많이 팔 수 있었을 텐데.
32	그가 곧 도착하지 않으면 그는 세미나의 시작을 놓칠 것입니다.
33	A: 어떤 부서가 Stuart가 일하는 곳인가요? B: 저도 알면 좋을 텐데요.
34	Wild Travel Company의 이익은 지난 10년간 매우 빠르게 증가했습니다.
35	Lawler 부인은 경영 관리상을 받을 만한 충분한 자격이 있었습니다.
36	가장 강한 열대성 태풍들은 허리케인, 타이푼, 또는 열대성 사이클론이라고 불립니다. 각각의 이름들은 모두 같은 것을 의미하지만, 세계 곳곳에서 다르게 쓰입니다. 만약 이런 큰 폭풍들이 에콰도르 근방의 대서양이나 태평양 바다에서 시작하면 그것들은 허리케인이라고 불립니다.
37	컨벤션 할인은 오직 소식지 메일 리스트에 있는 사람들에게만 제공됩니다.
38	아무도 당신의 컴퓨터를 쓰게 하지 마세요.
39	저희는 매일 사무실을 청소합니다.
40	그 회사는 투자자들로부터 신뢰할 만하다고 여겨집니다.
41	만약 궁금한 것이 있으시면, 저희에게 연락하는 것을 주저하지 마십시오.
42	올해 업계에서의 우리의 성장은 우리 업무 환경에 이만큼의 큰 개선을 할 수 있게 했습니다.

43	우리는 새 도서관을 지을 제안서를 제출했습니다. / 부서의 목표는 지역 관광객을 증가시키는 것입니다.
44	Chan 씨는 상을 받아서 행복했습니다.
45	Garcia Bistro는 건강에 좋은 에피타이저를 메뉴에 추가하여 업데이트 하면서 새 고객들을 끌어 오기를 바랍니다.
46	곧 당신에게서 소식을 듣길 바랍니다.
47	아직 일 시작 안 했나요?
48	내 스마트폰은 또 충전되어야 한다.
49	그는 실수 저지른 것을 자백하기로 선택했습니다.
50	모두가 방에 들어오는 부회장을 주목했습니다.
51	알래스카에 살면서 그들은 추운 날씨에 익숙해졌습니다.
52	당신은 소규모 사업 대출에 대한 많은 정보를 얻을 필요가 있어요.
53	Twitter와 Facebook은 커뮤니케이션과 사회 상호 작용의 주요 수단이 되었습니다.
54	맡기실 짐이 있으십니까?
55	우리는 은행에서 멈추어 ATM에서 현금을 좀 찾았습니다.
56	오직 몇몇 주주들만 작년 연례 회의에 참석했습니다.
57	새 매니저는 그녀의 스텝 각각에게 작은 업무들을 맡겼습니다.
58	A: 금요일 밤과 토요일 밤 중 어느 날 티켓을 원하시나요? B: 아무 날이나 괜찮습니다.
59	우리가 주문한 20개 아이템 중 하나가 분실되었고 다른 하나는 수송 중 손상되었습니다.
60	치과 검진은 나이든 사람들, 특히 치매 증상이 있는 분들을 위한 의료적인 검진이 포함되어야 합니다.
61	고용인들은 9시를 넘어서 회사에 도착하면 안 됩니다. 구체적인 회사 오리엔테이션은 점심 시간에 예정되어 있습니다.
62	Blackmore 씨는 다음 주에 주문할 것을 넌지시 나타냈습니다.
63	Jones 씨는 그의 사무실이 보수 중이라 Sharpe 씨에게 그녀의 사무실에서의 인터뷰를 잡을 수 있을지 물어보았습니다.
64	Lim 씨는 스스로 의회 지침을 쓸 예정인데, 인턴이 다이어그램을 만드는 데에 도움을 줄 것입니다.
65	Maple Road에서 사고가 있었습니다. 제가 늦은 이유입니다.
66	그들이 오지 않을 것 같은데.
67	만약 그렇다면, 그 개선으로 인해 모든 마을이 크게 이익을 얻을 것입니다.
68	저녁 식사는 Oxford 계열사에 새로 기용된 경영자를 환영하기 위해 마련될 것입니다.
69	Arizona의 여름은 무지막지하게 덥습니다.
70	새로운 연구는 당신이 원하는 것은 무엇이든 먹을 수 있고 그러면서 체중 감량도 할 수 있다고 합니다.
71	그들이 프로젝트를 효율적으로 진행했음에도 불구하고, 그들은 마감을 맞추지 못했습니다.

72	영화 〈로건〉은 매우 감동적이었기 때문에 매우 추천해요.
73	저는 프로젝트를 끝낼 시간이 충분하지 못할지도 몰라서 걱정 돼요.
74	Coleman 씨는 중요한 마감을 맞추기 위해 평소보다 사무실에 일찍 왔습니다.
75	그가 더 오래 기다릴수록 그는 더 화가 났습니다.
76	너도 알다시피, 그건 가장 인기 있는 아웃도어 의류 브랜드야.
77	Walker 씨는 쇼핑몰 도처에 배치된 카메라를 이용하는 법을 저희에게 알려 주고 있을 것입니다.
78	12개의 상영관을 포함할 새 G-MAX 영화관은 8월에 오픈하기로 예정되어 있습니다.
79	그들은 CV가 매우 좋은 최종 후보자 명단을 작성했습니다.
80	Browning 씨의 종합 비타민제는 그것의 건강 효능을 설명한 전단지와 함께 배송되었습니다.
81	A: 새 소프트웨어는 언제 설치되나요? B: 일주일 내로요.
82	최근 우리가 두 개의 새 보석 상점을 추가한 이후, 우리는 전보다 더 신중을 기해서 시설들을 보호할 필요가 있습니다.
83	A: 어디에서 구인 광고를 보셨나요? B: 회사 웹사이트에서 봤습니다.
85	Gertrude Ederle는 1926년에 영국 해협을 헤엄쳐 건넌 첫 번째 여성이 되었습니다.
86	우리는 추가 요금 없이 당신에게 새 책상을 제공할 수 있어서 기쁠 것입니다.
87	저는 회사의 모바일 부문 인터넷 광고를 맡았습니다.
88	출구 쪽으로 나가기 시작하시기 바랍니다.
89	광고 캠페인은 예산 제한으로 무산되었습니다.
90	저는 제 동료가 부재 중일 때 그녀의 고객을 배웅했습니다.
91	고고학자들이 그 도시를 발견했을 때, 도시는 몇 백 년 전에 버려져 있었습니다.
92	전화기 외에 그 회사는 송신기를 생산합니다.
93	그 이벤트가 공짜인 대신 당신은 먼저 등록을 해야 합니다.
94	여행을 마무리 할 수 있도록 즉시 저희에게 연락 주십시오.
95	Richman Language Institute의 코스는 스페인어, 중국어, 독일어 등 방대한 범위를 포함합니다.
96	양쪽 전략 모두 성공적일 수는 있지만, 그것들을 효율적으로 결합하기는 어렵습니다.
97	내일 아침 회의는 누가 주도하나요?
98	컴퓨터가 늦게 돌아가네요, 그렇죠?
99	그녀는 상사에게 그 팀에 나를 배정하지 않기를 요구했습니다.
100	시험에서 떨어진다면 넌 다음 달에 다시 시험을 볼 수 있어.

정답

* 각 답안은 해당 Unit의 내용을 기준으로 제시되었습니다. 대화체보다 폭 넓은 문맥을 적용하는 경우 제시된 답안 외의 가능성이 있을 수 있습니다.

Unit 001

❶
1. is
2. are
3. Is
4. Am
5. is
6. be
7. was
8. are
9. were
10. be
11. been

❷
1. You don't have to be afraid.
2. X
3. The children are doing their homework now.
4. Our headquarters are in Seoul.
5. The office is going to be cleaned tomorrow.
6. Where is she from?
7. X
8. Don't worry. Be happy.
9. X
10. I'll be back in an hour.
11. My house used be here.

❸
what is your dream? /
I want to be a nurse /
I want to be like my mom /
you'll be a wonderful nurse

Unit 002

❶
1. speak
2. take
3. don't smoke
4. go up
5. designs / manufactures
6. opens / doesn't close
7. flows

❷
1. Do you take Visa?
2. How do they do that?
3. Where does he live?
4. Does she drive an SUV?
5. How often do you call your parents?

❸
1. I usually get to work at 8:30 a.m.
2. She doesn't often wear jeans.
3. My dog is always happy.
4. He never shouts at others.
5. What do you usually do in your spare time?
6. I've always wanted to be an accountant.

❹
Koreans speak Korean / Italians speak Italian / what language do Canadians speak / Canadians speak English

Unit 003

❶
1. is doing
2. 'm using
3. are rising
4. 'm driving
5. 're selling
6. 're developing

❷
1. The air conditioner isn't working
2. I'm not sleeping very well
3. Are you calling from your cell phone
4. How's it going
5. They're not replying to my emails
6. Is Mr. Harris expecting me

❸
1. I remember
2. X
3. I like
4. X
5. I have a question

❹
He's not working

Unit 004

❶
1. have
2. 's having
3. 's getting
4. gets
5. works
6. is working
7. visit
8. 'm, visiting

❷
1. is always breaking down
2. are always forgetting
3. is always smiling and laughing
4. is always playing
5. is always telling
6. are always arguing

❸
1. is being so nice
2. is very nice
3. are being so mean
4. are being unreasonable
5. is sick
6. am being very patient

❹
My girlfriend is always fixing her makeup

Unit 005

❶
1. understand
2. 'm learning
3. 's / 's getting
4. 's / 's getting
5. are, looking
6. hear
7. 'm listening to

❷
1. have
2. 'm having
3. 're thinking
4. do, think
5. Are, seeing
6. see
7. smell
8. is smelling

❸
1. insist
2. promise
3. recommend
4. suppose
5. apologize

❹
Do you promise?

Unit 006

❶
1. finished
2. went
3. did, do
4. graduated
5. didn't realize
6. Did, study, were
7. didn't answer, was
8. ate

❷
1. When did Michael Jackson die
2. Where did the Vikings live

3. What did James Watt invent
　　4. How many books did Roald Dahl write

　　1. He died in 2009
　　2. They lived in Scandinavia
　　3. He invented the steam engine
　　4. He wrote 49 books

❸　1. used to
　　2. am used to
　　3. used to
　　4. are getting used to
　　5. would

❹　What happened to my favorite bakery

Unit 007

❶　1. was taking
　　2. wasn't paying
　　3. was wearing
　　4. was shining, were singing

❷　1. found, was looking
　　2. started, was driving
　　3. was chatting, crashed
　　4. noticed, was walking
　　5. invented, was working
　　6. were waiting, was negotiating

❸　1. left
　　2. was dancing
　　3. were playing
　　4. shouted, "Yay!"
　　5. was losing
　　6. hired

❹　I hurt my back while I was moving furniture yesterday

Unit 008

❶　1. haven't spoken
　　2. 've visited
　　3. 've lived
　　4. hasn't paid
　　5. has broken
　　6. 've seen
　　7. has broken down
　　8. hasn't arrived
　　9. Have, found
　　10. haven't done
　　11. 've made

❷　1. didn't sleep
　　2. has visited
　　3. moved
　　4. have never heard
　　5. have lost
　　6. liked
　　7. have never traveled
　　8. did you live
　　9. have you been
　　10. arrived

❸　you haven't met / I've heard

Unit 009

❶　1. Have you ever studied abroad?
　　2. Have you ever seen a celebrity in person?
　　3. Have you ever swum in the ocean?
　　4. Have you ever stayed up all night?

　　1. Yes, I have. I studied in Australia in 2016. or
　　　No, I haven't. I've never studied abroad.
　　2. Yes, I have. or
　　　No, I haven't. I've never seen a celebrity in person.
　　3. Yes, I have. or
　　　No, I haven't. I've never swum in the ocean.
　　4. Yes, I have. or
　　　No, I haven't. I've never stayed up all night.

❷　1. It's the first time I've seen a whale
　　2. It's the first time I've stayed in the Blueridge Hotel
　　3. It's the second time I've ever eaten sashimi
　　4. Interstellar is the best movie I've ever seen
　　5. This is the best steak I've ever eaten
　　6. He's the kindest person I've ever met

❸　1. The manager has already spoken to me.
　　2. He hasn't finished the November sales report yet.
　　3. I've already sent him an email.
　　4. The company has just announced it is going to close the Beijing factory next year.

❹　Have you learned / No, I've just started

Unit 010

❶　1. Did you see
　　2. Have you seen
　　3. has lived
　　4. lived
　　5. stayed
　　6. have stayed

❷　1. He's gone out.
　　2. Someone has eaten all the cookies.
　　3. She has bought a new car.
　　4. Someone has broken the window.
　　5. Someone has taken my shoes.
　　6. I've eaten a lot.

❸　1-b / 2-d / 3-a / 4-c

❹　I've already drunk

Unit 011

❶　1. We've loved each other for a long time.
　　2. Andy has known Amy since third grade.
　　3. Mr. Cruz has been a teacher for thirty years.
　　4. There has been a strong wind all day.
　　5. There has been a high-tech revolution in China since 1997.

❷　1. It's been 5 years since I last saw him.
　　2. It's been a year since I last went to the movies.
　　3. It's been a long time since we last visited him.
　　4. It's been over 10 years since Sia last ate meat.
　　5. It's been ages since I last went shopping.
　　6. It's been two weeks since he last called her.

❸ 1. She has lived in L.A. for 4 years.
2. They've been married for 7 years.
3. Steve Jobs has been dead since 2011.
4. I've known him since I was in elementary school.
5. How long have you had your cell phone?
6. How long have they been married?
7. How long have you been here?

❹ it hasn't rained / It's been sunny and warm since the moment I arrived at the airport

Unit 012

❶ 1-c / 2-d / 3-e / 4-a / 5-b / 6-g / 7-f

❷ 1. They've been dancing all night
2. We've been working on it for months
3. How long has he been waiting
4. They've been negotiating since this year
5. How long have you been looking for it
6. He's been watching them for hours

❸ She's been so upset

Unit 013

❶ 1. has been
2. has been working
3. 've been having
4. have been having
5. 've had
6. 've been collecting
7. 's been waiting
8. 's been
9. have believed
10. 've been dating
11. 've known

❷ 1. have been talking, haven't decided
2. haven't been feeling
3. Have, finished
4. 've been looking
5. 've been exercising
6. haven't been doing
7. have, read
8. have, been reading
9. Have, been crying, 've been peeling
10. haven't heard

❸ I've been working on it

Unit 014

❶ 1. I had seen him before
2. I had not sent them an email
3. there had been traffic jam
4. his late grandfather had left him a fortune
5. I had already had dinner
6. I had had my first cell phone for years
7. she had locked the door
8. they had never been to the amusement Park

❷ 1. had already prepared the dinner
2. said yes
3. had been smashed, called the police
4. had already left the house
5. opened their umbrella

❸ He had already turned into the road

Unit 015

❶ 1-e / 2-f / 3-g / 4-a / 5-c / 6-b / 6-d

❷ 1. had been waiting
2. had been trying
3. had been playing
4. had been working
5. had been developing

❸ 1. had been using
2. had known
3. had been working
4. has been using
5. had been looking
6. had already left

❹ He'd been sitting in traffic for three hours

Unit 016

❶ 1. I'm not going to accept the job offer.
2. I'm going to buy a smartphone.
3. They're going to spend the weekend in San Diego.
4. We're going to redesign our website.
5. It's going to hire 100 people.

❷ 1. We're going to be late.
2. It's going to rain.
3. The car is going to stop soon.
4. It's going to go bankrupt.

❸ 1. you see
2. X
3. I'm leaving
4. returns
5. X
6. X
7. get

❹ you're interviewing / What am I doing / is coming / Are we

Unit 017

❶ 1-e / 2-d / 3-a / 4-b / 5-c / 6-f

❷ 1. Will
2. Shall
3. Will
4. shall
5. will

❸ 1. I think I'll have an espresso.
2. I doubt she will accept the proposal.
3. I guess my boss won't be happy about it.
4. I wonder what happened to him.
5. I hope she doesn't mind waiting in the car.
6. I don't think I'll stay here tonight.

❹ 1-a / 2-d / 3-e / 4-c / 5-b

❺ it won't / it will be dry / will one chicken be enough / we'll need / will be

Unit 018

❶ 1. Are, doing
2. 'll send
3. Are, going to visit
4. 'll tell
5. are, going to call

❷ 1-a / 2-d / 3-c / 4-b

❸ 1. would
2. is about to
3. was going to
4. would
5. is to visit
6. was going to
7. wouldn't
8. are not to start

❹ was going to

Unit 019

❶ 1. will begin
2. will have finished
3. will be having
4. will be meeting
5. will leave
6. will be flying
7. will have arrived

❷ 1. will have been married
2. will have left
3. Will you be passing
4. will be taking
5. will have been waiting
6. Will they be attending
7. will be doing
8. will you have been working

❸ will have ended

Unit 020

❶ 1-e / 2-b / 3-c / 4-d / 5-a

❷ 1. have been
2. be
3. speak
4. have lost weight
5. Having seen
6. have rained

❸ 1. I'll send you the report /
I finish it
2. What you are going to do /
you go on vacation

3. He'll get back to work /
he's recovered
4. I'll keep trying /
I've learned everything
5. I won't believe it / I see it

❹ you've had

Unit 021

❶ 1. can
2. be able to
3. can't
4. be able to
5. be able to
6. can
7. can't

❷ 1. could
2. was able to
3. were able to
4. were able to
5. could
6. couldn't

❸ 1. X
2. X
3. being able to
4. can't, can
5. X

❹ was able to

Unit 022

❶ 1-c / 2-b / 3-a / 4-f /
5-e / 6-g / 7-d

❷ 1. could eat
2. X
3. could visit
4. X
5. could buy

❸ 1. could be
2. could have eaten
3. was able to arrive
4. could swim
5. could have called

❹ couldn't have done

Unit 023

❶ 1-b / 2-c / 3-d / 4-a
5-e / 6-f / 7-g

❷ 1. might go
2. might not have seen
3. might be
4. might not be
5. might have gone

❸ 1. X
2. X
3. might have been
4. might be taking a bath
5. X

❹ might have forgotten

Unit 024

❶ 1. She must be in love with him.
2. They must be having a party.
3. She must have changed her phone number.
4. They must not have been at home.
5. She must be reading a book or studying.
6. It must have been lost on the way.
7. The meeting must have been canceled.

❷ 1. must
2. may
3. must
4. must have been
5. might
6. must not
7. can't
8. must not
9. must

❸ must have picked up

Unit 025

❶ 1. I have to take
2. We have to go
3. do I have to arrive
4. Jessica and Naomi had to go
5. Does she have to work
6. They had to get
7. has to
8. I have to finish, It has to be

❷ 1. don't have to
2. mustn't
3. don't have to

4. didn't have to
5. mustn't
6. mustn't

③ 1. X
2. X
3. must/have to/need to
4. X
5. must/have to/need to
6. X
7. don't have to
8. mustn't

④ mustn't / don't have to

Unit 026

① 1. should visit
2. shouldn't cross
3. should knock
4. should eat
5. should email
6. shouldn't put

② 1-b / 2-d / 3-a / 4-f / 5-c / 6-e

③ 1. must
2. should
3. should
4. mustn't
5. should
6. have to
7. should

④ I think we should eat out tonight / I should have removed the steak from the grill earlier

Unit 027

① 1. X
2. should
3. X
4. X
5. should/must
6. should

② 1. My wife is supposed to make dinner tonight.
2. You're not supposed to take more than 3 books.
3. Cars aren't supposed to be on the bike path.
4. The newspaper was supposed to be delivered by now.

③ 1-c / 2-a / 3-b / 4-f / 5-e / 6-d

④ You're not supposed to park your car

Unit 028

① 1. we eat out at Paula's Kitchen
2. learn how to use Excel
3. he apologize to her
4. all employees not make personal phone calls during business hours
5. he be invited to the wedding
6. we have a word with the boss

② 1. keep
2. be
3. not neglect
4. refund
5. make
6. provide

③ 1-c / 2-b / 3-e / 4-d / 5-a

④ recommend that you see it too

Unit 029

① 1. Would you like
2. giving
3. May I
4. left
5. could

② 1. We could have dinner at The Plaza tonight.
2. Could you please turn down the TV?
3. May I ask who's calling?
4. Would you mind waiting a few minutes?

③ 1-c / 2-d / 3-e / 4-a / 5-b

④ 1-b / 2-c / 3-a / 4-e / 5-d

⑤ Could I use your name

Unit 030

① 1-c / 2-e / 3-g / 4-b / 5-a / 6-f / 7-d

② 1. If the traffic is OK, we'll get to the station in time.
2. If he's late again, I'll be angry.
3. If it stops raining, we'll go out for a walk.
4. If I see Jay today, I'll give him your message.
5. If the government raises taxes, people will consume less.

③ 1. If
2. when
3. when
4. if
5. if

④ Cats purr when they're happy

Unit 031

① 1. If the new S-phone wasn't/ weren't so expensive, I could buy it.
2. If she enjoyed his job, she would work hard.
3. If I had the key, I could open the door.
4. If you went to bed early, you wouldn't be tired in the morning.
5. If I spoke good French, I could work in France.

② 1-g / 2-a / 3-b / 4-e 5-c / 6-d / 7-f

③ If we didn't have this terrible flu / we'd go out skiing

Unit 032

① 1. If I had not lost my passport, I would be in Norway now.
2. If my brother had studied law, he would be a lawyer now.
3. If she had not been late, her boss wouldn't have been angry.
4. If he had not sold his car, he wouldn't have to take the bus every day.

② 1. had left
2. calls
3. had
4. would do
5. had been
6. did
7. would have bought

❸ 1-b / 2-d / 3-a / 4-e / 5-c
❹ If we hadn't had the flu / it would have been a wonderful vacation

Unit 033

❶ 1. The machine won't start working unless you press that button.
2. I won't call you unless I have a problem.
3. Book a room in advance in case the hotels are fully booked.
4. I'll keep some salad in case I get hungry later.

❷ 1. just in case
2. unless
3. Otherwise
4. as if
5. Supposing
6. as long as

❸ 1-b / 2-a / 3-c / 4-e / 5-d / 6-f
❹ in case

Unit 034

❶ 1. wish
2. wish
3. hope
4. hope
5. wish
6. wish

❷ 1. hadn't drunk
2. didn't drink
3. had
4. enjoy
5. had taken
6. could
7. would stop
8. hadn't bought
9. had been

❸ 1-b / 2-d / 3-c / 4-a
❹ I wish you would cook something else

Unit 035

❶ 1. you some tea
2. him my vacation photos
3. the whole situation to them
4. his old car to his neighbor
5. you the truth
6. a book for him
7. the file from the hard disk
8. you coffee
9. you to Mike Turner

❷ 1. made me clean the room
2. sent her an email yesterday
3. gave his report to the managing director this morning
4. Can you explain it to me
5. promised me a full refund

❸ 1-c / 2-e / 3-h / 4-b / 5-d / 6-g / 7-f / 8-a
❹ Can you get me some mayonnaise

Unit 036

❶ 1. is spoken
2. is grown
3. are often stolen
4. was invented
5. was written

❷ 1. was built
2. X
3. designed
4. was damaged
5. is collected

❸ 1. gone
2. married
3. born
4. interested
5. tired

❹ Where were you born / I was born in Lyon / Where is it located

Unit 037

❶ 1. 'm paid
2. has been fired
3. were invited
4. must be done
5. were being baked
6. had been stolen
7. will, be delivered
8. is being repaired
*영국영어는 loan phone을 주로 씀
9. be promoted
10. should have been saved

❷ 1. All our pies are made with fresh ingredients
2. Has he been taken to the hospital
3. The Mona Lisa was painted by Leonardo Da Vinci
4. When will tea be served
5. His cancer might not have been discovered

❸ What is this jacket made of / It is made of top-grade leather

Unit 038

❶ 1. It is commonly called Big Ben.
2. It employs more than 50 employees.
3. It was painted by Vincent Can Gogh.

❷ 1. was developed, have been, improved, enlarged
2. are collected, are dried, are called, are, shipped

❸ 1. heard
2. was given
3. lost
4. were defeated
5. received
6. was told

❹ be paid / pay / be paid

Unit 039

❶ 1. will be paid $120 for your old phone
2. was lent this book by Eugene
3. was told about the party by a friend
4. haven't been paid for the work yet
5. was taken to the hospital immediately
6. were promised delivery within 5 days of our order
7. was made to wait in the lobby for an hour

❷ 1. … will be given to the winner
2. X
3. X
4. I was given this sample …
5. X

6. ... make me feel better now
7. X
8. ... was elected chancellor twice

❸ was offered a position at Henson's / be given a good chance

Unit 040

❶
1. get
2. had
3. has
4. force
5. makes
6. lets
7. allow
8. learn
9. to sign
10. to express
11. repair
12. to leave

❷
1. What makes you think so
2. I'll have a mechanic look at my car
3. His ex-boss made him work overtime every day
4. I got my cousin to look after my dog while I was away
5. I want to allow only family members to see me on Facebook
6. I'll have someone bring your suitcases up to your room
7. Let me show you around our new house

❸ call

Unit 041

❶
1. have a pizza delivered
2. painting the kitchen
3. have my camera fixed
4. repair my car
5. had my phone number changed
6. have these pants shortened
7. have my teeth checked
8. cutting the grass

❷
1. cleaned
2. forwarded
3. had
4. taken
5. pierced

❸ 10 copies made / them spiral-bound

Unit 042

❶
1. was injured
2. 'm not scared
3. write
4. shocked
5. 'm surprised
6. frightened
7. open
8. were born
9. is worked

❷
1. It is said that there is a ghost in the theater.
2. It is reported that crime had increased over the past five years.
3. It is thought that empathy is a special emotion that only humans show.
4. The storm is expected to pass through Cuba.
5. Chocolate is thought to contain a lot of fat.
6. He is alleged to have robbed the bank.
7. Knowledge is considered to be power.

❸ didn't sign / was signed

Unit 043

❶
1. guarantee
2. neglect
3. seems
4. waiting
5. afford
6. threatening
7. claims

❷
1. What time have you arranged to meet her?
2. He offered to buy me a drink, but I refused.
3. I believe I deserve to be happy.
4. They agreed to give us more time.
5. He attempted to fix the TV but failed.
6. Sorry. I didn't mean to hurt your feelings.
7. The man appeared to be in his early thirties.

❸ My boyfriend tends to forget dates / he promised not to forget our 100th day anniversary

Unit 044

❶
1. I didn't ask you to do that.
2. Our boss doesn't allow us to wear jeans at work.
3. What are you expecting them to do?
4. Mr. Cruz gets his students to think critically.
5. Can you remind me to buy toilet paper at the supermarket?
6. I'm trying to persuade my grandmother to use a smartphone.
7. The doctor advised me to take a few days off.
8. He told me to call back later.

❷
1. He advised me not to buy the car.
2. My parents chose him to be my godfather.
3. X
4. I didn't want him to know about it.
5. The police officer ordered me not to leave my house.
6. X

❸ You seem to have something / I need you to be more considerate

Unit 045

❶
1. He's studying hard to pass his exam.
2. She works out at a gym every day to keep fit.

3. I need a day off next week to have the annual check-up.
4. I left early not to miss the train.
5. The union went on a strike to demand a pay raise.
6. Use a map not to get lost.

❷ 1. how
2. what
3. whether
4. when
5. who
6. where

❸ 1. I don't have time to argue with you.
2. He asked someone to bring a chair for me to sit on.
3. X
4. X
5. I don't have much to say, but thank you very much.

❹ I'm learning how to perform CPR

Unit 046

❶ 1-a / 2-d / 3-f / 4-g / 5-b / 6-e / 7-c / 8-h

❷ 1. It's difficult to drive on a rainy day.
2. Some wild berries are dangerous to eat.
3. It was selfish of you to eat the whole cake.
4. It's hard for me to read your handwriting.
5. I was scared to go to the dentist.
6. The news is sure to make everyone happy.

❸ seafood is unsafe to eat in the summer

Unit 047

❶ 1. calling
2. be paid
3. cheating
4. making
5. waiting
6. to give
7. postponing

8. to be
9. writing
10. losing

❷ 1. drawing
2. buying
3. crashing
4. making
5. Sleeping
6. doing
7. leaving
8. working

❸ failing

Unit 048

❶ 1. singing
2. replacing
3. waiting
4. shouting
5. yawning
6. developing
7. crying

❷ 1-d / 2-e / 3-f / 4-a / 5-b / 6-c

❸ 1. The video was not worth watching.
2. You can't keep me staying here.
3. I suggested not arguing about it anymore.
4. I went shopping with Mom this afternoon.

❹ to meet / to meet / meeting

Unit 049

❶ 1. X
2. to get
3. X
4. X
5. singing and dancing or to sing and dance
6. X
7. to come
8. working

❷ 1. tea to coffee
2. beer to wine
3. listen than speak
4. shopping online to going to a store or to shop online rather than go to a store

5. to have a private tutor rather than learn in a large classroom

❸ 1. I'd rather have a cat than a dog.
2. I'd rather she became a doctor.
3. I'd rather not say anything.
4. I'd rather you didn't say anything.

❹ to rain / to see

Unit 050

❶ 1. I wouldn't advise buying a used car.
2. I would advise visiting their website.
3. The landlord doesn't allow painting the walls.
4. I wouldn't advise buying from this seller.
5. We encourage applying as early as possible.
6. Most American college require sending talking one of the most common tests, the SAT or the ACT.

❷ 1. talking
2. saying
3. to meet
4. to call
5. to announce
6. talking
7. to explain
8. quitting
9. fighting
10. to lose

❸ 1. be cleaned
2. cleaning
3. cut
4. changing
5. be repaired

❹ using

Unit 051

❶ 1. Everybody agrees that money isn't everything.
2. I suggested going for a swim.
3. He didn't admit that he was scared.

267

4. His teacher encouraged him to read more.
5. She decided that it was time for a change.
6. He told me that he had seen a U.F.O.

❷ 1. be
2. meeting
3. using
4. host
5. have

❸ 1. in learning
2. of missing
3. to hear
4. of being forgotten
5. to say

❹ restarting

Unit 052

❶ 1. burning
2. go
3. play
4. following
5. shaking
6. bite
7. looking
8. rise
9. snoring
10. bang
11. hiding
12. slip

❷ 1. X
2. I couldn't help but look at his face.
3. Let me take care of the bill.
4. X
5. X
6. What made you change your mind?

❸ run

Unit 053

❶ 1. walking around the park
2. Opening the envelope
3. making me hungrier
4. (Being) Always hardworking and honest
5. Not knowing what to say
6. Having lived in London
7. (Being) Surrounded by her fans

❷ not wishing to / putting pressure

Unit 054

❶ 1. a, a
2. some
3. a
4. a
5. some
6. An
7. some
8. some

❷ 1. three bottles of water
2. two kilos of apples
3. three slices of bread
4. two bowls of rice
5. two spoons of oil
6. a bunch of bananas

❸ salad

Unit 055

❶ 1. people
2. knives
3. sheep
4. wolves
5. fish
6. volcanoes
7. teeth
8. children

❷ 1. is
2. Are
3. is
4. is
5. are
6. is
7. is

❸ 1. Mathematics is always difficult for me.
2. X
3. The books are on the shelves over there. or The books are on the shelf over there.
4. X
5. He wants to study economics in college.

❹ children / twins

Unit 056

❶ 1. A glass
2. email
3. hair
4. a hair
5. a cake
6. Chickens
7. space
8. experience
9. a loud noise
10. time
11. business
12. a hard time

❷ 1. a job or work
2. X
3. furniture
4. suggestions
5. X
6. X
7. baggage

❸ much luggage / goods / many bottles

Unit 057

❶ 1. the
2. a
3. your
4. any
5. This
6. some
7. that

❷ 1. any
2. some
3. any
4. Some
5. any

❸ 1. anyone
2. somewhere
3. anything
4. anywhere
5. sometime
6. someone
7. anytime

❹ anywhere / somewhere / anywhere / anything / something

Unit 058

❶
1. He has no brothers or sisters.
2. There is nobody here by that name.
3. I will tell no one about our conversation.
4. They bought no vegetables.
5. I have no ideas.

❷
1. a lot of or many
2. little
3. much
4. many / a few
5. a lot of

❸
1. X
2. Most of my friends…
3. None of us told…
4. X
5. Many of the kids…
6. X

❹ a lot of / a lot of / much / many / much

Unit 059

❶
1. each
2. All
3. everything
4. a tablet each
5. option
6. every
7. hand
8. every time
9. whole

❷
1. every student
2. Each member of the team
3. all (of) her students
4. all his life
5. They win every time
6. the whole summer

❸ every / whole

Unit 060

❶
1. Both
2. Either
3. Neither
4. both
5. either
6. either
7. both

❷
1. X
2. both intelligent and beautiful
3. neither of them came
4. either phone
5. X
6. neither Chinese nor Japanese

❸ most / any / none

Unit 061

❶
1. The other
2. the other
3. another
4. other
5. another

❷
1. another
2. other
3. other
4. another
5. Others
6. other
7. another
8. other
9. other
10. the other

❸ the other / the other

Unit 062

❶
1. The
2. The
3. a
4. The
5. a
6. a
7. the
8. the / the / the
9. the
10. an / the
11. the
12. a
13. the

❷

[ðə]	[ði]
1, 3, 4, (6), 7, 8	2, 5, 6

6. 미국 영어의 경우 [ði], 영국 영어의 경우 [ðə]

❸ an / the / The / the / the

Unit 063

❶
1. the Internet
2. The Kleins
3. Stanford University
4. the east / the west
5. television
6. the guitar
7. the blind
8. northern California

❷
1. X
2. the
3. X / X
4. X
5. The / X
6. the
7. the
8. X / X
9. X
10. the
11. X
12. the
13. The
14. X

❸ X / X / X / The / X

Unit 064

❶
1. Christmas
2. the Gloria Hotel
3. health
4. Google
5. The New York Times
6. Barak Obama / the United States of America
7. The television
8. the Museum of Modern Art
9. Penguins
10. Wednesday

❷
1. books
2. X
3. page 394
4. X
5. X
6. The Science Museum
7. The European Union

❸ X / the / X / the

Unit 065

①
1. church
2. classes
3. a single bed
4. bed
5. the prison
6. bed
7. school
8. college
9. a teaching college
10. a church
11. a science class
12. prison
13. the movies
14. The post office / the bank

②
1. house
2. work
3. office
4. home
5. company

③ college / college / high school

Unit 066

①
1. one
2. one
3. ones
4. one
5. ones

②
1. myself
2. myself
3. myself
4. yourself
5. himself
6. itself

③
1. they
2. Her
3. mine
4. their
5. mine
6. you
7. yours
8. they / they're
9. They

④ yourselves / yourselves

Unit 067

①
1. that
2. that
3. this
4. those
5. this
6. this / that

②
1. the government's
2. Patrick's
3. The last week's
4. South Korea's
5. 16 hours'

③
1. X
2. Who is the owner of this beautiful house?
3. They are Eugene's parents. or They are parents of Eugene's.
4. X
5. X

④ this

Unit 068

①
1. good to be home
2. essential to wear a helmet while riding on a motorcycle
3. fun to go to the movies on Saturday night
4. a pity that Erika couldn't be here tonight
5. hard to concentrate
6. seems that they're not coming
7. obvious to all that she is innocent
8. a rule to be up by 7:00 a.m
9. unlikely that they'll arrive before 6:00 p.m.
10. about a few minutes to download a video clip

②
1. It was his phone that
2. It is love that
3. It's the boss who
4. It was in Hawaii that
5. Was it in 2016 that
6. It is Peter who

③ I find it difficult to get to class on time

Unit 069

① 1-f / 2-c / 3-b / 4-d / 5-a / 6-e

②
1. thought so
2. think so
3. say so
4. Is that so
5. If so

③
1. I hope so
2. I don't think so
3. I suppose so
4. I'm afraid not
5. I guess not

④ I can't / Is it

Unit 070

①
1. a big old wooden table
2. a huge ice castle
3. the yellow brick road
4. a young American sales manager
5. someone sweet and kind
6. the last ten days

②
1. new
2. exciting
3. carefully
4. good

③
1. disappointing
2. exhausted
3. frightened
4. confusing

④ strange

Unit 071

①
1. Colorado is extremely cold in winter.
2. X
3. X
4. I trust you, and I always will.
5. … I also have a headache

②
1. well paid
2. badly organized
3. relatively easy
4. well qualified
5. totally different

③
1. He probably shouldn't drive.
2. It's no longer secret.
3. I still haven't received my package.
4. They've been waiting in line for 30 minutes.
5. The children had fun in the

pool all day.
4. yet / still

Unit 072

1.
   1. How
   2. What
   3. What
   4. How
2.
   1. Arizona
   2. Moscow
   3. The food
3.
   1. Whoever
   2. ever
   3. Whenever
   4. however
4.
   1. Even little kids know the difference between right and wrong.
   2. They didn't even have enough money for food.
   3. The band is even more popular abroad.
5. I thought he looked quite familiar. / You've even took photos with him. / You know that I can never remember people's faces.

Unit 073

1.
   1. Ms. Watson is a very patient person.
   2. There are so many stars in the sky tonight.
   3. It was such a terrible mistake.
   4. How did he earn such a lot of money?
   5. I'm in a very difficult situation.
2.
   1. such
   2. such
   3. so
   4. so
   5. such
   6. so
3. 1-f / 2-h / 3-g / 4-i / 5-a / 6-c / 7-e / 8-b / 9-d
4. The ceiling is so thin that I can hear almost everything

Unit 074

1.
   1. enough
   2. too
   3. enough
   4. very
   5. too
   6. very
   7. too
   8. very
2.
   1. You're too young to drive.
   2. There wasn't enough room for everyone in the car.
   3. He isn't experienced enough to get the job.
   4. She speaks too quickly for me to understand.
3.
   1. My room isn't big enough.
   2. She's got too little time to prepare for the presentation.
   3. The weather isn't good enough for a BBQ party.
   4. You're not walking fast enough. Hurry up!
4. I don't think he's talented enough.

Unit 075

1.
   1. colder
   2. better
   3. the fastest
   4. worse
   5. more dangerous
   6. Further
2.
   1. less, more
   2. least
   3. most
   4. fewest
   5. fewer
3.
   1. larger than the Atlantic Ocean
   2. the highest mountain in the world
   3. farther away from the Sun than Mars
   4. more strings than a violin
   5. the hottest planet in the solar system
4. louder/more loudly

Unit 076

1.
   1. is much/far/a lot/even/a little/a bit/ slightly more/less attractive than Paris
   2. are much/far/a lot/even/a little/ a bit/ slightly smarter/less smart than cats
   3. is much/far/a lot/even/a little/ a bit/ slightly more/less difficult than history
   4. is much/far/a lot/even/a little/a bit/ slightly more/less fun than playing video games
   5. is much/far/a lot/even/a little/a bit/ slightly more/less interesting than the Greek myth
2.
   1. more and more popular
   2. richer and richer
   3. more and more beautiful
   4. more and more
   5. faster and faster
3. 1-f / 2-d / 3-c / 4-b / 5-a / 6-e
4. more, more

Unit 077

1.
   1. run as fast as Andy
   2. eat as much as Sarah (did)
   3. as interesting as the/his new one
   4. last as long as I expected/had expected.
2.
   1. almost as high as
   2. twice as high as
   3. just as old as
   4. three times as heavy as
3.
   1. possible
   2. different
   3. far
   4. similar
   5. same
4. it doesn't look as nice as

Unit 078

1.
   1. that
   2. who
   3. that

    4. who
    5. that
② 1. (who)
   2. (that)
   6. (that)
③ 1. The hotel at which we stayed had more than 800 rooms.
   2. What's the name of the client with whom you had lunch?
   3. The exact shipping rates depend on the country to which your order is being delivered.
   4. This is the breakthrough for which we have been waiting.
   5. The world in which we are living is changing very fast.
④ that/which

Unit 079

① 1. , that I was reading
   2. , which surprised everyone
   3. who you were talking about
   4. , which was unusual for that time of year
   5. Speaking of which
   6. that was half price
② 1. I read four books during the summer, one of which I really enjoyed.
   2. The box contains 10 light bulbs, half of which are broken.
   3. I have eight nieces and nephews, all of whom are so adorable.
   4. There were a lot of people at the party, many of whom I had known for a long time.
③ 1. who
   2. that / which
   3. which
   4. that / who
   5. which
   6. who
④ which

Unit 080

① 1. that
   2. What
   3. what
   4. that
② 1. who
   2. whose
   3. who
   4. whose
③ 1. when
   2. why
   3. how
   4. where
   5. when

   1. Do you remember the day that you first met your wife?
   2. That's not the reason that I decided to resign.
   3. The calendar we use today started with the year that Jesus Christ was born.
④ when / who

Unit 081

① 1. on the wall
   2. next to the silver one
   3. on the table
   4. in Ontario, Canada
   5. with two doors
② 1. making smartphones
   2. happened last night
   3. sold in the U.S. in 2015
   4. found damaging museum property
   5. waiting for their flight
③ 1. who is
   2. that was written
   3. which had been
   4. that were painted
   5. which is
④ with

Unit 082

① 1. at
   2. on
   3. in
   4. at
   5. on
   6. on, at
   7. in
   8. In
   9. in, on
   10. at
   11. At, at
   12. In
② 1. next week
   2. X
   3. the day before yesterday
   4. X
   5. X
   6. in advance
③ Look, I'm free on the 28th. / I'm pretty busy next week, I'm afraid. / Say… on the 2nd? / Let's meet on Tuesday evening. / I'll see you at 7 at Thai Dreams.

Unit 083

① 1. while
   2. during
   3. for
   4. during
   5. while
   6. for
② 1-b / 2-c / 3-e / 4-f / 5-a / 6-g / 7-d
③ 1. after dinner
   2. a long time ago
   3. until noon
   4. in ten years' time
   5. before the meeting
   6. a week later
④ by

Unit 084

① 1. in
   2. on
   3. on
   4. at
   5. on
   6. at
   7. at
   8. in
   9. on
   10. in
   11. on
   12. in

13. at
  14. on
  15. in
  16. at
❷ 1. in
  2. at
  3. at
  4. on
  5. in
  6. at
❸ on

Unit 085

❶ 1. behind
  2. above
  3. across
  4. under
  5. beside
  6. between
  7. among
❷ 1. along
  2. through
  3. around
  4. up
  5. past
  6. off
  7. out of
❸ 1. They live somewhere near San Francisco.
  2. Go upstairs and get dressed for school.
  3. X
  4. Out hotel was very close to the beach.
❹ over / around / under

Unit 086

❶ 1. She was standing by the door.
  2. We were overcharged by $15.
  3. I'll be there by seven.
  4. You can contact me by email.
  5. I deleted the file by mistake.
  6. Domestic violence is prohibited by law.
❷ 1. The kid was frozen with fear.
  2. I'm looking for a bag with many pockets.

  3. Don't go. Just stay with me.
  4. I haven't decided what to buy with this money.
  5. Eva is a cute little girl with curly hair.
  6. I'll have a veggie burger with a garden salad.
❸ 1. with
  2. without
  3. by
  4. with
  5. By
❹ with

Unit 087

❶ 1. afraid
  2. take care
  3. full
  4. die
  5. proud
  6. consists
  7. approve
❷ 1. of
  2. of, for
  3. for
  4. for
  5. of
  6. for
❸ 1. for
  2. of
  3. to
  4. to
❹ for, of

Unit 088

❶ 1. damage
  2. invitation
  3. solution
  4. married
  5. apologize
  6. similar
  7. key
❷ 1-b / 2-d / 3-e / 4-c / 5-a / 6-f
❸ 1. at
  2. to
  3. at
  4. my question

  5. to the question
  6. at
❹ to / at / to

Unit 089

❶ 1. X
  2. as
  3. X
  4. around
  5. as
  6. about
  7. X
  8. X
❷ 1. over
  2. over
  3. above
  4. over
  5. above
  6. over
  7. through
  8. across
  9. across
  10. across
  11. through
  12. through
  13. over
  14. around
❸ over / like

Unit 090

❶ 1. gave, away
  2. take after
  3. hold, back
  4. looking for
  5. passed out
❷ 1. Take it off
  2. can I try this on
  3. hand it in
  4. Will you turn it up
  5. Rain gets me down
❸ 1. got off the bus
  2. looks after his brother
  3. breakthrough
  4. stands for Most Valuable Player
  5. getaway

④ left out / printed out the papers / throw, away / put off / made up / go on

Unit 091

① 1-g / 2-h / 3-f / 4-e / 5-d / 6-c / 7-a / 8-b
② 1. by the time
2. once
3. as
4. since
5. after
③ 1. If he doesn't change his attitude, …
2. X
3. X
4. … as soon as it stops raining.
5. … when I talk to girls.
④ when / before

Unit 092

① 1. neither
2. In addition
3. as well / too
4. and
5. so
6. either
7. and
8. too
② 1. or
2. instead
3. instead of
4. as well as
③ 1. Besides
2. Besides
3. Besides
4. besides
5. beside
④ and / or

Unit 093

① 1. but
2. However
3. but
4. but
5. however

② 1. in spite of
2. even so
3. Despite
4. while
5. Still
6. though
7. Although
③ 1-c / 2-e / 3-a / 4-b / 5-d
④ Despite

Unit 094

① 1. so I take the bus everywhere
2. as he had a lot of homework
3. cos I have to work late
4. because there were no more buses
5. because he speaks very fast
6. so he may not be able to go to work tomorrow
7. 'cause the oven was broken
8. since you paid for mine yesterday
② 1. because of
2. As a result
3. so that
4. due to
5. As a result
6. in order to
7. Thanks
8. In order
9. so
10. for
③ so that

Unit 095

① 1. Fortunately
2. To be honest
3. So
4. In my opinion
5. In fact
6. For example

Unit 096

① 1. sorry
2. recommended
3. certain

4. hear
② 1. you get better soon
2. watching TV is a waste of time
3. you missed it
4. you'll get the job
5. two people were killed in the fire
6. it costs too much
③ 1. to
2. That
3. that
4. to
5. that
④ The thing is that

Unit 097

① 1. No, I'm not.
2. Yes, it has.
3. No, not really.
4. I do.
② 1. What kind of
2. How far
3. Who
4. What
5. What time
6. How long
③ 1. Could you tell me where you come from?
2. Do you think you could call me a taxi?
3. Could I ask why you left your last job?
4. I was wondering if you could send me the information by email.
④ Are you going down / Could you hit basement level 4

Unit 098

① 1. He is
2. You did
3. You haven't
4. She did
5. It isn't
6. It is
② 1. isn't he
2. aren't we
3. can you / could you / will you /

274

won't you
4. am I
5. aren't I
6. don't you
7. don't you
8. did she
9. will you
10. shall we
11. will they
12. have you

❸ didn't they

Unit 099

❶ 1. Trish said (that) she would be back after lunch.
2. The man said (that) he worked/works for Microsoft.
3. Mom said (that) I could help myself to anything in the fridge.
4. My biology teacher said (that) a red blood cell takes/took 20 seconds to circulate around the human body.
5. Mike said (that) he had to be back in the office by three.
6. The boss told me to send the email immediately.
7. Amy asked Sarah not to tell others about it.

❷ 1. May both of you live a long and happy life together!
2. May he rest in peace.
3. May all your wishes come true!
4. May the New Year bring you happiness and success!

❸ ask you if you were interested in spiritual stuff. / They told me that I had some aura.

Unit 100

❶ 1. do I drive to work
2. have we seen such a beautiful view
3. will I speak to him again
4. will I give up
5. is she attractive, but she is also very smart

6. did she wash the dishes
7. had I arrived at the airport than I realized that I had forgotten my passport
8. was the coffee that I couldn't drink it

❷ 1. X
2. My father is a teacher, and so is my mother.
3. X
4. Here comes the winner!
5. May your new home be filled with happiness!
6. X
7. Had the phone been cheaper, ... *or* If the phone had been cheaper, ...

❸ Had we done anything differently last year

영어 Index

a/the 57(1,2),62-65
about 89(3)
    about/around/on 89(3)
across 89(5)
actually 95(2)
    in fact/as a matter of fact/
    actually 95(2)
all 59
allow 40(1)
although 93(3)
    although/though/even though 93(3)
and 92(1)
another 61
    other/another/the other 61
any 57(3,4)
    some/any/every+thing/
    one(body)/where/time 57(3)
around 89(3)
    about/around/on 89(3)
as 33(4-5),77,89(2),91(1),92(3),94(1,2)
    as if/as though 33(4)
    as long as 33(5)
    (not) as 형용사/부사 as 77
    as soon as 91(1)
    as well (as) 92(3)
    since/as 94(1)
    as a result 94(2)
ask/demand/insist 등 28(1)
at 82(3),84(3),88(2,3)
    at+시간 82(3)
    at+장소 84(3)
be able to 21(2,4)
be about to 18(3)
be born 36(2)
be going to 16,18

be to 18(4)
because 87(3),94(1)
    because of/thanks to/due to 87(3)
before 91(1)
believe/claim/consider 등 42(3)
besides 92(2)
both 60(1)
    both/either/neither 60(1)
breakfast/lunch/dinner 64(4)
bring/give/lend 등 35(3)
but 93(1)
buy/cook/get 등 35(3)
by 83(2),86(1),91(1)
    by the time 91(1)
can 21-22
could 21-22,24(4),29,31(1),32(1)
    could/couldn't have p.p. 22(2)
due to 87(3)
    because of/thanks to/due to 87(3)
during 83(1)
-ed 6
    -ed+시간표현 6(2)
either 60,92(3)
    both/either/neither 60(1)
    too/either 92(3)
elect 39(3)
enough 74
essential/imperative 등 28(2)
even 72(5),93(3)
    although/though/even though 93(3)
ever 30(4),72(4)
    who/what/which 등+ever 72(4)
every 2(4),59(3,4,5)
    every day/week/month 등 2(4)
fact 95(2),96(1)

in fact/as a matter of fact/
    actually 95(2)
feel 5(3)
for 83(1),87(2),94(3),95(1)
    for example 95(1)
force 40(1)
from 83(3)
get 36(2)
    get p.p. 36(2)
    사역동사 get 40(3),41
go 48(4)
    go -ing 48(4)
have 25,27(1),40-41,53(2)
    have to 25
    had better 27(1)
    사역동사 have 40(1),41
    having p.p. 53(2)
home 85(3)
hope 17(3),34(1)
however 93(2)
if 30-32,34(3),91(1)
    if only 34(3)
in 33(3),45(1),82(1),84(1),92(2),94(3)
    in case/in case of 명사 33(3)
    in order to 45(1),94(3)
    in+시간 82(1)
    in+장소 84(1)
    in addition/in addition to 명사 92(2)
-ing 3,7,47,53
    am/is/are -ing 3
    was/were -ing 7
    분사구문 53(1)
    having p.p. 53(3)
instead 92(4)
    instead/instead of 명사 92(4)

it 68,96(2)
know/like/seem/want 12(4)
let 40(1),52(3)
live 12(4)
look 5(3)
make 39(3),40(1),52(3)
may/might 23,24(4),29,99(2)
    may/might be -ing 23(2)
    may/might have p.p. 23(3)
    may/might as well 23(5)
means 55(3)
might 31(1),32(1)
mind 29(1)
must 24
    must be -ing 24(2)
    must have p.p. 24(3)
need 25(5),50(3)
    need to 25(5),50(3)
    need to be p.p./need -ing 50(3)
neither 60(1)
    both/either/neither 60(1)
news 55(2)
no 58(3,4),71(3)
    not any/no/none 58(3,4)
    no longer 71(3)
of 87(1)
on 82(2),84(2),89(3)
    on+시간 82(2)
    on+장소 84(2)
    about/around/on 89(3)
once 91(1)
or 33(1),92(4)
other 61
    other/another/the other 61
otherwise 33(1)

ought to 26(4)
over 89(4)
own 67(4)
prefer 49(4)
probably 71(2)
providing/provided (that) 33(5)
say 99(1)
    say/tell 99(1)
-self/selves 66(2)
series 55(3)
shall 17(2)
should 26,31(3)
    should have p.p. 26(2)
    Should you ~ 31(3)
since 11(1),83(3),91(1),94(1)
    현재완료+since 11(1)
    since/as 94(1)
so 69(2),73(2),94(2,3)
    so that 94(3)
some 54(3),57(2,3,4)
    some/any 57(3,4)
species 55(3)
such 73(3),95(1)
    such as 95(1)
suppose 27(2),33(6)
    (be) supposed to 27(2)
    supposing 33(6)
tell 99(1)
    say/tell 99(1)
thanks to 87(3)
    because of/thanks to/due to 87(3)
that 78,96(1)
    who/that/which 78
this/that 67(1)
though 93(3)

although/though/even though 93(3)
to 43-46,88(1,3)
    to 부정사 43-46
    to+방향 88(1)
too 74,92(3)
    too/either 92(3)
unless 33(2)
until 83(2),91(1,2)
used to 6(3),51(2)
    be/get used to 6(3)
very 72(3),73(1)
when 20(1),30,91(1,2)
whenever 91(1)
whereas 93(3)
which 78,79
    who/that/which 78
    ,+which/who 79(2)
    speaking of which 79(4)
while 83(1),91(1),93(3)
who 78,79(2)
    who/that/which 78
    ,+which/who 79(2)
will 17
    believe/be sure/expect 등+will 17(3)
    maybe/probably+will 17(3)
    won't 17(4)
wish 34(1),99(2)
    wish와 hope 34(1),99(2)
    wish+had p.p. 34(1)
with/without 86(2)
work 12(4)
would 29(1)
yet 9(3)

한글 Index

be 동사 1
    긍정/부정/의문문 1(1)
    현재/과거/완료형 1(1)
    축약형 1(1)
    be 동사 + 명사/형용사/전치사 1(2)

do type 동사 2

to 부정사 43–46
    to 부정사를 쓰는 동사 43(1)
    to be –ing/to have p.p. 43(2)
    동사+목적어+to 부정사 44(1)
    what/when/how 등
    의문사+to 부정사 45(2)
    주어+동사+to 부정사 45(1)
    명사+to 부정사 45(2)
    형용사+of 사람+to 부정사 45(3)
    형용사+to 부정사 46(1,2,4)

가정법 30–34
    if/when 30(3),34(3)
    if+ever 30(4)
    or/otherwise 33(1)
    unless 33(2)
    in case/in case of 명사 33(3)
    as if/as though 33(4)
    as long as/providing (that)/
    provided (that) 33(5)
    supposing 33(6)
    wish 34

감탄문 72(1)

과거 1,6,7
    be 동사 1(1)
    used to 6(3)
    과거진행형 7
    과거와 과거진행 7(4)

과거완료 14,15
    현재완료와 과거완료 14(3)
    과거완료진행 15

관계대명사 78–79
    who/that/which 78(1)
    ,which/who 79(1,2)

관계사절 80–81
    what 80(1)
    시간/때+when/that 80(2)
    how=the way (that) 80(2)
    that/which/who+동사, that/which/
    who+be –ing = –ing 81(1)

구동사 90

기원문 99(2)

다양한 뜻의 it 68

대동사 69

대명사 66–67
    –self/selves 66(2)
    성별이 불특정한 경우 66(4)
    's/of 67(2)

도치법 100

동명사 47(2)

동사와 문장 35,44(2),47–51
    자동사와 타동사 35,44(2)
    동사+ing 47(1),48(1)
    to와 ing 모두 사용하는
    동사 49(1,2),50(1,2),51(1)
    to만/ing만 사용하는 동사 49(1,2)

명사 54–56
    셀 수 있는 명사 54(1),56
    셀 수 없는 명사 54(2),56
    단위로 나타낼 수 있는 명사 54(3)
    단수와 복수형이 같은 명사 55(3)

주로 복수로 쓰이는 명사 55(4)

미래 16–18
    현재진행형과 현재시제 16(4,5)
    be going to 16,18(1)
    will 17–18
    be about to 18(3)
    be to 18(4)
    미래진행형 19
    미래완료형 19(4)

부사 71–74
    부사의 위치 71
    강조부사 72
    very/so/such 73
    enough/too 74

분사구문 53

비교급과 최상급 75–77
    비교급 and 비교급 76(3)
    the 비교급 ~, the 비교급 ~ 76(4)
    최상급 앞과 뒤에 오는 표현 76(6,7)
    as 형용사/부사 as 77

사역동사 40–41
    make/force/have/get/
    let 등 40(1),41

수동태 36–39,42(3)
    수동태+by 36(1)
    수동태+여러 시제 37(1)
    조동사+수동태 37(2)
    make+대상+동사의 수동태 39(3)
    believe/claim/consider 등+
    수동태 42(3)

의문문 17(1,2),19(3),23(1),29(1),97–98
    will 의문문 17(1),19(3)
    Shall I/Shall we 17(2)

May I 23(1),29(1)

Would you like to 29(1)

간접의문문 97

부가의문문 98

전치사 82-89

시간 전치사: in/on/at 82

시간 전치사: for/during/while/until/by/from/since 83

장소 전치사: in/on/at 84

장소 전치사 85

방향 전치사 85(2)

전치사를 쓰지 않는 표현들 85(3)

기타 전치사 86-89

접속사 91-95

when/after/until 등 접속사 뒤 시간 표현 91(2)

although/though/even though 93(3)

because/since/as/so/as a result 등 94

제안하기 28-29

예의 바른 요청 29

조동사 21-27,29,31(3),32(1),37

can/could 21-22,31(3),32(1)

may/might 23,31(3),32(1)

must 24-25

mustn't와 don't/doesn't have to 25(2)

have to 25

should 26,27(1),31(3)

had better 27(1)

(be) supposed to 27(2)

It's time 주어 -ed 27(3)

조동사+수동태 37

지각동사 52

can't help -ing/but 52(2)

한정사 57-65

a/the 57(1,2),62-65

some/any 57(2)

some/any/every+thing/one(body)/where/time 57(3)

not any/no/none 58(2,3,4)

most/some+of 58(6)

all/whole/every/each 59

both/either/neither 60

other/another/the other 61

현재 2-5,16(4,5)

시간표현 + 단순현재 2(4)

현재진행형 3

단순현재와 현재진행형의 차이 4,5

현재완료 8-13,20

현재완료와 과거시제 8(3),10

현재완료+never/ever 9(1)

현재완료+just/already/yet 9(2),9(3)

현재완료진행 11(1),12

현재완료+since 11(1)

현재완료와 현재완료진행형 13

현재완료와 현재시제 20(1)

과거를 표현해야 할 때 20(2)

형용사 1(2),70

be 동사+명사/형용사/전치사 1(2)

형용사의 일반적인 순서 70(1)

명사+명사의 형태로 된 하나의 표현 70(4)

형용사로 쓰이는 -ing/-ed 70(5)

279